THE ULTIMATE SPIRITUAL ADVENTURE!

From the Book:

"She had no way of knowing where she was, or even when she was. Rather than traveling in a straight line, time seemed to dance upon the moonbeams. Gradually, however, the breaking waves grew louder until their sound was that of thunder, and the sparkling moonbeams became sharper and brighter until they were transformed into lightning. Ariana ran aimlessly through the endless night, not knowing where to go or if there was anywhere to go. She made for some hills in the distance, and saw the flickering light of a candle or campfire beckoning from the mouth of a cave. In desperation, she hurried to the hollow as if it were the only hope of shelter in all the realms of the cosmos. As she entered, a little man with big ears, bald head, and brown skin, dressed only in a simple white shawl and loincloth, smiled the warmest welcome she had ever received in any realm. She knew instantly who he was, and forgot all about her loneliness, the Teacher, and the abyss that the reading had uncovered in her soul."

From the Readers:

"*Into the Fire* is a personal journey into your soul. This book will challenge your beliefs and inspire you to have the courage to love."

—Patricia Hass
Southfield, Michigan

"I really enjoyed *Into the Fire*. It introduced me to the concepts, the myths, and the realities behind the world's major religions in a way that I could understand, appreciate, love, and enjoy."

—Jon Collins
Tetbury, England

"I absolutely adored *Into the Fire*! While reading this book, I have not felt that I'm reading for a class, but my own enjoyment. It makes the reader feel as if she is on an intimate exploration of religion. It is an awesome book!"

—Shawny Syme
Farmington Hills, Michigan

"Unlike ordinary fiction, there is an undiluted nugget of wisdom on every page. And unlike ordinary nonfiction, this gem is made accessible and applicable to real life."

—Lori Hile
Chicago, Illinois

"After reading *Into the Fire*, I finally understood the major religions and how they are related. The book proved to be a great resource when I recently adopted my 5-year-old son from India, helping me to understand the complicated Hindu caste system from which he came."

—Daniel P. Durci
Howell, Michigan

"I keep coming back to *Into the Fire* again and again. It has been a mile-stone in my life. It's riddled with truth, and has inspired me wherever I go."

—Dave Falconer
Milford, Michigan

BY
JAMES
COOK

INTO THE FIRE

WORLD
RELIGIONS
AS LIFE,
CHALLENGE,
POWER
AND
LOVE

THIRD
EDITION

Pearson
Custom
Publishing

Dedication

To my children, Elisha and Kelila,
and to one who wishes to be nameless,
but who lives deep in my heart:
For love and inspiration in all.

Acknowledgments

Most of the Zen stories are drawn from Irmgaard Schloegl's
Wisdom of the Zen Masters (New York: New Directions, 1976).

The story of the autistic child is from Barry Kaufman's
Son-Rise (New York: Harper & Row, 1976).

The story of the Belgian woman is a loose adaptation from
William Styron's *Sophie's Choice* (New York: Random House, 1979).

The movie mentioned in Chapter 6 is Richard Attenborough's *Gandhi*.

Cover art is by Y. S. Hanoosh.

Printed in the United States of America

10 9 8 7 6 5 4 3 2 1

Please visit our website at www.pearsoncustom.com

ISBN 0–536–62903-X

BA 993016

PEARSON CUSTOM PUBLISHING
75 Arlington Street, Suite 300, Boston, MA 02116
A Pearson Education Company

A Note To the Reader

A historical novel is an attempt to make a historical period come to life in the imagination of the reader. *Into the Fire* is an attempt to make the spirit of the five major contemporary religions, as well as religion itself, come to life in the minds and hearts of its readers.

One's religion is what one holds to be of supreme value and ultimately real. Scientific materialism is the religion of most people in the modern world. Pagan polytheism was the religion of most people in the ancient world. However different they may seem on the surface, both these world views have one thing in common: they are about competition, for survival as the bottom line, power as the meaning of it all, and pleasure and glory as the icing on the cake.

Pagan polytheism developed as human beings broke away from their aboriginal roots, where harmony with nature was the keynote, and sought dominance over their environment. Unlike the human ego, however, the human soul does not feed upon power. It seeks a more profound understanding of life, one that sees human existence as an intimate and essential part of a larger truth, a truth embracing the entire breadth and depth of the universe. And so Hinduism and Judaism arose, the one emphasizing the mystical unity of all being, the other the moral righteousness and concern of a transcendent and almighty God. Once started, this drive toward universal relevance, moral grandeur and ultimate meaning could not be stopped; so the cultural religion of Hinduism gave birth to Buddhism, while Judaism mothered Christianity and Islam.

Today, most people in the world belong nominally to one of these five religious traditions, yet most still live as if pleasure and competition for power were what life is all about. We are "consumers" who devour life rather than give ourselves to it. At heart, the world religions are different ways of giving oneself to life.

Certainly, this self-giving has its dark side, as the history of religion, with its overtones of fanaticism, persecution and brutality, makes painfully obvious. Yet we do not really have the choice of being religious or irreligious, because religion is a dimension of our being. The human soul can never be satisfied with a way of life that ignores the call of the spirit.

Ariana, whom you will shortly meet, is the spirit of the coming age. She is also the human soul, desperately seeking a way of life that makes for greater life, rather than death. What she finds and what she decides will have more effect upon the future of the world than all our scientific discoveries, technological advances, and political and economic systems put together.

We are all Ariana. This book is an invitation to you to take spiritual responsibility for yourself. It offers a survey of your spiritual possibilities, shows you their ramifications, and asks you to make an informed and conscientious decision about the meaning of life from the depths of your heart. The alternative is taking the path of least resistance; and, even as modern science affirms with its law of entropy, that is the path to death.

Ann Arbor
April, 1999

CONTENTS

INTRODUCTION: THE CONTEST

Imagination is the key, the way, the light.

Love is the force, the power, the life.

To follow the way of imagination in the passion of love

is what we are discouraged from doing

from the moment we come into the world.

To follow the way of imagination in the passion of love

is what we must do if we are to have a world.

As far back as we humans can remember,

we have been sizzling over love's flame.

Now it is time to leap into the fire.

Ariana's Theme

In a light that was bright but not blinding, on a field that was solid but not bruising, the young woman screamed and the children laughed as she feigned inability to tag anyone so she no longer would be "it." Everyone slid in the grass and rolled in the mud until the pursuer, in mock exhaustion, threw herself onto the biggest and blackest puddle of all. All the children followed, giggling and tickling their victim until Ariana begged for mercy. Then it came.

Nothing changed exactly, not the light, the wetness, the colors, the warmth, nor even the joy in their hearts; but she knew and they knew she had to go.

High on a hill overlooking the fields of antiquity shone the light that had summoned her. It was a brilliant light, yet did not hurt the eyes; a light the like of which is practically unknown to us earthbound creatures, but whose call was more intimate to her than the aura of her own being. She glided swiftly up the incline, feet barely touching grass and rock, until she came into the presence of the angelic being who had tutored her as far back as she could remember. At first she moved to embrace the austere yet amiable spirit, until she noticed the stranger beside him. The newcomer was unusual in these heavenly parts in that he gave off no light, no color, no warmth at all. Vibrationally he was utterly neutral; and this, more than the fact that she did not know him, caused her to turn solemn and wary, like a child meeting a prospective stepparent.

The angel, noticing her perplexity, smoothed over the awkward moment with a simple introduction. "This is the Teacher," he smiled, and she nodded at the newcomer, who nodded back, more as if in imitation than acknowledgment, it seemed to her. If she had been among her friends she would have made some wisecrack like, "Monkey see, monkey do?" that would have dissolved them in laughter and let the stranger see that his reserve did not intimidate her. However, here she was intimidated, and felt it best to take refuge in silence.

The angel knew exactly what she was up to. "Aren't you going to ask him what he teaches?" he whispered conspiratorially as he leaned forward and enveloped her in his warm yet bracing glow. The stranger, however, did not give her a chance to inquire. "We have business, you and I," he said to her. The angel at once was gone, and for the first time since the dawn of becoming she lowered her eyes before the intensity of another's.

He sat and invited her to join him.

"It's time for you to marry."

Though she had always known this moment would come, she was yet so shocked that all she could do was nod.

"The suitors surround the field and await my signal to begin the contest."

"What contest, sir?"

She knew he knew she would not understand what he said, and wondered why he went to so much trouble to confuse her. She also had never addressed someone as a superior, and it made her feel confused—both frightened and safe, if one could imagine such a paradox.

"The contest for your hand in marriage."

"How many suitors are there?" she asked, feeling that any number would be either too high or low, too overwhelming or insulting.

"Five," he replied.

"Who are they?"

"Before we deal with them, you should meet your children."

She was too astonished to speak. Even in the heavenly realm, there was a certain temporal propriety, if not order. How could she meet her children before giving them birth?

"Look down," he commanded, and as she did she understood what he meant. All the countries of the Earth, that realm whose spiritual significance was out of all proportion to its minuscule dimensions, lay before her in all their diversity. Overspreading that diversity, however, was a pall of lassitude and fear that united the children of the Earth in common despair.

"Look closer!" he insisted.

She strained to see, but that only caused the vision to recede.

"No!"—you fool, the tone in his voice seemed to add. "To look closer you need to stop trying."

She was not sure how to follow these instructions, but something she did or ceased doing worked, and she found herself looking into the lives of the earthbound. There was some joy and cheer, but an overwhelming amount of misery, fear and despair. "My children," she whispered, more to herself than the Teacher.

"Not until you marry."

"I don't understand," her voice trembled, referring as much to the strange maternal feeling welling up from deep within as to the question of marriage.

"Do you know who you are?"

She admitted that the question had never much occupied her. She was who she was.

"You are the spirit of the coming age."

"Upon Earth, do you mean?" She had heard that the earthbound were great ones for marking time off into times and seasons.

"Throughout the universe," he replied.

She wanted to inquire how she could be so important, but was certain it would only invite his sarcasm. "What must I do?" she asked instead.

"That is for you to decide. But if you wish to nurture your children,"—she nodded as he spoke—"you must choose with whom you may generate the most life."

"My husband?" she inquired.

He nodded in return, again, it seemed to her, as if in imitation.

"And it is my job to show you the candidates."

It was maddening how he stood there expectantly without blinking an eye, knowing full well that there was only one question she could possibly ask. "Who are the candidates?"

"The spirit of the old age, of course."

"I thought you said I had a choice." She waited for him to ask the obvious question, but his was the more stubborn will.

"How can I have a choice if there is only one?"

"The spirit of the old age is many."

"And I am only one." She hoped for an explanation, but sensed none would be forthcoming. "Will you introduce them to me?" she asked.

"Certainly." Gesturing with his right arm, he called out, "Ishwara!" and immediately a spirit of tremendous energy, passion, and joy appeared. He looked like an earthbound soul as, now that she thought of it, did the Teacher himself; but he possessed a concentration of power and vitality that was to the helpless children of darkness as their sun to an inert stone. He bowed low, kissed her hand, and stood at a comfortable attention before her.

"Buddha!" cried the Teacher, and the next to appear was a slender young man who was definitely of and not of the Earth at one and the same time. What he lacked in passionate vitality was more than made up by his air of winsome gentility. Ishwara would be an unsurpassed lover, but Buddha, she speculated, an extremely congenial mate.

As Buddha, with a friendly bow, took his place next to Ishwara, the Teacher announced the next candidate.

"Yahweh!"

This time, however, no one appeared. Instead a wind rushed over her, a spirit of exquisite peace and unyielding challenge.

"Might my husband be invisible?" she asked herself, and of course the Teacher answered.

"Reality is not what is seen, but what does the seeing."

"And who else?" she queried, not in the mood for his epigrammatic wisdom.

"Allah!" he exclaimed, and again no one appeared; but a feeling of majestic, awesome, and soul-shaking music arose, as if from a distance, and filled the interstices of existence until everything and everyone seemed to be dancing to its command. She was so enraptured that she barely noticed the Teacher's final introduction.

"Kristos!" she heard him proclaim; but she remained enthralled by Allah's symphonic power until the mood was abruptly broken by the deepest, most penetrating pair of eyes ever to look into her own. She did not know how long she returned his gaze before her field of vision broadened to take in the rest of his being; but, when it did, she saw that he was an ordinary man, much like the Teacher, but with a lack of vibration more justly labeled reticent rather than neutral. It was as if he held himself back for fear of intruding, yet everything so restrained gushed forth in concentrated intensity from his eyes. All in all, his was at once the most troubling and compelling epiphany of all.

"So now I must choose," she mused, her aura tingling to such unaccustomed authority.

"You may do so," said the Teacher, "if you wish to choose unwisely."

"But you said I had to decide!" she retorted in frustration. "There is no pleasing you."

"You don't exist to please me," he replied with an unshakable equanimity that only raised her anger to the boiling point.

"Then I will please myself," she nearly whispered.

"You don't exist to please yourself," he countered.

"Why, then, do I exist?"

"That is what you must find out before you can choose wisely."

For the first time since they met, she admitted to herself that she might learn something from this teacher. "How shall we proceed?"

"Simple. Each of your suitors will woo you in turn. At the end, you will make up your mind."

"Simple indeed." She breathed deeply of the excitement in the air, knowing it was not hers alone. "I'm ready."

"Oh, one more thing." The Teacher smiled, but whether at what he was about to say or her own change of heart she could not tell. "I will be your chaperone."

"Is that necessary?"

"I will be there to make sure that the focus remains squarely upon reality."

"What is reality?" she challenged.

Suddenly Ishwara and she were alone.

"That is the mystery," he agreed. "Shall we explore it together?"

CHAPTER I.

HINDUISM

The scholarly controversy over the historical origins of Hinduism is bitter and long-standing, complicated as it has been by Western cultural chauvinism and Indian nationalism. Before the discovery of the remains of Dravidian cities at Mohenjo-daro and Harappa in the early 1920's, many Western scholars cavalierly dismissed the legends of a great indigenous civilization existing in India before the coming of the Aryans. Nowadays the pendulum of scholarly fashion is swinging in the opposite direction, and many historians, especially but not exclusively Indian, are claiming that there was no Aryan invasion and that Hinduism is entirely a product of the Indian subcontinent. There is evidence and cogent argument on both sides of this scholarly divide, of course, but it seems to me that there are too many disparate elements in Hinduism for it to have arisen out of a single cultural milieu. Perhaps the Aryans were not responsible for the demise of Harappan civilization. Perhaps nature, in the forms of climactic change, famine, and drought, was the primary agent of its doom. Nevertheless, the hypothesis that still makes most sense to me is that, in the second half of the the second millennium B.C.E., the Aryans overwhelmed India culturally if not militarily, providing the religious forms that gave new shape to the mystical substance of the pre-Aryan civilization once it reemerged into the light of history with the Upanishads.

1. The Marriage

Before she had time to say yea or nay, she found herself hurtling through a suddenly empty universe, and at the same time growing in size and translucence until she filled that universe; or seemed to fill it, because she had no way of really knowing, no longer being able to see any part of herself, or perhaps, not having any part to be seen, and not having anyone to tell the difference. It was all like a sweet and pleasant dream, as if she were a babe in her mother's womb.

Then the dream gradually turned into a nightmare. As she literally hung out everywhere and nowhere, a strange anxiety crept upon her, as if something or someone were looking over her shoulder, if she had had a shoulder to be looked over. In an uncontrollable spasm of fear, she felt an undeniable urge to become impregnable.

To be without fear, one had to be without danger; but likewise, to be without danger, one had to be without fear. To be without fear, one had to be without thought; because no matter how objectively safe one was, one could still imagine threats. To be without danger, one had to be without sensation. One cannot be hurt when one cannot feel hurt. However, could one be destroyed without feeling hurt? Then one must be hard, harder than anyone or anything that might strike, stab, burn, tear, or compress. What was hard, without sensation and thought, but still was? Imagination, the source of anxiety, also provided the answer.

For hundreds of eons she dreamt of herself as a rock, reveling in the security identification with that form brought. Finally, however, her life, her consciousness, dormant but still the most real "thing" in her, grew bored with a rock's limited or, should one say, non-existent possibilities; and she struck a compromise between fear and desire of life. The initial forms this compromise took were cautiously vegetable; but eventually, over a period of millions of years, she ventured into animal form. She transmigrated through every species, from ant to rabbit to muskrat to water buffalo, and even tasted of other animals' flesh as mighty lord of the jungle. No one of these incarnations could truly satisfy the spark of awareness, the *atman*, in her, so eventually she found herself in human form. Now she was an animal without any protection save what wit and cunning could fashion, but there was no going back.

Through more thousands of years she passed from one human form to another. Over many lifetimes her spirit began to awaken to the fact that she had but two choices: she could live for the happiness and security that came to her from the things she found in the world, or for those moments of peace and inner joy that had little or nothing to do with what went on around her. The way of identification with the rock now struck her as safety bought at the price of imprisonment. The way of identification with the animal brought momentary satisfaction of desire, but afterwards emptiness and unrest. It seemed as if there must be another way, but she had no idea what it could be, only brief flashes of intuition, as if a memory of something were remembering her.

Then came a turning point. She incarnated as a dark, exquisitely beautiful princess in a land renowned for the industry, wealth, cleanliness and sophistication of its people. They were not noted, however, for their military might, so the inevitable happened. Raiders massed on the borders and, when there was no retaliation against their exploratory forays, poured through the mountain passes and surrounded the capital. The princess, outwardly calm but inwardly feeling an eerie mixture of fear and expectation, sat in her private study awaiting the enemy assault. Her father's soldiers would meet the barbarians on the ramparts and die, but here she would encounter them on her own terms. Here, even if there were no way around death, she would at least have the opportunity to pit her spirit against their flesh.

She sat through the night and most of the following day, sometimes heeding the sounds of battle as the fighting drew steadily nearer, but most of the time drawn into an inner quiet that felt like the hush of her spirit before death. At sunset of the second day, the silence was broken by the entrance of a solitary warrior. He was taller and brawnier than any at her father's command, and the sword and shield he wielded made the weapons carried by the two guards at the passageway look like child's toys. With a quick lunge and swifter slash of his blade, the fiery barbarian, with hair like the sun and eyes like the sky, dispatched the slaves and turned to her in lusty triumph.

"I am your lord," he said, in a language utterly foreign but unmistakable in its meaning.

She neither bowed nor protested, but met the proud look on his handsome visage with two pools of infinite depth where her eyes had once been, pools in which, she could see from a sudden tremor through his body, he feared to drown.

"I will be your slave," she returned, though she knew he could not understand a word she said, "but I will not be in your service. You see, I had a vision just before you entered. It was as if I were a child again, sitting beside a pond on a calm and sunny summer day; and high above, on a lonely mountain peak, was a fairy-tale castle. I wanted to live in that castle more than I've wanted anything in my life. To me it meant everything—fun, joy, peace, adventure, wisdom, love. But there was a problem."

"What was it?" came a strange and undoubtedly masculine voice out of the passageway's deepening twilight. As she stared, she made out another tall and light-skinned figure approaching. It was another barbarian, but this one was obviously no warrior. His shaved head and assured yet self-restrained manner led her to conclude that he was some sort of priest. "What was your problem?" he quietly persisted, as if he were accustomed to being obeyed.

Addressing herself to the warrior, who had respectfully but not slavishly bowed to the priest, she continued as if there had been no interruption. "The castle was perfectly reflected in the still, clear pond."

"So you have to decide," interrupted the priest, "which castle is the real one, and which the reflection."

"Should I choose the one high overhead," she explained, again without acknowledging the priest, "which would require a difficult and dangerous climb; or the one right before me, that seems I need only reach out and touch?"

"Let me guess," the priest laughed. "I've made it my business to familiarize myself with not only your language, but also your philosophy and customs. Knowledge of an enemy is more powerful a weapon than brute force," he added parenthetically, despite or perhaps because of her apparent lack of interest. "You chose the image rather than the reality."

"We all have," she finally turned to him. "That's why we are here. We look for fulfillment outside ourselves, when peace can only be found deep within."

"The spiritual mountain!"

"Yes, the spiritual mountain," she echoed, not knowing or caring if he was indulging in priestly condescension. "You think you have conquered us, but in reality it is my spirit that summoned you here."

"For what purpose?" The priest, surprisingly enough, seemed absolutely serious.

"To free me from the concerns of this illusion so that I may devote myself entirely to the spiritual quest."

"You are a dreamer," he smiled, "and a beautiful one at that. I'm sure my friend here will be more than happy to relieve you of such concerns, if by 'illusion' you mean what pertains to flesh and blood."

"I mean whatever comes from without," she clarified, not caring if he believed her or not. "You see, our people are urbane and sophisticated. You are barbarians. We farm and build great cities, with magnificent baths and sewage systems to keep ourselves free of pollution. You maraud and wander with your stinking herds. Through your *soma* and magic, you seek power and ecstasy in this life, with no belief in the next. In the world we cultivate harmony, and in meditation we go deep within, breaking the ties of sense that bind us to the otherwise endless round of death and rebirth. We worship the Great Mother who gives life, while your gods are all brutal and domineering males who bring death!"

"Not all," the priest mused. "I myself have always had a particular affection for the rosy goddess of the dawn."

"We are civilized people who know how to preserve language in writing, and who build magnificent edifices and well-ordered cities. You are barbarians who sing lusty hymns to your gods and fight magnificently against anyone whose possessions you covet. You are expert at tearing down, but haven't the least power or desire to build up."

She waited for signs of anger from her audience. She knew that the enemy was extremely proud, so proud that they called themselves *aryans*, the "noble ones." She knew that their simple society, unlike her own economically multifaceted and socially stratified one, was divided into three groups: the priests (*brahmin*), nobles and warriors (*kshatriya*), and merchants and traders (*vaishya*), in order of descending prestige; and that all real work was left to women and slaves. She knew that the warriors, of whom the blond giant who had slaughtered her guards was an excellent specimen, were vain and constantly on the lookout for any pretext to pick a fight. She knew that the priests, to which group her interlocutor had to belong, were proud of their sophistication and learning, as well as their ability to maintain the cosmic order through ritual and sacrifice. It was a perfect opportunity.

The warrior had wiped his sword with the skirt of his tunic, but, eying her, hesitated to return it to its sheath. The priest, too, stared at her, quite possibly because he wanted to drink his fill of her beauty before she disappeared from his sight; but she had no idea whether he expected her to go into the tent of some mighty noble or down to the grave. It was the priest who finally broke the uneasy silence. "What do you propose?" he asked warily.

"A marriage between my people and yours."

He laughed. "You are hardly in a position to make such a proposal, and I am certainly in no position to agree to it."

"It doesn't matter," she replied with quiet but intense conviction. "It will happen. My people are too cultured, too beautiful, too mystical for you barbarians not to take us to wife."

"But it would be a marriage of fire and water!" The priest was no longer smiling. "You are so obsessed with ritual purity that some of your holy men hesitate to harm a fly. We, on the other hand, see the connection between animal sacrifice and cosmic order, and so slaughter animals without number, consuming them in Agni's divine fire to generate the power that maintains the cosmos. You are in love with death, and so fear convinces you that you are chained to an endless series of lives. We embrace our one life and our one death. Why should we quench our holy flame in your sacred river?"

She met his fear with chilling calm. "Water drowns fire, but fire also evaporates water. Either way, the visible is taken up into the invisible."

"Why should we want to be taken up into the invisible?"

"Would you rather be like him?" She nodded toward the warrior and he grinned in return, no doubt thinking certain arrangements were being made. In a way he was right, but to be right for the wrong reasons sometimes was worse than being outright wrong, because the rot was hidden beneath the surface. She smiled at the priest, knowing that he was thinking the same thing.

"If you are right," he finally responded, "if it was indeed your spirit, the spirit of your people, that summoned us here, then everything will happen as you say no matter what I or anyone else thinks. What do you want of me?"

"Earthly marriage is a makeshift affair." The young princess spoke with the authority of an elderly matron, but the priest offered no challenge to her wisdom. On the contrary, he attended to her every word with the utmost respect. "We put so many safeguards around it because we don't trust it. There are no safeguards to be put around spiritual marriage. All one can rely upon is the thing itself. My spirit brought you here, but your spirit chose to come. Will you go only half-way with your conquest, or play it out to its logical end?"

"Logic?" the priest echoed ironically. Are we still in the realm of logic?"

"I would not know my lord," she answered in coy humility. "Cosmic order is your territory."

And with that, the priest took the princess' hand and gave it to the warrior. That was in northern India, present-day Pakistan, sometime in the second half of the second millennium B.C.E. She lived out the rest of her life as a concubine, but one of a special sort who never indulged in domestic gossip and infighting, and who spent the bulk of each day sitting alone in quiet inwardness. Most unusually of all, she received visits periodically from a famous and influential Aryan priest who, it was rumored, solicited her counsel before all his major decisions.

2. Karma

From that time forth, the Aryan and pre-Aryan peoples blended into one; or, to be more precise, they eyed each other warily, discovered qualities in each other's culture and understanding of life that were to their mutual liking, and finally came together and gave birth to a new culture, Hinduism. To be sure, the "father" in this marriage, the conquering Aryans, remained dominant in the partnership; but, as so often happens in such patriarchal arrangements, the "mother," who had been ravished and enslaved in body, in turn ravished and enslaved her master's spirit.

Ariana continued to pass from one human embodiment to another; but no longer did she wander aimlessly, an animal on two legs with a gender and a brain that was painfully self-conscious, agonizingly aware of its own flaws, limits, and weaknesses. Now she had a focus, a goal, and a way to reach that goal. If the outer world was too absurd to be bearable, and if the inner world could not be turned outward without it too becoming unbearable, without it too ceasing to be inward, why not leave the outer world behind? Why not take refuge in the soul? This was, however, easier said than done.

Suicide was no help. She tried that several times, only to find herself, after a suitable period of torment in a hell, back in the world as a puling, diaper-soiling baby. Nor was it possible simply to ignore the world. Someone or something always intruded, like the barbarians when she had been a princess. Finally, even when she did manage to arrange for herself a life of solitude, her own thoughts would not be stilled and inevitably would drive her back to human society to find some distraction. Her intimations of peace were unmistakably real, but they also had a life of their own apparently independent of her will. The inspiration that came to her the evening of the pre-Aryans' downfall eventually petered out, and she was close to despairing of ever finding a way out of this endless round of death and rebirth, this hellish maze taking her down one blind alley after another.

Eventually, however, she began to discern a pattern. In one life she was an untouchable who picked dead animals up off the streets. She—or rather "he," because she was a man in this lifetime—found himself outside a temple, when his attention was caught by loud shouts of triumph and joy. Despite the fact that outcastes were not allowed anywhere near the temple because the touch of an untouchable, or even the touch of an untouchable's shadow for the priests, was the spiritual equivalent of being showered with human excrement, he could not help himself. Not only was there the fascination of the forbidden, but also a spiritual warmth and camaraderie that he had never known. He managed to spend the rest of the afternoon, without being seen, sitting at a chink in the temple wall and drinking in the sights, and even more so the blessedness, of the worship within. It was not until he sought to slip away in the shadowy twilight that his presence was noted. Some children had been playing around his unattended cart and spread various members of its deceased occupants all over the temple grounds. When their elders emerged from the *puja*, they caught him as he returned to the cart. If they had taken time for reflection, no doubt they would have come up with a more torturous method of execution. Mercifully, they were so incensed at the desecration of the holy place that they immediately stoned him to death.

After that sorry episode, Ariana had to spend what seemed like hundreds of lifetimes in the most humiliating of incarnations, as highwaymen, washerwomen, prostitutes, and drunkards, all in foreign lands and all without hope of spiritual advancement. In one embodiment she even became king of a mighty nation, one she knew in her soul would eventually rule practically the entire world, including India. Yet her India was more beloved to her because it was the one society on earth focused on escaping the weariness and triviality of the world. To be king of a foreign land was simply to have the lion's share of that weariness and triviality.

When finally her soul returned to India, again as an untouchable, she would not go near a temple. Unfortunately, her outer self, again a male, sometimes had his own ideas. Then there ensued a struggle that generated nothing but misery for all aspects concerned. However, once her soul had learned the lesson, it was relatively easy to inspire her incarnation to follow. She realized that every deed brings with it certain consequences. They may not come immediately, but they will come, because action gives disposition to the soul. Just as if one walked north one would eventually come to the ice and snow of the Himalayas, so too when one did evil one eventually came to an evil end.

Thus, those who did evil became evil and attracted evil thereby. Those who did good became good and attracted good thereby. Action (or *karma* in the Sanskrit, the language of the Noble Ones, the Aryans) was the way in which the soul, the atman, mired itself in the world, succumbing to the endless round of death and rebirth. She discovered how to accumulate good karma and avoid bad karma, to do what was given her as an outcaste, so that finally she might place her feet, so to speak, on the social ladder and climb, lifetime after lifetime, toward something she only knew, by toil and anguish, what it was not.

3. Caste

The society of the Noble Ones to which her soul had finally gained admission was a kaleidoscopic maelstrom of fear, desire, lust for power, and passion for liberation from passion; but counteracting this chaos was an order neither imposed nor intrinsic, but spiritually inspired. The priests, or *brahmin*, were its mentors, its spiritual guides, who had proved themselves through many lifetimes to be expert at bringing what could be thought, seen, felt, heard, and smelled into harmony with what could not. They did everything from conduct the sacrifices that made the women and fields fertile, to formulate the most abstruse understandings of the nature of truth and illusion, being and non-being. Most important of all, they set the ground rules for everyone else, for they alone had the wisdom to order society toward the spiritual goal.

Next came the *kshatriya*, the nobles and warriors, whose duty was to protect the society from those deluded peoples who would conquer and destroy it. To them was entrusted both political and military power, to be exercised within the cultural limits, however, set by the priests.

The brahmin and kshatriya were high-caste.

The third class was the *vaishya*, the merchants and traders and land-managers, who provided for the material needs of the society. The wealth that they amassed was theirs to spend, so long as they paid generous fees to the priests and ample taxes to the nobles, as well as subsistence wages to the simple laborers below them.

The brahmin, kshatriya and vaishya were upper-caste. Their numbers were in inverse proportion to their social significance, making up less than a tenth of the people.

The vast majority of the population formed the *shudra*, the peasants and laborers, because in a farming society with the simplest tools and methods there was much work requiring many hands.

The shudra were low-caste.

And finally, there were the *pariah*, the outcastes or untouchables. As far as she could tell, they were a bit more numerous than the upper castes combined. Ariana well remembered her lives in this penal colony of the soul. Those who seriously violated the mores of this most perfect of social orders, along with their descendants, were shunned by society. The most serious transgression, of course, was marriage with someone of another caste. Intercaste marriage led to utter confusion of caste. The pariah were assigned work befitting their spiritual lassitude: cleaning toilets and latrines, collecting garbage, scavenging, and any task involving the handling of dead flesh, animal or human; so they were also the tanners, butchers and undertakers. They lived apart, in marshland and near cremation grounds. They were not permitted to own anything of value. They cooked and ate with broken crockery, and drank, bathed in and cooked with brackish water.

The priests taught everyone the spiritual significance of this hierarchy.

Everyone and everything owes its being to the great spiritual sun of *Brahman*. Just as a raindrop refracts the clear light of the sun into all the colors of the rainbow, so too does the pyramid of delusion, fear and desire have a prismatic effect upon the clear light of being. And just as all the colors in the world are various combinations of the three primary colors, so too is the infinite multiplicity of phenomenal existence the result of the interweaving of the three strands of being, or *gunas*, the primary refractions of the pure light of absolute being.

The purest and best is *sattwa*, the light of being. To sattwa belongs the blue of the sky, the knowledge of the mind, the contemplation of the seer, the wisdom of the sage, and the patience of the spirit. Those, like the priests, who are predominantly sattwa are even-tempered and alert, thoughtful and self-restrained, calm and lovers of peace. They eat food to sustain life, not to indulge their palates, and so partake only of healthful fruits and vegetables. They are content with doing the duty to which their karmic destiny leads them, and they find happiness in solitude and contemplation.

If sattwa is the light of being, *rajas*, the second guna, is its heat, its energy. Human beings dominated by rajas, like the nobles and warriors, are passionate, lustful, proud, arrogant, and insatiable. Whether in diet or love, they always seek the pleasure of the moment. They do not eat to sustain life so much as to please their palates, so they indulge in salt and spices, and are connoisseurs of all manner of condiments and meat. In love, their tendency is toward absolute devotion until a woman is conquered, and then they look for another, more enticing challenge. On the other hand, they are magnificent warriors, and, if properly educated, can be prodigious builders and energetic administrators; for they worship and live for honor and glory. The yellow of the spleen belongs to rajas, but so does that of a golden harvest or a benevolent sun.

The third and last guna is *tamas*, the darkness without contrast to which there would be no light. Tamas is the ballast of being, sheer existence devoid of all other qualities, the being of a rock. Its color is the red of the blood, of blind instinct. Those dominated by tamas are concerned with material security and prosperity more than the power and pleasure of rajas or the enlightenment and peace of *sattwa*. They always seek the path of least resistance, and will do anything to keep self-awareness to a minimum. Pleasure to them is release from pain, and understanding simply confirmation of their own triviality. They are attracted to starchy and unwholesome foods. If left to themselves, they sink into utter spiritual darkness.

Thus human beings, through their own karma, arrange themselves in a spiritual hierarchy. It is only fitting that human society should mirror that hierarchy. Only in this way can order triumph over chaos, and the structure of human existence serve rather than impede the great quest for spiritual liberation.

The caste system that the priests devised, therefore, served and reconciled what in most cultures are continually at odds—society's need for stability, and the individual's drive for growth and self-transformation. The beauty of it all, which Ariana readily appreciated, was that here was achieved no mere compromise or balance between collective and personal necessity. By going to the spiritual root of the matter, Hinduism discovered the ultimate identity of self and other, individual and society. One's true self was to be found and one's society was to be maintained through dedication to *dharma*, the duty assigned to one's station in life. Only through dharma could one advance spiritually, and only through dharma could social and indeed cosmic order be preserved.

The priests explained that the realm of *maya*, the phenomenal veil hiding consciousness from its own true being, is like a prison. Even if a king's favorite artist were to poach in the king's deer park, he would have to spend his days digging in the royal mines and his nights in a cage with the rest of the criminals. One might bemoan the waste of a great talent, but justice takes precedence over utility, because justice is the very order of the cosmos. Human dharma is simply imitation of cosmic *rita*, by which all find their proper place in the universal scheme of things.

The lesson to be drawn is that, no matter how highly gifted in intelligence or aesthetic sensibility, one born a shudra or pariah, for example, should be content with his lot. A superior soul in an inferior caste certainly has done some terrible wrong in a previous lifetime, and can not go on to the higher castes without first paying its karmic debt. To ignore that debt is to court disaster; for, in the spiritual realm as in the phenomenal, it is no less true that not to go forward is automatically to go backward. Ariana even heard it said that some souls go back to animal existence or worse, though she herself never experienced such a regression and had no idea if it were possible.

What the priests said made sense to her. Tamas was sloth, resistance, inertia, and to overcome it one needed energy, passion. Rajas was energy, but energy without direction was destructive, not only of itself but all that got in its way. Sattwa was guidance and understanding, and so it belonged in authority. Since the priests were predominantly sattwa, they should guide everyone else. Since the nobles and warriors were predominantly rajas, they should defer to the priests but rule over the rest. Since the merchants and laborers were, in increasing measure, predominantly tamas, they should serve the priests and the nobles, the one with their minds and the other with their bodies. Finally, since the untouchables, the pariah, were almost pure tamas, it was only right that their lives be given over to the most degrading and spiritually polluting tasks.

Thus the caste system formed a spiritual ladder from earth to heaven, from the seen to the unseen, by which a soul might climb to liberation. And how did a soul do that? Those lost in the inertia of tamas learned discipline. Those on fire with the passion of rajas learned honor and responsibility. Those content with the self-contained wisdom of sattwa learned that the truly ultimate reality could be reached not by dwelling in oneself, but only by going beyond oneself. The great light of Brahman, the universal absolute, and the little light of atman, the essential self, were both one light; but that identity of atman and Brahman, of inner and outer being, self and the God beyond the gods, could only be realized through transcendence of the false self with which the soul had come to identify. Dharma, duty as prescribed by caste, was the only way of going beyond the false self. Only by working one's way up the ladder of spiritual development from laborer through merchant and noble to priest, from the darkness of tamas through the heat of rajas to the light of sattwa, could the soul lost in delusion ever be in a position to make the final leap to Brahman, the ineffable bliss and peace of being itself.

4. The Four Stages of Life

Over many lifetimes, Ariana saw the wisdom of the priests at work. The society of the Hindus, of those living in the Indus River Valley, was unlike any other on earth. Certainly, other societies had different social classes, hierarchically arranged not only according to wealth but also birth. In other societies, priests held positions of influence and even leadership. Those foreign priests, however, were nothing like the Indian brahmin. They knew nothing of Brahman, the ultimate reality, or atman, the essential self, much less of the identity of the two. They knew nothing of maya—how this phenomenal world of touch, taste, hearing, seeing, feeling, and even thinking, was nothing but a veil hiding Brahman from atman. Thus they pursued the vanities of maya, even in religion; while the priests of Hinduism built a society as Ariana's princess long ago had known they would, focused on one goal—liberation from the wheel of death and rebirth. It was as if they had lowered a rope to one drowning, and she could not have been more grateful.

Though her attention, at least in her soul, was now solely upon transcendence of the phenomenal world, she now understood not only how it was necessary to order that world in order to go beyond it, to form it into a ladder upon which to climb above it, but also how the spiritual focus alone could bring intrinsic and lasting peace. First of all, if everyone held one little incarnation in the phenomenal world to be the only life one lived, all would, like the original Aryans, maraud and kill to get what they could before their time was up. The only social peace would be the peace of convenience, of honor among thieves; and when the thieves had no more victims to rob, they would turn on one another. Second, if each individual had his own spiritual focus but did not contribute to the maintenance of the social order through work and raising a family, then the only thread leading through this labyrinth of delusion would be snapped, and everyone would be trapped.

Thus Hindu culture had two overriding imperatives: first, to reach spiritual liberation; and second, to maintain a social order keeping the way open to spiritual liberation. From one lifetime to the next, Ariana witnessed how these imperatives gradually took hold of a chaotic land, weaving vastly different cultures and sub-cultures into a harmonious pattern whose keynote was inner tranquility. Certainly, people continued to seek wealth and pleasure, but added to the centrifugal power of these worldly goals was the centripetal force of *dharma* and *moksha*, social duty and spiritual liberation. And certainly, the society continued to be divided up into thousands of occupational and special-interest groups; but by turning each group into a sub-caste, birth into which determined not only one's social status but type of work, diet, and range of marriage partners as well, the borders of each group were clearly marked and each group's place in the scheme of things clearly defined. Of course,the reality never quite matched the design, for nothing in the realm of maya could be perfect. Brahman, the invisible absolute, alone was perfection. There continued to be infighting among the various castes, and occasionally even untouchables sought a short-cut out of their dharma. Nevertheless, she began to feel that, in time, the tiny beam of light that Hinduism brought into the world would grow to illuminate the entire cosmos.

Particularly powerful to her was the priestly concept of the Four Stages (*ashrama*) of life. It was as if the Aryan penchant for order and the inchoate mysticism of the pre-Aryans had, in their fusion, undergone an alchemical transformation. Each culture had been after the quick fix, the one materially, the other spiritually. Their marriage had taught them, as so many marriages do, both the power of patience and the value of repetition. Just as a blood or grass stain upon snowy cotton necessitated repeated washings, so too did karmic impurities deep in the soul require incarnation after incarnation of slow, steady and balanced effort in order to gradually work the soul free. From one lifetime to the next, the balance in this effort was maintained through the Four Stages of Life.

Since the Four Stages were for bringing the individual soul into harmony with the cosmic pattern of order leading to liberation, the priests explained, only the upper-caste males, the priests, nobles, and merchants, were expected or even permitted to fully realize the ideal of balanced existence the *ashrama* signified. One first had to come into harmony with the cosmos before one could embody the harmony of the cosmos. Nevertheless, the ideal exercised a benign and purifying influence upon the entire culture.

The first stage was that of the student, *brahmacharya*. A brahmin boy at the age of seven, a kshatriya boy at the age of eleven, and a vaishya boy at the age of twelve would be sent away to school—again, an *ashram*, but this time signifying a community devoted to a spiritual purpose. These schools were staffed by priests and located, like boarding schools anywhere, away from the distractions of the larger society, especially that of the opposite sex. In these schools a boy would learn the overwhelming importance of Hindu culture for the spiritual health and social harmony of his world, and specifically what his job would be to help preserve that culture. Such education would take only a year for a vaishya, who would learn the family business by doing it at home; and two years for a kshatriya, who would be educated in the arts of war and/or government by his father or his father's appointed representatives; but a brahmin boy would spend as many as twelve or thirteen years in the ashram. He not only received a more in-depth philosophical training, since he would be one of the society's spiritual guides; but he also had to learn the specifics of whatever branch of priestcraft his sub-caste was assigned. Some priests practiced medicine, learning the role of regimen and diet in maintaining health, as well as the use of herbs, massage, baths and poultices in restoring it. Others developed skill in discerning the fine points of custom and law that inevitably came into dispute. Most, however, specialized in several of the numerous sacrificial rituals by which the priests had maintained the cosmic order from time immemorial. The rituals themselves were repetitive and relatively simple, but it was necessary to memorize long passages of the *Vedas*, the holiest scripture, to chant in accompaniment. These rituals, and the chanting that went with them, established a harmonic vibration by which the entire society kept itself in spiritual tune, and so it was from these rituals that all blessings, material as well as spiritual, ultimately flowed.

The second stage, that of the householder or *grihastha*, followed logically from the first. The boy would return home, at thirteen if he were kshatriya or vaishya, or twenty if he were brahmin, and take up the work of a man. He would marry the woman of the head of his clan's arranging, she would come to live with him in his clan's compound, and he would have children and go about the business for which he had been born and trained.

These first two stages, Ariana realized, were to be found in one form or another in every society on earth. Every culture educated its children, reserving higher learning for those who would become its movers and shakers; and when those children grew, it required that they contribute to the maintenance and improvement of society. Most societies, however, stopped there, regarding education as serving productivity, and often making productivity, if not an end in itself, at least a stop-gap in the place of an ultimate end, as though if human beings stayed busy enough they might forget the absurdity of their lives. The latter two stages of the Hindu schema, though restricted to the upper castes and especially the priests, relativized the daily round of earning and spending, working and playing, and pointed to something beyond.

The third stage was that of the forest dweller (*vanaprastha*), or withdrawal. When an upper-caste male saw his sons' sons, he might leave the family home, taking his wife with him if he pleased, and go into the wilderness. He would live in a cave or makeshift hut, grow a few vegetables and gather nuts and berries and roots, and occasionally receive visits from his family. If his wife were with him they would live as brother and sister, no longer engaging in sexual intercourse. In any case, he would spend the bulk of his time in prayer, meditation, and study of the scripture, preparing for the moment of death, which was a supreme opportunity to face the spiritual enemy of delusion, overcome one's attachment to the phenomenal world and make great spiritual advancement. Some sages even claimed that dying with a holy name of God prayerfully on one's lips, a name of one of the many personal faces of absolute being, ensured total spiritual liberation.

The fourth stage of renunciation, that of the wandering ascetic (*sannyasa*), was for those who would go even further, but was reserved in theory for the brahmin. A priest who had seen his sons' sons would perform his own funeral ritual, signifying that he was dead to his family and his world. Then he would shed all but the most necessary clothing (and in southern India it was so warm that the *sannyasi* often went naked), including his sandals, and leave his home on foot, traveling at least two-hundred miles away. Never, at least in his present lifetime, would he come within the radius of two-hundred miles of his former home. In a society in which one could live out one's life in a village and never know anyone from a village five miles away, this ensured that he would never meet up with anyone who knew him again.

Then the sannyasi would simply wander. If passing through a wilderness, he might feed on nuts, roots, and berries. If among people he would, without soliciting, permit them to earn spiritual merit by dropping scraps into his wooden begging bowl; and he would eat whatever he was given with supreme indifference. Most important of all, he would not talk to anyone and no one would talk to him, but he would remain in perpetual contemplation of ultimate being.

Not too many men undertook the strenuous discipline of *sannyasa*, but the fact that it was the ideal climax of human existence gave tremendous dignity to old age and maintained the culture's spiritual focus. The sannyasa ideal also reminded everyone, including the priests, that caste was an emergency measure for a spiritually fragmented universe. Even though the priests forbade anyone but from among their own number to take up the life of the wandering ascetic, the practice by its very nature could not be controlled. As the priests themselves taught, a sannyasi was beyond name and caste. So, once one discarded social persona and took up the beggar's bowl, one's caste standing was impossible to determine. A sannyasi was regarded by everyone as a "god-upon-earth". At death, everyone else's body, because it would otherwise pollute the earth, was cremated. Only two kinds of bodies were pure enough to be buried in their mother earth—that of an infant and a sannyasi.

5. Women

Through many lifetimes Ariana worked her way slowly up the caste ladder, occasionally even ending her life as a sannyasi, but never quite focused enough to die with a name of God reverently on her lips. Actually, one should say "his" lips because, for some unaccountable reason, except for an occasional incarnation early on, she had not been a woman since as pre-Aryan princess she had brought her Harappan culture into spiritual marriage with that of the "noble ones," the Aryans.

Then, just as she seemed to be reaching the finish line, just as she had completed a lifetime as a dedicated and successful priest, she found herself beginning a new cycle of incarnations as women. And not just women! There came rebirth after rebirth as outcastes! As before, Ariana was aware of herself between incarnations, like a sleeper who awakens briefly between nightmares; but in embodiment her awareness seemed to be split, and at times her deeper Ariana-self was overwhelmed and seemingly lost, only to reemerge at death. She nearly despaired, because it seemed that all her patient effort had gotten her nowhere.

Being an untouchable woman was not too different from being an untouchable man. Life was an endless round of dirty, humiliating and exhausting work punctuated by exhausted and restless sleep, with an occasional and perfunctory coupling, usually initiated by her man, in-between. The one great difference was that she had to bear the children. This was done often in silent and solitary agony, because no one cared to hear her troubles, not even herself.

Life as a laborer, a shudra, was better. Though generally she gave birth in the fields, the work was healthier and the daily round was frequently punctuated by festivals in honor of one or another of the many Hindu goddesses or gods. Also, though again her place was usually in the home when not in the fields, whenever her work was done and some other woman in the household agreed to tend to her children, she might visit the temple of her chosen god, Vishnu, who was in her estimation the noblest and handsomest of all the deities, which was no trivial thing given that there were, she had heard, three hundred and thirty million of them. Best of all, she no longer had to endure the isolation and shame of untouchability, but could roam freely throughout village and town without fear of being beaten or stoned to death for drawing too near the dwelling places of those ascending the noble ladder of caste.

Best of all were her lifetimes as a vaishya, especially as a merchant's wife. Deep in her soul, she marveled at the change that had come over her. As the pre-Aryan princess nothing had brought her joy but the dream of spiritual liberation from the pettiness of phenomenal existence. Now she positively took pleasure in that pettiness, finding in it a refuge from the disturbing question that was coming more and more to haunt the inner recesses of her being: what if there were no way out? What if the ladder of caste turned back upon itself? What if the round of death and rebirth were truly endless? Busy with the endless detail in the day-to-day running of her husband's business, she forgot about the deeper endlessness of doubt and despair. Not even in the temple, where she immersed herself in the festive ritual, did it rise to the surface of her awareness.

It began to seem to Ariana that she might go on in this split between superficial contentment and profound desperation for all eternity, when two successive shocks brought both sides into violent confrontation.

As a kshatriya, the consort of a powerful noble, she was able to continue her program of worldly distraction with a vengeance. Surrounded by numerous slaves and maidservants, she made it her business to manage the personal life of everyone who came within her orbit. This she did not in an unkindly way, and often with satisfactory and even welcome results for all concerned. Nevertheless, it gave her a sense of power that made her feel at once satisfied and guilty, as if she had been caught making love with the handsome young knight who commanded her husband's guard and who evidently adored her. She felt that something had gone awry, that she was off her spiritual track; but she had neither the will nor the wisdom to set things aright.

Then, out of the blue, her world came tumbling down. Her husband and liege lord died in his sleep. He was a relatively young man who had proved himself a tireless hunter and formidable warrior, and there was no evidence of foul play, so there was only one possible explanation for his death. She had committed a sin of omission or commission that had brought bad karma upon him. There was only one way to expiate the guilt, and that was to commit *sati*, the act of a "virtuous woman"—throwing herself on his funeral pyre.

She did not have much time to make up her mind, only a few hours, as bodies decayed rapidly in the subtropical heat. Her children did not try to persuade her, as was usually the case in such a situation; but their silence was more effective than pleas and tears, because she knew it would go on the rest of her life if she did not take upon herself the duty of a high-caste Hindu widow. As her husband's body was being raised for transport to the cremation ground, she sat herself in the litter next to his. This action, in and of itself, did not betoken a decision one way or the other; but the glow of resignation in her eyes was an unmistakable beacon to all who knew her. Her sons, silently and gracefully, as befitted their upbringing, relieved the slaves of their burden and carried their mother to the place of her death. She was moved by this gesture, even though she knew it had a double meaning. It signified that they were grateful for the honor and spiritual merit that would accrue to the family on account of her sacrifice; but they would also be in place to force her to follow through, to do the right thing, if she should happen to change her mind.

The cremation ground was forbidding and eerie—a fitting place to meet death. When the double-littered party arrived, the slaves immediately set the body upon the raised platform around which piles of faggots had already been arranged; while she, without needing instruction from a priest, took up position at the innermost circle of the spectators' perimeter. It seemed like no time at all before the priests had mumbled the necessary prayers and the flames were climbing up the wood pile to devour her dead husband. Someone handed her a flask, and she drank deeply of a strange, at once sweet and sour-tasting liquid that seemed to clear her head. Suddenly the flames exploded into a thousand shooting stars, and a hand gently pushed her forward. Somehow she could see all her sons in her peripheral vision, even though some were standing not to either side but behind her; and their uniformly stern faces made her realize she was going to be with her husband. That thought, more than any fear of the fire, caused her temporary panic; but when she sought to flee, the flesh-of-her-flesh firmly barred her way. She was grateful for their patience. She had heard of women in her position changing their minds at the last moment and having to be dragged, kicking and screaming, to their dharma. Her sons knew her well enough to understand that, once she realized there was no way out, she would do with dignity what needed to be done.

Her final sensation in that particular embodiment was that of melting into a searing pain. After that, rather than finding herself in the company of her husband, her god, her highest master, there was a season of oblivion, and then immediate rebirth.

Her next lifetime was as a brahmin, a member of the priestly caste; but again she was a girl baby, and her family was unusually poor and insignificant. On the other hand, she herself was extraordinarily beautiful. Beloved and favored by parents and siblings alike, hers was a happy childhood, despite the necessity of making do with the minimum of food, shelter and clothing. Her father, it seemed, had had the double misfortune of not having any influential uncles or cousins, and of being extraordinarily stupid. Thus at ashram he had barely managed to learn a single ritual, the purification of a (spiritually) polluted well, and the scripture that accompanied it, and he was prone to make mistakes. Only the poorest villages that could afford no better hired him for that particular ritual; and it was only through the kindness or class-solidarity of his fellow priests that his own village accepted his muddled version as good enough, and that the well became unclean often enough for him and his family to get by.

One day, when she was eight, the most powerful and important priest of the village came visiting. When he left, she went with him. He was old, and his wife had recently died. From the time their little girl could walk, he told her parents, he had noticed her. Now that there was a place for her in his life, it would be to the advantage of both families to enter a marriage alliance. He would get a pretty young wife and, through association with him, they would no longer be poor and insignificant. Her parents immediately assented, but at first suggested a period of betrothal until she had become a woman. He pointed out to them, however, that should he die in the interim without having actually married their daughter, all the benefits accruing to them through the proposed alliance would be lost. Noticing that they still hesitated, he assured them that he would take good care of their hearts' treasure, and said what never should have needed to be said, that the marriage would not be consummated until she reached puberty. She knew all these details because he repeated them over and over again on their walk to his home, not, she sensed, out of intentional cruelty, but simply garrulous senility.

The marriage ceremony was unusually hurried, no doubt because her parents saw that the bridegroom might fall over any minute. Normally there would have been months of preparation culminating in a celebratory feast attended by all their relatives and friends, if not their entire sub-caste. The old priest himself, however, was adamant. The marriage was to be today, immediately, or not at all. So the sacred fire was lit and she was summoned to walk around it with the man to whom she would be shackled the rest of her life.

She knew what her parents had done, but she did not blame them. Yes, they had bartered her away like a prize cow, but what other hope did the family have? Why else had she been so privileged, so exclusively fattened and groomed?

The rest of her life proceeded as she foresaw. Before she had opportunity to lose her virginity, she was already a widow in a house filled with strangers who, if they were male, looked upon her with unrealizable lust, or, if they were female, regarded her with petty but deeply ingrained jealousy and mistrust. She tried to take some comfort in the social and financial boost her abortion of a marriage gave her siblings; but, as she grew old, a bitterness took hold of her soul that death could not extinguish. When she crossed the threshold between being and non-being, Ariana found herself back in the heavenly realm sitting opposite a smiling Ishwara; and though she was surprised, she could not smile back.

6. Yoga

He addressed her without wasting time on pleasantries. "The problem is that it is all a dream."

She stared at him, paralyzed by the conjunction of total comprehension and utter disbelief.

"All of it," he repeated.

"It can't be! There must be a way."

"There are many ways."

"Then why can't I find one?" she demanded of him with an intensity born of despair.

"Look around you," he chuckled. "Maybe you already have!"

"This is the goal, simply to return to the place whence I came?"

"If so," he put the implication into words for her, "what would I or anyone gain by marrying Ishwara? You are right. This is not the goal. It is merely a way station."

"If this is not the goal," she rejoined angrily, "then why have you been wasting my time this way?" It was clear from the tremor in her voice that anger was only a device to keep herself from dissolving into tears. "Why have you been wasting the time of hundreds of millions of Hindus?"

"Because before you were not ready to walk the true path. Now that you have exhausted every possible shortcut, you will have the patience to master the real way."

"Tell me the real way."

"In your play with the spirits of the earthbound, did you ever hear of *yoga*? You know, something to do with meditation, and tying oneself up into knots?"

She did not laugh.

"Actually, the *asanas*, the stretching exercises and unusual postures, are intended to help one sit in meditation for long periods without being distracted by pain and numbness. They also include sitting postures that enable the practitioner to lock the spine in place so that one may remain upright even in deep trance."

"Trance?"

"The actual going beyond," he explained. "*Samadhi*. When you were a princess way back at the dawn of Hindu civilization, you experienced it for one brief but glorious moment. You have been trying to recapture that moment ever since."

She nodded slightly but firmly, knowing that, however else Ishwara might deceive her, this was the absolute truth.

"You have been trying to climb the ladder of caste out of the labyrinth of *maya*, but there is no ladder."

"The whole point of the ladder," she laughed bitterly, "is to realize there is no ladder? The importance of caste is that caste is absurd?"

"You put the paradox nicely," he complimented her.

Her bitterness was not in the least diminished. "What do you mean by saying it is all a dream?"

"Have you ever dreamed?" He had the most annoying habit of answering a question with a question.

"I am a spirit," she stated the obvious.

"Yes," he persisted, "but just now, when you were incarnate, did you dream?"

"Yes, but I have no way of knowing if any of that was real, so I can't know if that was a real dream."

"That's just it!" Again his infuriating smile. "You had no way of knowing, and neither does anyone else." He paused for effect, but she would not give him the satisfaction of surprise. "When one dreams, one may experience entire universes of people, places, and things. Isn't that so?"

She nodded.

"And one may also live through histories of whole civilizations?"

She nodded again.

"And one dream may follow hot on the heels of another, so that one may live many lives in a single night. Where do all these dream worlds go when one awakens?"

"I don't understand. What do you mean?"

"Well, then, if that's too difficult a question, where do they come from? "

"I still don't know what you mean. They don't come from or go anywhere. They just appear and disappear."

"Creation out of nothing, eh?" he smiled. "Who is the creator, then?"

"The dreamer, of course."

"So, when you dream at night, you self-consciously create the dream the way a storyteller creates a story?"

"Of course not! Dreams just happen."

"But what do they mean?" he insisted.

She had never thought about it. "I suppose they are our hidden fears and desires."

"So all the millions of different persons, places, and things in a dream are different aspects of the dreamer?"

"Yes, I suppose you could put it that way," she assented, but with the disdain of the plain thinker for the intellectual.

Ishwara looked deep into her eyes, and for the first time, despite her anger, she admitted to herself that she might one day love him. "Consider this possibility," he said. "There is but one being, one dreamer, and we are all dream figures in his dream."

"But that would mean that you and I are the same being, that there is no 'we,' only 'I!'"

"Precisely," he confirmed, "with exception of the business of 'I.' Where there is no 'we,' there is no 'I.' "

"Then what is there?"

"Being itself, existence itself, what Hinduism calls *sat*."

"Sounds boring."

"You prefer what you've been living thus far?"

Ariana cast down her eyes, feeling crushed between the Scylla of tedium and the Charybdis of despair.

"Think, Ariana!" Ishwara exhorted her. "Was it boredom that led you to begin the endless round of rebirth?"

She remembered back to the time before time, when she had been everything and no-thing. "No, it was fear."

"Fear led you to identify with a form that gave you the illusion of security but no pleasure. From that point on, your existence was an endless series of compromises between the two. You can have both serenity and fulfillment, Ariana, you can have it all, if you will only stop living in a dream world. Realize that you *are* what you seek, and the forms in which you have unprofitably invested yourself will dissolve."

"Leaving what?" she asked sarcastically. "What is beyond all that is?"

"Absolute being," he replied.

"Being!" she mocked. "Define it for me!"

"It can't be defined," he said calmly.

"Just as I thought!" she cried in empty triumph. "Sheer and meaningless abstraction!"

"Only if one regards it as abstraction," countered Ishwara readily, as if he not only expected but welcomed this criticism. "Let me explain something to you. We're using words, right?"

Again, not only the statement but the questioning of the obvious. Nevertheless, she nodded because she wanted to see what he was getting at.

"There are two ways of understanding words: they define reality or they point to reality. The West has taken the first approach—whatever can't be defined is not real. The East has taken the second." His facial expression remained bland, but his tone could only be described as a verbal wink. "The West on this point is positively insane. A lot of what Westerners call mysterious, mystical, and even irrational in Eastern religion is nothing more than common sense. If what can be defined alone is real, then tell me, how do you define color to the blind, or music to the deaf? All definition ultimately depends upon some experience to which the words of a definition point. If one doesn't share the relevant experience, one won't understand anything in the definition except its verbal, that is to say its logical, form, and that is sheer abstraction!"

He gave her a moment to think. "So," she finally responded, "you're saying that the West has trapped itself in a tissue of abstraction that it calls reality, whereas what everybody knows to be real is dismissed as unreal because it can't be defined, only pointed to?"

"You are quick!" he beamed.

"But isn't that what *maya* is all about?"

"Yes, to be caught up in the dream, in the abstract representation of the self," he agreed. "But it goes deeper than thought or language. Like a dream, we don't just call it real or think it real. We feel, experience, live, and breathe it as real."

"So, to go beyond it," she continued his thought, "one must go beyond all thought, feeling, sensing, even the breath of life itself?"

"Exactly."

"But you still haven't answered the question—why bother?"

"To reach pure awareness, for which all that is is but a dream."

"So, it does exist!" she cried.

"No, it is existence itself."

"But how does one get there?" she demanded, ignoring his metaphysical subtleties. "What's the good of just showing a rope to a drowning person? Throw me the line!"

"Are you prepared to pay the price? Are you willing to go beyond yourself? Will you be the dream figure who insists on awakening even if it means your own disappearance?"

She nodded more decisively than she had ever done anything in her life. "I am."

"Then I will tell you the way, and then show you the ways."

"Proceed as you see fit," she encouraged him. "I am entirely at your disposal."

"It will mean death. The way of yoga, of union with God, of realization of one's true identity as the God beyond the gods, is also the way of breaking identification with your ego, your dream-self, and that is the way of death. One can experience death without dying, and one can die without experiencing death. The spiritual path involves the recurrent experience of death."

"I am ready," she assured him.

"That very statement shows that you are not," he declared. "You can never be ready. That's why death is death."

Again, she simply nodded.

"Alright," he seemed convinced, "if you give yourself entirely into my hands, I won't have to leave you to your own devices."

"Is that what you did before?"

"You had to come to the end of self. I have prepared for you several 'dreams' designed to show you the essentials of each path. My hand will be upon you in all that you think, feel, say, and do."

"I simply go along for the ride?"

"That's what you were doing anyway," he laughed. "Only now I can show you how to get where you want to go."

"Then all ahead full!" She returned his laugh, feeling a warmth that could well blossom into full-blown love.

"One more thing before we proceed," he said. "There are essentially four spiritual paths. I am going to show you them all, because it is crucial that you understand how diversity is not incompatible with unity, how different paths can all lead to the same goal. It is equally important to understand, however, that just as one may choose not to wear shoes of the proper size but cannot choose one's shoe size, so too one may choose not to take the proper spiritual path but cannot choose which path is right for oneself. That is determined by one's temperament."

"What are the four paths?"

"*Jnana*, or knowledge, for the thinker; *Bhakti*, or devotion, for the emotional type; *Karma*, or action, for the person of action; and finally *Raja*, the royal road, the yoga of power."

"One has to be one or another?" She felt the universe closing in on her again.

"Not at all!" he assured her. "One's path is determined by how one relates most spontaneously to life. The emphasis is upon the spiritual cutting edge, but one must bring one's whole self along. And remember, you don't have to stuff yourself into one of the four categories as if they were boxes to be shipped to a spiritual destination. They are simply points of reference by which to orient oneself. In traveling, physical or spiritual, it is crucial to know not only where one is going but also whence one comes."

"They all go to the same place but from different locations?"

"Exactly! Yes, you do learn well. But again I digress. An individual need not fit neatly into a particular category. One may be, and almost certainly is, a blend of some sort. Nevertheless one usually finds a dominant tendency. In a soul that is close to full self-realization, however, all paths join into one."

She looked down for a moment, sounding the depth of what he was saying, and then looked once again into those deceptively cheerful eyes of indeterminate hue. "I think I understand," she said, and with that the adventure began.

7. Jnana-Yoga

She was a queen, something like a latter-day Alexander the Great, only the Greece that her father had united and whose forces she led was the entire Western half of the Earth. She was engaged in the conquest of the Eastern half, with the goal of bringing the light of modern rationalism into the dark night of Oriental mysticism.

Her armies were poised on the enemy's frontier, and no one on either side doubted the outcome. It was the eve of her final victory, and she had planned to spend it visiting her troops; but she had been summoned back to headquarters by her most trusted aide, and therefore knew something required her immediate attention.

When she arrived and was told why her outing had to be cut short, she wondered aloud if a turn in the trenches might not do the formerly reliable chief of staff a world of good. It seemed some Hindu holy man had requested an audience, no doubt to toady up to the future empress of the world. For some unfathomable reason, her aide had been impressed. Since returning to the front that night was out of the question, she decided she might as well see for herself what manner of man had unsettled so balanced an officer.

The holy man was dressed like a typical brahmin, complete with loincloth and shawl, cloth sandals, and sacred thread over the shoulder. She had heard they never took off that thread, not even when bathing or making love.

The man joined palms and bowed, and was about to begin his spiel when she preempted him. "I've often wondered why you Hindus venerate cows. I've heard you believe your ancestors reincarnate in the beasts."

The priest smiled. At least he had a sense of humor.

"In point of fact, your Majesty, despite the superstition of some thoughtless peasants, a soul that has reached self-consciousness as a human cannot revert to a lower level. The cow is the living symbol of the divine mother. She is gentle and peaceful, and we derive butter, milk, cheese and fuel for our fires from all that she naturally excretes."

"Who excretes, the cow or the divine mother?"

"The fact that you had to ask," deftly countered the priest, "is itself the answer to your question."

"Then they are one?"

"They are one."

"Symbolically?"

"Spiritually."

"I seem to remember a similar attitude toward animals in our own antiquity," she mused. "But you said something disparaging of your laboring class. Do you priests really think you are naturally superior to everyone else?"

It was clear from his bearing that the man undoubtedly did.

"I did not come here to defend my civilization, your Majesty," he replied.

"What did you come here for?"

"To attack yours."

Of course she burst into laughter. "What do I do now, surrender?"

"I'd much rather you put up a fight."

She leaned forward. "I must say, this is the most interesting conversation I've had in ages."

The young priest smiled. "It will get even better, your Majesty, I promise you. But don't you think that, if I am attacking, you should summon your army?"

"I believe I can defend against this assault on my own."

"No doubt, your Majesty," the priest bowed; "but, in doing so, you would do me too great an honor."

She looked at the priest for the longest time, not knowing herself whether her next move would be to guffaw or to order the guard to cut off his head. At length, she smiled. "Alright priest, you win. I'll summon my army, just as soon as you tell me what you mean."

"Your best philosopher," he replied in absolute seriousness.

"You think I'm not capable of taking you on?"

"Why should we fight, your Majesty," the priest deeply bowed, "when at heart we are allies?"

"You and I?" she exclaimed. "Impossible!"

"You have come to destroy reason in the name of reason—that is what I will show you."

Her quizzical expression signaled him to proceed.

"I will demonstrate that it is not our culture that is imprisoned in the darkness of unreason, but yours."

"We the irrational ones?" she snapped. "We?" And then she laughed. "Alright, let the contest begin!" She bade her guards fetch the Professor, and then asked the priest, "What are the stakes? Surely you had something specific in mind."

"I have perfect faith in your Majesty's generosity and integrity," he replied. "I need only show you the truth of the matter."

She offered the priest a seat and some fruit and wine, and by the time they finished their repast the Professor had appeared. She explained the general nature of the contest, and then asked the priest what ground rules he proposed.

"Only one, Majesty: that each of us be judged on his own merits, that we be forbidden to argue on the basis of precedence or authority."

"No footnotes?" she smiled.

"Exactly," he smiled back.

"Impossible!" the Professor protested. "Are we to ignore the wisdom of the great thinkers of the past? Are we to reinvent the wheel?"

"Pardon me, your Majesty," said the priest, "but by his logic one could equally well argue that, because the ancients did it, we have no reason to eat or make love, only digest and have babies. Real thought always goes back to the beginning."

"Then I have a compromise to propose." She looked over both men with open curiosity, as if each were a specimen of some rare species of insect. "You, priest, wish to go back to the beginning. You, my dear Professor, wish to profit from the wisdom of our forebears. Why don't we take our wisest and most ancient of forebears as the standard by which the debate will be judged? The question here is which philosophy is truly rational, that of the West,"—here she gestured toward the Professor, who drew himself up to his full height—"or the East." The priest bowed without need of further cue. "Gentlemen, let Socrates be your judge."

Without waiting for the priest's acquiescence or his queen's permission, the Professor took it upon himself to begin.

"Socrates was a man who held reason to be supreme. He criticized the blind beliefs and superstitions of his time, and for that reason he eventually was put to death. His chosen deity, Apollo, was the god of science, music and light. Moreover, he held that open discussion, not mystical introspection, is the highway to truth. If Socrates is the standard, your Highness, you have no choice but to condemn this Hindu culture, with its mumbo-jumbo about mysticism, meditation, and reincarnation, to death!"

The Professor sat down, evidently satisfied that his opponent had been trounced before even opening his mouth.

"Your Majesty, may I cross-examine?" the priest asked.

"Of course! There will be nothing but due process here."

"Sir, I have heard something of this Socrates. He lived in the fifth century B.C.E., did he not? And his native city was Athens, in Greece?"

The Professor nodded on both counts.

"It's said he had some form of spiritual guidance, which he called his *daemon*. Isn't that so?"

"Yes," the Professor replied, "but that was nothing more than his way of talking about his conscience. The daemon would tell him what not to do, but never what to do. Doubtless he was speaking about moral guilt in a way his superstitious contemporaries could understand."

"What sort of thing did this daemon forbid Socrates to do?" continued the priest.

"Most notably, it forbade him to take part in the political life of Athens, a most unusual abstention in so democratic a society."

"Then such participation would have been morally wrong?"

"What are you talking about?" the Professor snorted. "I never said any such thing! The active participation of citizens in their own governance is a cornerstone of our Western civilization."

"Then forgive me, dear Professor, my logic must be faulty. It seems to me that, if Socrates' daemon was nothing more than his conscience, and if it forbade him to take part in the political life of Athens, then such participation must have been evil."

"Your logic is not faulty," the Queen interjected, while the Professor sat in flustered silence.

"There is something else I have heard about Socrates," the priest resumed. "Something about a prophetess, an oracle."

"The Oracle of Delphi," explained the Professor. "An extremely prestigious institution in ancient Greece, held to speak for Apollo. On the advice of the Delphic Oracle, the Athenians were once persuaded to abandon their city to the invading Persian army so their navy could have a free hand to destroy the Persian navy and sea-borne supplies in the battle of Salamis, a turning point in history that saved Western civilization from Oriental barbarism."

The priest smiled. "What did the oracle say of Socrates?"

"That he was the wisest of men!" The Professor could not have spoken with more pride had the oracle been speaking of himself.

"What do you Westerners call your wise men? We use the term *Jnana-yogi*, one who follows the spiritual path of knowledge."

The Professor took a moment to reflect. "I suppose 'philosopher' is as good a term as any."

"Such as yourself?" the priest said, and the Professor nodded. "What does that mean, 'philosopher?'"

"Literally, it means 'lover of wisdom.'"

"Literally?" queried the priest. "Not in its present usage?"

"No, no, 'lover of wisdom' is as good a definition today as it was twenty-five hundred years ago."

"Then I submit to you," pounced the priest, "that you are not a true philosopher."

"Before this goes any further," the Queen intervened, "someone will have to enumerate the characteristics of a true philosopher."

"A thinker," the Professor declared. "Someone whose reasoning is not swayed by anything but logic itself."

"Do you agree?" she asked the priest.

"I would say that a philosopher is someone who perceives reality through thought. I suppose we mean the same thing."

"I have a litmus test for determining who is a true philosopher," the Professor said. "It was developed by another of our wise men, Anselm of Canterbury, and it's called the Ontological Argument for the Existence of God."

"You are violating the terms of the compromise," the Queen objected.

"I'll allow it, your Majesty," conceded the priest.

"It's quite simple, really," the professor continued, almost boyishly eager. "If God may be defined as the greatest possible being, then a being with all possible perfections, including necessary existence, would be greater than a being with all possible perfections minus necessary existence. Therefore God exists necessarily, by definition."

"As long as the concept of God is not self-contradictory," added the Queen, and the Professor smiled condescendingly as his star pupil demonstrated what she had learned.

"So, priest," she added, "what do you think?"

"I think the truth of the argument, like that of all brilliant arguments, is self-evident. Of course God exists."

"But the argument?" insisted the Professor. "Are you convinced by the argument?"

"Is that the test of a true philosopher," the priest queried, "to accept this argument?"

"No, but at least to take it seriously, not to dismiss it out of hand as mere word-play or abstraction. How many times have I heard my idiotic pupils say, 'That's just an idea'? Just an idea? My God, we see with ideas!"

"Philosophical people do," the priest added. "Other people have other ways."

The Professor went on as if he had not heard.

"The idiots' thoughts are like pretty balloons they select for their pleasing shapes and colors, and carry around in their heads all day to make themselves feel good."

"And then you have the fanatics who think they are thinkers," the priest added. "To hold to fixed ideas, rather than allowing thought to be fluid and perceptive, is like putting on a pair of spectacles that systematically distorts vision and then driving out on one of your superhighways."

"One crashes and burns," said the Queen, but the Professor still seemed not to have heard. "Bringing this tete-a-tete back to the point, it seems that is what your civilization is doing, priest, with its fixed ideas about reincarnation, karma, caste, and spiritual liberation."

"Ah, but your Professor has only described half of a philosopher!"

"What do you mean?" The Professor certainly heard that remark.

"Sir, would you give us the pleasure of hearing Socrates' entire story?"

"I told the whole story," the Professor lied.

"But you left out details, and I've heard you Western wise men have a saying: 'The truth is in the details.' "

"Yes, we do," he agreed, "but that means relevant details. I didn't describe his features or mention his hair color, but I said everything that has bearing upon the present issue."

"Your Majesty," the priest persisted, turning to the Queen, "would you fill in the details?"

"I'd be happy to. When Socrates heard the god had named him the wisest of all, he laughed, not out of disrespect, but because he thought Apollo surely must have been joking. Of all human beings, Socrates certainly knew that he himself knew nothing."

"Whereas your philosophers claim to know everything?"

"But that was all Socratic irony!" the Professor protested.

"Oh, I see," rejoined the priest. "If something tallies with your idea of Socrates, it is factual; if not, it is ironical."

"To proceed with the story," said the Queen, cutting short the budding squabble, "Socrates decided that the god had given him a mission."

The priest smiled, but remained silent.

"He was to prove Apollo was jesting by seeking out real wisdom. A stonecutter by trade, he had always spent more time than his wife would have liked engaged in philosophical discussion; but now he gave up his work almost entirely in favor of a higher calling. He spent his time talking with anyone, rich or poor, native or foreign, to find out the purpose of human existence."

"Yes, that's the origin of the Socratic method," observed the Professor.

"If I may be so bold, your Majesty?" asked the priest.

She nodded.

"Pardon me, Professor, but I don't see any 'method' in Socrates at all. He simply was a man seeking sincerely after the truth of human existence who thought, quite naturally, that the best place to look was among his fellow humans. People want to find a method to life, it makes life easier to control; but there is none."

"Still spouting your irrational mysticism?" hissed the Professor.

The Queen was tempted to say that she rather agreed with the priest, but she was enjoying the fray too much to give one side a decisive edge over the other, so she went on with the story.

"Wonder of wonders, Socrates discovered that, though numerous people thought they understood what life was all about, upon closer questioning they proved not to know what they were talking about. This futile quest for wisdom made him so popular that, after years of popping everybody's pretty balloons,"—she smiled at the Professor in recognition of the source of this metaphor—"he was brought up on capital charges, found guilty, and executed."

"I heard he committed suicide," the priest remarked.

"Not at all!" said the Professor. "That was simply the Athenian method of execution, having the condemned drink hemlock. They thought it absolved them of blood-guilt, but it was no more suicide than when a condemned individual in our society doesn't wrestle with the executioners while being injected with poison or strapped in an electric chair."

"I also heard that he could have escaped any time before or after his trial, up to the fateful hour."

"That's so," confirmed the Professor. "He thought that running away from his country would be betrayal even if he were the victim of injustice, seeing how Athens had nurtured him, both physically and intellectually, even more than his mother and father."

"He also knew that the same thing would happen to him anywhere else," the Queen added sardonically, "people being what they are."

"Yes," said the priest, "but wasn't the essential reason he stayed that we humans have no real reason to think death evil, and thus no reason to fear it? That death may even be a positive good, releasing the soul from bondage to the body?"

The Professor eyed the priest warily. "Yes, but he identified the soul with reason."

"Or he identified reason with the soul. Tell me, dear Professor, have you no reason to fear death?"

The Queen laughed, and the Professor reddened. "Are you so free of fear yourself?" he shot back at the priest.

"You already know the answer to that by my coming here."

Not even the Queen laughed at this irrefutable rebuttal.

"Tell me, priest, you said that the Professor had hit upon only half of genuine philosophy."

"Yes, to perceive reality through thought."

"What's the other half?"

"Let me illustrate," he bowed to her and then turned to the Professor. "I imagine, sir, that you are what is known in the West as a 'professional philosopher?' "

"Yes, I am a professional," the Professor replied with a resurgence of pride.

"And by that you mean that you teach philosophy in an ashram?"

"A university," the Professor corrected.

"A university. And you write articles for professional journals that can be understood only by other professionals?"

"I understand the importance of popularizing," replied the Professor, "to the extent that it is possible, the findings of rigorous thought; but yes, the bulk of my publication has been in professional journals."

"And you belong to a professional organization, attend professional conferences, present professional papers, and even hire yourself out as a professional consultant?"

"Yes, yes, primarily to computer software developers and occasionally to lawyers and businessmen. But what is the point?"

The Queen was already smiling, but she did not dream of spoiling the punchline.

"You say that philosophy is love of wisdom," answered the priest. "That would make a philosopher a lover of wisdom, would it not?"

"Yes, of course."

"Then what is a professional philosopher?"

The Professor was genuinely puzzled. "I don't understand, I've already told you."

"Put it together," the priest insisted.

The Queen could hold back no longer. "A professional lover of wisdom."

"And what is a professional lover?" asked the priest, still addressing the Professor. The latter rose, looking as if he would have killed the priest that moment if the task were not beneath his exalted intellectual status, and strode from the room without so much as a perfunctory "By your leave" to the Queen, who was laughing so hard she took no notice. After she quieted a little, the priest said, "The worst prostitutes are not out walking the street. At least ladies and gentlemen of the night don't deceive themselves about what they are doing."

"And I, O wise man, am I too a prostitute?"

"That you will decide today, your Majesty, by how you deal with me and my people. If I convince you that we do represent the light of reason in the world, and yet you go on to destroy us simply to complete your empire, you know as well as I what you then would be."

"You've driven your foe from the field and you have already half-convinced me to spare you," she responded, not at all taking his candor amiss. "But only half. You have convinced me that genuine wisdom is to be found as much in the living as the thinking of it; but show me how your way of living and thinking is wiser than ours."

The priest smiled, as if she had fallen into a trap he had been preparing all along. "Like thinkers everywhere, your Majesty, we Jnana-yogis tend to complicate matters when we talk among ourselves; but the gist of it all is simple. Within ourselves we find the realm of the soul, and outside the phenomenal world. What is the essential reality of each, and how are they interrelated? That is the question upon which we focus."

"It seems like the question for everyone," she admitted.

"First, let us consider the world. Let us look for its reality. That reality must be eternal, absolute, and unchanging."

"Socrates' disciple, Plato, said as much; but I've never understood why reality could not just as well be temporal, relative, and in flux."

The priest reflected, as if he had never considered this possibility. "Think of this, your Majesty. Suppose right this moment, in the twinkling of an eye, you found yourself a scullery maid scrubbing on her hands and knees. What would you conclude?"

"That I was a peasant who had been dreaming she was a queen."

"And then everything changed once more, and you were on a chariot charging into battle? What would you conclude then?"

"That I was a warrior who had been dreaming he was a scullery maid dreaming she was a queen."

"And when would you think you had come to the real you?"

"I see. When the changes stopped. Very well," she added, "I'll concede your point that reality is absolute, eternal and unchanging. Proceed."

"Where do we find this reality? That's the question," he continued. "Is there any thing that could be this reality—a tree, a rock, a mountain, a star?"

"Of course not," she replied. "A thing is relative to other things, and no thing is unchanging."

"Your Professor has trained you well," he said, but his ironical tone really meant that she had trained herself well. "Is reality, what we call *Brahman*, the phenomenal world taken as a whole?"

"Of course not. That too is in constant flux."

"What about our knowledge of the world? Is that what is ultimately real?"

"Some people like to think it is," she smiled, remembering the Professor's face when he got the punch line; "but no, knowledge of the phenomenal world is constantly changing, even scientific knowledge."

"Even more than that, your Majesty, what you Westerners call 'science,' which you proudly trumpet forth as the highway to truth, is but one perspective, and a very narrow one at that. Wasn't it one of your own physicists who showed you that all knowledge is relative to the viewpoint taken by the knower?"

"The Heisenberg Uncertainty Principle," she cited. "So then, where do we find this ultimate reality, this Brahman?"

"We don't, your majesty. The most one can say is that it is *netti, netti*—'not this and not that.' "

She stared at him, beginning to get an inkling of what he was up to. "What about the self? Do we define that too as absolute and eternal before we look for it?"

"Not at all, your Majesty," he laughed appreciatively. "As you yourself imply, that would hardly be philosophical. We assume that reality is unchanging because that is all it can be; but the self, in our experience of it, could be many things. To keep ourselves honest . . ."

"Not to assume what we are trying to prove!"

"Yes, not to assume what we are trying to prove, we must begin with common human experience. Let's look at the possible candidates. Is the body the true self?"

"Of course not," she said. "Otherwise, when one lost a leg, an arm, or even a hair or a fingernail, one would be less of a self."

"Exactly! And there is another reason, your Majesty, which I think you of all people would be the last to overlook. Does an automobile drive itself?"

"I can control my body; therefore, I am not my body."

He nodded. "Next, the emotional self. Is that the true self?"

"I can control my emotions; therefore, I am not my emotions."

"Next, the mind," he continued, "the intellect. Is that, as our dear Professor might have us believe, the true self?"

"I cannot control my mind," she pondered. "Can I?"

"It depends upon what you mean by 'mind,' your Majesty. Here we mean 'intellect,' the ability to develop and follow a chain of reasoning according to logic."

"I can develop that ability, but I cannot control it. Logic is what it is."

The priest looked intently into her eyes. "Think carefully, your Majesty. Wasn't it one of your own wise men who proved that every system of logic rests upon at least one assumption that can't be proved in the system?"

"Goedel, the mathematician," she replied. "So we cannot choose whether or not to think logically, because thought by definition is always logical; but we can choose the logic according to which we think."

The priest smiled. "And so one can control the intellect, and the intellect cannot be the controlling self. Finally, the ego, the sense of individuality distinct from everything and everyone else. Is that the true self?"

"It must be!" she laughed. "There is nothing else left!"

"Again, think it through, your Majesty. Have you ever told an acquaintance all about yourself? And when you were all through did you feel any closer, as if you had revealed your true self?"

"On the contrary, I felt much more distant."

"Look into my eyes," he commanded, for the first time daring to omit formal recognition of her royalty. "Abstract from everything that sets you apart from me: height, weight, gender, personality, etc. What's left?"

She shook her head in ignorance. "Nothing. What could there be?"

"There's nothing only if you're talking about what is seen, but what about the unseen?"

"Awareness," she whispered. "Pure awareness."

"Where do we find the true self?"

"*Netti, netti*—not this, not that."

"And when two things one thought were totally different and distinct, like self and world, have the same definition, what should one conclude?"

"That they are the same!" she smiled excitedly. "Bravo, priest! You have pulled the mystical rabbit out of the metaphysical hat! Neither absolute being nor essential selfhood are to be found in the realm of experience, so they must both be in the realm of the experiencer. They are not in any sense objects of experience; therefore, they must both be subjects of experience. There is no differentiation in pure awareness, and thus there is only one subject of experience. Therefore absolute being and essential selfhood..."

"Brahman and atman."

"Yes, Brahman and atman, are one!" Then she frowned. "But so what? It's all abstraction."

"Not for a genuine philosopher! A genuine philosopher perceives reality through thought. For a genuine philosopher, metaphysical insight and personal self-realization go hand-in-hand. If you were a genuine philosopher and realized your body were not your true self, you would not spend all your time and energy building a nest and feathering it with the latest in technological toys to keep your body housed as comfortably as possible. If you realized your emotions were not your true self, you would not be the slave of every whim, mood, or passion that blows through you. If you realized your intellect were not your true self, you would not be so quick to denounce as irrational those whose basic assumptions differ from your own. And," his voice heightened as if he were about to deliver the *coup de grace*, "if you realized your ego were not your true self, you would not be seeking the false greatness and the insanity of world conquest!"

"I can still have you executed!" she declared angrily.

"Just like Socrates," he smiled.

Then everything changed before her eyes and she found herself looking into the eyes of Ishwara. "I would have killed you," she said flatly.

"Perhaps the path of thought is not for you. Ready for the next dream?"

She took a deep breath, nodded, and said she was as ready as she could imagine.

"Remember, now," he reminded her, "the goal is to break identification with the false ego self and realize one's true identity as absolute being."

"That's the key, isn't it, to Jnana-yoga—one can't find ultimate reality because one is ultimate reality."

"Yes. As it says in our *Upanishads*, writings almost as ancient and sacred as the *Vedas*, 'The true seer cannot be seen, the true knower cannot be known.'"

"But can the true lover be loved?" she laughed.

He looked at her with new seriousness. "You are about to learn," he said, somewhat ruefully, "how that too cannot be so."

8. Bhakti-Yoga

Next she found herself in what could only be called a dream montage.

It was as if she were at all the temples of India at once, witnessing and even empathically experiencing the *puja*, or worship, going on in each. She thought that perhaps this path of devotion, or *Bhakti*, indeed was for her, for she already understood two things: one, that the people worshiping in these temples were in love; and two, that they were in love with the god or goddess they were worshiping. That was the key to Bhakti, so much simpler than the spiritual path of knowledge. It was falling in love with God. That was why the Hindus so thoroughly enjoyed their rituals of devotion, and why they had so many objects of devotion.

To take first things first, falling in love lifts a person right outside of the ego-self. One's universe, which formerly consisted of oneself at the center and everything else at the periphery, now shifts, and the beloved takes center stage. Indeed, one finds oneself not only willing, but wanting, to do things for the beloved which when not in love one would never do, even if offered a million dollars or threatened with a gun to one's head!

Furthermore, love not only instills the desire to come out of oneself. It also gives the energy. When in love, one can go without food, sleep, the amenities of life, what have you. The only thing one cannot go without is love. When in love, one feels as if one can move mountains; and, occasionally, one does.

Most important of all, love spontaneously liberates the self from pride and fear, awakening the soul to a larger life. Love does not fight desire, but fulfills it. Since the genuinely emotional person never does anything except spontaneously, for such a person the only way to spiritual liberation is falling in love with God.

This spontaneity was the reason for the legendary three-hundred and thirty million gods of India. What had been so puzzling when the priests first taught her this number now became perfectly clear.

"Yes," she heard Ishwara's voice, though she could not see him. "Parents may order a child to marry, but it would be absurd for them to order their child to fall in love."

Indeed, she thought to herself, it would be the one way to keep a child from falling in love.

"But isn't that what the Western religions often place themselves in the self-contradictory position of doing—ordering their adherents to fall in love with God?"

Now the answer came without her even hearing it.

One had no control over the matter.

"And if one tries to have control over the matter?"

One killed the love.

"And so going to church, mosque, temple, or synagogue becomes a boring duty."

Rather than an exciting and intimate tryst.

"Precisely."

And just as in the Western ideal of romantic love there was a beloved for every lover, so too in the Hindu ideal of devotion there was a god for every devotee.

"Three-hundred and thirty million."

Ariana pondered the utter simplicity of it all. It really said everything about Hinduism that, while one's marriage partner was determined by caste and parental arrangement, one was free to worship God in any form one pleased. It would be as absurd to denounce others for not worshiping one's own chosen deity as for a lover to denounce all other lovers because they were not in love with her own beloved.

Ishwara reappeared. "There is one criterion," he cautioned her. "One cannot simply worship God in any form. The difference between genuine worship and demonic worship is that genuine worship takes one out of one's narrow ego-self and into the ultimate reality of the spirit, which is pure bliss and love. In demonic worship one's ego becomes one's god."

"That, too, is relative in a way, isn't it?" she asked. "What may be demonic for a devotee far advanced upon the spiritual path may be genuine worship for someone further back?"

"Certainly. In fact, worship of any sort becomes demonic when one reaches the penultimate step to liberation."

"What do you mean?" she asked with a sense of foreboding.

"All in good time," he assured her.

She knew the extent to which she had come to trust him by her willingness to wait.

"I'm reminded of an earthbound soul with whom I became particularly good friends," Ariana mused. "She was a Hindu, and a *brahmin*. When a young girl in her early teens, she told her father she had had enough of spiritual freedom. She had had enough of being told she could worship God in any way she pleased, or even not worship if she so desired. She wanted order in her spiritual life. She wanted definite instructions as to the proper way of worshiping God. She was going to become a Roman Catholic. Her father said, 'You wish to become a Catholic? You see that as your spiritual path? Then by all means, do so!' Of course, it would have been a different story had she told him she was going to marry a Catholic."

"Of course," Ishwara nodded; "but, as you are beginning to understand, the body must be disciplined and restrained so that the soul may be set free."

"I'm beginning to understand that is what you believe. I'm not sure I understand it. Not at all sure."

He bowed, and she picked up the thread of her story.

"Anyway, this girl became a Catholic, went to Catholic school and mass on Sunday, received the sacraments—the works. And, looking back on it, she was certain that the priest who baptized her was convinced he was converting a heathen idolater to the one true faith. However, in her own mind, and in the mind of her father, she never ceased to be a Hindu, and was simply taking a further step along her spiritual path. After she had taken it, she went on to the next and left the Catholic Church behind."

She fell silent, a feeling of peaceful joy coming over her at the realization that, while human beings may form their exclusive clubs and claim their monopolies on salvation, there were as many ways to God as people willing to walk them.

Ishwara did not really break the silence, but gave it voice. "Roman Catholicism and Eastern Orthodoxy are the most sophisticated Western forms of Bhakti. One may worship God not only as young man or father, but as baby or woman as well. And if the devotee is not moved by any of these forms, he or she may look to any of the multifarious saints."

"One is not supposed to worship them," she smiled. "Not even the mother of God."

"Ah," Ishwara returned her smile, "you are right! But in religion what one actually does is what counts, and what one merely is supposed to do counts not at all."

"One thing disturbs me."

"Only one thing?" he laughed.

"What about the statues, the idols? I have heard Hindu philosophers say they are merely symbols, but I don't see how symbols could arouse such ecstatic fire!"

"Never ask a philosopher to explain the logic of love. The statue used in *puja* is neither symbol nor idol, but a place where the deity may take up residence at the invitation of its devotees."

"The god or goddess comes into the statue?"

"Yes, and leaves when the worship ends. Of course," he smiled, "there are temples in India in which the worship never ends."

"That must be awfully pleasant for you," she laughed suggestively. "I wonder, under which of your three-hundred and thirty million aspects might I fall in love with you."

"In reality, all of them may be reduced to three."

"Do you mean the Hindu trinity I've heard so much about? Let me see . . . Brahma, the creator; Vishnu, the preserver; and Shiva, the destroyer."

"The *trimurti*, but again you are mixing devotion with philosophy. That was some thinker's way of explaining to the multitudes the eternally cyclical character of existence. Whether of ants or galaxies, every birth is a death, and every death a rebirth. Let me show you the three deities who have won the hearts of Hindus." He assumed the full-lotus position—back straight, legs crossed and feet on thighs—and then sank, or appeared to sink, into a profound meditation.

She had no way of knowing how much time went by, for everything had disappeared. The universe seemed to be empty of all but the two of them. Indeed, the universe seemed not to exist. Gradually, she forgot everything about being Ariana, or the spirit of the new age, or the object of so much flattering attention. And gradually, in her loneliness, a desire awakened that came to possess her entire being. She was now Shakti, the consort and active manifestation of her beloved Shiva, the god of mystical power. She wanted her lord to make sweet love to her, but he was drinking deeply from the well-spring of being. As she sat waiting, eon after eon, she eventually dissolved into tears. Brahma happened to come by and ask what was wrong, and why Shiva, who had been assigned the creation of animal life, wasn't doing his part to populate the earth.

Shakti could only shake her head and turn away in shame. Looking unaccustomedly severe, Brahma assured her that he would take care of things and left. When he failed to return, she cried even harder; but then she decided that, if sexual union with her lord were denied her, she could at least enter into spiritual union. So she went into meditation herself, and attained a measure of both oblivion and peace.

Meanwhile, Brahma had not been idle. He knew that confrontation would never work with so mighty a god as Shiva; and besides, it held the potential of vast destruction. No, there was only one way—Kama.

Kama, whose name means "desire," goes by many forms; but on that day he happened to be a chubby, cherubic little figure with wings and a bow-and-arrow. To be pierced by one of his arrows was to be filled with passion for the next person of the opposite sex one encountered. He is the twin brother of the Western Cupid. Brahma saw the situation as a problem to be resolved, but Kama regarded it as an opportunity to be exploited. He was something of a joke among his peers; but were he to overpower Shiva, his prestige would soar.

Kama's ambition proved overreaching. Though he had been in deep trance meditation for countless ages, Shiva sensed Kama's approach and zapped the prepubescent troublemaker with his third-eye energy (something like a laser beam from between the eyebrows) before the latter could let his arrow fly. Nevertheless, this was no great disaster for Kama, for desire cannot be destroyed, only sublimated. Furthermore, the mischievous deity had accomplished his purpose. Like a man in the desert coming upon water, Shiva now noticed his long-forgotten Shakti. They made love as love has never been made before or since. They copulated as horses and gave birth to the horse species, and as lions and gave birth to the lion species, and so on, down through all the animal species, until earth teemed with their progeny and all Shakti's eons of tears and lamentation were requited.

Ariana came out of this dream feeling wonderful, though also surprised to find herself not in Ishwara's arms, but sitting opposite him just as she had been when it had begun. "It was all a dream?" she asked with both relief and regret.

"It is all a dream."

"So Shiva is the identity of the sexual and the spiritual energies?" She took refuge in abstraction.

"Yes, Shiva's and Shakti's symbols are the *lingam* and the *yoni*, the shaft of light and the sacred clearing that receives that shaft."

"If one's passion is aroused by passion, then one loves Shiva."

"Exactly."

"What of the other two?" she asked, unable to bear this place where intimacy and distance seemed to coincide.

"You are an intrepid adventurer," he remarked, but without a smile. He must have sensed how she was succumbing to the ambiguities of the situation. "We shall proceed."

This time the waiting period between waking and dreaming was shorter. She was learning how to keep disbelief out of the way of exploring the universe opening up to her. Besides the excitement of discovering new possibilities of being, she felt a growing sense of responsibility. The entire future of the earth, perhaps of the entire cosmos, might rest upon her choice of suitors. It was not only fair, but positively crucial, that she give each candidate a just and empathic hearing.

In the next dream she was a he. Ariana became Arjuna, the mighty warrior of ancient India. He was riding in a chariot alongside Krishna, his friend and fellow prince, returning from a fruitless parley with Duryodhana, the evil cousin who had usurped the share of the kingdom rightly belonging to himself and his four brothers, the sons of the dead King Pandu, the Pandavas. Names and personalities, however, did not seem the issue here. Arjuna's heart ached with the knowledge that shortly he would be fighting and killing men he had known and loved from childhood, noble warriors whose only crime was their sense of duty to their liege lord.

Arjuna looked at Krishna, wondering why he was involved in this battle. After all, he had no personal stake in it. Kin to both parties in the dispute, he could just as well have stayed out of it. Instead, he chose to make both sides a most peculiar offer. One army could have his soldiers in alliance, while the other could have himself, though in a purely advisory capacity. Always trusting in brute force, Duryodhana, of course, had snatched at the extra soldiers. Krishna, however, had left the final decision up to Arjuna. How could Arjuna, in all honor, not have chosen his friend over anonymous soldiers?

At this point much of the dream became blurred, as if someone else were in control and had decided this part was not significant. Then she beheld an image of Krishna, though in a form that beggared description, swallowing up Duryodhana's evil hordes. "I am Vishnu," he was explaining, "and wherever darkness threatens to overwhelm the light, I come into the world with my divine power to conquer the forces of chaos and bring order back to the cosmos."

Ariana awakened. "That was brief," she remarked lamely to Ishwara, who was studying her with serious but inscrutable intent.

"We will return to that one later," he explained. "Now do you understand the power of Vishnu?"

She nodded. "He is the hero who rights all wrongs. And the third?"

Another dream came as answer. She was once again a man, and a devotee of the goddess Kali, Shakti in her dark aspect. Even though Kali had skin the color of poisoned blue, wore a necklace of human skulls, and carried a chalice of human blood from which she drank so copiously that the scarlet liquid ran from her lips, she was still his divine mama, the spiritual mother who had nurtured him all his life and weaned him from attachment to his ego and its playthings. There was something still missing, however, but he did not know what it could be. He had become a naked flame feeding on its own substance, burning with devotion for the goddess. Sitting in meditation, he invoked her presence, as he had done a thousand times before.

"Ramakrishna!" she called to him.

"Help me, mother, help me!" he begged piteously. "What do I still lack?"

"It's not that you have too little, Ramakrishna," she answered her supplicant. "It's that you have too much."

What did the goddess mean, he wondered? He owned nothing, was nothing. What was he not understanding?

"Too much by one, Ramakrishna. Destroy me, and you will destroy you. Then there will be only the One."

A sword appeared in his hand. Without hesitation, the yogi slashed his beloved Kali to shreds, and so entered ultimate spiritual liberation.

Ariana returned. "Ramakrishna!" she murmured. "The nineteenth century Hindu saint!"

"Do you understand now?" Ishwara demanded. "I am but the face of Brahman, the being you yourself ultimately are. I am the lucid dreamer, the dream figure who knows he is the dreamer, and so I am not bound by karma, the logic of the dream. Karma rules over duality. If you too wish to be free, you too must overcome duality."

"I could never destroy you!"

"Of course not. What I am and what you are is indestructible. But someday, if you became a Bhakti-yogi, perhaps only after thousands of lifetimes, you would destroy the me who was the object of your devotion so you might unite with the me that you are."

"I don't understand," she protested, on the verge of tears.

"It's simple," said Ishwara. "Every spiritual path is like a ladder one climbs and then leaves behind. One uses thought to transcend thought, feeling to transcend feeling."

"The true knower cannot be known, the true lover cannot be loved."

"Yes," he affirmed, "but the true lover can become love."

"I don't see how I can be love without my beloved!"

"That's because you're clinging to the personal dimension of your being instead of going beyond it."

"I suppose I'm not cut out for this path," she excused herself.

He admitted no excuse. "On the contrary, you are discovering what death is all about."

"You said there were two other ways?"

"Yes, but one must pass through death no matter which path one takes. And it will be no different with your other suitors."

"I know." She looked into his eyes. "I wasn't trying to escape."

He laughed. "Then let's go on to the way of action."

9. Karma-Yoga

Almost instantly Ariana was again Arjuna, back on the battlefield between the two armies. This time the reluctant warrior was on his knees, weeping and declaring that he would rather die than kill any of his kinsmen, former teachers, or friends.

"But you know they are wrong," Krishna was saying. "You know, whatever the personal motivation of each individual, their cause is evil. It isn't just a matter of who rules India, but what. Is India to fall into chaos and ruin, as it most certainly will under that greedy and self-serving Duryodhana; or is it to enjoy peace and prosperity under you, the Pandavas?"

"I agree. Our cause is just; but what will that matter if we destroy society in the very act by which we hope to save it? What evil can be greater than killing one's kinsmen?"

"The evil of a warrior turned coward," answered Krishna.

Arjuna raised himself threateningly.

"If I did not know you were simply trying to provoke a reaction, I would kill you right now."

"So," laughed Krishna scornfully, "you would kill me for insulting you, but you would not kill men who are destroying India?"

Arjuna once again collapsed in the dust. "If only I knew that it would do any good," he moaned. "If only I knew that it would not have the effect opposite to that intended."

"You cannot know!" hammered Krishna. "The results of your actions are not in your hands. But if you fail to act you need not worry," he added sarcastically, "because what you would be fighting for will already have died. You must follow your duty as you know it in your heart. Otherwise, there is no hope left."

"My duty," Arjuna mused. "You say these foes are evil, yet they too believe they are obeying the call of duty."

"I say their cause is evil. They are good men, most of them, trapped by delusion into defense of an unworthy lord."

"How do I know that I too am not self-deluded?"

"You can't, so what one can't know one had best forget. You must act according to your light, they according to theirs."

"So, it's all relative?" Arjuna despaired. "Right and wrong are simply what we choose them to be?"

Suddenly, Arjuna and Krishna dissolved, leaving Ariana and Ishwara in their place.

"Have you heard of Winston Churchill and Mohandas Gandhi?" Ishwara continued, as if the transformation were a matter of insignificance.

"Yes, the Prime Minister of England during World War II, and the little Hindu who led India to independence."

"Why don't you try them on for size?"

In a twinkling, she found herself in the self of Winston Churchill. It was, for London, an unseasonably warm midsummer's night, whose peace was disturbed only by an occasional air-raid siren that turned out to be false alarm. Ignoring the warnings, he chewed absentmindedly on a half-lit cigar while studying the latest statistics from the War Office. The struggle was going badly. The enemy was fire-bombing London, and every day both the civilian and military casualty lists were lengthening at an alarming rate. Worse yet, German U-boats were sinking a large percentage of the supplies England needed not only to carry on the war, but to exist. Suddenly, one of his aides appeared at the door. There was news from India. That troublemaker Gandhi had called upon Britain to relinquish control of India, the linchpin of her empire and the key to its defense against the Axis Powers. What timing!

"Throw him in prison!" the prime minister ordered. Then he went back to thinking about Germany. "We have to see this through to the bitter end," he whispered to no one in particular. "God knows, we can't let barbarism conquer the earth."

Meanwhile, on the other side of that same planet, Mohandas Gandhi, known to the entire world as *mahatma*—"great soul"—was preparing to face imprisonment and even death in opposition to the very same empire that Churchill regarded as the guarantor of civilization. The British had turned a deaf ear to his pleas for understanding and compromise, and had patronizingly declared war upon Germany for India rather than wait for India to do it herself. Yet he would not fight violence with violence. If Churchill faced the monster of Nazi Germany with an air of righteous and resolute defiance, Gandhi faced Churchill with a love that was so certain of its own triumph that it had no need to fight.

Gandhi thought violence self-defeating. Churchill thought nonviolence irresponsible. Neither, however, understood the world at all like that egocentric monster, Adolf Hitler. Both men differed over right and wrong, but both truly desired to know the one from the other, and to follow the path of righteousness. Hitler, however, did not even ask the question.

"This path you are showing me now," she found herself questioning Ishwara, "is about doing what one believes is right?"

"Yes," Ishwara appeared, and the dream figures evaporated. "Karma-yoga is the path of action, of work in the world. It is for the individual who finds meaning in life neither through philosophy nor religious devotion, but the good he or she may do."

"It consists simply of doing what one believes is right, rather than what would be more convenient, fulfilling, enjoyable, etc.?" This seemed almost too simple, until she thought about how difficult it had always been for anyone to do even that.

"There is one other requirement, as you have already seen. If one worries about success or failure, reward or punishment, one will be lost. The Karma-yogi acts without regard for the fruits of action."

"Otherwise, one would be paralyzed," she observed.

"That is one pitfall. Let me illustrate the other."

This time she found herself a young lawyer in France at the time of the revolution, who joined the party against the king because he hated the death penalty, much employed by the royalist regime. Indeed, he could not stand the sight of blood. Both hard-working and brilliant, young Robespierre rapidly rose to leadership of the revolutionary party. When he reached the top, however, he looked around and saw that the movement which stood for liberty, equality, and fraternity, the noblest ideals known to the human race, was in danger not only from enemies without, such as England and Prussia, which had declared war upon revolutionary France, but also from enemies within. In addition to royalist agents actively working to undermine the new republic, there was a large population of aristocrats, mostly politically passive, who nevertheless formed a seedbed of opposition. Worst of all were the factions within the party itself, threatening to tear the revolution apart. In the end, the formerly tenderhearted youth knew that either he must watch his beloved, earth-shaking revolution die or take drastic measures. He instituted what came to be known as the Reign of Terror, in which tens of thousands of men, women, and children died, some of whose only crime was having aristocratic blood, and in which Robespierre himself eventually perished under the blade of the guillotine.

Ariana returned from this dream extremely sobered.

"What have you learned?" Ishwara asked.

"That good men can work the greatest evil because they are good."

Ishwara nodded. "Men of high principle who do not tie the ethical knot, who do not hold as absolute the individual rights of fellow human beings, are playing with fire."

"But he did hold such rights to be sacred!" she cried.

"In the abstract," replied Ishwara. "He sacrificed reality to an abstraction. He would never have done so had he recognized the limits of human action and entrusted the end to God."

"Action without regard for the fruits of action," she remembered. "So, it is best to practice Karma-yoga in the spirit of Bhakti-yoga?"

His humor returned like the sun through the clouds. "You are becoming a regular yogini," he smiled.

"This path of action seems quite simple," she smiled back, "but one thing still confuses me. You say that, to be a Karma-yogi, one must act without regard for reward or punishment. Does that mean one must forego all reward? If so, how is one to purchase food and shelter? How live?"

"It is a question of priorities," answered Ishwara. "Action without regard for the fruits of action does not mean action without fruit. All action has fruit. That is the meaning of the law of karma. And on the mundane level"—again he smiled—"one may work for a living and still be a Karma-yogi. The important point is to do the work that one feels to be most meaningful in the spiritual sense, most creative and beneficial to the world, even if that means making less money than one otherwise would. And above all, do not let money become the be-all and end-all of one's work. If one ever encounters a situation where the question is that of meaning vs. money..."

"Such as a judge offered a bribe?" Ariana interjected.

"Yes, or a superior threatening to fire you if you don't cooperate with the boss's fraudulent business methods. In such situations, one's priority should be clear. If one chooses money, or even survival, over duty, then one is not a Karma-yogi."

"That too bothers me. You have said that duty must be determined by individual conscience, but what about Arjuna? Weren't you asking him to fight simply because of his social class?"

"All real duty has a social as well as individual aspect," replied Ishwara.

"But the individual aspect in Arjuna's situation was at odds with the social. In that case, which is one to choose?"

"Was it?" asked Ishwara. "Let us see." And immediately he was Krishna and she Arjuna, back on the famous battlefield of Kurukshetra.

"If I fight," Arjuna was protesting, "how can I know I will not do more damage to the fabric of human society than if I do not?"

"You cannot know," declared Krishna. "You can only trust in the nature that I have implanted in you. You can only trust in me. If your nature is to be a warrior"—he paused and looked searchingly into Arjuna's eyes—"and you know that it is, then to refuse to fight, to refuse that nature, will be to set up a conflict within yourself."

Arjuna once more looked over the enemy lines, and imagined his friends' and kinsmen's bodies littering the open field and their blood soaking into the dusty earth. Even if it had to be, he still wanted no part in it. "Then let me be at war with myself!" he cried. "I can't fight my own people!"

"There is a path for those who subordinate nature to principle, and thus find the higher nature beyond principle," said Krishna with equanimity. "That is Karma-yoga. And then there is a path for those heroes who undertake the most perilous struggle of all, who attempt to conquer nature unconditionally. That is Raja-yoga."

Once again they were Ishwara and Ariana, and she was filled with an excitement and a trepidation the like of which she had never known.

10. Raja-Yoga

"The path I am about to show you is the most dangerous of all," Ishwara announced. "If the spiritual quest may be likened to climbing a mountain, then the paths you have already explored—Jnana, or knowledge, Bhakti, or devotion, and Karma, or action—are, despite their sorrows and sufferings, like roads that wind gently around the mountain. Raja-yoga, the royal path, is like scaling the cliff face. If one falls while on the other paths, one merely picks oneself up and keeps going. If one falls while on this royal path, one descends into hell; and the higher the point from which one falls, the deeper the hell."

"I do not understand," Ariana said. "Why is it so very dangerous?"

"Because it deals directly with power. If improperly used, nothing is more spiritually destructive."

"Physically and mentally as well," she added.

"The spirit encompasses all of these," he rejoined. "Don't you realize that yet?" He took her silence for assent. "Are you ready?"

"Wait!" she cried. "If this path is so very dangerous, why take it?"

"Because it is the most direct route."

"For an embodied as well as discarnate spirit, jumping off a cliff is the most direct route to the valley below," she retorted; "but for the embodied spirit, it's suicide!"

"I see you won't be satisfied with any shortcut answer!" he laughed, easing but not dispelling the rising tension. "Though it is true that, if one gives one's all, Raja-yoga can lead to spiritual liberation in a single lifetime, it is also true that your question reveals a failure to grasp what I've already taught you, that you can no more arbitrarily choose a spiritual path that will work for you than one can arbitrarily choose one's shoe size."

She struggled to piece it together. "Jnana is for the thinker, Bhakti for the lover, Karma for the doer . . . What else is there?"

"Power," he declared, "and the spiritual path of power must be dangerous! Why do people climb mountains, jump out of airplanes, launch themselves into space?"

"Because they are crazy?"

"Because they seek power. Power and danger go hand-in-hand. They define each other."

"Power accrues to those who court danger," she said, "and danger to those who seek power?"

"Exactly," he affirmed, "and most poetically phrased."

"So," she concluded, blushing at the compliment, "Raja-yoga is spiritual sky-diving."

"Not precisely. The world got along fine before the invention of parachutes and airplanes, but the world gets along dismally when power-oriented individuals do not take a spiritual path."

"I have an inkling of what you mean, but I'm still not sure I get it."

"From a spiritual perspective, what is a power-tripper actually doing?" he asked.

"Playing God?"

"Yes," he affirmed; "or, to put it another way, one identifies with Brahman, or absolute being, before one breaks identification with the ego. Thus one who plays God while still identifying with the body falls prey to what Western psychology terms paranoid schizophrenia. Any threat to the body is an attack upon God, and therefore must be flushed out and ruthlessly suppressed. Simultaneous identification with emotions and the absolute yields self-validating passions. All anger is divine wrath, and its object utterly evil. All desire is divine love, and whatever thwarts it also evil. The intellectual power-tripper thinks divine thoughts, and anyone who disagrees is wicked or stupid or both. And finally, the deified ego is the dictator whose only reason for existence is to lord it over others."

"You have just described ninety-nine percent of the human race," she remarked in painfully amused despair.

"Not quite," he smiled. "Actually, power-oriented people, whose temperament might best be described as 'heroic,' make up only a small part of humanity. Their influence, naturally, is out of all proportion to their numbers. They do a great deal of harm, but also a great deal of good; and human society, especially its Western half, does not make things easy for them."

"Isn't that their karma?" she queried, nothing subtle about the sarcasm in her voice.

"The karma of the victimizer is also the karma of the victim."

"Pardon me, but I have a hard time feeling sorry for such people."

"Pity is not required," he admonished, "merely awareness that Western culture provides some sort of spiritual path for the philosopher, the lover, and the doer, but none for those who relate to life in terms of power. Certainly it is their responsibility to find one for themselves, but life would be so much easier for everyone if they had a little encouragement. After all, what is the general attitude toward people of power?"

"Donald Trump," she stated.

"Excuse me?"

"A famous billionaire in the West, an American. My friends in the heavenly mansions told me about him. He certainly is not to be pitied; but still, a few years ago, when his money was secure and growing, everyone admired him. Now that his fortune is on the wane, many of those same many despise him."

"My very point!" Ishwara declared. "When they succeed, they are loved, and when they fail, derided. Is it any wonder they will do anything to succeed?"

"But is there really another way," she wondered, "a third alternative?"

"Raja-yoga," he assured her, "the spiritual path of power. Do you wish to talk about it, or experience it?"

"Talk is safer," she laughed.

"And therefore would not do justice to the most dangerous path of all, so shall we begin?" He sat for what seemed like an eternity looking questioningly into her eyes.

"Why is nothing happening?" she asked, breaking the lengthy silence. "Every time you ask if we should begin, something happens and we begin."

"No dream can show you what Raja-yoga is about. In Raja-yoga, discipline and experience go hand-in-hand. You must go into meditation."

She obliged by adopting the full-lotus posture, legs crossed and feet resting upon thighs, and closing her eyes.

"At the base of your spine you will find the *kundalini*, the 'serpent power,' coiled in sleep."

"The libido," she said, opening her eyes. "The instinctual energy. I heard about it from the earthbound spirits."

"Close your eyes," he ordered, calmly but firmly. "There are seven centers of spiritual energy in the body. Or rather, the body exists within an aura of spiritual energy with seven nodes."

"Yes, I've heard about those as well. They are the seven chakras."

"*Chakra* simply means 'wheel,'" he continued, "but here we are talking about the power centers of the spirit. In reality, there is no power. Brahman is neither powerless nor powerful. Brahman simply is. All power involves action, and all action belongs to maya, the sphere of delusion. Do you remember the gunas?"

She nodded. "The three strands of being produced by the refraction of the pure light of Brahman."

"The chakras are the permutations of the gunas. The way out, however, is also the way home. The consciousness of most human beings is a schizoid distortion of the pure awareness of the atman. The life force is asleep. It awakens only in severe crisis, and then strikes out blindly and brutally. The spiritual faculties are divorced from the life-force, and therefore weak and ineffectual. Thus most human history is carried on the shoulders of the few who develop their creative resources. The majority live in relative stagnation, punctuated by periods of mass insanity."

"Like wars and revolutions that destroy much and change nothing?" said Ariana mournfully.

"Exactly," agreed Ishwara. "The whole point of any spiritual practice is to energize the chakras with the kundalini, and spiritualize the kundalini by raising it up through the chakras. In the other paths, this vitalizing of the spirit and spiritualizing of the flesh happens naturally and unselfconsciously. The Raja-yogi deals with these forces directly."

"It's about energy refinement, then?" she asked, no longer able to pretend she was meditating and again opening her eyes.

He seemed not to notice. "Yes. When seen in that light, the process is simple. Starting at the lowest level, you awaken and experience the energy, master it, and then sublimate it to reach the next level, like a step-lock canal in which the water is dammed up in order to take it to a higher level."

"Or a video game!" she laughed, feeling oppressed by his gravity.

"Yes," he replied seriously, "but instead of testing hand-and-eye coordination, here the balance of energy and self-discipline is in question. Undirected energy is dissipated, and misdirected energy is destructive."

"I see."

"I'm not sure you do." His words were harsh, but his voice sorrowful. "The chakra system has been much ridiculed by Westerners, but as a model for understanding what it means to be human—indeed, what it means to be—it is unsurpassed in subtlety, wisdom, and depth."

"I'm not a Westerner, or an Easterner for that matter," she reminded him. "Why do they laugh?"

"Because they have divided human being into various aspects, and then transformed these aspects into airtight compartments. Any way of thinking that reverses the process they consider superstitious and irrational. The mind is for the psychologists, the body for the biologists, and never the twain shall meet; or worse, the former is made an epiphenomenon, an excrescence, of the latter."

"That's changing," she said hopefully.

"Perhaps," he mused. "But let us get on with it! Nothing teaches like experience." He finally smiled, though a trifle demonically, she thought. "Close your eyes!"

She did so immediately, and what before had been simply a heavy darkness, a boring passage between waking and sleeping, seemed charged with intense possibility. She felt a certain power, a certain energy, but it was raw and undeveloped, having not only the redness but the psychological "feel" of blood.

She found herself imagining what it was like to be a soldier the first time in battle. One moment there was the quiet camaraderie and warmth of her fellows, and the next it seemed as if all hell had broken loose. The enemy artillery pounded their lines, and she kept her face buried deeply in the dirt, lest she glimpse any body parts of the soldiers whose unearthly screams signaled their dismemberment. When it was all over, she discovered she had evacuated her bowels.

Next, she was running through a battlefield, and bombs were exploding all around her. She saw her comrades hesitate and die, but she ran without thought for herself or anything else, allowing instinct to be her guide. Coming upon a shell crater, she took a moment to rest and felt something warm and sticky flowing from her side. She was wounded, and had not even realized it! Nevertheless, she got up to continue the fight. Gradually, her garb changed from a soldier's uniform to the robe of a martial artist. Instead of scampering through a barrage, she found herself standing and fighting, countering the deadly missiles as if they were kicks and punches. Then they were kicks and punches, and she was fighting the king of the demons for control of the cosmos. After she defeated the tyrant, all beings throughout the universe knelt to her in subservience. For a moment she relished the feeling of total control. Then she realized that, if she retained that control, she would be as depraved as the demon king she had vanquished. As soon as she abdicated her throne, she felt the energy in her bowels expand like crimson waves in all directions, and for the first time in her existence she felt genuinely physical, situated in concrete reality more intimately than sense experience would allow. At length she opened her eyes, and there was Ishwara. "It was so real!" she murmured.

"So real," he queried, "or more real?"

"It felt more real," she admitted; "but if that's so, why are you here and not there?"

"I am there, and in reality, not form. I am the energy itself."

Ariana pondered. "Why did I soil myself?" she asked, curious rather than ashamed.

"It was the opening of the root chakra. Soldiers regard this common phenomenon as a sign of cowardice, but in reality it is the beginning of courage. Fear is the awareness of danger. Courage is the ability to deal with danger. One cannot deal with danger if one is not aware of it."

"Fear is the beginning of wisdom."

He nodded.

"Why didn't I feel the wound?" she asked.

"Because you were in a state of trance, or *samadhi*."

"Trance?" she echoed. "But it did feel so real!"

"If reality is reached through the senses, as Westerners believe," answered Ishwara, "then to go within is to escape reality. If sense-awareness is maya, a veil of illusion hiding reality, then one attains reality by transcending the senses."

"And the blood?" she continued. "I don't mean the blood of the wound, but the blood I felt pumping through me. It was raw energy, crimson incarnate!"

"The first chakra holds the energy of tamas, the material dimension. Its color is red. This is the energy of the warrior in battle. To master it is to master one's fear, to learn the secret of one's own survival. The lesson to be learned here is courage."

"Lesson?"

"We could also call it the mechanism of sublimation."

"Let's stick to lesson," she smiled.

"And what is the essential lesson, what the greatest courage?" he asked.

She answered almost before she knew what she was saying. "To renounce the fruits of that power and to harness it to the spiritual task."

The basic pattern of the first chakra repeated itself in all the rest. She passively experienced the energy of the chakra, learned to master it, successfully resisted the temptation to abuse it, and then sublimated it to the next higher level. As she went along, the intensity increased and so did the stakes. As in climbing a mountain, the higher one climbed upon this spiritual path of power, the farther one could fall. And, as in the refinement of material energy, a step up was an increase in energy concentration. The energy of the chakras, however, was not spiritual as opposed to material, but a spiritual that included the material. As Ishwara had put it, it encompassed all dimensions of her being; and so its sublimation was at once profound and comprehensive self-transformation.

If the first chakra carries the energy of personal survival, the second concerns that of survival of the species. Located just above the genitals, its color is orange, being a combination of rajas and tamas, energized matter or impassioned flesh. It is, in other words, the energy of sexuality. The abuse of this energy is to use it only to attain pleasure, or worse, gain power over others. The lesson to be learned from it is the instinctual or intrinsic unity of the life force in all living things, as well as intimate and profound union with another.

Ariana experienced herself as a lover pining away for her absent beloved, and as a mother not hesitating for an instant to sacrifice herself for her endangered child. Finally, she was a psychologist whose wealthy and influential clients found her attractive and with whom she was tempted to expend herself in the pleasures of the flesh so as to further her career. She resisted the temptation, and the sexual energy contained and controlled, she discovered, deepened into friendship, and so carried her to the next plateau of spiritual struggle.

If the sacral center is fire, the emotional center is pure warmth. It is located at the solar plexus, a little above the navel, and its dominant color is yellow. Here is the emotional nexus of being, and the lesson to be learned is empathy, or the ability to feel what another individual is feeling, to not only appreciate but enter into another's subjectivity, and so overcome the artificial barriers that create the delusion of multiplicity. Empathy is the beginning of all true humanity. Without it, there is no true morality. Jesus said, "Do unto others as you would have them do unto you." Confucius and Buddha said, "Do not do unto others as you would not have them do unto you." Muhammad said, "Wish for your brother what you wish for yourself." And, in the Native American tradition, it is said, "Do not judge another until you walk a mile in his moccasins."

Ishwara's teaching method here could have been described as "stereo-optical." She experienced a variety of personae and situations from the dual viewpoint of an analytical and judgmental consciousness, on the one hand, and a sensitive and open one, on the other. Invariably she discovered that it was the latter form of awareness that not only proved more creative and effective in resolving interpersonal crises, but also more accurate in assessing the truth of a person or situation.

The mastery of this chakra yields the ability to win friends and influence people as no amount of positive thinking can. The temptation, she well understood by now, is to use that power to preen one's personal pride, minister to one's insecurities, or satisfy one's ego-desires.

Over and over again she was tested, as a politician, a schoolgirl, a monk in a monastery, etc.; and each time the temptation was essentially the same, to use this newfound popularity for her own benefit. Once again she overcame temptation, and so finally felt the warmth expand from her solar plexus to envelop the entire cosmos. Totally out of touch now with her sense-awareness, and therefore deep in what that sense-awareness called "trance," she was more and more in touch with life s spiritual reality.

The next level is centered at the heart. She remembered her Hindu friend who had practiced Roman Catholicism once telling her that Christ was a master of the heart-chakra energy. As a combination of rajas, or emotion, and sattwa, or intelligence, its color is green, and it has to do, as anyone might guess, with love. The lesson one has to learn to master this energy is selfless love, or compassion.

She found herself in situations similar to those experienced at the emotional level, only this time they demanded of her a more crucial and active role. If before she had been a mother whose child had stolen from the cookie jar, for example, this time she was a mother whose child had been arrested for dealing drugs. If before she had had a husband who was irritable at the end of the workday, this time her husband was an alcoholic who beat her and abused her children. There was no dual perspective either, because love was not a matter of learning but doing, not of understanding but willing. She understood each situation through her feelings. The only question for the heart was whether she would listen to pride, fear, and desire, or to love.

Ariana discovered a marvelous desire in love, so marvelous that it was at this chakra that she came closest to falling into the hell of which Ishwara had spoken. In one experience she was a woman who fascinated the most fascinating of men, but who toyed with relationships until she met someone who saw through the game she was playing and loved her despite herself, so to speak. It was not that he was willing to do anything for her, for he was a man of strong conviction; but he would forgive her anything and love her no matter what. In other words, he was completely at her mercy without being at her beck-and-call, and the temptation to torture him with the tension between acceptance of the sinner and rejection of the sin was almost overwhelming because the opportunity was so rare. In the end, however, she gave herself up to his love, and felt the vitality of the heart chakra envelop her and her entire world.

Going deeper or, if you will, higher, the next step is the throat chakra. Will and feeling are not enough. Intelligence has to direct will, or even the good-hearted will go astray. Thus intelligence is the next step toward the essence; and intelligence, pure sattwa, is centered in the throat rather than the brain because intellect is facility with concepts. Every concept is a word, and every word a concept.

Sattwa, the blue light of intelligence, has two aspects, creative expression and truthful communication. The throat chakra is therefore the center of both philosophy and art. Since Ariana was already as accomplished in both fields as a spirit undergoing preparation for embodiment could be, she only needed three experiences to get the point and move on.

The first was as a brilliant but struggling young artist who was offered a fortune to work with an advertising firm. She joined the firm, but continued her own art on the side. One day, she was assigned as client a business lobby seeking to prevent congressional legislation regulating the commercial exploitation of animals. She told her superior, one of the partners in the advertising firm, that in good conscience she could not work on this account, and requested reassignment. He told her to work on it in bad conscience, then, because the business lobby in question was one of the advertising company's best customers. It was clear to her that a life of hardship on the street might be the only alternative to pocketing her principles, but nevertheless she resigned. Ariana immediately felt an expansion and intensification of the blue aura of the chakra, a kind of symbolic and conceptual interconnection with the cosmos.

The second experience was similar, only she was a philosopher who was being asked to trim her "bold but counter-intuitive" ideas for publication in a journal. No one but professional philosophers read the journal in question, but if she did not publish her article she would lose her teaching position at the local university with practically no hope of finding another. She compromised as much as conscience would allow, but in the end decided to have a go at desk-top publishing.

The final experience at the throat chakra was simple, direct, and terrifying. She was a sorceress who could create or destroy anything merely through the proper verbal formula. At first, she thought she would only use this power for good, but found that everything she tried had disastrous consequences. She bestowed abundant food upon the earth, but hoarders gathered it up and, after underselling legitimate farmers to force them out of business, charged such exorbitant rates that the economies of the poorer nations were destroyed, enabling the richer nations to enslave them. She transformed weapons into flowers, but governments simply resorted to biological warfare and all but extinguished human life on Earth. Finally she renounced her power altogether, and so moved on to the penultimate level of spiritual development, the third-eye chakra.

Ariana knew that the third-eye energy was famous in mystical traditions the world over, but now she discovered why. It unites the first and the last, the highest and the lowest, the alpha and omega, sattwa and tamas, and so its aura is purple. This most powerful and dangerous of energies is generated by, and in return develops and intensifies, direct insight into the deep-structure of the phenomenal world.

Anyone who masters this energy can manipulate the phenomena of that world, can create and destroy at will.

At this level she had only one experience, but it summed up and raised to an infinite power all that had gone before. She was a guru/scientist or a scientist/guru, uniting in her brilliance the best of the wisdom of both West and East. The world was under attack by an alien power from the remote reaches of the galaxy. The invader's weapons were so superior that the Earth's might as well have been toys. There was only one hope for the planet—Ariana. The secretary-general of the United Nations, to which all sovereign countries had subordinated themselves in face of the alien threat, knew that Ariana had the ability to devise the ultimate weapon, one that, by neutralizing the strong force that bound atoms together, could unravel the very structure of the phenomenal world in the proverbial twinkling of an eye. Since such a weapon worked by disrupting the space-time nexus, its effect could not be localized, and the Earth would be destroyed along with the entire cosmos. The secretary-general assured her, however, that the "Night of Brahma," as the doomsday machine was code-named, would never actually be activated, only used as the ultimate threat. The aliens, extremely rational beings, would never risk the annihilation of the universe simply to lord it over earth, no matter how beautiful or rich in natural resources the tiny planet might be.

Ariana thought of her children, her husband, her parents and siblings. The threat was so palpable, so immediate. If the enemy succeeded in its conquest, as at that point seemed a foregone conclusion, human beings would become to the aliens what pets and workhorses were to humans. All that her race had struggled over centuries so painfully to achieve in the way of peace, democracy and human dignity would be erased so thoroughly it might as well have never been. On the other hand, how could she build such a weapon no matter what was at stake? The dilemma seemed perfect in its insolubility.

In the end, Ariana offered to pretend she had built the Night of Brahma. If all he wanted was a weapon that would never be activated, she told the secretary-general, in that way he would get the threat with an automatic safeguard against its realization. When he rejected her offer, saying there could be no substitute for the weapon itself, she started to see the walls of fear he had built up around himself and his world, and gradually his figure receded into the distance on the purple stream of third-eye energy that shot forth from between her eyebrows, giving her the spiritual equivalent of x-ray vision into the very essence of life. She saw there was nothing to fear, because what dies never really lived, and what lives never truly dies. With that understanding, she entered into the final stage of self-realization, known as *nirvikalpa samadhi*, samadhi without duality.

There was no test to be passed at this level, no temptation to overcome. She had been climbing a mountain, but now she was at the top. The kundalini had dropped back down to its original home at the base of the spine, but this time it was not sleeping but coiling in order to strike. Suddenly, like a fire or electrical charge, it shot up her spinal column, opening up the chakras as it went and giving her a sense of unutterably intimate connection with the entire cosmos, and burst through the crown of her head. Then the pure, clear light of Brahman came pouring through the opening, filling her being with wisdom, bliss, peace and light. At that point, just as she was thinking to herself that she could stay in that state forever, her eyes opened and Ishwara was smiling into them with his own. "I was beginning to hope it was real," she said wistfully.

"It was," he assured her, "but your path to it was not. You have had the experience. Now you must undertake the discipline."

"Meditation?" she whispered.

"Yes, meditation," he said tentatively.

"But it can't all be done in meditation," she continued. "All those experiences would have to be real."

"You still don't get the point," he chided. "It is not the experience that has to be real. It is you who have to be real. One yogi has to go out and range over the entire world. Another can do it all sitting in a closet."

"What about us?"

"There ultimately is no 'us.'"

"Then why do you want to marry me?" she queried. "In your universe, what can we be together that we cannot be apart?"

"There is no apartness," he maintained with irritating consistency; "but, to answer your question in the spirit in which it was asked, I have saved that part for last."

11. Tantra

What happened next was the most paradoxical experience she had ever known. Ishwara began to change into a woman, a dark-skinned and ravishingly beautiful woman, and yet he/she remained Ishwara. Simultaneously, though she did not know what was happening until the metamorphosis was almost accomplished, Ariana changed into a light-skinned and extremely large-nosed, ugly man with the shaven head of a priest, while yet remaining Ariana. Along with the physical change came a corresponding psychological one. A new set of thoughts, feelings, and memories was, as it were, superimposed upon her old ones without at all obliterating or even obscuring the latter.

"The ritual is to become one with the goddess," Ishwara's female form was saying.

"What goddess?" suddenly came out of the priest's mouth.

"Can't you feel her?" the woman encouraged. "If you cannot feel the goddess, how can you undertake the great work? You have eaten the forbidden food and drunk the forbidden drink. You have washed yourself in brackish water and played among the ashes of the dead . . ."

"Yes," interjected the priest, "what more can you ask of me? Haven't I shown my disregard for duality, my indifference to the pairs of opposites that constitute maya?"

"You know why we are here," she persisted.

"But you are pariah!" he trembled with the contradictory passions of fear and desire. "How can I touch what is untouchable?"

"I am the goddess," she smiled, and Ariana could feel the priest melting, beginning with his groin. "Besides, this is not the first time you have undertaken the ritual of identity. Indeed, I hear you are a real master!"

"I have never done it with an outcaste," he said flatly.

"There is no caste." She moved closer. "There is no 'you' and there is no 'I.' There is only the One."

Then she kissed him, a long, lingering kiss that seemed to cool rather than inflame. In the act of intercourse that followed, the woman took the active role. As she enveloped the priest, he remained sitting with his back straight, yet absolutely relaxed and still, having abandoned his initial reluctance and totally surrendered himself to possession by the kundalini in its sacral permutation. Given the circumstances, his calm struck Ariana as truly amazing. As for her and Ishwara, it was not clear to her whether they too were actually making love or simply going along for the ride. Ariana finally decided to take her cue from the priest and let happen what happened.

With eyes open, she experienced the experience of the priest. With eyes closed, she felt Ishwara deep inside her. Gradually, however, the difference between the two disappeared, and Ishwara making love to her was the same as the lovely chandala making love to the brahmin. The tension was rising for everyone, and everyone was remaining relaxed in the midst of it. She was not certain of all that happened next or what it all meant, but she did understand that the priest, upon reaching the point of greatest excitation, suddenly and shockingly exerted his will and, with a mighty effort, succeeded in preventing ejaculation. The sublimated kundalini shot up the spine and out the crown chakra, and then the utter bliss of Brahman poured through. She experienced this spiritual release as well because she too, without really knowing how, had sublimated her orgasm. All she understood was that it was a matter of going deep, of keeping oneself below the surface of passion's ocean so the waves did not overwhelm. Then the explosive force of the sublimated orgasm sent her straight to the ocean floor, where all was calm and at peace.

She had no idea how long she rested in that bliss, but when she finally opened her eyes, Ishwara was nowhere to be seen. She had been ready to declare her love, and so was distraught at finding the Teacher sitting opposite her in what had been Ishwara's place.

12. Transcendence

"What are you doing here?" she asked before she could catch herself.

He did not appear to take offense. "I said I would be your reality-check."

She wanted to ask who would check his reality, but after her gauche opening did not dare.

"What happened to Ishwara?"

"He has shown you what you needed to see. Do you have any questions?"

"Why can't Ishwara answer my questions?"

"It's best that a disinterested third party handle the summing up."

Ariana reflected. "The marriage between the Aryans and pre-Aryans proved fruitful. Do I really understand that aright, that the rigid order of Hindu society frees the soul from preoccupation with things of the world so that it may concentrate on things of the spirit?"

"It may be regarded that way," he replied in a perfectly neutral tone, "or it may be seen as a instrument by which the upper castes enslave the rest of the population."

"What do you think?"

"There is a third possibility," he said noncommittally. "Perhaps it's a way to escape from life by burrowing within oneself, just as the typical Westerner escapes from self by immersion in life."

"But all these are simply equal possibilities," she remarked, smiling sardonically.

"Of course," he smiled back, and once again she thought she might possibly like him. "Are you ready to continue the contest?" he inquired, with more warmth in his voice than she had hitherto noticed.

"I'm not sure," she said, and closed her eyes to think. "It was so real!" she murmured, without opening them. "The going beyond was so real!"

"Of course it was," he agreed, without a trace of irony. "It is real. It is the reality of the inner depth."

"And in the final experience . . ." Her voice trailed off, lost in ecstatic memory.

"The tantra," he remarked, and she reopened her eyes.

"Tantra?"

He nodded. "The spiritual harnessing of the sexual energy. The Hindu tantra consists of a small family of Hindu sects that, I think, are important because of their attitude toward sexuality. As you learned firsthand, Hindu society, like most societies in history, has been strongly patriarchal and puritanical. Wherever sexuality is denied its proper spiritual significance, women likewise are devalued."

"I noticed that," said Ariana, "but I don't understand why. Do men think women more sexual than themselves, or what?"

"Yes, men tend to project their sexuality onto women," replied the Teacher, "but there's more to it than that. Women are closer to their sexuality than men. For woman, sexuality is nature. For man, it's achievement."

"In your opinion," she bristled.

"Yes," admitted the teacher, "but not only in my opinion. In many societies, women are held to reach sexual and emotional maturity long before men. In many aboriginal societies, women marry around twenty years of age and men around forty."

"Men stay celibate for so long?" Ariana said unbelievingly.

"No, no!" replied the Teacher, again as if she were stupid. "They engage in sex practically from puberty on, but are only permitted to enter a committed relationship when deemed mature enough to handle it."

"And I suppose the widows enjoy themselves with the younger men," she said slyly.

"You catch on quickly," he laughed, and her anger dissipated. "The tantric sects equate the sexual and spiritual energy . . ."

"Shiva!" she interjected, remembering.

"Yes, Shiva. However, they do so not merely in theory, but also in practice."

"You say the tantra is a tiny part of Hinduism," she remarked.

"Yes, in size, and a despised part. It involves violation of caste in many ways: the eating of forbidden food and drink; sex outside marriage for some purpose other than procreation, probably between members of two different castes or between a caste Hindu and an outcaste; and defiance of a host of lesser taboos. In fact, the tantra pretty much ignores caste. Many of its gurus are untouchables. In turn, many Hindus pretend it does not exist."

"Then why did Ishwara end with it? Do you think he was trying to tell me that the position of women is changing in India?"

"There can be no doubt that it has changed," he nodded vigorously, "as well as that of the untouchables. Whether it has changed for the better, however, is open to question. With the British came railroads, industry, and ideas of democracy and social equality that turned caste from a social ideal into a national embarrassment, as well as making it, and the traditional form of education that went with it, highly impractical and inconvenient. For better or worse, India is a much different place today than it was two-hundred years ago when the British took control, more different than many Hindus are willing to accept."

"What do you mean?"

"Many upper-caste Hindus want to enter the modern world economically, politically and militarily, and stay socially and religiously within the feudal confines of caste. Just like poor whites in the American South during the heyday of racial segregation, many shudra cherish their social superiority to the untouchables more than the prospects of advancement a more egalitarian system would offer them. The untouchables, on the other hand, just like African Americans, have come to resent their traditional degradation, and are actively working to better their lot. Though the existence of a pecking order among them weakens these efforts, it has not prevented them. The result has been a conservative backlash in the form of violent and often lethal repression that is shrouded in a conspiracy of silence on the part of Indian journalists and government officials."

Ariana felt the grief in his voice, as if he took these injustices personally. "And women?" she reminded him.

"Upper-caste women tend to be much better educated today than in the past, though their brothers still receive priority. In liberal social circles, women are regarded as men's equals, but nowhere else. Sati was outlawed by the British and died out in the nineteenth century, yet in some parts of India there has developed a variation upon this theme. A man will marry for his wife's dowry, and six months or so down the line push his wife into the bread oven so he may keep the dowry and move on to his next victim. This is murder, of course, but difficult to prosecute because, given the patrilocal character of the Hindu family, the only witnesses are usually the perpetrators own blood-kin. Also, as an interesting variant upon the Western genre of technocratic horror, Indians are taking advantage of modern obstetric techniques to selectively abort girl-fetuses."

"So, despite equality on paper," said Ariana, "women are still second-class citizens."

The Teacher nodded. "Monogamy is the rule in Hinduism, and the ideal of Hindu marriage is one of mutual consideration and respect. Arranged marriage, however, is still the dominant practice; and child marriage, though illegal, still goes on."

"What about the Four Stages of Life?" she asked, and he brightened a little, as if relieved to move on to another subject.

"As an ideal, it still exercises considerable influence; but, as a practice, it is much more honored in the breach than in the observance. Take the third stage of withdrawal. Traditionally, one left one's home when one's sons were grown and ready to take over, and thenceforth dwelt in solitude. Today population in India is so dense that every uninhabited place is uninhabitable. I know of more than one Hindu parent who has alienated the affection of his or her family by 'withdrawing' while still in the household. To spend most of one's time in prayer and meditation while living among people who are busy with the affairs of daily life, especially the raising of children, is emotionally taxing on all parties concerned."

"If everything that Ishwara showed me is dying, dead, or ossifying," she protested, "why did we go to all the trouble?"

"Because you can't have any idea of what Hinduism is today or what it might be tomorrow unless you know what it has been. Besides, not everything he showed you is dying."

"Yoga?" she guessed.

"Precisely!" he confirmed. "When the caste system is dead and forgotten, there is no doubt that Hindu spirituality will live on. What form it will take, however, is impossible to say. If Hinduism's spiritual openness and diversity of religious expression is truly one-half of a psychologically symbiotic relationship, then the death of the other half cannot leave it unaffected. We can see the truth of this in the rise of Hindu fundamentalism, a phenomenon one might think almost a contradiction in terms. Social change breeds insecurity, and insecurity breeds philosophical rigidity. Is Hinduism in the process of exchanging social for ideological conformity?"

"I imagine that is something only Hindus themselves can decide."

"Certainly," he smiled. "On the other hand, one might regard future developments as the playing out of the inner logic of the Hindu tradition."

"Do you ever give an unequivocal answer?" she laughed, despite the feeling of irritation he engendered in her.

"If you think I'm bad," he grimaced with mock malignity, "wait until you encounter our next contestant!"

CHAPTER II.

BUDDHISM

As the echo of this exclamation faded into the stillness of the empyrean, she suddenly felt as if someone were behind her. Turning instinctively, she saw the winsome figure of Buddha standing, with hands folded, as if he had been there forever. Turning back to compliment the Teacher for orchestrating so striking an entrance, she discovered that he had disappeared. Good riddance, she thought to herself, though she had to admit that, beneath the surface of contempt, her feelings toward the Teacher were far more ambivalent than she was willing to let on. In any event, her relationship with the "grand inquisitor," as she had already dubbed him in her mind, was at that moment of purely academic interest. After all, she thought, she might never see him again, though she knew in her heart that she would. Now, however, she had the chance to enjoy the company of the charming and handsome Buddha.

With him there were no preliminary theatrics, as with Ishwara. He sat her down on a comfortable patch of soft grass. There was none of the intensity born of sexual tension so noticeable in her relationship with Ishwara. He played congenial host to her role of honored guest, valued friend to valued friend.

"Tell me," she smiled, not out of politeness, as for a stranger, or coyly, as was her wont with men, but out of a feeling of genuine companionship. "I have heard something about your teachings, but your viewpoint never struck me as all that different from Ishwara's."

"At first the primary difference between Hinduism and Buddhism was not so much philosophical as social," he replied with frank seriousness, a refreshing change from the Teacher's acerbic irony and even Ishwara's love banter. "As Gotama in ancient India . . ."

"Gotama?"

"Buddha, as you know, is a title."

"'Awakened one?'"

He nodded without a trace of either pride or self-effacement. "Gotama was the name of my family, my clan."

"What was your personal name?" she asked, wanting to be on as familiar terms with him as possible.

"Siddhartha," he replied, and then added with a smile, as if he had been reading her mind, "but I prefer to be called Gotama."

"Gotama it is, then!"

"Unless you prefer Sakamuni," he offered.

"Where did that come from?"

"It's the way the Chinese pronounce Shakyamuni, sage of the Shakya tribe, my tribe."

"Gotama will be fine," she laughed. "Now for your first test: Pick up the thread of your discourse where I interrupted you."

"As young Gotama in ancient India twenty-five hundred years ago," he complied flawlessly, "I had no time for the priestly magic that turned the idea that we are all manifestations of the one and only *Brahman* into a system of hierarchy and caste. I also had no patience with mystical veneration of barbaric hymns to primitive gods."

"You didn't believe such gods existed?"

"I didn't believe it made any difference whether they did or not."

"Oh, I see. You were concerned with only the one true God, Brahman."

"No," he declared with uncharacteristic vehemence, "I'm not concerned with any god, many or one! Nor, to save time, am I concerned with the soul, the world, or any other 'ultimate' reality."

"What are you concerned with?"

In reply, Gotama told a story. "One time one of my disciples, a brash but gifted youth, cornered me and demanded an answer to his questions. He wanted to know if there was a God or not, if there was a soul or not, if the world had a beginning and if it would have an end, and if there was life after death. He berated me for being the enlightened and all-knowing spiritual master who nevertheless always answered a question with a question."

"What did you tell him?"

"Naturally, I answered his question with a question."

She shook her head in amused disbelief.

"I asked him what he would do if his house were on fire. Would he hunt up the blueprints or the title deed? What would you do?" he addressed her.

"Save myself," she laughed. Somehow obvious questions were not so irksome when they came from Gotama's lips.

"And what would you do if shot with a poisoned arrow—seek to know the caste and ancestry of the one who shot the arrow?"

"Get medical attention," she replied as expected.

"So too," he went on, speaking both to her and that obstreperous young disciple of long ago, "life is on fire with craving. It is poisoned with suffering. Don't be concerned with abstractions like *Brahman* and *atman*, God and the soul, or speculation about the duration of life or the universe. The concrete task is before you, to find the way beyond suffering."

"To go beyond," she echoed. "So, it is simply Hinduism without caste?"

"I said that the differences were primarily social rather than philosophical in the beginning," he explained patiently. "It was my fault that you did not understand, because I forgot to mention that I was speaking only of apparent differences. In truth, what took me out of the Hindu society into which I was born was a radical departure in fundamental understanding of the nature of reality."

He was long-winded, but the complexity of his ideas required verbal as well as mental expansiveness in which to develop. And no matter how he went on, she much preferred the gentle regularity of his voice over the staccato interrogatories of the Teacher, in the same way one would prefer sitting next to a gurgling brook to being sprayed by a riot hose. Whether she liked it better than the playful fire of Ishwara she could not say.

"You seem so certain of that, but I still don't see the difference," she remarked.

"It only stands to reason," he replied. "Buddhism lasted in India well over a thousand years. If it had had no distinctive philosophy, no distinctive spirituality of its own, it would have been reabsorbed into its mother."

"I thought it was," she observed.

"In part, but chiefly it was destroyed. White Hun invaders in the sixth century and Muslim invaders from the ninth century on burned monasteries throughout northern India and put many monks to the sword."

"They did the same to Hindu priests and temples. Or so I have heard."

"True, but Hinduism, for all the richness of its temple *puja*, is centered on the home. Every household has its altar and sacred fire. Also, though at one point Islam controlled all of India except the Deccan, a strip of land along the coast, the Hindus retained a base of operations in the south from which to regroup and reconquer northern India. Indian Buddhism was centered in the north and upon its monasteries. Their destruction was irreparable."

"You speak as if you had no self-interest in it."

"In what?" he asked, apparently missing her gentle irony.

"Buddhism."

He smiled. "No self-interest, because there is no self."

For the first time since meeting him she considered the possibility, so contradictory to his aura of cheerful compassion, that it was all an act, and that his serenity was the product, not of spiritual enlightenment, but a gigantic ego-complex.

"So, you are beyond self?" she queried.

"You misunderstand me," he smiled, as if he too, like Ishwara, knew what she was thinking. "Not 'beyond self,' and not 'me.' But let me begin my explanation from the beginning. To be fair to Hinduism, though I and my followers tend to think of our philosophy as more practical and realistic, the differences between us and the Hindus really originate in a difference in root metaphor. Hindus would simply deny that human existence is like a house on fire. For them, it is more like a maze, a labyrinth, even a hall of mirrors."

"A fun-house!" she laughed sardonically, remembering her time with Ishwara.

"Yes, like a fun-house. And if one is trapped in a labyrinth, it makes sense to try to figure out its layout."

"The path of knowledge."

"Yes, *Jnana-yoga*," he confirmed. "Or to call for help."

"Devotion."

"*Bhakti*," he nodded. "Or to demolish the walls and force one's way out."

"Is that *Karma* or *Raja-yoga*?" she laughed. "Work or power?"

"Metaphors have their limits," he smiled, "but I would think that *Raja-yoga* would be more like laying charges against the walls and hoping one survives the blast."

"The big bang!" she laughed even harder, remembering the *tantra*.

"You will see," he said with just a hint of suggestiveness, "that we have our own version in Buddhism."

"I can hardly wait," she said, and then immediately wished she had not. The tone of friendship between them she felt to be so special was slipping away. However, again as if he could read her thoughts, Gotama kindly returned to the straight-forward exposition she found so reassuring.

"To sum up, Hinduism is the most metaphysical of religions. It not only holds that there is such a thing as metaphysical reality, but that the metaphysical is the only reality. Buddhism, on the contrary, isn't concerned with metaphysics at all, but with overcoming suffering, which can only be done by awakening to the nature of human existence here and now."

"A more psychological approach?" she suggested.

"Yes, that's a good way to put it."

"So, you don't think there are any gods?"

"Oh, there are plenty of gods, and demons as well. There are all sorts of entities in the phenomenal world. There are simply none outside of that world. There is no God beyond the gods, no *Brahman*, no absolute being."

"Nothing unchanging?" she queried.

"Absolutely no-thing," he smiled. "All is *sunyata*—emptiness, no-thingness, the void."

"A field of potentiality," she added, "as the physicists say."

"And there is nothing but *samsara*," he continued. "Change, flux."

"Energy?"

"If you will, energy."

"I knew a physicist among the earthbound spirits. It sounds like what he said, that it is all just structured energy."

"'Energy equals mass times speed of light squared,'" he quoted. "As Einstein said, and the Western scientists proved with their atomic bomb, matter is simply energy in relatively stable form. Disrupt that stability, and there is more than enough energy in a cubic centimeter of 'empty' space to destroy an entire city."

"And energy is just another way of talking about change with no-thing changing," Ariana added.

Gotama smiled appreciatively. "Yes," he said, "but the notion of Western science is not identical to our own. It's too narrow and limited. We do not deny the spiritual dimension of life, but simply reject the idea that it is an absolute reality apart from the flux of the phenomenal world. If one is to find peace, one must do it in the midst of that flux."

"How does one do that?" she asked.

"There are many different ways, many different ideas. Though each likes to claim me as its own, they all arise from the basic philosophical viewpoint to which I gave utterance."

"The Four Noble Truths?"

"Yes," he smiled, apparently pleased that she had heard of his teachings, "we will come to those. While we are here, though, let me tell you a story to illustrate the crucial difference between Buddhist and Hindu spirituality. It's a true story about an experiment conducted by some Western scientists. They took two volunteers, a Hindu *yogi* and a Buddhist monk, hooked up each in turn to one of those machines that reads out brain waves . . ."

"An electroencephalograph," she assisted.

"An electroencephalograph," he echoed. "You are of the new age! Each man, in turn, went into his own style of meditation, and each emanated the slow, what I believe they call alpha, rhythm. Then, in turn, they fired a pistol next to the ear of each meditator."

"Ouch!" she winced. "That would be like a thunder bolt!"

"When the pistol went off next to the Hindu *yogi*, there was no change in the brain wave pattern."

"I don't believe it!"

"You should," he admonished her. "You know what deep trance is like. He wasn't present to his senses."

She nodded in understanding.

"When the pistol went off next to the Buddhist monk, there was a sharp jump in the pattern, but then it went immediately back to the alpha rhythm."

"It registered, but he didn't panic."

"Yes," he agreed, "no emotional trauma."

"I can imagine what my pattern would have been like!" she laughed. "I'm all over the charts just thinking about it."

"So you see," Gotama pointed out the moral of the story, "we don't seek to go beyond ordinary awareness, but to find the point of balance within that awareness."

"You still haven't explained to me what you mean by 'no-self,'" she reminded him.

"Think of an onion," he said. "According to the Hindu conception of an eternal and immutable soul, or *atman*, if you peel away the layers of the onion . . ."

"What layers?" she interjected, his gentility giving her license to be direct.

"In the case of Hinduism, the physical, emotional, intellectual, and personal dimensions of being," he explained patiently. "Peel these away, and one comes upon a hard core of selfhood, or pure awareness, which remains the same in all the changes the empirical self goes through. According to my conception, the Buddhist conception of *anatman* or "no-self," the empirical self consists of five *skandhas*, or heaps: sensation, perception, feeling, thought, and consciousness. Peel these away and one is left with nothing."

"Or no-thing?" she asked archly.

"You do learn quickly," he laughed.

"And you do believe in reincarnation, don't you?" she persisted. "Otherwise, if you really only want peace, why don't you just blow your own brains out?"

"Yes, we believe in reincarnation, of a sort," he replied, not the least bit offended. Ariana realized that she was trying to break down his facade of abiding serenity. She now wondered if it was a facade.

"According to Ishwara," she asked less belligerently, "reincarnation is like the soul putting on and off a body the way one puts on and off clothing. If there is no soul, what's reincarnated?"

"Let me give you a different metaphor," he said. "If you have a row of candles, and you pass a flame from the first on through to the last, is the flame of the last candle the same as that of the first?"

"This is a trick question," she laughed. "I never answer trick questions."

"You are right," he affirmed. "The question doesn't make sense, because 'same' and 'different' apply to things, and fire is not a thing. There is no thing like a soul passed from one lifetime to the next. As with the flame, there is only a chain of causation, a transmission of energy."

"And what is the flame that passes through the cycle of death and rebirth?"

"Craving. Extinguish the craving, and no more rebirth. That is nirvana."

"So if 'self' doesn't exist," she asked, "who is 'Ariana'?"

"What is the Ganges?" he countered.

"Always answer with a question!" she laughed. "Okay, I'll take the bait. It's a river in India."

"Is it called the Ganges because it always has the same water in it?" he went on.

"No," she answered, "because the water flows along the same route."

"Or suppose you arrange a pile of dominoes into a nice, neat row," he said. "You show it to me. What would I say?"

Ariana pondered. "Where's the row?"

Again Gotama laughed. "Yes, 'row' is an abstract term denoting the arrangement of the dominoes. In reality, there is no row."

"What is there, then?" she asked.

"Successive states of existence," he replied. "*Samsara*. Each state gives rise to the next in a causal chain that can be broken only by the cessation of craving. That cessation is *nirvana*."

"What is nirvana like?" she asked.

"That cannot be told," he replied, "any more than one can explain color to one born blind. But I can say this: though nirvana is a wholly negative concept, it is a positive reality. However, it is not a positive reality in the samsaric sense . . ."

"What do you mean?"

"The phenomenal world, just like the phenomenal self, is samsara—flux, change. Buddhists use the term *maya*, but it doesn't really fit Buddhism philosophically, because it means the veil hiding ultimate reality, and in our thinking there is nothing to hide. Therefore, nirvana is not real in the samsaric sense, but neither is samsara real from the viewpoint of nirvana."

"I never thought I'd admit this to anyone," she laughed, "but the Teacher was right! It is impossible to get you to give a straight answer!"

"The only way to know what nirvana is like," he replied congenially, not at all offended, "is to go there. And the only way to go there is to walk the path."

"Show me this path, and maybe I will."

"It begins and ends with me, but along the way it branches out into several paths."

"So why don't we begin with you?" she suggested, and Gotama responded by telling his story.

1. Gotama and the Four Noble Truths

He was born sometime in the middle of the first millennium B.C.E., the son of the chief of the mighty Shakya tribe, in the foothills of the Himalayas. According to legend, and Gotoma would not say whether the legend was true, there were signs and wonders and prophecies at his birth indicating he would grow up to be a universal monarch, king of all of hitherto war-torn and disunited India; or a *buddha*, an enlightened one. Like most fathers, the king wanted his royal kshatriya son to follow in his footsteps; so he took measures to ensure that the boy would never set out on the spiritual quest. From his earliest days, Gotama knew nothing but enjoyment and adventure. His father built him an enchanting pleasure garden, sent away to a distant kingdom for a most beautiful wife, and in short order he and his ravishing bride produced the first of what seemed certain to be a multitude of beautiful sons and daughters. Gotama knew bliss such as no mortal ever had because, in addition to all these joys and unbeknownst to himself, his father the king had ordered his soldiers, on pain of death, to keep the crown-prince from any sight of poverty, sickness, old age, and death. The soldiers did their best, and everything was falling out as the king had hoped, but then the gods intervened. The gods wanted Gotama to become a buddha because they themselves did not know the way to enlightenment and wanted him to teach them!

Thus in four days a god appeared to him successively as a poor man, sick man, old man, and dead man. One could imagine the shock, something equivalent to being raised in heaven and waking up one morning in hell. Unlike a typical Westerner, Gotama did not regard the suffering and death he had discovered as something to be ignored or fixed. The misery was to him a window looking into the very heart of existence. Even more, he did not see himself as apart from the evils. They caused him to realize that his self-indulgent princely life was merely the other side of the coin. He himself would one day grow old or take ill and die, and the more he had possessed of life's good things, the more painful would be their loss. The greater his enjoyment of life, the more agonizing would be its end.

Gotama knew that he could not escape the pall this experience cast over his entire world. He could not run away from suffering, but had to come to grips with it.

"That is your first noble truth," Ariana observed.

"Yes," Gotama assented, "that all is suffering, or, in the Pali dialect, *dukkha*. Nothing is fulfilling or satisfying. Everything is changing and without substance."

"A cheery outlook," she commented. Gotama smiled sadly in response, and then continued with his story.

That night, not wishing to create a disturbance and, he confessed, afraid that his resolve would weaken were they to implore him to stay, Gotama bade his sleeping wife and son farewell and went off into the forest with nothing more than a loin cloth and beggar's bowl. For a time he lived under the successive guidance of the two greatest yogis of the day, and they taught him the Second Noble Truth, that craving and clinging are the roots of suffering.

"Why?" asked Ariana. "What is the connection, exactly?"

"We feel empty, without substance, so we try to fill ourselves up with food, sex, drugs, money, prestige, and power, but nothing works. The more we devour, the emptier we feel."

"I see. And clinging?"

"From the time we are little, we feel so helpless and alone, so ephemeral, that we hold on to whatever we think is big, eternal, and unchanging—parents, teachers, lovers, careers, and eventually, in the face of death, the idea of God. But everything is passing, and so we suffer. We are like a man in a runaway canoe hurtling down the rapids who grabs onto an overhanging branch. It hurts to hold on, and sooner or later either his strength must give out or the branch will break."

"So what is one to do," Ariana wondered, "go with the flow?"

"We already do. That's the dilemma."

"Yes, I see," she said. "The problem is how to get out of the stream."

"That is the problem," he agreed. The yogis told him that the only way out of the samsaric stream was to root out craving and clinging, and that this could be done only by overcoming them with one's will, by asceticism.

"So if one never gives in to craving and clinging, if one refuses to act out of fear and denies oneself one's desires, one will go beyond suffering?" she asked doubtfully.

"Yes, that's it precisely," he affirmed.

"Why can't there be healthy desires, healthy attachments?" she queried. "After all, isn't the need to overcome desire just the fear of being hurt when you lose what you desire?"

Gotama agreed that that might be so, and said some of his followers had been led by that very question on a most paradoxical path. At that point in his life, however, he was grasping at straws, willing to try anything to overcome the bleak despair in his soul. And try anything he did, with a vengeance. He became the most famous ascetic in the forest. He went for months subsisting on only one bean a day, until his ribs protruded through his skin and one could almost see his backbone through his belly. He drank little, slept little, and sat or stood for hours in the most contorted yogic *asanas* in the hot sun or chilling rain. Gotama was so celebrated for the extremity of his austerities that half-a-dozen young men—like ancient "groupies," Ariana thought—followed as his disciples without his wanting or even welcoming them. For several years he lived in this way, fighting to overcome the many-headed monster of desire; but the harder he fought, the stronger his enemy seemed to grow. He continued to increase his efforts, thinking that sooner or later the craving for life would be broken. As it turned out, his life was broken first. One day, after an extended fast, he collapsed. His disciples did nothing, thinking this was simply the final stage in his conquest of self. After all, one of his own former teachers had held that the ultimate act of holiness, the one overcoming all *karma*, was to starve oneself to death. Gotama, however, was in utter despair. Even more bitter to him than the knowledge that he was dying was the realization that he was no closer to solving the problem of suffering than when he had set out from his father's palace years before.

"Why?" Ariana cried. "Because starving yourself to death hadn't worked?"

"It seemed I had tried everything," answered Gotama, "explored every logical alternative. If craving is an inner monster, a beast that threatens to devour us . . ."

"I suppose someone in the grip of an addiction is being devoured by that inner beast," she interjected.

Gotama nodded. "If craving is an inner monster," he resumed, "there seem to be only two ways to deal with it. Either give it what it wants, so it will go to sleep and leave one in peace awhile . . ."

"That's what most people do," said Ariana—"self-indulgence."

"Yes," he agreed. "One may live in self-indulgence, or one may live in self-denial."

"Deny the beast what it desires," she said. "Master it with one's will."

Again he nodded. "I had tried both, and neither had worked. Craving had turned out to be such a beast that, whether one fed it or starved it, it grew. That's why I was in despair."

Ariana studied his face, and saw the shadow of the heartache that had possessed him. She impulsively took his hand, and he went on with his story.

While the "holy man" lay there, a bag of bones in the dust, a passing maiden took pity upon him and offered him a bowl of milk. He knew that, if he took it, he would be admitting hopeless defeat, but there was no virtue in hiding from oneself or others what was undeniably true. As he drank, he felt the nourishment course through his veins like warmth through a frozen limb. His disciples left him, thinking he had succumbed to temptation; but he did not care, because he felt he was on the verge of a dawning realization.

He had tried what appeared to be every logical possibility to still desire, either indulging or suppressing it. Still, he knew there had to be a way without really believing it. Now he both knew and believed it, and it would come to him very soon. This is the Third Noble Truth, that there is a way to still craving and clinging and go beyond suffering.

Gotama arose, bathed, and exchanged his worn-out loincloth for a swami's saffron robe. Then he sat under a bodhi tree, a tree with large overhanging and thickly matted branches used by lovers for trysts and holy men for meditation because it provides protection against both weather and prying eyes, and fell into deep-trance meditation.

Gotama was a shining example of a *Raja-yogi* who, as Ishwara had put it, could do it all while sitting in a closet. He did not really know whether this meditation lasted one night or several weeks, but in that time he mastered all the *seven* chakras and overcame all the temptations associated with each. Again, the gods took a hand in this. Mara, the tempter, sought to seduce him with everything from culinary delicacies and ravishing dancing girls to unsurpassed knowledge of all mysteries and rulership over all the kingdoms of the earth. After achieving the ultimate trance state, *nirvikalpa samadhi*, the floodgates of memory were opened and he remembered all his past lives, about many of which he later told his disciples, who passed them down to their children and children's children until finally they were compiled into the *Jataka Tales* that are so popular with Buddhists today.

For example, in one life he was a crane who proved his seniority to a giraffe and an elephant by pointing out that he himself had dropped the seed that had grown into a seedling over which the elephant had walked, and into a tree upon whose highest branches the giraffe had grazed. In another, he had been the king of the monkeys who had sacrificed his own life to save his fellow monkeys from hunters. In a third, he had, as a young man, given his body to be eaten by starving lion cubs. Finally came his present life as Gotama. His childhood and youth passed through his mind, right up to the present moment. When it came to remembering that he was remembering, and remembering that he was remembering that he was remembering, he grew dizzy and opened his eyes. Then he knew that excessive searching for the way within oneself was just as much of a dead-end as excessive searching outside oneself. If craving was the problem, trance meditation was no solution, only a temporary escape. It was then that he hit upon the Fourth Noble Truth, the Middle Way.

At this point in his narrative, Gotama fell silent. At first Ariana thought he was simply building up to the grand climax; but, as the silence lengthened, she began to wonder if something had gone wrong. "Gotama," she called to him as if he were on the other side of a great chasm, even though he was sitting only a few feet away.

"I'm sorry," he smiled at her, mentally shaking himself out of his reverie. "I was just thinking about all the different directions in which my followers have taken my teachings down through the centuries."

"I noticed something," she ventured, hoping a brief change of mental scene might revive his powers of communication. "You think just like a physician."

He smiled in appreciation, signaling that she was on the right track.

"The First Noble Truth is the diagnosis—the world is poisoned with suffering. The Second, that craving and clinging are the roots of suffering, is the etiology or cause of the disorder. The Third, that there is indeed a way beyond suffering, is the prognosis, or probable outcome. And the Fourth, the Middle Way, is what I bet you anything is the cure. Am I right?"

"Yes, you are right," he brightened.

"You know something else I noticed?" she continued. "The Third Noble Truth, which seemed to me at first to say nothing that couldn't be said with just the other three, is the key. Everything depends on the prognosis. If a doctor decides that a patient is incurable, the most that can be done is to make her as comfortable as possible until she dies. But if the doctor figures the patient can be cured, he might put her through living hell to bring her back from the dead!"

"You have hit upon it exactly!" he affirmed. "That's what sets our philosophy apart from philosophical pessimism! You know," he lowered his voice as if she were a fellow conspirator, "when they first encountered Buddhism, many Western philosophers thought it a way of committing spiritual suicide, an embracing of oblivion. That is because *nirvana* literally means 'extinction,' and they confused the extinction of craving with the extinction of the soul. In fact, the soul cannot be extinguished because it does not exist! They themselves had stopped short with the first two of the Four Noble Truths. If life is an incurable disease, they concluded, we should make ourselves as comfortable as possible until it ends."

"'Eat, drink, and be merry,'" she quoted from somewhere, "'for tomorrow we die!'"

"Yes, for tomorrow we die," he echoed poignantly. "Or tomorrow we are reborn. East or West, it all amounts to the same thing. Is there a way beyond the dualities, the self-contradictions of life?"

"Is there?" she challenged.

"Are you willing to go through hell to get there?" he quoted her playfully.

"Lead on!" she cried, as if going into battle. "With a friend like you by my side, I'm willing to go anywhere!"

The radiance of his answering smile assured her that he felt the same way.

2. The Way of the Elders and the Eight-Fold Path

"The question is," he pondered, "how should we begin."

"A wise man once told me," she laughed—"or was it a little bird?—that it's always best to begin at the beginning."

"Theravada," he said, and when she made an inquisitorial face he added, "the Way of the Elders."

"Sounds like the beginning," she encouraged him.

"Actually, it was one of many philosophical schools of early Buddhism," he said, "all with the same basic understanding of life, and collectively called by their opponents within the Buddhist tradition *Hinayana*, or 'small raft,' usually translated into Western tongues as 'lesser vehicle.'"

"I can't imagine what these opponents called themselves," she said with pointed irony.

"We'll come to that later," he smiled. "Anyway, partly because of its purity, and partly due to a period of undisturbed incubation in the island kingdom of Sri Lanka, Theravada alone survived, and then went on to conquer most of Southeast Asia."

"Most?"

"Actually, just about all but Vietnam. Myanmar, Cambodia, Thailand, and Laos are essentially Theravadin countries. The reason Vietnam went over to the Mahayana, the 'Greater Vehicle,' is its close historical and cultural association with China."

"Yes," she added, "long before the Vietnamese fought the Americans and the French and the Japanese for their freedom, they were fighting the Chinese. Still, I suppose influence is influence, however you come by it. But I guessed from what you've said that southern Asia went Theravadin, and northern Asia Mahayana. Why?"

"I could give you all sorts of fancy philosophical reasons," he answered, "but the simple truth is that the Theravadin missionaries were too set in their ways to survive in the north. They went barefoot and wore nothing but the light saffron robe, even in the severity of the northern winters. And they refused to eat meat, even when that was the only food available. Furthermore, the practical and down-to-earth Chinese regarded the monastic practice of begging as sheer laziness, and had great difficulty finding meaning in the almost exclusive focus upon a transcendent spiritual goal like nirvana. The Mahayana missionaries were much more adaptable."

"If the Chinese are so down-to-earth," asked Ariana, "why did they accept Buddhism at all?"

"They believe in making provision for all possibilities," Gotama readily replied. "They already had Daoism for nature, and Confucianism for society, but nothing for dealing with a transcendent spiritual reality. Mahayana Buddhism satisfied this need."

"Then why did Theravada win out in southern Asia?"

"Because Theravada emphasizes monasticism, the cultivation of holiness for its own sake, something the less severe climate of southern Asia gives its people the luxury to pursue without so much concern for 'practicality.'"

"So tell me," she said, "what is the Theravadin ideal of spirituality? What is the 'Way of the Elders?'"

"That's one of the issues I was considering how to present without misleading you. You see, the basis of all Buddhist philosophy is the Four Noble Truths, and especially the Middle Way or Eight-Fold Path. Yet Mahayana brings in other elements that, from the Theravadin standpoint, not only modify but actually corrupt the original teachings."

"Do you agree?" she asked pointedly.

"There is something to be said for having a variety of paths," he replied with intense seriousness, "as long as they all lead to the desired goal."

"So do they or don't they?" she persisted.

"That is for the ones who take them to decide."

"You've done it again!" she laughed. "The Teacher wasn't wrong about you."

He smiled, almost shyly, she would have said, if she had not already enjoyed with him so long and intimate a conversation. "I am going to explain the Eight-Fold Path from a Theravadin perspective. You must see for yourself, when we get there, if and how the Mahayana differs in its understanding of the Middle Way."

"Fair enough," she smiled in return, "especially since I know I won't get a better deal out of you."

"The Eight-Fold Path is enumerated variously in the tradition, but the way that best fits the Theravadin philosophy is right understanding, right attitude, right effort, right action, right livelihood, right meditation, right concentration, and right mindfulness."

"Am I supposed to memorize all that?" she pouted. "I do remember that every step begins with 'right.'"

"That's a beginning," he laughed, "and I will make it easier to retain the rest. Memory is really a function of understanding. If you absorb something's meaning, then it becomes a part of you. If not, you can carry it around in a mental box, but you won't have any use for it and eventually will, quite rightly, discard it. So, to the end that you understand this path, the first thing that must be said is that these eight 'folds' are steps, not stages. One does not take them in succession. They are phases of one movement along the spiritual path."

"Inseparable, then?" she asked.

"Not exactly. One may choose not to engage in the path fully; but if one does, one must attack on all eight fronts."

"The kshatriya is coming through in you," she laughed. "As Ishwara might say, caste will out."

"I admit, I am a warrior," he smiled. "Though perhaps the metaphor of 'athlete' will make things easier for you to comprehend."

"Whatever works."

"The Eight-Fold Path divides conveniently into three aspects—wisdom, compassion, and spiritual discipline. Like the three legs of a stool, they are mutually supportive."

"I wish more people understood that," said Ariana ruefully, "especially in the West, where everyone seems to think that three stools, each with one leg in a different corner, are as good as one stool with three legs."

"You are right!" he nodded vigorously. "Specialization has become the West's special brand of insanity. Not only do people specialize in a certain occupation. They specialize at being a certain type of human being."

"Yes!" she agreed. "You have the airhead with a heart of gold, and the genius with a heart of stone, and the 'religious' person with no real heart at all."

"Compassion without wisdom is sentimentality," said Gotama, "and wisdom without compassion is arid abstraction. As for piety without either wisdom or compassion, what is it but a clanging cymbal or a sounding drum?"

"To paraphrase one of the West's own holy men," she laughed.

"There is much to be learned from them," he said seriously. "It's a pity the West has ignored what its own most profound philosophers have had to say."

"They are not known as 'philosophers,'" she remarked. "They are known as saints. That gives everyone the obligation to worship them and the license to ignore their teachings."

"This split between philosophy and religion is another sign of insanity," Gotama said, shaking his head. "But I was explaining to you the Eight-Fold Path." Then he went on to describe each of the three divisions in turn.

Wisdom has to do with basic assumptions. Right understanding simply means that one has come to understand the necessity in one's life for such a path. In other words, one appreciates the truth of the Four Noble Truths. With the exception of a few fanatics who are the Buddhist equivalent of evangelical Christians, Buddhists do not preach, "All is suffering" the way many Christians preach hell-fire and damnation. His followers have no desire to bring people to despair. Rather, the Middle Way is offered as a possibility for those who have come to the end of possibility, who are already in despair over samsaric existence. If one were not, one could still find something of value in certain aspects of the Eight-Fold Path, but one would have no reason to walk it. A training manual for a certain sport is of interest only to those who, for whatever reason, decide to take up that sport.

Right attitude, as Gotama explained it, fits the athletic metaphor quite closely. It involves both trust and faith. Just as an athlete who does not trust her trainer should find another trainer she can trust, so there is no point in setting out on the Eight-Fold Path if one does not trust in the wisdom of the Buddha. Gotama was emphatic in pointing out that the trust he requests is not blind belief, but a practical and provisional giving of the benefit of the doubt until one is in a position to judge for oneself from actual experience. Even more important than trust in the Buddha, however, is faith in oneself. "Just as an athlete training for the Olympics might as well not even bother unless she believes she can win," he declared, "so one can get nowhere on the spiritual path unless one has faith in oneself!"

The third "fold," right effort, she expected would be self-explanatory; but Gotama said he was not so sure, especially where the West was concerned. "People have no difficulty understanding how an athlete can accept a rigorous physical regimen and forego social life in order to win a gold medal at the Olympics or, even better, make millions of dollars in professional sports; but how can monks give up family and friends and lead such ascetic lives for something as trivial as finding the meaning of life? It has no market value, and it can't even be put in a trophy case!"

It was the first time she heard sarcasm in his voice. It was not to be the last.

"To be fair, I have no doubt that such people think the spiritual life a waste of time because of their own despair, because they feel there is no meaning to life; or, if there is, they themselves are incapable of reaching or living it. The right attitude was expressed beautifully by Jesus of Nazareth, when he said that the kingdom of heaven is like a pearl of great price for which a man went and sold everything he had so he could buy it!"

"You really do find truth in Christianity!" she marveled.

"Much truth!" he affirmed. "For example, the Gospel tells of a rich young man who comes to Jesus and says, 'I have kept the law since I was a youth. What yet do I lack to achieve perfection?'"

"Conceited, wasn't he?" she observed.

"Apparently not," said Gotama. "The Gospel says that Jesus looked upon him and loved him, because he saw that he was sincere. So Jesus told the young man to go and sell everything he had, give the proceeds to the poor, and come, follow him."

"Ouch!" she grimaced.

"That's how the youth took it," said Gotama regretfully. "He went away in sorrow."

"What else could one expect?" said Ariana. "How many people are capable of such a sacrifice?"

"Yes, he didn't understand," replied Gotama, "and you don't understand either."

"Understand what?"

"No sacrifice was involved!" he declared with startling vehemence. "Jesus was offering him the greatest gift imaginable! All he had to do was throw away his toys and baubles so as to make room for it!"

She bowed her head. "I understand," she said softly. "I really do."

"So you see," he concluded, instantly back to his accustomed equanimity, "while right effort is not a function of right attitude, since one may simply be lazy, if one really believes in the possibility of the spiritual quest, the strenuous effort it demands will appear perfectly in keeping with the goal to be achieved."

"Now we come to compassion," she said after a pause, to let him know she was following his exposition.

"Yes, right action and livelihood are the same here as in *Karma-yoga*. They mean leading an ethical life, just as Ishwara explained it, and that includes following what one knows to be right in one's daily work."

"So, you were eavesdropping!" she laughed. "Or should I suspect conspiracy?"

"Both," he smiled. "There are no secrets here, and ultimately we all work together." Then he continued his explanation.

"In the Buddhist tradition there are five prohibitions, akin in moral status to the Ten Commandments in the Judaeo-Christian tradition. They are not to harm life, which means not only no killing of humans, but animals as well; not to lie; not to steal; not to take intoxicants; and not to abuse sex, which for monks means celibacy and for lay-persons no fornication or adultery. To these are added five more prohibitions for monks, against eating after the noon meal; sleeping on a soft bed; handling gold, silver, or precious gems; wearing fine clothes or jewelry; and dancing or attending shows. These are moral guidelines, however, not absolute commands of a just but severe deity. While strictly enforced in the monastery—otherwise, what would a monastery be for?—the ordinary people do their best with them so that they might do even better in a future life."

"So, what I have heard is true," Ariana interjected. "There really is no morality in the Western sense in Buddhism."

"It depends how it's understood," he said. "If by 'morality' one means ethical absolutes, you are right. There is no irredeemable sin, and no irredeemable sinner. But if one means common human decency, our tradition is shot through with it. To go back to our earlier metaphor, an athlete may train hard and give her all in every competition; but if she does not eat properly, get enough sleep, and abstain from liquor, tobacco, and drugs, she will never be truly great, even if she has all the talent in the world. So, too, an individual may have tremendous spiritual insight and meditate sixteen hours a day. If she treats other people badly, she will never progress on the spiritual path."

"I'm beginning to see how wrong so many Westerners are about Buddhism," she said, "how wrong they are about all Eastern philosophy. They think that, because it is mystical, it must also be irrational."

"The oneness of being is a self-evident truth," Gotama declared.

"And so many Westerners who fall in love with Buddhism are even worse," she went on. "They talk about meditation as though it were making some adjustment in one's head, after which everything in life will be 'groovy.'"

"Nothing could be further from the truth," he agreed.

She smiled gratefully. "I see now that it's as much about purifying one's heart as one's mind."

"For Buddhism," he clarified, "mind and heart are the same thing. And they are centered, not in the brain, but the heart."

As they spoke, the atmosphere began to change in what for Ariana was a most unusual way. If she were an earthbound soul, she simply would have thought the sun was going down; but heaven was lit with a spiritual light, so there was no sun to go down.

"Dimming the lights?" she inquired coyly.

"Yes, twilight is a good time for spiritual discipline," he replied.

"Spiritual discipline?" she echoed, not certain if she was disappointed or relieved. She found Gotama attractive, but in a comradely, even brotherly way.

"Spiritual discipline is the third and final division of the Eight-Fold Path. It is the fire that generates the light of wisdom and the warmth of compassion. Only someone living a monastic lifestyle can truly undertake it, which is why the wisdom of the ordinary lay person never goes beyond common sense, and his compassion beyond accepted decency."

"It hardly seems fair that only the monks can attain genuine spirituality."

"It's not like Hinduism," he explained, "where you have to be born into the brahmin caste to be a priest. Anyone who is willing to accept monastic discipline can become a monk."

"Even women?" she asked, thinking this religion, compared to others she knew, was too good to be true.

"That," he bowed his head, "is one of my greatest disappointments. Originally, I accepted women as well as men into the order. To me, there was no spiritual difference between them, any more than there was between caste Hindus and untouchables. But then, after my death, as Buddhism grew from a rebel movement outside the mainstream culture to a large and respectable part of that culture, it took on the patriarchal coloring of the society with which it had come to terms. Women were excluded from the monasteries, and the monks even recopied the record of my teaching, putting words into my mouth to the effect that women in the Order would cause the genuine teaching of the Buddha, the *dharma*, to decay twice as quickly as it otherwise would."

"I did not know it was supposed to decay at all," she said.

"The common Theravadin belief is that, while certain extraordinary individuals are finding their own way to nirvana all the time, a full-fledged buddha, one not only able to reach enlightenment but also willing and able to teach others the way, comes along every seven thousand years."

"Comes from where?" she asked. "Heaven? Sent by God?"

"Remember," he laughed a trifle condescendingly, "as far as we are concerned, there is no 'God.' The Theravadin belief is that a man . . ."

"Necessarily a man?" she queried.

"In Theravada, yes," he replied. "A man, not a god or son of a god, works his way up over the course of many lifetimes to buddhahood."

The Jataka Tales," she said.

"Yes, the *Jataka Tales,*" he confirmed. "On his way up, he is a *bodhisattwa,* literally a 'being of light.'"

"As in the guna sattwa?" she asked.

He nodded. "Only here the term bodhisattwa is taken to mean 'one destined to enlightenment' or, more precisely, 'one destined to buddhahood.' Once he reaches enlightenment, a buddha establishes a monastic order, the *samgha,* to preserve and propagate his teaching. After he goes beyond . . ."

"A euphemism for death?" she asked.

"Not precisely," he answered. "A buddha is beyond death as well as rebirth. Anyway, after he leaves samsara, his teaching begins to decay, until over the course of millennia it is entirely lost. Then, seven thousand years later, another buddha appears."

"It's a cycle, then?"

He nodded.

"An endless cycle?"

"Such questions do not tend toward edification," he replied gently.

"So, there are no nuns," she said glumly.

"Officially, no;" he qualified, "but unofficially, yes. There is a large movement in Theravadin countries seeking recognition from the religious establishment."

"An establishment, no doubt," she commented, "consisting entirely of men."

He nodded.

"So they think they are preserving the true teaching by keeping women from becoming nuns?" she asked.

"Yes," he replied, "for longer, at any rate. The irony is that this exclusion of women from the monasteries is really a sign of the corruption of the true teaching."

"I'm beginning to think that irony is what life on Earth is all about," she remarked caustically. "There's something else I've wondered about. The monks beg instead of working for their food. Isn't that right?"

"In the Theravada, yes," he answered. "And you think that's taking unfair advantage of the poor peasants who make up the majority of the population in Buddhist countries, who spend their days, sunup to sundown, doing backbreaking labor in the fields?"

She nodded.

"If that were so," he asked, showing irritation with her for the first time, "why doesn't every man become a monk?"

"There are ways the upper crust keeps the underdogs down in every society. Repressive mechanisms," she said, repeating a phrase she had heard in one of her conversations with the earthbound.

"Yes, certainly," he said testily. "As in Western society where people pay individuals millions of dollars to play children's games with balls of various shapes and sizes, or to sing and tell jokes and play-act to make them forget the troubles that will never go away unless they face them. There you have the mechanism of competition, the aristocracy of talent. This of course is not exploitation. But when monks who spend most of their day in meditation, who provide a spiritual focal point for their society, who keep open the path to enlightenment, and who forego the pleasures of sex and other social amusements beg for enough food to keep themselves alive for one day, that is exploitation."

It was her turn to bow her head. "I'm sorry," she whispered. "You're absolutely right."

He smiled as if the storm had never been. "Now that the lighting is right, would you like to try Theravadin meditation?"

She bowed semi-formally. "Master, I am at your disposal."

At that moment everything was transformed, and she was back in one of those experiences she had begun to think might have been the provenance of Ishwara. She was an American youth who had traveled to Sri Lanka to become a *bhikkhu*, a monk; and she, or rather he, was receiving instruction from an elder monk.

"The first step in spiritual practice is right meditation," the elder was saying as they sat cross-legged opposite each other on meditation cushions in an otherwise bare and open-aired room. "You have already learned this, or you would not be here."

"I don't understand," the American said, feeling perfectly at ease with this stranger who was not a spiritual master, but simply someone with more experience.

"In essence," the elder monk explained, "right meditation means that you arrange a time and place for daily sitting, and when that time comes, you go to that place and sit. You don't get up to eat because you forgot to eat breakfast, or to relieve yourself because you forgot to visit the outhouse. You don't give up because you feel bored or foolish. Everyone who meditates seriously experiences and must deal with all such feelings at one time or another."

"How does one deal with them?" the American asked.

"That's the next step," the elder beamed, as if at a prize pupil."Right concentration. Once you make the commitment to sitting, you learn to focus your mental energy. And the best thing to focus on, because it is natural, rhythmic, and always with you, is your breath."

"What do I do with my breath?" the youth asked. "Is this a relaxation exercise?"

"Nothing," the elder answered. "Nothing. You do nothing with your breath. Simply watch it—in, out, in, out. Watching it will make it quiet, but don't try to change it directly. Would you like to try it?"

The monk clapped his hands, and immediately both men half-closed their eyes, straightened their spines, and went into meditation. The young American started out thinking that the task of watching his breath would be easy; but after only what could have been no more than fifteen seconds, he found himself wondering about how his body would adjust from three meals a day to one. He pushed this thought out of his mind, only to have it replaced by images of the girlfriend with whom he had broken up just before deciding to try to get his head together by staying for a while in a Theravadin monastery. Then these images were superseded by speculation about what it would be like to spend one's entire life as a monk, and gratitude that Buddhist monasteries, unlike Christian ones, welcomed transients as long as they lived by the monastic rules. Just as the elder clapped his hands again to signify the end of the meditation, he remembered he was supposed to be focusing on his breath.

"It's hard," he said to the elder, and it was clear from the latter's smile that he understood what the newcomer meant.

"When distractions come," the elder said, "you have several choices. Let us suppose you are in meditation and find yourself thinking about food. You can go to the refrigerator and grab a snack."

They both laughed, since the monastery had no refrigerator.

"That would be self-indulgence. It is not the Buddhist way. You could use willpower to force the temptation out of your mind. That would be self-denial, and that too is not the Buddhist way. You could go into deep-trance . . ."

"The Hindu way?" the American interjected.

"Yes," confirmed the elder, "but not the Buddhist way. Finally, you can simply note the distraction, and then go back to your breath. That is the Way of the Elders, the Buddhist way."

"It seems so simple," the youth remarked, "so gentle."

"It is, which is why we have no system of master and disciple here. We are all *bhikkhus*, disciples of the Buddha. Our path is safe, sure, and without need of a spiritual overseer."

"Where does it lead?" the youth wondered.

"Why don't you follow it," the elder invited, "and find out?"

The youth, charmed by the old man's cheerful serenity, took him up on the proposal. He fell into the rhythm of morning begging and afternoon and evening mediation as if he had been born to it. The months went by, and then the years; but his original anxiety that his life was slipping away without his ever having really tasted what the world had to offer, an anxiety that had brought him to the monastery in the first place, lessened with the passing of each "inactive" year. It was as if, when he had arrived, he had been a leaf floating on his own stream of consciousness. Sometimes that stream had been stagnant in boredom and indecision, and sometimes it had been a raging torrent of anger and frustration; but, in any event, he had always been at its mercy. Now, however, through what his fellow monks called the practice of "bare awareness," he was lifted out of this stream, slowly but surely, and deposited safely on its shore. It still eddied and flowed, but now he could watch it go by with the freedom of complete indifference.

"And that is the final stage," Gotama was saying as the monastery dissolved and she came out of her reverie. "Right mindfulness. When you are breathing, know that you are breathing. When you are walking, know that you are walking."

"Wouldn't it be a wonderful world," she laughed, "if, when people were talking, they knew they were talking?"

He laughed too. "Once you reach the point of perfect objectivity, perfect detachment from the contents of your consciousness, you have achieved paranirvana, enlightenment while still in the body. The only desire left in you is your body's natural craving for food, drink, shelter, and rest. You give the body its due but, when you die, even that craving is snuffed out."

"Nirvana?"

He nodded. "No more death, no more rebirth. The chain of causation has been broken, the fire of craving has gone out."

"And nothing more can be said about it?" she concluded for him.

"No," he shook his head, "nothing more."

"So, that's Buddhism," she said wistfully, not wanting him to leave so soon.

"Theravadin Buddhism," he corrected. "Except for one final point. Because Theravada is so singlemindedly focused upon the monastic life, the ordinary Buddhist who works and raises a family tends to turn to non-Buddhist religious practices to find meaning and assistance in everyday life. Thus religion in Theravadin countries tends to run on two tracks, the monks benevolently tolerating indigenous rituals and beliefs in matters relating to anything other than the ultimate spiritual goal."

"They make a virtue of necessity," Ariana commented.

"Yes, one could see it that way. The kind of Buddhism we will examine now arose from the desire to bridge this gap between monks and laity, and to make Buddhism an all-embracing spiritual fold."

3. Mahayana: The Greater Vehicle

"That's why it's called the Greater Vehicle?" Ariana asked.

"Imagine you are a lower-caste Hindu in ancient India who converts to Buddhism," Gotama responded, "because you have fallen in love with someone of a different sub-caste and hope to find a community in which you can be accepted and married. In leaving the Hindu fold, however, not only do you cut yourself off from your family, but you make yourself an untouchable, and so are forbidden to enter a Hindu temple ever again, even if the monks who lead your new community do not discourage it. Now, each of the four yoga-margas of Hinduism is analogous to one of the three divisions of the Eight-Fold Path. Which yoga is missing from that path?"

"Wisdom is Jnana, compassion is Karma, and spiritual discipline is Raja," she answered. "That would leave Bhakti, the path of devotion."

"And what is the most popular yoga in Hinduism, or indeed, in any other religious tradition—the spiritual path followed by most of the laity?"

"Bhakti," she replied. "So, Theravada bought purity and simplicity at the price of completeness."

"Nothing is lacking for the monk, only for the laity," he said.

"Who make up the vast majority of the population," she persisted.

He smiled. "That is why we have the Mahayana. One could call it 'democratic' Buddhism."

"As opposed to the spiritual aristocracy of Theravada?"

"One could see it that way," he admitted, "and proponents of the Greater Vehicle tend to do so."

"And Theravadin Buddhists look down on the Mahayanists as upstarts," she guessed. "I know, it's all too human."

"Yes," he confirmed, "they actually claim that the Theravada is much older than the Mahayana, which they regard as a degeneration of the original teaching. The claim may be true, when it comes to philosophical and institutional development; but with regard to actual practice, the roots of Mahayana go back to the very beginning."

"To your own lifetime?" she wondered. "I thought you discouraged worship, especially of yourself."

"I did," he smiled, "but that sort of thing is impossible to stop. It began innocently enough, in the practice of paying respect still widespread in the Theravada."

"I thought the Theravada discourages devotion," she said.

"It does," he explained. "Theravadin 'paying respect' is exactly what it says, the religious equivalent of a military salute. Not only do monks and laity pay respect to me by bowing before my statue, but lay people pay respect to monks, and monks of lesser seniority pay respect to monks of greater seniority. For the laity especially, however, the lack of an object of worship left a spiritual vacuum where *Bhakti* used to be. This vacuum was filled by Mahayana."

"But how did a Buddhist Bhakti develop without temples and statues," she wondered aloud, "without a focal point for worship?"

"It didn't," he explained. "After I died, my relics were distributed among *stupas* all over northern India."

"Two questions, " she said. "Relics? Stupas?"

"In a religious sense, relics are remains or pieces of personal articles associated with saints and holy men."

"Remains?" she queried.

"Yes, bits of bone, teeth, or hair," he said. "The rest of the body, as you no doubt know, disintegrates."

"What pieces of you were preserved?" she asked, making a face.

"As far as I know," he replied, "some slivers of bone, but mostly scraps of my robe and bits of my begging bowl. The stupas in very ancient India, before the Aryans brought their custom of cremation, were burial mounds. By my time they were used . . ."

"No, don't tell me, let me guess!" she laughed. "They were used for housing relics!"

"Exactly!" his smile blossomed into a chuckle. "It may strike you as a strange custom, but relics were never as important in the East as in the West, where in the Middle Ages they provided the staple attraction for the medieval equivalent of the tourist industry, pilgrimages."

"Yes, I know," she agreed. "I've heard that enough pieces of the true cross, the one upon which Christ was crucified, were bought and sold to build a small city. And Perugia and Assisi were fighting over the body of St. Francis before he was even dead!" She shook her head. "Yes, it all comes back to me. Undoubtedly an unpleasant topic whose remembrance I subconsciously repressed."

"These stupas containing my relics became centers of popular devotion after my death," he resumed, not without a hint of appreciation for her sarcasm. "Add to that the influence of Greek culture a few hundred years later, and of Christianity a few hundred years after that, and you get Mahayana Buddhism."

"Quite a recipe!" she marveled. "I had no idea it contained all those ingredients."

"Many people don't. Some Buddhists are positively offended by the idea. Generally, however, they are converts from the Judaeo-Christian tradition. There is plenty of evidence, however, if one is willing to open one's eyes. For example, both I and the monks who followed after me forbade my representation in sculpture or painting in any form other than empty footsteps."

"Yes," she said, pretending to study him. "Empty footsteps—I can see the resemblance."

"Shortly after Alexander the Great conquered northern India, however, in the latter part of the 4th century B.C.E., statues supposedly of me but actually in the Greek style started popping up all over the place. And where there was Greek art, there was bound to be Greek philosophy. You see, the Mahayana is lay-oriented. That is its dominant characteristic. Second to that, however, is the metaphysical character of its philosophy."

"Why couldn't it have gotten that back from Hinduism?" she wondered.

"Because Hindus and Buddhists were engaged in bitter philosophical controversy throughout the latter's stay in India. They did influence one another, but mostly negatively. For example, the Hindus came to claim me as an incarnation of the god Vishnu . . ."

"Like Krishna!"

"Yes, like Krishna. Only they said I had purposely given a demonic teaching to test the faithful Hindus and draw away the weak, cowardly, and traitorous."

"Talk about co-optation!" she laughed.

"However," he continued, "all other things being equal, the Indian mind, especially in both its Hindu and Buddhist manifestations, is supremely open to influence from anyone and anywhere. It does not ask about pedigree, but takes ideas on their own merits. It is a well-known fact that Alexander's soldiers exported all facets of Greek culture to every part of Asia through which they passed. Given the highly metaphysical character of Greek philosophy in the Hellenistic period, and add to that the fact that the Mahayana developed philosophically in precisely those areas of northern India where Greek influence was strongest, I fail to see how anyone could doubt that Mahayana was influenced by Greek thought. It must be added, however, that whatever ideas the Mahayana philosophers took from their Greek counterparts, they made thoroughly their own."

"And the Christian influence?" she inquired.

"The third most notable characteristic of the Mahayana is that, in addition to its paradoxically metaphysical non-metaphysics, it also developed a non-theology of compassion very much like the theology of love in Christianity."

"What do you mean?" she asked.

"Have you yet grasped what a metaphysical idea is?" he returned.

She pondered. "A basic definition of reality?" she hazarded.

"Very good!" he commended. "And what is the concept that defines reality according to Buddhism?"

"Emptiness," she answered. "No-thingness. The void."

"Mahayana adds another potion to the brew," he twinkled. "It promotes compassion from being the chief moral virtue to being one of the two metaphysical principles of Mahayana philosophy."

"How can that be?" she queried. "The two hardly go together!"

"That's a matter which has been debated down through the centuries," he replied. "Mahayana asserts the truth, or at least the utility, of both."

"Is it deliberately self-contradictory, then?" she asked in frustration.

"In a way, yes," he said mischievously. "At the very least, deliberately paradoxical. When the intellect is shipwrecked upon abstract contradiction, then the intuition has a chance to see the truth."

Ariana had no idea what that meant, but she had no desire to pursue the matter. "And you say that Mahayana is like Christianity?" she asked, steering the conversation to shallower waters.

"You will see when I describe the basic ideas of Mahayana, and then I will let you judge for yourself."

"How do you know it didn't work the other way around?" she challenged, not quite understanding why she suddenly felt so strongly about this issue, unless she hoped that heated argument would lead to heated passion.

"Buddhist missionaries reached Syria and Egypt in the second century B.C.E.," he admitted, "but their influence was confined mostly to abstruse philosophical circles."

"But how did Christian influence get to India?" she rejoined.

"If we can believe the legends widely accepted in India but largely rejected by Western scholars, it was brought by St. Thomas in the first century."

"The doubting Thomas?" she asked. "The one who wouldn't believe that Jesus had risen from the dead until he could touch his rabbi's wounds?"

"The very one," he confirmed. "Of course, even if Christianity didn't get to India until the fourth century, it still would have been early enough to have influenced the development of Mahayana."

"And of course it came into India through those centers of Greek culture where Mahayana philosophy developed," Ariana surmised.

"Of course," he bowed. "Now, do you wish to find out what Mahayana is all about?"

"I'm dying to know!" she said half-mockingly.

"I warn you," he said with only half-mock seriousness, "I will be greatly simplifying. The Mahayana tradition is incredibly complex, and the three ideas I have distilled as its essence all have histories of development and transformation we'll ignore here."

"I think your simplification will be more than enough for me!" she laughed.

"Well then, let us begin!" he cried, and immediately she was at the start of another experience. She was once again a "he," once again that young American monk who had ended up devoting his entire life to the quest for enlightenment. Finally she reached paranirvana, and shortly thereafter died. With death came the realization that she was free to go on to nirvana, to leave the cycle of death and rebirth forever behind. Before doing so, however, she took one last look at the madness she was abandoning, and was more impressed than she had ever been before with the variety, intensity, and sheer ubiquity of human suffering. Instead of going on to the still eye in the samsaric storm, she found a way into embodiment as someone destined to be a bag lady on the streets of a major Western metropolis. After that, she incarnated as a politician who led his country to democracy. Gradually, she developed the knack of picking out the karmic "place" where she could do the most good. She vowed never to take the escape route of nirvana until all sentient beings, all beings capable of suffering, were saved.

Upon making that vow, she was back with Gotama. "This is more powerful than Theravada," she murmured once she realized where she was. "Definitely more powerful. It's as if an ex-con were to return to prison as an inmate simply to help his fellow inmates, or a psychologist were to become a patient incognito in a mental asylum!"

"You have just encountered the Mahayana conception of a bodhisattwa. The Mahayana bodhisattwa is pure compassion, like a Christian saint, no?" He smiled, and she remembered what he had said about the influence of Christianity upon the development of Mahayana Buddhism. "Also like a Christian saint, bodhisattwas are objects of devotion. For reasons you shall see, to the ordinary Mahayana Buddhist bodhisattwas seem much closer to everyday life than buddhas. One can pray to them not only to help one reach ultimate enlightenment, but for the rain to fall or stop falling, to help the crops grow, so that one's wife will give birth to a son, etc."

"So, bodhisattwas are objects of devotion, and bodhisattwahood a human possibility."

He nodded. "For those who reach enlightenment."

"Did I truly agree to return over and over?" she wondered.

He nodded again. "A bodhisattwa vows to return not only once, or a hundred times, or a million, but as often as it takes, until all sentient beings are saved."

"That means not only my dog," she laughed, "but the fleas on my dog!"

"You have a dog? Perhaps she is a bodhisattwa."

Ariana studied his face for a moment, uncertain whether or not he was serious. Then he broke into a broad grin.

"We philosophical Buddhists, just like philosophical Hindus, hold that once one reaches human self-awareness, there is no retreat; but, within humanity, a bodhisattwa could be anything; and so, anyone could be a bodhisattwa, from president or king to untouchable or pauper. Bodhisattwas do not come to preach Buddhism, however. Buddhism is not about accepting a doctrine, but awakening to reality."

"It reminds me of something I once heard in a movie."

"You watch movies?" he laughed.

"I am the spirit of the new age, aren't I? Anyway, the film was just a dinner talk between a theater director named Andre and an actor."

"*My Dinner with Andre.*"

"So, you watch movies too," she kidded. "One thing Andre said always stuck with me—that a fellow director and friend of his thought of New York as a concentration camp where the guards and the inmates were the same people."

"Not just New York," said Gotama. "That defines all of samsara. Only, I prefer the metaphor of an insane asylum. People hold to be true what is false and false what is true. They regard as real what is unreal and unreal what is real. They value what is worthless and despise what is valuable. Insanity."

"Gotama," she asked, "have you ever known a person who, simply by his presence, could calm a riotous crowd and cause people who were losing their heads to focus on what needed to be done in a crisis?"

Gotama smiled ironically.

"Oh, I'm sorry," she cried, "you are such a person!"

He bowed. "And so were Mahatma Gandhi, Mother Teresa, and Martin Luther King! A bodhisattwa does not preach an abstract truth. A bodhisattwa brings the aura of sanity into an insane world."

"Wouldn't the Theravada see what the bodhisattwa gives as a spiritual crutch?" she wondered.

"Absolutely," he agreed. "The motto of the Theravada is the final words I spoke before I died: 'Work out your own salvation with diligence.'"

"To quote a great man!"

They both laughed.

"And wouldn't the Theravada say it's impossible for someone who had reached paranirvana to come back?" she continued. "When you were teaching me about the practice of bare awareness, I got the image of a see-saw. Pain isn't suffering, only half of it, which is why you were so shocked when you encountered sickness, old age, poverty and death. It was the contrast between what you had experienced of life, all the pleasures, and what you had yet to experience, sickness and death, that was so shocking. Suffering is not in the pleasure, and not in the pain, but in the ups-and-downs from one to the other."

"If you see that," he smiled, "you must also see nirvana from the Theravadin perspective."

"That's easy," she returned his smile. "It is the only point at rest on the see-saw, the center point between pleasure and pain."

"Yes, the fulcrum," he confirmed.

"So, the Mahayana idea of a bodhisattwa requires moving the fulcrum, and then it's no longer the fulcrum."

"You mean that it is impossible to bring the sanity of nirvana into the insanity of samsara?"

"Something like that," she frowned uncertainly. "Not that I think that's right. I don't know, but I wonder what a Mahayana Buddhist might say in reply."

"That Theravadin philosophy holds the logic of pleasure and pain, suffering and release to be absolute," he answered. "Mahayana philosophy holds the logic of compassion to be more fundamental. Think back to your experience just now. When you were in the position to choose, was there any doubt in your mind or heart that you had to go back and assist the suffering, no matter what?"

"No, but what if that's not possible?"

"By what standard of possibility?"

"Oh," she said softly. "I see." She pondered for a moment. "I've thought of something else," she brightened, certain that this time she had hit upon a dilemma not to be so readily resolved. "To go on to nirvana when one could help others is regarded as selfish, yes?"

"That tends to be the Mahayana attitude," he confirmed; "hence the titles, 'Greater' and 'Lesser.'"

"To enter nirvana, however, one must be beyond self," she continued.

"Yes," Gotama agreed. "In the Mahayana conception, the bodhisattwa keeps himself in samsara by holding onto the illusion that there are selves who are suffering and in need of salvation. From the point of view of nirvana, however, there is no self."

"So," she pounced, "if going on to nirvana is selfish, and those who reach nirvana must be selfless, the only ones who can go on to nirvana are those who choose not to!"

"I see," he said noncommittally.

"And you can't say that because in nirvana there is no self, it doesn't make any sense to say someone who chooses nirvana is selfish, since you've already said that Mahayana Buddhists regard the Theravadin ideal as selfish."

He nodded measuredly. "And one also cannot say that a bodhisattwa lives with the illusion of choice," he said, "since then he would cease to embody wisdom."

She looked at him blankly.

"Surely you see that that is the very heart of your criticism?" he pointed out. "Or were you wiser than you knew?"

"The latter, I think," she laughed. "Why don't you explain my wisdom to me?"

"The fundamental issue is whether a bodhisattwa has a real choice. If he does not, then what becomes of his famous compassion?"

"I understand!" she exclaimed. "If I fall in love with someone who pushes me out of the path of a speeding car, risking his own life in the process, I don't know if I'd stay in love if I found out that he hadn't been concerned about me at all, that he had accidentally knocked me out of the way after he was pushed in front of the car by someone else. You're right," she concluded in both pride and chagrin. "I was wiser than I knew."

"So, Ariana, are you convinced by your own critique?" he asked. "Is the Mahayana ideal of compassion a pipe dream?"

"Yes," she nodded solemnly, "I don't see any way around it."

"But you do have a question to ask me, Ariana, don't you?"

Suddenly they were a middle-aged couple lying in bed on a Saturday morning, and she found herself rolling over, nestling into his arms, and asking, "Honey, why did you fall in love with me?"

"Well, back in our college days," he replied, "after I had just finished another in a series of disastrous romances, I was sitting outside the student union, feeling lonely, when I decided to give love another try. Just then a group of women walked out of the union, and you looked as good a choice as any, so I decided to give you a try."

She sat stunned for a moment, not believing her ears, and then turned abruptly and started kicking and slapping . . .

The next thing she knew, she was in the same bed with the same husband, only this time he was saying, "Honey, I fell in love with you the way a stone falls to earth!" This sounded better to her, but then she realized he was saying that he would stay with her as long as no more attractive heavenly body came within his orbit! Again, she ended by hitting and screaming.

"So which is it?" Gotama asked as she "awoke" from the experience. "Is love a matter of choice or necessity?"

"It's both!" she cried. "No, it's neither. I don't know!" She was on the verge of tears.

"You do know," he said. "All love is a paradoxical conjunction of freedom and necessity. I have known people who have made themselves miserable by convincing themselves that love was impossible for abstract reasons like those in your criticism. When one is faced with such criticism, one has a choice. Is one to regard something that we all experience as impossible, or is one to regard the dilemma as a paradox pointing to a reality that doesn't fit neatly into any logical construct? The issue here is not rationalism versus irrationalism. It is, rather, insanity versus sanity. Are we to dismiss experience that does not fit our preconceptions of life as irrational? That is the clinical definition of delusional schizophrenia."

"I don't get it," she said.

"The categories 'rational' and 'irrational' may be applied to how we think about and respond to experience, but experience itself is neither rational nor irrational. It simply is. Was Socrates crazy because of his daemon? Was Joan of Arc crazy because she talked with invisible saints? Were those who followed Hitler any the less crazy because they could see the man to whose voice they gave heed?"

"I understand," she said thoughtfully. "I think the attitude comes from natural science. It divides experience into empirical and non-empirical, cognitive and non-cognitive, valid and invalid, objectively meaningful and subjectively meaningless. Those who make science their religion do just what you say—split experience into rational and irrational."

"It is a defense mechanism," he explained, "against an uncontrollable world. But life is not about control, is it? And it's not about being out of control, either. Maybe if we let go, we would find we had nothing to fear. That is awakening."

"Is there more to Mahayana?" she asked, eager for further revelation.

"More after awakening?" he laughed. "As a matter of fact, we have only just finished with the first basic idea. The second has to do with my nature."

"You?" she wondered. "I thought you were a bodhisattwa! Wasn't that what you were telling me?"

"According to the Mahayana, a buddha is quite different from a bodhisattwa. Do you remember when I told you that Mahayana brings metaphysics back into Buddhism?"

She nodded vaguely, wishing he would get to the point.

"In Mahayana Buddhism there are many buddhas, and each is a metaphysical no-self embodying what can't be embodied, the emptiness or non-absoluteness of nirvana."

"Come again?" she asked.

"They reason like this," he continued, obviously frustrated at his inability to put the indefinable into words. "To know is to be—this is a given in almost all Eastern philosophy. The quality of one's consciousness is the quality of one's being, and vice-versa."

"A more general version of the idea that wisdom and compassion are one," she observed.

He smiled, pleased that she was catching on. "The next point, believed by all Buddhists, is that a buddha is all-knowing. The Theravadin philosophers hold that I became all knowing when I attained buddhahood. Now, if being and knowing are one, and a buddha knows everything . . ."

"Then a buddha is everything!"

He nodded. "And if a buddha is everything, then a buddha must be eternal. Since one cannot become eternal," he concluded, "a buddha must have existed from all eternity."

She thought for a moment. "It makes sense on its own terms, but are you giving the reason for the belief, or its rationalization?"

"I confess I don't know," he laughed, "and I don't think anyone really does."

"I thought you knew everything!"

"Everything that can be known," he rejoined playfully. "Since everything is no-thing, there is no-thing to be known."

"Socrates is Buddha!" she laughed, but the seriousness of his look made her wonder if, once again, she was saying something wiser than she knew.

"According to Mahayana, there are many buddhas throughout the nirvanic realm. As one of them, I chose in my compassion to enter the samsaric realm to aid sentient beings in their quest for enlightenment."

"Like Jesus, who came down from heaven," she half-whispered.

He nodded. "And at the end of this world age, another buddha, the Lord Maitreya, will enter embodiment and lead the forces of light in a spiritual struggle against the forces of darkness, overcome the darkness, and set up a buddha-realm on earth that will last 3,000 years."

"The Second Coming!" she marveled. "Is this a common belief among Mahayana Buddhists?"

"It takes many forms and bears many interpretations," he said, "but yes, I would say it is common."

"What do you mean by a buddha-realm?" she inquired.

"That's the third basic idea of Mahayana Buddhism," he replied. "But a picture is worth a thousand words, and an experience is worth a thousand pictures . . ."

Once again, she found herself in an earthbound situation without knowing how she got there or where she was going. And, once again, she was a man. He lived outside the imperial city in Japan, and operated a stone masonry business that served the emperor himself. One day, a youth of modest dress and demeanor came into his office and told him about a way to reach enlightenment that would not require the arduous life of a monk. All he need do was take one of the celestial buddhas as his patron and chant the name of the selected buddha for an hour or so each day. When be died, he would be reborn into the buddha's "pure land." There he would enjoy the most delicious food, the most delightful drink, and the best sex he had ever known. What was more, he would be guaranteed eventual enlightenment, and there would be no more samsaric rebirth.

The stone mason thought it over, and then asked sharply if all one had to do was chant. The young man assured him that chanting alone would set up the mystical connection with his celestial patron, as long as he continued to lead a decent life of hard work, marital fidelity, and charity to the poor.

The stonemason was skeptical, but tried it and discovered all the young man had told him to be true. When he died he was reborn into a heavenly realm where existence was sheer delight. Then, in due course, there was no more existence—only, if one can imagine such a thing, delight itself.

As he changed into a she and Ariana returned to her tete-a-tete with Gotama, the feeling of delight lingered. "That was wonderful!"

"So you like the Mahayana pure land," he laughed.

"I liked whatever that was," she assented, "but is it possible? I mean, as a reality? And even if it is possible," she added before he had a chance to reply, "isn't that the easy way out? What is a 'pure land,' anyway?"

Gotama looked at her in eloquent silence.

"I ask too many questions, don't I?" she said sheepishly.

"Not at all," he laughed again. "I was just wondering in what order to answer them."

"Do whatever you think best," she smiled. "I'll trust your judgment."

"Not to belittle the originality of your thought, but rather to assure you that you are on the right track, all your questions have long been anticipated by Theravadin criticisms. There are essentially two issues here: Is the Mahayana concept of a pure land religiously harmful, and is it metaphysically possible?"

"Succinctly put!"

"To argue the Theravadin side of the first point, suppose I was a teacher in a typical university, and I told my students at the beginning of a term that they had two options: one, they could come to class, take the exams, turn in their papers and receive whatever grade they earned; two, they could never come to class, write no papers, take no exams, and receive a perfect grade. How many people would choose the former alternative?"

"Not many, I would guess!" she laughed.

"So too here, the Theravada would argue. You asked where pure lands come from. According to the Mahayana, they don't exist naturally, but by the grace of a buddha and the merits of bodhisattwas."

"Like the Roman Catholic purgatory!" she interjected. "It exists through the grace of Christ and the merits of the saints. Or so I've heard."

"Yes," said Gotama. "And it is also a half-way house, like a pure land. When one dies without being good enough to go to heaven or bad enough to go to hell, one's soul is purified in purgatory so that one may enter heaven. But there is a crucial difference," he grinned.

"In purgatory, purification comes through suffering," she said. "In a pure land, by pleasure."

"Yes," he replied, "and that brings us back to the main point. If one provides a spiritually easy way, a Theravadin might argue, just about everyone will take it."

"Just about!"

"Then who will be left to provide the merits to make the easy way possible?"

"So," she proclaimed, "the argument shows that the idea of a pure land is both religiously dangerous and logically self-contradictory!" Then she frowned. "But I bet you have some sort of paradox up your sleeve."

"The Mahayana rebuttal to this criticism would be two-pronged," he replied without flinching at her sarcasm. "On the one hand, one might say a pure land is the easy way, but look at what happens in a Theravadin country where the 'hard way' is maintained. The people pay lip-service to the monks and the idea of nirvana, but real life is presided over by a bevy of deities and spirits who have nothing whatsoever to do with Buddhism. The idea of a pure land makes the spiritual ideal realizable, and therefore meaningful, for the average lay person. One may say it also corrupts that ideal, but one is always free to pursue it in whatever one believes to be its pure form. Indeed, one might wonder about the purity of those who did pursue the ideal if their only reason for doing so were that no easier way was offered. The idea of the pure land enables Buddhism to exercise a benevolent influence upon the daily life of the ordinary person, where it exercised practically no influence before."

"It makes sense," she conceded, "but everything you say makes sense one way or another. Do you really believe what you are saying now, or do you believe what you said before in favor of the Theravada?"

"You're asking me to choose between my children," he smiled ever so slightly. "I merely brag about them both. It's up to you to decide if you like one more than the other."

"I understand your point," she responded noncommittally. "What's the other Mahayana response to this criticism?"

"You said that just about everyone would choose not to attend class?" he asked.

"Yes," she nodded warily.

"That 'just about' is a significant admission. Most people would take the easiest way offered, but some would not. To give another instance, you've talked with many Christians, haven't you?"

"Yes, more than any other group. There were more of them than any other religion among the earthbound with whom I studied."

"Incidentally, would you have gone to class if you had been offered an easier way?" he asked ironically, almost sarcastically, she felt, without giving her a chance to answer. "What, according to most Christians, is the goal of being a Christian?"

"Going to heaven," she answered readily.

"You have no doubt about that?"

"No, it was all most of them ever talked about."

"And yet," he declared, "it may be argued that a medieval Christian saint expressed the genuine spirit of Christianity when he said, 'Better hell with Christ than heaven without.'"

There was complete silence for a moment. "I see what you mean," she said solemnly.

"So, in every religious tradition—indeed, wherever one finds humans—there are two kinds of people: those who take the hard way, even if an easy one is offered . . ."

"The saints!" she whispered.

". . . and those who make of even a hard way an easy one. There are the minority, who give of themselves completely, expecting nothing in return; and the majority, who give of themselves as little as possible while wanting everything in return. The Mahayana solution is brilliant in its simplicity. Why not have those who wish to get everything receive it from those who wish to give it?"

"The Greater Vehicle!" she cried, and he nodded his encouragement. "It's just like a big ocean liner! The buddhas are like the ship's officers, the bodhisattwas like its crew. On an ocean liner only the officers and crew need know where they're going and what they're doing, or do any work. Everyone else goes along for the ride."

"They do have to keep order," Gotama added, "and trust in the wisdom of those sailing the ship."

"Yes, they must lead an ethical life," she remembered, "and have faith."

He watched her intently while she reflected upon all she had heard.

"But is it possible?" she asked at length. "You still haven't answered that question."

"You mean, are the metaphysical assumptions underlying the Mahayana idea of the pure lands self-consistent?" he translated good-humoredly. "They are; and, also, they are far more profound than one probably would guess."

"If every pleasure is accompanied by pain, and samsara is the see-saw between the two, how can a place of pure enjoyment exist?" she queried.

He laughed. "I see you'll have to learn your lesson the hard way!"

"Another experience?" she asked in some trepidation.

"No," he laughed even louder, "another demonstration of the relativity of logical and ontological systems to the basic assumptions upon which they rest."

"Ontological?" she asked, trying to remember what Ishwara had said about the word.

"It's Greek for the logic or structure of being. Most of us carry around models of reality in our heads that have a logic of their own, corresponding with the logic of reality only at the most obvious poiĺnts."

"So, reality does have logic!"

"Yes, certainly," he admitted freely, "but a logic of infinite dimensions. To attempt to reproduce that logic with finite logic, which is all the intellect can do, is like trying to reproduce a circle with only straight lines. The more sides one adds to a polyhedron, the closer it will approximate to a circle; but a polyhedron of no matter how many sides will never be a circle."

"What does all this have to do with pure lands?" she protested.

"Think of nirvana not as the fulcrum or balance point between pleasure and pain, but as the sheer intensity of life. How many people on earth can look at the sun for any length of time without damaging their eyes?"

"Very few," she answered uncertainly, hesitating to go with him when she could not see where he was heading. "A few saints and yogis."

"Think of nirvana as the sun, the smiling sun of the Buddha."

As he spoke, his face indeed looked radiant, so radiant that it almost hurt to look upon him.

"Imagine you have been out the night before indulging in intoxicating drink, and now you are lying in bed with a hangover."

Her head began to ache and her stomach felt queasy.

"You are curious about the weather, and so you go to the window and open the blinds; but the sun is so bright it causes your head to throb, and so you retreat to the cellar. The light is still too bright; but, luckily for you, the cellar leads into a network of underground caverns. You go deep down into the caverns to sleep it off; but when you awake, you linger, because the darkness is so cool and refreshing. Finally, you are getting chilly and decide to leave, but your eyes have become so accustomed to the dark that the light leading the way out of the tunnel hurts them. Instinctively you retreat back into the cavern, where you rest your eyes in the dark. Gradually the cold gets to you and you start to leave once again, only to be stopped once more by the pain caused by the light. You continue to go back and forth . . ."

"The see-saw," she whispered.

". . . until you forget there ever was a way out, much less green earth under the open sky."

"Nirvana," she whispered again.

He nodded. "The relation of the Theravadin to the Mahayana perspective may be likened to that of Newtonian to modern physics—the former represents a limiting case of the latter. From the Mahayana viewpoint, the Theravadin experience of nirvana as the still point between pleasure and pain is not invalid, merely limited. Ultimately, samsara is samsara not because it changes, but because it contradicts itself."

"I thought I was following," she said, "but now you've lost me again."

"Since you watch movies, I assume you're familiar with television."

"Yes!" she laughed. "I like the detective shows and Saturday-morning cartoons."

He continued in absolute seriousness, evidently not willing to risk distraction from the thread of his logic. "What is the common human image of pleasure?"

"I'm not sure what you mean."

"Isn't it the intensity of life? Take beer commercials and cigarette advertising . . ."

"You watch the tube and read magazines?" she cried in amused disbelief.

"I am aware of all that goes on in this universe," he stated without the hint of a smile.

"You were asking about beer and cigarette advertising," she said, humoring him. "Like the beautiful girl puffing away on a wild south-sea island, or the handsome hunks sky-diving into a vat of fresh-brewed ale?"

"I'm not sure I remember either of those," he softened, "but you get the point. They are images of life, and more than that, of the intensity of life. However, in reality what effect do tobacco and alcohol have upon an individual?"

She saw it in a flash. "They lower the intensity of life. So people convince themselves that they are after intensity . . ."

"No," he corrected, "they really do desire intensity."

"Alright," she conceded, "they really desire intensity . . ."

"Because it alone yields genuine fulfillment," he added.

"But they settle for the reduction of intensity . . ." she paused, knowing he would complete the thought she could not.

"Because, in their present spiritual debility, the genuine pleasure of life is simply too painful."

"So what they really embrace," she concluded, "is not life, but death."

"And that is their self-contradiction, their insanity—the insanity of samsara."

"What does all this have to do with the pure lands?" she asked, too impressed by the profundity of the thoughts he had presented, however, to be flippant.

"A pure land is a place of controlled intensity—controlled by the buddha and bodhisattwas whose pure land it is. In a pure land, the intensity of each individual's experience is calibrated precisely to a point just above his or her customary measure. Thus, everything is delightful without being overwhelming, and the individual is led by degrees to higher intensity."

"How calibrated?"

"Form is what moderates intensity."

"That is why it's a land and not merely a state of awareness?" she ventured.

"Precisely," he concurred. "To go beyond form is to enter pure intensity."

She marveled at the complexity needed to arrive at such simplicity. "And that is the Mahayana concept of nirvana?"

"Not concept," he corrected. "Intuition. I am presenting an ontological justification of their way of seeing."

"What about the spiritual implications?" she queried. "It seems to me that, if one gave oneself to this 'intuition' with the same discipline and determination that Theravadin monks give to their version of the Middle Way, one could explore a lot of new worlds."

"Absolutely, and that is what we shall do now." He bowed to her. "Forgive me for being austere, but sometimes charm gets in the way of truth."

"I have no doubt that I, in turn, have given you plenty of opportunity to exercise patience," she smiled. "One thing more. Since there are few Buddhists left in India, where is Mahayana to be found today?"

"In northern Asia," he replied, "primarily China, Japan, and Korea. Also in Vietnam."

"Even in China, Vietnam and North Korea?" she queried. "Under the Communist regimes?"

"The Communists have suppressed the institution of Buddhism, but they cannot destroy its spirit." He lowered his head in pained silence, then looked up in a sad smile. "If you are ready, we will act upon your suggestion, and explore the most esoteric form of Buddhism of all—the *Vajrayana*."

4. Vajrayana: The Diamond Vehicle

"Not another *yana*!" she laughed, both to take his mind away from unpleasant thoughts and to relieve her own discomfort at he, the Enlightened One, having them.

"It depends upon how you look at it," he smiled wanly. "Most people, Buddhist or not, categorize Vajrayana as an independent tradition in its own right. Since so much in Buddhism comes in threes, it being the number of process—as opposed to the Hindu 'four,' which is the number of stability—they think it fitting that there be three major forms of Buddhism. However, I regard Vajrayana as a sub-tradition of Mahayana. One finds in it all the major Mahayana concepts."

"Bodhisattwas, preexistent buddhas, and pure lands," she enumerated in only half-mock pride.

"Very good!" he laughed, weakly but genuinely.

"So, why do so many people regard it as a third branch of Buddhism, then?" she asked.

"First of all," he replied, "because it's geographically isolated. There is some Vajrayana Buddhism in Mongolia, but in Tibet it was the state religion before the Chinese Communists took control in the 1950's. They crucified monks and destroyed monasteries."

Again he lowered his head; and this time, when he raised it, his expression was a paradoxical blend of resignation and determination "Tibet will be Buddhist again when they lose control."

"I hope so," she said cautiously, wanting to assuage his grief but not so eager to play the prophet. "What does 'Vajrayana' mean?" she asked, enjoying the way he was not in the least perturbed by what to others had always been her annoying habit of abruptly changing the subject.

"It has three meanings," he replied, "which is quite in keeping with its unashamed embrace of life's dualities and their dialectical integration—'lightning vehicle,' 'thunder vehicle,' and 'diamond vehicle.'"

"What do you mean by 'unashamed embrace of life's dualities?'" she asked, quoting exactly because she did not understand what he had said well enough to even paraphrase.

He looked at her meaningfully. "The Vajrayana is tantric Buddhism."

"That's why they had to go all the way to Tibet!" she laughed. "Unashamed, indeed!"

"There may be something to what you say," he responded seriously. "The tantra is a notorious practice in India, and perhaps the Buddhist yogis who carried it to Tibet sought out so remote and mountainous a land to ensure against disturbance."

"Buddhist yogis?"

"Yes," he said. "The Tibetan laity are, for the most part, average, everyday Mahayana Buddhists who are devoted to buddhas and bodhisattwas, and who hope to go to a pure land when they die. Vajrayana proper, however, is a monastic form of Buddhism, and its practitioners might just as well be called 'yogis.'"

"I thought they were *lamas*," she said, remembering a bit of trivia she had learned from the earthbound.

"A rose by any other name," he smiled. "Yes, that is the term for a Vajrayana guru, a spiritual master who heads a community of monks. There are also yogis who practice the tantric rituals, and may or may not be monks."

"They may marry?"

He nodded.

"So, this is tantric yoga," she said, "just like in Hinduism?"

"No, not exactly," he replied. "Since the tantra is the national religion, there is no shame attached to it as such, only to certain practices that have been rejected by the mainstream."

She made a face. "I don't think I'll ask."

"That's probably best," he laughed. "But the mainstream practices are probably more wholesome than those in the Hindu tantra. There is a greater tendency, for example, to form long-term bonds, and even marriage, with one's sexual partner. And there is perhaps a greater emphasis upon meditation as an alternative to ritual."

"What do you mean?" she inquired.

"I'll show you," he said, and with that she was back in another experience.

This time she did not feel in embodiment, but rather as if she were in someone else's dream. She found herself dressed in extremely revealing silk, and hovering like a cloud over what had to be a monk entering meditation. Right before her eyes he constructed, simply by concentration, a pleasure garden. She regarded this feat as indeed miraculous, until she realized that he was certainly performing it "in his imagination," in whose subconscious reaches she at the moment seemed to be stationed. He spent what must have been hours meticulously working and reworking every detail. Finally, when all seemed in readiness, he called, without opening his mouth, a name that somehow was her name, though it was not 'Ariana.' She instinctively responded by coming forward and, as in the Hindu tantra, making love to him rather than he making love to her. At first, she felt tremendous excitement; but then she noticed that he was intentionally quiet, and she likewise focused on the profound center of her own arousal. Her excitement was gradually transformed into an intensity that was superficially agonizing but deeply pleasurable all at the same time. It was movement toward a climax that never came. There was no release, physical or, as in the Hindu tantra, spiritual. Instead there was an intense expansion and deepening of her being. If the Hindu tantra was like climbing into a rocket ship and blasting off into deep inner space, this Tibetan Buddhist tantra was more like having the rocket blast inside oneself.

After an indeterminable length of time, Ariana separated from the yogi and returned to the fringes of his consciousness. This time, however, she was aware of him and his physical reality as well. He was sitting in a large hall tightly packed with monks all sitting in meditation! Even if someone had been looking at him, which nobody was, he would not have been able to know what his fellow monk had just experienced, except perhaps by the slight suggestion of a smile that hovered over his features. When Ariana returned to awareness of Gotama, she felt that, in a small but real way, something inside her had permanently changed.

"Any questions?" he asked, after giving her a moment to mentally settle.

"Why the lightning and the diamond?" she asked. "Why *Vajrayana*?"

He returned her question with a question. "How is a diamond formed?"

"Out of carbon, under tremendous pressure, over many centuries deep in the earth."

"To the Vajrayana, the ordinary awareness is a lump of coal, dark and opaque, impervious to spiritual enlightenment, and therefore of no greater utility than to fuel the fires of existence."

"Sounds elitist," she remarked.

"Or challenging," he rejoined. "The Vajrayana holds the goal of human existence to be the transformation of that ordinary consciousness, that nearly worthless rock, into a glittering, gleaming diamond."

"Sounds beautiful," she mused, "but what does it mean?"

"In associating with earthbound spirits, did you ever meet any who had survived imprisonment in a concentration camp, service in a grueling and dehumanizing war, an earthquake and its aftermath, or some such traumatic experience?"

"Many," she answered pensively, remembering the terrible stories.

"What does such an experience do to a person?" he asked.

"That depends on the person!" she exclaimed.

"That's true," he acknowledged; "but, in general, such an experience usually affects a person in one of two ways."

"Makes you or breaks you," she said succinctly, not at all comfortable with the topic.

"Precisely!" he agreed. "And what determines the outcome in each individual case?"

"You yourself."

"How does the individual determine the outcome?" he persisted.

"I'm not sure. Will-power?"

"Perhaps, but let me give you a different explanation," he replied, "the Vajrayana explanation. Such an experience destroys the ego. If one is identified with the ego, one will be broken with it. If, on the other hand, one is centered spiritually, one can only grow from such an experience, because the breaking down of the ego would then also be the building up of the spirit."

She reflected upon her recent experiences. "I suppose that makes sense," she said ambivalently.

"A crisis opens up the inner recesses of the self," he affirmed. "In any crisis, one has three basic choices. One may regard the situation as a threat, and so shrink back from the inner opening as if it were an abyss. In doing so, one also shrinks one's self-consciousness to the point of sheer immediacy, shutting out everything that is not on the surface."

"Hysteria?" she offered.

"Yes, hysteria," he agreed. "Or one may go in the other direction. One may leap into the abyss, leaving the pain and uncertainty of the world behind, taking refuge in an inner reality far beyond the triviality of everyday concerns."

"Dissociation," she said. "Or, perhaps, Raja-yoga!"

"Yes, from the Buddhist perspective the deep-trance meditation of Hinduism is but a disciplined method of escaping from reality."

"Either way," she remarked, "it seems to me that one is escaping from reality. But, of course, what is reality?"

"That's something one must experience for oneself," he asserted. "The point is, one cannot do so as long as one's consciousness is dissociated from itself, as long as one's awareness is fragmented. Most people are like mirrors broken into a thousand pieces."

"And Vajrayana is a way of putting the pieces back together again?"

He nodded.

"It sounds worthwhile," she said, "but it also seems abstract. It doesn't seem real to me."

"I suppose you have never been in a crisis situation," he said, the half-smile on his face only serving to emphasize his seriousness.

"Oh, lots of them!" she exclaimed, and then reflected. "But I suppose they never touched my inner core."

"That is yet to come."

She brightened. "So you don't think I'm impervious?"

"Not at all," he said matter-of-factly, "but it is not my place to initiate you into those depths."

"Whose place is it?" she wondered.

"That you will discover when it happens. But let me try a different tack. In your socializing with the earthbound, did any psychologist ever happen to mention the phenomenon of 'state-dependent' memory?"

She searched her own memory, to which, until this contest began, she had always had remarkably easy access. "Let's say you were drunk last night," she explained with more than a hint of irony. "Today, after you've sobered up, you don't remember what you did the night before. Tonight, when you get drunk again, you remember what you did when you were drunk last night, but not today when you were sober. Am I right?"

"Do you speak from experience?" he laughed.

"I refuse to answer on the grounds that it might tend to incriminate me," she also laughed.

"In any event," he said, "you are right, and this phenomenon has been observed to apply to all varieties of so-called altered states of awareness, whether induced by drugs, emotion, meditation, or what-have-you. It is the rare individual who carries memory over from one state to the next."

"In other words, human consciousness runs on multiple tracks," she observed.

He nodded. "It is, to borrow a technical term, 'multiphasic.'"

"And that's what you mean by fragmented awareness?"

"Yes. Science, however, only reveals the way things are. It doesn't really tell how they came to be or, even more important, what they should be."

"And crisis, trauma, pressure . . .?"

"Intensity!" he interjected.

"Alright, intensity," she conceded doubtfully. Intensity is the way to put all the pieces back together?"

"It provides the opportunity," he answered, "but only for those who are spiritually centered. For those identified with the ego, intensity is destructive. That is why they run from it, even if, in their heart of hearts, it's what they truly desire. Therefore, one cannot even take the first step along the tantric path, at least not safely, until one has broken identification with the ego."

"What is the ego?" she complained. "You keep using the word, but you've never defined it."

"Perhaps you've just not heard me," he smiled with what struck her that moment as insufferable condescension. "Each type of Buddhism understands the illusion of I-ness somewhat differently, but a general working definition may be 'self-image.'"

"I see," she said quietly, unable to escape the logic of this definition despite her flash of resentment. "When one gets a 'fix' on oneself, one automatically misses oneself."

"A very Theravadin way of putting it," he continued to smile. "I've noticed you have a tendency in that direction."

"I like its simplicity," she said, not smiling.

"In Vajrayana, the ego-self is the illusion that a fragment of the self is the whole self. Or, to return to the original metaphor, it is the lump of coal mistaking itself for a diamond. The basic idea is simple." He looked at her meaningfully. "It is to take all the different dimensions of awareness that, in the ordinary person, are dissociated from one another, and make of them the perfectly regular facets of a glittering diamond. A diamond shines because its facets are transparent, and because each facet is perfectly reflected in every other facet. The goal is not to reduce every dimension of awareness to one, but to interconnect them, to open up the channels of communication, resulting in perfect clarity."

"Nirvana," she queried, "Vajrayana style?"

"Yes, the attainment of the buddha-body, which is immortal, indestructible, and not bound by the limitations of matter, space, and time. The thunderbolt signifies its power."

"A pleasant belief," she commented, and the flash of anger in his eyes, something only a short time ago she would have thought impossible, signaled that her sarcasm had hit home. "What I don't understand," she demanded, as much to fill up the moment because she was afraid of where his wrath might lead as to comprehend, "is how one can get rid of one's ego before one begins. It's like starting a race at the finish line."

"You must listen carefully," he said evenly. "I did not say one has to rid oneself of one's ego, but that one has to break identification with it."

"What's the difference?" she demanded. "Aren't the ego and the identification with the ego the same thing?"

"Perhaps from the Hindu perspective," he conceded; "but, from our standpoint, the ego has a life of its own apart from the genuine self."

"I thought there was no self!"

He sighed and looked at her as if she were a foolish little child.

"You are catching yourself up in words," he admonished. "Self, no-self, these are used to point. What's important is the reality, not what is used to point to it."

"But I'm not seeing!"

"No, you are seeing. What you see doesn't fit into your logic, that's all. Allow it its own logic, and there will be no difficulty."

"So, tell me," she said, after forcing a few deep breaths, "what is the reality?"

"The reality is a consciousness whole and undivided, with many different facets that illuminate one another."

"I see," she said, and this time she really did. "And how does one achieve it?"

"Through controlled intensity."

"Just like a pure land!" she clapped her hands.

"Yes, just like a pure land. In a way, the Vajrayana is trying to establish a pure land on earth."

"And the controlled intensity," she continued, pleased with herself but not wishing to show him, "is generated by the tantric practices, especially the sexual ones?"

"Yes," he confirmed. "How is energy generated?"

"It's not," she replied. "Energy is neither created nor destroyed."

"Yes, I too know the laws of thermodynamics," he rejoined with some impatience. "I said, 'generated!'"

"I don't know," she pouted. "A billion ways!"

"But every one of those billion ways involves the same basic process," he declared—"the creation of a differential. And the greater the differential, the greater the energy released. For example, stretch a rubber band and you create a differential. The farther you stretch it, the greater the differential. Roll a stone up an inclined plane and you create a differential. The higher and steeper the gradient, the greater the kinetic energy released when you allow the stone to roll back down again. Electricity has positive and negative charges—that is a differential. The greater the charges, the greater the differential and therefore the greater the voltage produced when the charges are connected. From waterfalls to thermonuclear reactions, the generation, or if you will, transformation of energy requires the creation of a differential."

"It's setting up a state of tension and then releasing the tension," she added, and he nodded approval.

"Therefore, what would be the most natural way for human beings to generate the kind of spiritual energy that can be directed, not only toward escape from one dimension of awareness into another, but the obliteration of all obstacles to the integration of awareness? In other words, where in human nature does one find the greatest differential?"

"Good and evil?" she answered immediately, unable to imagine a more intense opposition.

"Perhaps," he responded. "In the Hindu tantra, what has generally been known as the tantra of the left hand involves the actual ritual practices, especially the sexual, as opposed to those involving only the imagination in meditation, because the rituals are violations of marriage and caste. In Tibet, where there is no caste, the tantra of the left hand has much the same meaning today. Several centuries ago, however, one sect generated tremendous psychic tension by engaging in acts its practitioners themselves fully recognized as evil. Through a discipline that mimicked spiritual centering, this tension was converted into energy that supposedly was then used to develop spiritually, as with the regular tantra."

"Mimicking?" she queried. "Supposedly?"

"It was not, nor can it ever be, an authentic spiritual path," he said decisively, "because it fractures the heart, whereas genuine spirituality makes the heart whole."

She pondered. "What, then, of the polarity of life and death? Does that fracture the heart?"

"No, that is both a powerful and spiritually productive differential," he said. "For example, monks will often meditate naked in the snows of the frigid Himalayas. As Western observers have attested, those who do it right will be generating such energy that one can dry wet towels on their bodies."

She did not wish to ask what happened to those who did it wrong.

"But the greatest differential in human nature," he continued, "the most powerful source of energy, is that between man and woman." He smiled. "Haven't you and Ishwara demonstrated that? And in the Tibetan tantra, the goal is not transcendence but integration of the personal. Thus, though most practitioners are monks who stick to the celibate right-hand path, a yogi and his wife will perform their spiritual discipline together, in their marriage. That is of the essence of the Vajrayana."

"Is there more to the Buddhist tantra?" she asked, returning his smile.

"In essence, there is but one more truth for you to fathom. The greatest differential in the cosmos, mirrored by that of male and female, is that between heaven and earth!"

"The Lightning Vehicle!" she murmured, and then a lightning bolt split the empyrean and a peal of thunder cast her into a dream-like sleep in which grotesque monsters were repeatedly dismembering and devouring her body. Strangely, she was not so much frightened as confused by it all, and prayed to some nameless divinity for clarity and light. Then she was awakened by the clanging of a gong.

5. Zen

Upon the sounding of the gong, she found Gotama had been transformed into a rotund but nevertheless austere old man with no hair and a big stick. He brandished this stick at her, saying softly but with absolute seriousness, "I will give you fifty blows if you can say it, and fifty blows if you can't say it." Ariana at first had no idea what 'it' was, but then she realized he could only be referring to the way to spiritual enlightenment. She said, "The Noble Eight-Fold Path," thinking that would be just enough to have said it, namely, point to it, without saying it, namely, wrap it up in a neat verbal formula. He hit her anyway.

Then she found herself as a monk walking with another monk. They were discussing their master's fifty blows when they came upon a river that had to be forded. On the bank sat a lovely young woman dressed in the finest of silks and obviously in a quandary over how to cross without spoiling her dress. Without hesitation, Ariana's companion hoisted the woman onto his shoulder and waded through the muddy but relatively placid water to the other shore, where he set his beauteous burden down and continued on his way. Ariana, hurrying after him, upbraided him for violating one of the strictest rules for a monk—absolutely no physical contact with a member of the opposite sex. Not only had he broken the rule, but he had dishonored the monastery and everyone in it. Ariana went on like this for almost an hour, deathly afraid that the taint her companion had brought upon himself would, by association, make her unclean as well. Finally, the other monk turned to Ariana, seized her eyes with his own, and said quietly, "I'm not the one who is carrying that woman. You are."

Then Ariana remembered back to her girlhood. A mountain immortal, one of the wise men who achieved lasting youth through the esoteric use of minerals, incantations, and herbs, had promised her supernatural powers if she would only follow him without question or protest. For a lass who had little to which to look forward but a life of oppressive labor in the fields, the prospect of powers beyond even those of the emperor was irresistible.

At first, the experiences through which the wild sage took her concerned no one but herself. There were trials by fire and by water, tests of courage and endurance which she passed with relative ease because her desire to be more than she was was so burning. After a while, however, the focus shifted from her to other people. She had to watch a dog cruelly whipped, and then a defenseless man even more cruelly beaten. Finally, she was taken to what must have been the deepest hell, where her master revealed her own parents heartlessly tortured by demons. Realizing that the path of the supernatural required not only going beyond nature but actually making war with it, she let out all her pent-up disgust and fear in one agonized scream. Immediately she found herself at home again, her parents safely asleep in their bed.

She stopped seeking supernatural powers after that, but she still yearned to be more than what everybody else was. It was not until her school made a field trip to the local Buddhist monastery, however, that she discovered another way to pursue her ambition. The monks, sitting in complete stillness in long rows in the meditation hall, did not much impress her, but the magnificent dragon that overlooked their endeavors did. It was not a real dragon, her schoolmaster made haste to assure her when he saw how it filled the girl with awe; but this statement only confirmed a truth that she had long since suspected, that schoolmasters did not see reality, they only read about it in books.

The girl found a crevice in a corner of the hall from which she could gaze upon the dragon without being disturbed by demands to participate in the other activities her teacher had planned. Indeed, she became so lost in the painting that she did not notice when the schoolmaster sounded his whistle, rounded up his charges, and left the monastery. She did not realize that she sat there with the dragon all that night and into the following day, completely absorbed in the greater life she found there. Finally, a monk approached and gently whispered in her ear. He asked whether the girl would like to hear the story of how the great dragon had come to be. He told of a master artist from a distant province who had heard of the wonderful dragons dwelling in the monastery. The artist knew immediately that all his work thus far had been but preparation for capturing the essence of a real dragon, the cosmic overlord that united in its being the knowledge of heaven and the wisdom of earth. When he arrived at the monastery, there was nothing to be seen.

"So he made it up?" the girl asked, as if it had all been a hoax.

"Not at all!" replied the old monk. "He learned how to see the dragon; and not only see it, but hear, smell, and touch it as well."

"How?" asked the girl excitedly.

"By disciplining his imagination, as those people are doing right there." He gestured toward the meditating monks. From that moment, she knew that the spiritual life was for her.

Once she entered a monastery, Ariana worked hard. Not only did she meditate for hours on end, but she learned to read as well, and then devoured all the sacred texts in the monastery library. Thus the rebuke from the monk who had carried the girl across the river was especially hard to bear, coming as it did from a relative newcomer who wasted most of his time joking with the senile monks and playing with the urchins who hung around the monastery gates. Nevertheless, she fell silent because she felt there was some merit to what her comrade had said, and scripture emphasized that wisdom could come from the strangest quarters. Until she herself saw a live dragon and learned its ways, she would apply himself to her studies and hold her tongue.

When the traveling companions arrived at their monastery, there was no time to rest from their journey. "Kyogen!" one of her friends cried out, "there is important news!" At that point Ariana realized her soul, or 'no-soul,' had once again incarnated as a male. Her, or rather, his upset at his fellow monk's impropriety in carrying the beautiful damsel suddenly made sense. On hearing the news, all memory of having been Ariana was lost, and the transition, more gentle than those with Ishwara, was nevertheless complete.

The master had died while they were away, and a new master been installed, a woman! Kyogen had thought no one of importance took nuns seriously. The majority of the monks regarded women as too weak and sensual for the strenuous demands of monastic life. Now they were to have a female master! Kyogen had to see this for himself.

After Kyogen was admitted to the master's presence, they exchanged bows and the new abbess courteously expressed the hope that he would be staying on since, after all, he had been the late master's star pupil. Kyogen, who could not but be impressed by the new master's just assessment of his true worth, said that he would remain for a while, implying a trial period. The new master bowed deeply and thanked him profusely, saying she hated when people went away. Indeed, it was most fortunate that Kyogen had dropped by, because she was certain that he, with his tremendous knowledge of scripture, could help her with a question that had bothered her for years: "Where do we go after we die?"

Kyogen couldn't remember any pertinent passage, which would not have surprised Ariana since Gotama had made a point of dismissing such metaphysical questions, but which puzzled and exasperated Kyogen, who thought all wisdom lay in scripture. All that night and through the next day he ransacked the library, gradually arriving at the certainty that, if he could solve this one mystery of death, he would finally see the dragon. Then, as it became clear that his search would be fruitless, he became convinced that the new master was toying with him. He rushed to her chambers, managing to calm himself before entering her presence. He begged humbly to be told the answer to her question, but she said that that would deprive him of the pleasure of finding it out for himself. Finally, he grabbed her by the throat and she laughed, saying that perhaps he thought if he killed her she would give him the answer from beyond the grave. He lifted his hand and gave her a resounding slap. Then, realizing what he had done, he gathered up his few things and left the monastery, knowing that he would now never be able to see the dragon.

Kyogen wandered until he was taken in by an old woman, a widow, who had been looking to keep a monk so she could gain spiritual merit before she died. For several years he was able to devote himself to conquering the mighty anger that had driven him to strike his new master, in his mind the worst sin a monk could commit. In his meditations, he replayed that moment over and over again, and then juxtaposed it with what he knew of the Buddha's life. Gradually his imagination narrowed its focus down to the single moment in Gotama's existence that Kyogen intuitively felt was the key to the contradiction of his own character, so lost in darkness and so lusting for light—the Flower Sermon.

The story was a simple one. Gotama announced one day that he was going to give a public sermon at a certain field at noon the next day. By the following midmorning, the field in question was packed with people from miles around who had heard of the new holy man and wanted to see for themselves if he was really as powerful as rumor made him out to be. As the sun reached its zenith, an expectant hush fell over the crowd and Gotama appeared in their midst. They sat comfortably, expecting several hours of solid entertainment. There was no way of knowing whether he planned it or acted on the spur of the moment but, instead of speaking, the Buddha simply bent over, plucked a flower that grew at his feet, and held it up for all to see. Then he turned and left the disappointed crowd behind. Only one of the Buddha's disciples got the point, but Kyogen's own tradition traced its origin through that disciple back to the Buddha's Flower Sermon. That was the beginning of Dhyana Buddhism, the Sanskrit term that means "meditation" and that, through a series of mispronunciations, became the Chinese Ch'an and the Japanese Zen.

That was as far as Kyogen's book-learning would take him. In holding up the flower, the Buddha had pointed to its "suchness." What was suchness? The essential reality of anything as revealed to experience before the vivisection of experience through analysis, reflection, classification, and all the other tools we use to cut into bite-size pieces the reality that ultimately only makes sense when one takes it whole.

He remembered his former master asking him, "What was the suchness of a flower?" He had replied, cogently enough, that if it could be put into words, the Buddha would have done so. Then, as so often he had had to do with Kyogen, the master tapped his forehead sharply with his fly whisk and said, "Yes, yes, of course! Nothing can be put into words, any more than a country can be put into a map or a real dragon into a painting. Words point, that's all. So what word would you use to point to the suchness of a flower?"

"Beauty," he said.

"Yes," the master confirmed, "the beauty of which the Christian master Jesus spoke when he said, 'Consider the lilies of the field. They neither work nor weave, but not even a king in all his glory is dressed so finely as they.'"

"This Jesus," Kyogen had asked in surprise, his experience of Christianity confined to the intolerant bigotry of missionaries, "he was a master?"

"A perfect master," the old man nodded. "Take a child, for example. What is the suchness of a child?"

Kyogen considered the possible candidates. "Innocence," he finally selected.

"And what did Jesus say of children?" the master continued: "'Let the little ones come to me, for of such is the kingdom of heaven.'"

"A beautiful sentiment," Kyogen observed with barely disguised condescension. He liked Zen because it wasn't sentimental. Was his master also growing senile like the other ancients in the monastery?

"There's nothing beautiful about it!" the master exclaimed. "From the moment we are able, we do whatever we can to get away from childhood, going so far as to poison ourselves with tobacco and liquor to prove our 'maturity.' And we treat our children as if, without our guidance and the imposition of our standards and values upon their suggestible natures, they would become little monsters. But Jesus says that children don't need values inculcated in them because they are the value, the value of life. We in Zen go even further and make the infant the standard."

"How so?"

"When hungry, we eat. When thirsty, we drink. When tired, we sleep. To do whatever is natural with all ones heart, that is the way of the baby!" He paused. "My question to you, dear Kyogen, is what is the suchness of the self?" His eyes twinkled mischievously. "What is the suchness of your self? You should know, since presumably you have lived with yourself most of your life."

He stared blankly into his master's laughing eyes. He knew it was not enough to repeat, "When I'm hungry I eat and when tired I sleep." He knew to himself he was much more than these animal appetites. The easy way out was a trap for those who were not honest. "I don't know," he finally said.

The master nodded in satisfaction. "That's your *koan*."

"My what?" Kyogen had asked, even more mystified.

"Your koan," laughed the master even louder. "A bit of nonsense only you take seriously. We all of us have such nonsense—it comes with being human. In wrestling with one's own particular bit of nonsense—in other words, in passionately trying to make sense out of one's nonsensical passion—one wrestles oneself to a standstill."

"What happens then?" he queried, and the master replied that he would find that out when he had exhausted himself.

Day by day, Kyogen puzzled over it all. His master had given him a koan: "What is the suchness of the self?" But then the new master, the woman, had asked him, "Where do we go when we die?", and in agreeing to look for the answer he had tacitly accepted her guidance. Was her question a new koan for him? If so, did it hold the key to the old one?

Days passed into years, and Kyogen gradually forgot about everything else but solving the riddle of the self. One day he was cleaning the weeds and rocks from a long disused vegetable plot. Just as he was dumping a barrowful of refuse into the compost, a crow flying overhead burst the silence with one loud, piercing "Caw!" Kyogen looked around as if he were seeing everything for the first time—the land, the trees, the sky, the compost heap. It all revolved in one gigantic circle of life. He was a part of it. How could he ever have thought any differently?

About this time the widow, who actually made a profit off of Kyogen because of his insistence upon working, both to earn his keep and as part of his spiritual discipline, decided to take in another monk. By doubling her investment, spiritually speaking, she hoped to double her return. Instead of a favorable rebirth in this world, as she had previously desired, she began to set her sights on a pure land.

The only trouble was that every monk she came across refused the offer once he learned that another monk was already in her keeping, and that there was not enough work around her tiny farm for two. What she originally had thought a selling point became the single obstacle to the realization of her scheme, until she found a monk from another land, Ceylon, who had come to Japan at the request of Ceylonese merchants who missed the spiritual comfort and security the presence of monks, their own kind of monks, gave them. The merchants had since returned home, but he had decided to stay. He did not tell her why, but she knew it was a safe bet to assume he liked feeling unique. This suited her fine. All she had to tell him was that all the other monks had spurned her invitation because they would rather work than meditate, and he was hers.

Because of his vanity, however, doubts lingered in her mind. Was it so very innocent in a holy man? What if he was not really a holy man? He was mature, even old as the average life span went; and if she were looking for another husband, she could have done worse. Yet what more could a husband give her than what she already had in Kyogen, except for demands for service and sex? No, she wanted another holy man to hedge her bet. When it came to destiny and the afterlife, one could not be too careful.

So she decided to test him. She had a beautiful young niece who visited from time to time, and one morning she bade her take the foreign monk his breakfast. "And make sure you show him the hospitality any foreigner would expect from a woman," she added meaningfully. When her niece embraced the monk, he rebuked her sharply, saying that sap did not course through dead wood, so why was she wasting her time.

The monk chuckled to himself about his clever double entendre, leading the girl to believe he was impotent when he was really saying that the sap of craving no longer was the substance of his life. The joke, however, was on him; for when the widow heard how the monk had treated her niece, she threw him out and, in a fury, set fire to the still perfectly serviceable hut she had built for him.

Since Kyogen was unaware of all these events except the fire, whose necessity the widow ascribed to infestation by ants, she decided she should see if she had the genuine article in him as well. When the beautiful young girl embraced him, he hugged her back in an unmistakably fatherly way and laughingly asked her what her old fox of an aunt was up to. The girl said that he must have heard about what had happened to the other monk, after all. When the blank expression on his face convinced her he had not, she told him the whole story. At the end, he proclaimed her aunt a real Zen master, sent the girl on her way with a basket of freshly picked cucumbers, and bade her tell her aunt to let him know when she planned the next bonfire, as he had a new recipe for vegetable kebob that he was certain would cook up deliciously over the open flames.

Needless to say, the widow herself had a good laugh, and Kyogen was not kicked out of his hermitage. Shortly thereafter, however, he knew it was time to return to his former monastery.

The nun was still in charge, and she greeted him with a cheery, "What took you so long?" For several years he enjoyed the luxury of devoting himself to his own personal discipline, but on her deathbed the nun named him her successor; and, after all she had done for him, he was in no position to refuse, especially after their final interview, in which she once again managed to change his life.

He was sitting in his most dutiful posture, squatting on his haunches so he could instantly be of service should need arise. He was telling her how inadequate he felt for the task she was bequeathing to him, and asking if in her mind he was particularly lacking in any area—all the sort of thing the crown prince would say to the dying king, but Kyogen really meant it. Suddenly, with an astonishing surge of energy, the master jumped out of her bed and bustled about the room sniffing and making a face. "There's a real stench here!" she cried. Kyogen thought she had gone out of her mind, for he smelled nothing. Then she sniffed at him and yelled, "Aha! I found it! You really wreak of Zen!"

Those were her last words. The attendant physician, who had heard the ruckus and come running, said the strain of this final effort must have been too much for her, but Kyogen knew that she simply had said all she had to say and had no more reason to stay.

Whether because of his predecessor's final testament, his new position of authority, or the conjunction of both he could not say, but after that Kyogen began to notice things about the monastery he had been oblivious to before. The masters no longer had much of a personal relationship with their disciples, as had been the rule in his youth. There were far too many monks now. Not only had Zen become fashionable, but the monastery doubled as a "finishing school" for the teenaged children of affluent adults. Even the koan, that tool for literally shaking an individual's world, had been transformed into a system of "examinations" with "correct" answers kept absolutely secret and known only to the senior examiners, of whom Kyogen of course was the chief. Life in the monastery was beginning to resemble what he saw in the Western spy films, with disciples expending their time and energy toward discovering not only what koans would be presented to them, but also what were their solutions.

In short, the spirit of Zen seemed to have abandoned the monastery, and it was fast dissolving into insanity. Worse than the abandonment of the spirit of Zen was its corruption. What most people meant by "Zen" nowadays, including those who practiced it, was Theravada with a spice of paradox. In other words, they were no longer seeking the total engagement in life demanded by his masters. On the contrary, they established as their spiritual ideal aloof, superior, and most important of all, secure detachment.

At last, Kyogen made a crucial decision. He left the monastery, he left Japan and traveled east across the ocean to the West, a directional paradox whose symbolic significance of rebirth through death was lost on all his protesting disciples. In America, he was welcomed with open arms by a small Zen community in a large city. He found his new disciples charming in their ignorance, prodigious in their arrogance, and boundless in their energy. It truly was the New World to him, a place where he could forget about tradition and get about the business of living. It was not that he had been unable to make a fresh start. As far as he was concerned, there was and never had been anything to start. It was that the essential remained the essential wherever one went, only this was much easier to see with a change of unessentials. His familiar past and unknown future canceled each other out, leaving the present free to be what it always was when one did not get in the way—pure adventure. In short, Kyogen entered a second childhood, but there was nothing senile or debilitated about it. And this new zest for life was not at all diminished by a doctor finding that he was suffering from a relatively unusual form of heart disease that could take him at any time without warning. When he learned of it, Kyogen actually laughed at how all the pieces were fitting together.

It just so happened that, a few months after arriving in his new home, Kyogen was invited to speak at an annual interfaith banquet of Protestant and Catholic clergy. Apparently, they wanted to spice up the bill-of-fare with some tidbits of exotic Oriental wisdom. The invitation struck Kyogen like a revelation. He declined for the present year because he did not speak English and had no desire to be watered down by a translator, but he said that he would be willing to take the podium next year.

In the interim, Kyogen was as happy as the proverbial clam and frisky as a newborn puppy. He had a new koan! No longer would he permit his more serious disciples to practice their Japanese on him. He instead would practice his English on them. He took several courses, all at once, in every kind of English—written, spoken, colloquial, even slang. He attended classes, watched American television, did programmed self-study on the Zen center's computer, and fell asleep with language tapes playing through a Walkman on his head. More than learning how to speak American, however, Kyogen took it upon himself to eat American, act American, dress American, even sleep American. In addition, he worshipped American by visiting every type of church. A devotee offered him a water bed, and he did not refuse. By the end of the year, he felt he was ready, though he was still uncertain about what he had gotten himself ready for. He had no idea what the Christian priests and ministers desired or expected. They had asked for Zen, and they were going to get it. In other words, Kyogen was not going to plan his presentation at all. His own buddha-nature would lead him in clarifying theirs.

Kyogen arrived at the banquet hall several hours early, wishing to bring his spirit into communion with the spirit of the place where he was to be such an honored guest. His disciples, knowing that a favorable appearance would lead to an increase in contributions and prospective converts from the Christian community, had encouraged him to dress in his most formal of ceremonial robes. He, however, insisted upon jeans and a sweater. Thus it was that, when he was unable to produce any documentary proof of his identity, the private security guard turned him away at the door.

When Kyogen returned to the Zen Center, he found his best robe freshly starched sitting in the middle of the meditation room floor. He had never liked these formal robes, so stiff that they could stand up by themselves; but now he smiled as if the costume were an old friend. Everything, indeed, had a way of falling into place.

When Kyogen returned to the banquet hall, the same guard who had turned him away before simply smiled and called up to his boss on his walkie-talkie that the guest of honor had arrived. Kyogen was ushered to the front of the large hall by a Catholic priest who identified himself as the secretary of the Interfaith Council, and who sat him down between himself and the Methodist minister who was chairing the council that year. Dinner was taken up almost entirely with small talk about mutual acquaintances (there proved to be none), Japanese cooking (Kyogen knew how to boil rice), and Japanese weather. Kyogen predicted a storm was coming, and his dinner companions smiled politely, thinking no doubt that his English was still rough because the weather was expected to be nearly perfect for the foreseeable future.

Finally, Kyogen's moment came. He rose, walked to the podium as breezily as if he were back in the Zen Center, lifted that same podium, set it aside, and then sat cross-legged on the table upon which it had rested. At first, he was tempted simply to look at everyone without saying a word; but that would have been cheap imitation of the Buddha. Then he wondered if some simple phrase might express the essence of the occasion. Finally, remembering the lesson of the fifty blows and realizing that "saying it" was as much a part of the way as not saying it, he decided to do the one thing he had not considered doing because it was what everyone expected, and yet was what he had wanted to do all along.

"I want to talk," he said, "about Zen."

And he did. He told them of his struggles as a young monk, his failure to appreciate his master, the necessity to see the living dragon. As he went on, several people yawned. "Perhaps I am not making sense to you," he chuckled. The question was greeted by polite and icy smiles. "Let me tell you a story," he said, and then he went on to tell them how his last master had behaved on her deathbed, and how she had found him stinking of Zen. At the end of this story a hand went up, and Kyogen was asked what on earth he meant. They had thought they were getting an authentic Zen master, but instead here was a phony who not only seemed not to know anything about the subject, but also to hate Zen as well. Kyogen replied evenly, neither smiling nor frowning, that he begged their indulgence to translate the story into Western terms.

"Suppose it is Sunday," he began, taking silence for assent, "and you are preparing for church service. The doorbell rings, and standing on your doorstep is Jesus Christ, come to pay you a little visit on the sly. You put an arm around his shoulder and say, 'Good buddy, you came just in time! I'm going to show you that we've kept the faith!' You are going to take him with you to church. When you arrive, you direct him to the front pew, so everyone will see you're good friends with Jesus. You pour your heart into the service, giving the most powerful sermon about the evil of sin and the necessity of faith in Christ. Nevertheless, your eye keeps wandering to ascertain how Jesus is reacting, but his face gives nothing away. At the end, you are so anxious that you forget about formal farewells to individual members of your flock. Instead, you grab Jesus' hand and take him someplace you won't be disturbed so you can ask the question you've been dying to ask—'Well, Jesus, what did you think?' 'It was interesting,' he replies, enveloping you with his eyes, 'and parts of it were even moving. There was only one problem. It stank of Christianity!'"

The silence in the room leapt from apathetic to stunned. Taking advantage of that silence, Kyogen quietly removed his robe without anyone trying to stop him. "When I came without this robe," he said, "you would not let me in. It seems you do not wish me to stay, so I leave you with what you wanted." Kyogen set the robe upright on the table and walked with measured step the length of the room. Strangely enough, as he walked, the hostile faces of the foreign clerics changed to the smiling faces of all the monks he had known over the years. Kyogen felt a sharp stab at his heart, and he realized he was literally about to discover the answer to the riddle his last master had proposed, the one that had driven him nearly to kill her.

"Kyogen!" his old master was calling. "Kyogen!"

Old now but with a young heart, Kyogen came running. When he arrived at the Great Hall, the Master was seated on his throne-like chair with a chessboard arranged before him. A young man, a stranger, had taken the side of the black. It was obvious the Master wanted Kyogen to take the white. "Play!" he ordered them both, pulling out the ceremonial sword that Kyogen had never seen unsheathed before. "The one who loses, loses his head!" Kyogen drew back, but the Master insisted. "Play!" he bellowed. "If you lose, I promise you will be reborn in a pure land."

So they played, each knowing that the Master had both the legal authority and, from the look in his eye, the will to execute his judgment. At first Kyogen was losing, but then he rallied as his opponent made one foolish blunder after another. Just as Kyogen was about to place the enemy king in mate, however, the Master sliced through both board and table with the sword, and Kyogen instantly realized that his opponent, who appeared to be nothing more than a pampered rich boy, had been throwing the match. "You have learned the two essentials," said the Master, smiling at the newcomer, "discipline and compassion. Now you need merely apply these lessons and awakening is yours."

Awakening! That's what it was all about! Kyogen had always been the instrument of others' awakening. Had his turn come at last?

Without knowing how he got there, Kyogen found himself hanging over an abyss, the only thing keeping him from death a single shrub that was slowly coming free of the anchoring earth. At the end of this shrub to which he clung was a single blue flower, whose nectar dripped down upon his crown. Slowly, agonizingly, he threw his head back, a most unnatural position under the circumstances, and sucked greedily at the viscous liquid. Never had he felt so alive as at that moment when the roots broke free of the sheltering earth and both Kyogen and the tree plunged to their deaths.

Ariana, who had become almost completely identified with Kyogen, took several moments to realize who and where she was. "Gotama!" she finally whispered, looking into her friend's concerned but smiling face. And then she added, "The movie."

"You have a penchant for non-sequiturs!" Gotama laughed. "What movie?"

"The Theravadin monk who pushed the girl away, the one the old lady threw out . . ." she continued, straining to make him understand. "He had a movie playing in his head. We all have movies playing in our heads."

Gotama nodded. "And, of course, we both know who the hero of that movie is."

She smiled. "I am! Me, myself and I—the ego!"

"What was the plot of this particular movie?" he asked.

"That's easy!" she replied. "He was the spiritual hero who had conquered craving and attained perfect detachment. The girl was the final test to certify his status. She wasn't a person to him, just an object. It wouldn't have mattered really, if he had done the opposite and satisfied his lust. Either way, he still would have been caught up in his own self-image."

"Self-imaging might be better, don't you think?"

She nodded. "I see that we do it, and I see why we do it, but I don't understand how it works."

"If you knew that," he said, "you'd know how to stop it."

"If this ego, this image-maker, obscures the reality of the self," she reasoned, "then maybe one has to first find out what that reality is."

"But if that reality is obscured by the image-maker, how can one find it without first getting rid of the image-maker?" he reasoned further.

"Oh, I hate this!" she cried. "Everything goes in circles!"

"Abstract thought always goes in circles," he said calmly. "Take a leap beyond it. Try insight."

She did not say anything, for at the moment this suggestion seemed like a cruel joke.

"In your commerce with earthbound spirits," he asked, "did you ever notice how the younger ones tend to group in pairs, and how many of those pairs will spend hours doing nothing but laughing at everyone and everything?"

She nodded.

"Why do you think they laugh?"

"Because it's all very funny," she said in bitter jest.

"Exactly!" he unexpectedly agreed. "And why is it all very funny?"

"Because it is, that's all."

"Because they are observing it," he went on. "Life is extremely funny when we look at it from the spectator's viewpoint. Take sex, for example. Nothing is more serious when one is engaged in making love, but what could more sardonically funny than Shakespeare's image of the beast with two backs? People kill themselves for love, but it's also the stuff out of which Shakespearian comedies and TV sitcoms are made!"

"So that's the key," she mused. "Kyogen said as much. Engagement is the key."

"Yes," he agreed, "people observe because they are afraid to engage."

"Why?"

"Oh, all sorts of reasons. Take your pick. This person has to watch himself all the time or he's afraid he will lose himself. That person wants to step back to be able to chart a course through dangers in the offing. Still again, like our hypothetical adolescents, one does not like being regarded as a fool. To sit back and watch life is a psychological defense against being watched. The illusion is that, if one is laughing at everyone else, no one can be laughing at you. To find the way, to awaken, one has to have the courage to be a fool, like Kyogen. When Kyogen was asked the question, 'Where do we go when we die?,' he could have given the correct, the textbook answer."

"'Such questions do not tend toward edification,'" she quoted.

"Yes," he affirmed, he could have given that answer, but it would have been a lie because he was concerned about where we go when we die. Indeed, Kyogen was concerned about finding in the scripture an answer to every possible question. It was part of his self-imaging, his nonsense. The question of where we go when we die, however, goes right to the core of self-imaging, so it was a particularly appropriate koan. One can allow the nonsense to fall away like a leaf from a tree by focusing on the deep and quiet rhythm of one's being—that is one style of Zen meditation, the one favored by the School of Gradual Enlightenment. Or one may, as in the School of Sudden Enlightenment, meditate upon a koan. A koan is a particular bit of nonsense that arouses and engages one's passion. In wrestling with the koan one is wrestling with oneself, one's self-image; and, as you discovered, if one is not sweating after a half-hour, one isn't meditating properly. Since one is wrestling with oneself, one naturally wrestles oneself to a standstill. That is the 'Great Death.'"

"I don't understand!" she cried in such distress that she had to wonder if she really did understand.

"As Jesus put it," he clarified, "unless a seed dies, no life can come from it. This is the cracking of the egg, the germination of the seed. One has sought the meaning of life through one's passion, but since one has invested oneself in nonsense . . ."

"What nonsense?" she asked pointedly.

"Fashion, sports, automobiles, stamp-collecting, computers—whatever you will," he replied.

"Oh," was all she could say.

"One doesn't find life's meaning in such nonsense," he resumed, "and so one ends up in despair. At that point, if one neither kills oneself nor loses oneself in dissipation, nor tugs on the seedling out of impatience . . ."

"What does that mean?" she interjected.

"Much of what goes by the name of 'education' and 'spiritual discipline' is like pulling on a plant to make it grow," he replied. "If, like Kyogen, one remains quietly attentive, the despair will be like a seedling that can be uprooted with a simple tug of the hand, but which, if allowed to grow, will break open the heart the way a flower cracks open concrete!"

"It sounds painful!" she said. "Painful and difficult."

"Only for those who have abandoned their true nature," he affirmed, "and so allowed their hearts to ossify. For a baby, and therefore for a human being, total engagement in life from the passion of the heart is the most natural thing in the world!"

She pondered. "And when this seedling of awareness breaks through the surface of consciousness—that is awakening?"

His answering nod was almost a bow. "We are heart," he declared. "We are the passion of the heart, but we squander our passion like intoxicated millionaires on cheap and tawdry hopes, fears, beliefs and desires. We must allow passion to find its natural center, its home again in the heart. One can not do that by cutting passion off. One can do it only by withdrawing from the petty and superficial. The investment of the self, however, is always strong. Therefore the withdrawal is slow and gradual, or quick and violent. These are the two sides of passion, and passion is the suchness of the self—the passion of the heart."

Again she pondered. "So, Zen differs from Theravada in engaging in rather than disengaging from this nonsense we call life?"

"To engage fully from the heart," he confirmed. "To live the passion of the heart."

"I thought passion was a spiritual fetter, even for Zen."

"Words, again!" he laughed. "I guess you are still Kyogen—he had to be told everything thrice. Passion such as most human beings experience and live is destructive, but one may regard this fact in one of two ways. For Theravada, passions are a disturbance, a movement of what should be at rest. To reach enlightenment one must calm them, and the only way to do that is to detach oneself from them, to remove the investment of self that is the source of their energy. What happens, however, when one puts a dam in front of a gently flowing river?"

"The river backs up, floods its banks, and eventually either breaks through or overflows the dam with tremendous force," she replied.

"That is how Zen sees passion," he said. "It is pure spontaneity, but if we attempt to block its flow in any way, it becomes destructive."

"Reminds me of Freud."

"Yes, in a way, but Freud saw this passion of life as blind and self-centered, an engine without intelligence. For Zen it is the only real intelligence."

"The life force?" she ventured.

"It is beyond the life-force. One can't put it into categories because categories deal with abstractions, and it alone is real. It is the *Dao*, the Way that embraces life and death."

"The mystical unity!"

"Only from a Western perspective, for which everything is mystical that does not fit its mechanical and arbitrary criteria for determining what is real. A young but famous samurai once came to a Zen monastery to discuss philosophy with the equally famous master. The samurai was a Confucian in orientation, which meant, among other things, that honor and propriety were of supreme importance to him. When he was ushered into the presence of the master, who by the way was of peasant stock, the young nobleman bowed, expecting a bow in return. Instead, the master slapped him so hard that the stunned warrior backed into the hall, enabling his assailant to slam the door in his face. No doubt the samurai would have killed the master to erase the stain upon his honor, but a young monk who happened to be passing convinced him that it was all a misunderstanding, and offered to make amends by brewing him a cup of tea. Just as the knight was about to sip his tea, his host jostled his elbow, causing him to spill it all down his silk robe. Instead of apologizing, the monk challenged the samurai to show him his way, but the samurai had no idea what he should do. 'Then let me show you our way!' the monk declared. What do you think he did?"

"Meditate?"

"He wiped up the tea."

"It's just about reality, then," Ariana said after a lengthy silence. "Accepting reality."

"Not accepting it," he corrected. "The reality that one accepts is always outside and apart. Zen is about living the reality that one is."

"The passion of the heart," she murmured.

"With emphasis upon 'heart.' Remember, engagement is not the same as busyness. Someone may sit on the board of six corporations, have a large family, and keep up an endless round of social and business affairs and still not be engaged in life at all. One may live alone on a mountaintop and be totally engaged."

"I think I see what you mean," she said tentatively.

"Two lovers may make love with a great deal of flurry and commotion, and not be truly involved with each other. Two lovers may be absolutely still and be totally involved."

"That I understand," she smiled, "and that's the difference between stinking of Zen and living it."

He laughed. "Yes, or to see it another way, formal religious practices, whether meditating or singing hymns, preaching, and receiving sacraments, are crutches. Who should use crutches?"

"Cripples."

"And what happens to healthy people who use crutches?"

"They become crippled."

"So," he concluded, "in the world one sees the interesting spectacle of crippled people running to and fro, seeking to persuade and even force healthy people to use the same crutches they do; and, if the healthy people refuse, they are destined for eternal darkness or damnation to hell, and sometimes even tortured, imprisoned, or murdered in this present existence for good measure."

His words struck a deep and somber chord. "But there is no hell."

"There is only sleep and awakening," he affirmed. "Zen is not concerned about anything else. The essential idea of Zen is that nirvana and samsara, peace and process, realization and action, are one. You can reach the highest heaven, but if you are not awake, you might just as well be in a garbage dump. You can fall to the deepest hell, but if you are awake, you've got life's essence."

"The nectar and the abyss!"

He nodded. "The basic ideas of Mahayana—bodhisattwas, preexistent buddhas, and pure lands—all occupy the Zen universe, but only as furniture. The life of Zen is to be found nowhere but in the here-and-now. The only way one can be in the real here-and-now, as opposed to the cheap, abstract imitation so popular today, is by going to meet it with all of oneself, leaving nothing behind to keep an eye out for danger or opportunity. There is no substitute for total engagement from the heart!"

"And here I thought Buddhism was about objectivity!"

"According to Zen, authentic subjectivity is genuine objectivity."

"Woody Allen in *Love and Death*," she laughed.

Gotama smiled. "He got it from Existentialism—Western Zen."

"There's one thing that still puzzles me."

"Only one?" he laughed. "I guess I'm not a real Zen master!"

"The old woman," she said. "The widow."

"Whenever a Zen story pits an old woman against a monk," he explained, "you can be ninety-nine-point-nine percent certain that the woman is in the right and the monk in the wrong. She is the Dao."

"Then what about the test?" she asked. "How could he have passed?"

"He couldn't," Gotama declared. "No one could. That's why it was a perfect Zen test—damned if you do and damned if you don't."

"I know the feeling," she frowned.

"Think of the earthbound spirits, or even of your own intimate relationships with other spirits," he said. "Have you ever known of a situation in which a woman felt that her man was not emotionally connecting with her, and she tried to talk about it?"

She nodded. "All he can do is ask what he's done wrong—did he forget their anniversary, or is he spending too much time at the office? He just doesn't get it."

"Yes," agreed Gotama, "no matter what he says, he's wrong, because he is looking for a behavioral solution to a problem of awareness, and no such solution is possible. One looks for such a solution because a change of behavior is so much easier than a change in oneself."

"So women are natural Zen masters?" she brightened.

"It's not that easy," he laughed. "Women tend to think that all one need do is understand how one is feeling wrong, and the problem will solve itself."

"But feeling isn't right or wrong!" she protested.

"Exactly!" he said. "To realize that there is no solution because there is no problem, only each moment to be lived from the heart—that is awakening."

"I understand," she said. "I have seen the dragon."

Gotama bowed deeply, and she bowed in return. When she raised her head, the Teacher was sitting in Gotama's place.

CHAPTER III.

JUDAISM

1. Yahweh

By now such changes had become, if not routine, at least common enough for her to look forward to what was coming and not dwell in regret at losing what had gone. The Teacher sat in silence, his face inscrutably expressionless, evidently waiting for her to speak. She too sat in silence, her own face as inexpressive as she could make it. She would wait him out with a game of tweedledum-tweedledee.

"We turn now to the West," he said, apparently not interested in games. He spoke like a schoolmaster introducing today's lecture topic. She wondered, if this really were a courting, where all the romance was to be found.

"Where's Yahweh?" she asked. "Why doesn't he do this himself?"

"He's here. Can't you feel him?"

The Teacher spoke in a hushed and reverent tone of which she had thought him incapable. They both sat still and silent, and she felt a subtle variation upon the paradoxical theme of challenge and peace that had first come to her in a gentle breeze in this very same clearing what seemed like ages ago. Or was it the exact same vibration, and simply she herself that had changed? The peace seemed more precious, the challenge more real.

"Yahweh has asked me to interpret for him," he explained.

"Oh, I thought you were here for a reality-check," she remarked, not bothering to soften the sarcasm.

"That is no longer necessary," he said, without taking offense, "as you are getting to the heart of things quite nicely on your own."

"What I have been through . . ." she stammered. "I can hardly take credit. But why you? Are you one of the Chosen People?"

"Yes," the Teacher replied, "and no. Let it suffice that Yahweh trusts my understanding in these things. He knows I will not misrepresent him."

"Is it only to be talk, then?" she said, feeling bored already.

"Oh, no, I'm sure he has planned for you a great variety of experiences. They will require orientation, however, orientation and interpretation. Both are of the very essence of Judaism. Do you know what fundamentalism is?"

"Religion out of a book."

"Religion is the book. The absolute truth is set down in black-and-white, and one need only read and obey."

"That is the Jewish attitude toward scripture?" she asked, uncertain what he was getting at.

"That is the opposite of the Jewish attitude toward scripture. What is a word?"

She hesitated, annoyed at herself for not following and at him for not making it easy to follow. "A concept, an idea."

"True, if one asks what a word is about," he agreed, though she felt more for her sake than that of the truth. "But what is a word literally?"

"A sound. Marks on paper."

"So what is the literal meaning of a word?"

"Nothing. Literally, a word is meaningless."

"Yes," he said with satisfaction, "words have meaning only as we interpret their meaning. Thus Judaism rejects the idea that there can be such a thing as a holy book from which God's will may be read straightforwardly. Without interpretation there is no meaning, and without meaning there is no communication."

"So there's no such thing as Jewish fundamentalism?"

"There are Jewish fundamentalists, but no Jewish fundamentalism."

"What does that mean?" she challenged, wondering what kind of game the Teacher was playing. "And if that's so, how can you say Judaism says such-and-such at all? Maybe what you really mean is your interpretation of Judaism!"

"Certainly, I am giving you my interpretation," he replied evenly. "Even if I gave you someone else's interpretation, it would still be my interpretation of that some-one's interpretation. As I said, Yahweh trusts my interpretation, but you don't have to. If it doesn't ring true to the experiences through which he takes you, develop your own interpretation. You have to do that anyway, even if everything I say to you makes sense, in order to make my ideas your own."

"So the point is there's no getting around interpretation," she concluded, and he nodded approval. "But didn't you also say something about orientation?"

"Yes, orientation is the preparatory part of interpretation, because the way one understands something depends as much upon how one approaches it as what one does when one arrives."

She understood what he was saying, but she could not imagine why anyone would choose to put so simple a matter in so convoluted a form. She would have dropped the whole thing and moved on to the next suitor were she not so intrigued by Yahweh himself. "I'm ready whenever you are," she finally announced.

"First of all," he began, "Judaism is a form of ethical monotheism; indeed, the oldest form known to history."

"That's very interesting," she observed. "What's ethical monotheism?"

"The belief in one God, a personal God, who is good and all-powerful, and who requires justice and righteousness from the human race."

"So we are not all God?" she queried, thinking of Hinduism. "Or the equivalent?" she added, thinking of Buddhism.

"That's mystical monism," the Teacher explained, "the idea that ultimately all beings are one being."

"It's more than an idea!"

"You're right," he agreed, "it's an experience; but so is ethical monotheism. In fact, each simply emphasizes one of the two sides of common human experience."

"I don't see how that can be possible."

"Think of an intimate relationship between a man and a woman. In the passion of sexual union, the two become as one self. In day-to-day living, what is important is the relationship of two selves. Which is the truth of the relationship?"

"Both are."

"That sounds fine in theory," he said, "but in practice can one really have it both ways? The choice is between living as two selves or as two extensions of one self. Is there a third option?"

"Not when you put it that way," she admitted, "but I'm sure there are other ways to put it."

"Do you have another way to put it?" he challenged. She shook her head. "If you don't, then arguing that way is as valid as drawing credit on a possibly existent account that, whether it exists or not, is not your own."

"There you go again," she protested, "making things more complicated than need be! Why can't you just say, 'Drawing credit on an imaginary account?'"

"Because that would be inaccurate," he replied coolly. "The account in question may actually exist. I'm not in a position to foreclose on that possibility."

She thought about it for a moment, and then smiled. "You're right. I suppose logic isn't one of my strong points."

"Logic is to the mind what muscles are to the body. If one's logical thinking is underdeveloped, one can't go anywhere or do anything mentally. If it is overdeveloped, one becomes a powerful but very limited thinker. The point is to be logical enough to assist thought without getting in its way."

"Is that your way of saying I'm not really so stupid after all?" she laughed.

"You ask the necessary questions. That can hardly be called stupid."

"So, Judaism is a form of ethical monotheism," she prompted, feeling uneasy at the unmasked affection with which he said this last remark, especially since he was not among those eligible to be her spouse.

"Yes, it emphasizes relationship. God creates the world . . ."

"God is Yahweh?" she interjected.

"Yes, as long as we are dealing with Judaism, God is Yahweh. God creates the world, and here is a significant point. This world is not an illusion, a veil hiding the true reality, as in Hinduism; nor is it essentially a place of suffering and dissatisfaction, as in Buddhism. The world is real, and it is good."

"I can understand the reality part," she conceded, "but there seems to be at least as much wrong with it as there is right."

As soon as she said this the reality before her dissolved, and the multicolored mists reformed into a place whose beauty outshone any of the heavenly realms she had ever seen. Trees and shrubs of infinite variety abounded, and instead of passing through seasonal changes, they were perpetually flowering and bearing fruit. She herself was not bodily present to this scene but, strange to say, it was bodily present to her. She was aware of two human figures in the garden, though again, they were not aware of her. They were the most beautiful humans she had ever encountered, spiritually as well as physically. She knew because there were no barriers to her awareness—the entire scene in all its aspects, inner as well as outer, was present to her.

The couple had just finished making love, so beautifully that Ariana would have cried had her eyes been available, when she felt the presence she had come to associate with Yahweh. They obviously felt it too, and arose with joy to greet their creator. Yes, at that point it was unmistakably clear to Ariana that Yahweh had made all the beauty before her, again both the inner and outer. Yahweh's "breath" caressed his creatures so lovingly and playfully that it was impossible for them not to feel like his children. They romped and played through the garden. At length they came upon what certainly was the most majestic tree of all, and Yahweh "told" them this tree was not for them to eat. Ariana understood he was taking a calculated but unavoidable risk. She knew that all these trees were incarnations of life's varied possibilities, and this particularly awesome one embodied the tragic possibility of turning against life. All possibilities had to be in this garden of life, or there could be no life. The freedom to do good was also the freedom to do evil. Nevertheless, the command, necessary as it was, set up a tension within the man and woman, the tension between "should" and "want" that, as she knew from her experience with Eastern religion, sooner or later would lead to a deeper, less ego-oriented sense of self, on the one hand, or destructive rebellion on the other.

Ariana had never felt so helpless as she did in watching the process of speculation, mistrust, envy and suspicion by which the couple turned against the love that not only had given them birth, but was the ongoing source of their life. The catalyst for this betrayal was a magical serpent who embodied a wisdom too proud to submit to love. The motive, however, was simple lust for power. The serpent told the couple that, if they ate the forbidden fruit of the Tree of the Knowledge of Good and Evil, they would not die but, on the contrary, would become like God. In a way he was telling the truth, because they would know what it was to carry responsibility for their actions, but what they understood by this "being like God" was power with no responsibility. They ate of the fruit and immediately a darkness, visible only to the spiritual eye, fell over the garden. It was not Yahweh who had exiled the human race from the garden, as their holy books claimed. It was humanity that had exiled itself.

Ariana was back with the Teacher. Now I know what you meant by 'orientation.' It has never been explained to me that way."

"And perhaps," he smiled, "you also understand why Yahweh trusts me to represent him."

She nodded solemnly. "So the original sin was not disobedience?" she said.

"No, it was the betrayal of love for the sake of power."

"Power-tripping!"

"Yes, power-tripping. Power-tripping destroys any personal relationship, whether between human and human or human and God. Life goes on when one loses a relationship with another human being. However, when one loses one's relationship with God, one loses the source of one's life. Through sin, the betrayal of love, we have cut ourselves off from our very life's blood. And not just ourselves. We are creation made conscious of itself. The life of God flows to creation through us. Unless our relationship with God is restored, all of creation is doomed."

"I understand," she said solemnly; "but why do humans turn this loving God whom they have betrayed into a tyrant?"

"Isn't that what they do with the human lovers they betray?" he answered sardonically. "Once one buys into the power game, that's all one sees in anyone else. Adam blames Eve. Eve blames the serpent. God gave Eve to Adam. God gave the serpent to Adam and Eve. It's obvious who's to blame."

She nodded. "The question, then, is whether God will take us back."

"No, that was never a question for Yahweh," he asserted. "The real issue is how can Yahweh lead us out of the insanity of power-tripping and back to the world of genuine relationship. What is the first step in establishing any personal relationship?"

"Empathy," she replied. "Without it no personal relationship is possible."

"But before that?" he persisted.

She thought for a moment. "I suppose the very first step is to make contact."

"Yes, so simple in theory, and yet in practice so difficult, especially for a spiritual being who seeks relationship with people who have repressed their spiritual perception."

"So what did Yahweh do?"

"According to Judaism, he chose a people to be the instrument of his divine revelation."

"The Chosen People," she said meaningfully.

"Yes, the Chosen People. Chosen not for privilege, however. Every people on earth thinks of itself at one time or another as chosen for privilege. Do you know how a sword is made?" he asked, true to his annoying but increasingly endearing habit of indulging in apparent non sequiturs.

"No," she laughed, "I haven't the faintest idea."

"One begins with metal," he prompted. "Where does one get metal?"

"Out of the earth."

"Well, let us suppose you are part of a vein of beautiful red iron ore," he continued, and as he spoke she actually felt herself become part of the earth. "Someone seeking to make a fine sword takes you instead of the iron ore next to you. If iron ore could talk, you might say to the rest of the ore that you had been chosen, but the ore had to be taken from someplace."

Ariana could still hear the Teacher's voice, but she had become the ore in question. The only thing to compare to it was her initial experience as a rock on the Hindu ladder of reincarnation.

"Next, the ore is processed," he continued, "to filter out the impurities. More precisely, it is smelted, subjected to tremendously high temperatures that cause it to liquefy, and the dross to rise to the top."

Ariana felt all this happening to her, but since she had the lowered awareness of a mineral, she was just able to bear it, as in a dream where, no matter how excruciating the agony, one's real self is not touched.

"Finally the dross is skimmed away and the metal is allowed to cool. As it cools, it is not simply molded, but beaten into shape. Otherwise it would be brittle. It is the beating," he emphasized, just as the blows upon Ariana were coming particularly hard and heavy, "that gives the metal its tensile strength."

After he pronounced these words, Ariana returned to her accustomed state.

"Now," smiled the Teacher invitingly, "would you like to be one of the Chosen People?"

"'I have tested you in the fires of affliction, says the Lord,'" she murmured. "'I have formed you like gold in the crucible.'"

He bowed his head as if to hide a look of pain and sorrow. "Something like that."

"Then why do so many of the Jews I meet say that God chose them because they were somehow better than the rest?" she asked. "They even say that, when God was looking around for a people with whom to make a covenant, they were the only ones who would sign without reading the contract. That sounds to me like they're the only people who trust God."

"That story is to be found in the Talmud, the commentary on the Torah," he said.

"Torah?"

"The Jewish Bible is what Christians call the Old Testament, with some books in slightly different order. It is called the *Tanakh*, an acronym formed from the first consonant of each word designating its three major divisions: the Law, or *Torah*, the Books of Moses, the first five books of the Bible; the Prophets, or *Nevi'im*, which includes not only such obviously prophetical works as Isaiah, Jeremiah and Ezekiel, but also the books of Samuel and Kings; and all the rest, the Writings, or *Ketavi'im*. The Torah is the most sacred part, and its books—Genesis, Exodus, Leviticus, Numbers, and Deuteronomy—were the earliest to be admitted to scriptural status. That was back toward the end of the fourth century B.C.E. The Prophets were not canonical until the end of the third century B.C.E., and the Writings until the end of the first century C.E. That's why, in the Christian Gospel, Jesus always refers to scripture simply as 'the Law and the Prophets.'"

"Is it all right to talk about Jesus here?" she asked. "I thought he was the black sheep of the family."

The Teacher laughed. "He's as much a part of the Jewish tradition as the Christian. And since Judaism, like Hinduism, has been primarily a cultural tradition, how one lives has been the primary issue, not how one thinks. There are perhaps as many attitudes toward Jesus of Nazareth in Judaism as there are Jews. That doesn't concern us here, however. You'll be meeting the real Jesus soon enough. Now it's time to meet his people, the people without whom he would not have been possible." And then he told her their story.

2. The Chosen People

Sometime in the latter half of the second millennium B.C.E. a small group of barbarians, the Hebrews, escaped from forced labor in Egypt and made their way to what was then known as Canaan, the later Palestine. Joining with some ethnically related indigenous tribes, they set about the painful business of carving some living space out of a land where competition for survival, let alone territory, was fierce. Over the course of several centuries their religion welded them into a united people, and the strength of this unity enabled them to subdue and exterminate their enemies.

Around 1,000 B.C.E. these Hebrews, who now called themselves 'Israelites' after their legendary patriarch who reportedly had wrestled with God, formalized their union by unanimously accepting the authority of a king. The first king, Saul, laid the groundwork, but it was his rival and successor, David, who more than anyone else was responsible for transforming what was still in many ways a loose confederation of tribes into a nation-state; and it was under David's son, Solomon, that Israel reached its cultural, political, and military apex, growing into what later generations would enviously look back upon as the people's one and only empire.

Israel's fall was as meteoric as its rise. After Solomon's death around 930 B.C.E., the empire fractured into a northern kingdom, which inherited the name of Israel as well as ten of the original twelve tribes, but broke away from the House of David; and a southern kingdom, which consisted of two tribes: Judah, the largest and most powerful of all the tribes, the tribe of David and Solomon; and Benjamin, the weakest and smallest, the tribe of Saul. The southern kingdom was known as Judah (from which are derived the terms 'Jew' and 'Judea'), and kept, for better or worse, the lordship of the Davidic dynasty.

Like any two brothers, Israel and Judah got along much better with strangers than each other. The two centuries they existed side by side were years of uneasy alliance at best, and at worst, outright civil war. Sometimes they would join together against a common enemy. More often one would join what should have been a common enemy against the other. Finally, history itself intervened in the form of the Assyrian Empire (roughly present-day northern Iraq), which overthrew Israel around 722 B.C.E. and carted away to its capital, Nineveh, everybody who was anybody of the fallen kingdom—the nobles, the intelligentsia, the businessmen, etc. Thus began the legend of the Ten Lost Tribes of Israel. The Dutch explorers to the New World thought their descendants were to be found among the American Indians, and they also recently have been identified with native Ethiopian Jews. No doubt someday the tabloid journalists will discover them on the moon. There is no mystery about these ten tribes, however. They suffered the same fate as all the other little peoples of the ancient Middle East: if not annihilation, then assimilation.

By keeping very still and by playing off one cat against another, the mouse that had once been the lion of Judah managed to outlast its northern brother by nearly one-hundred and forty years. In 586 B.C.E., however, a briefly resurgent Babylonian Empire, after overthrowing Assyria, did to the southern kingdom of Judah what its predecessor had done to Israel. Its soldiers destroyed Jerusalem, including the temple Solomon had built, and carted everybody who was anybody off as slave to Babylonia (present-day central and southern Iraq). Thus began what came to be known as the "Babylonian Captivity," though it well might not have been known as anything, because the Jews came perilously close to cultural extinction. It is fashionable to speak of the Chosen People as languishing in Babylonia, but what really happened was much more dangerous. They thrived. Thus in 539 B.C.E., when the enlightened Cyrus of Persia overthrew the Babylonians and not only permitted, but encouraged and assisted, those Jews who wished to return to Jerusalem, the wonder is that any took him up on on the offer.

Those who bravely returned to a land not wanting them, having no place for them, and to a city in ruins, came to be known as the "faithful Remnant." From this point on, the idea that the true Jew is not just born a Jew but remains faithful in the face of temptation and persecution, became prominent within the tradition. The Remnant rebuilt Solomon's Temple, along with the rest of Jerusalem, and gradually reestablished Jewish hegemony, under Persian overlordship, over Palestine.

For two hundred years the Jews enjoyed semi-autonomy within the Persian Empire. Then, in 331 B.C.E., on his way to points east, Alexander the Great took this crossroads of three continents for himself.

The Hellenistic culture of Alexander's day was like American culture today, only with taste—everybody wanted it. The Jews were particularly vulnerable to its attraction, because Greek philosophy appeared to be approaching, in its own cerebral way, the same monotheistic outlook at which the Jews had arrived in their more experiential fashion. On the other hand, the Jews were equally sensitive to the dangers Greek cosmopolitanism posed to their status as a people set apart, not to mention the religious and moral threat of Greek polytheism and hedonism. On balance, however, attraction probably outweighed aversion, and it might have only been a matter of time before the unique culture of the Jews went the way of so many other unique cultures of so many other little peoples in a suddenly Graecophile world.

The Greeks, however, got pushy. They tried to force their religion upon the Jews, even going so far as to set up pagan idols in the Jewish temple's inner sanctum, the Holy of Holies. In 165 B.C.E. Judas Maccabeus (nicknamed "the Hammer"), along with his four brothers, led a small and under-equipped but fanatically determined band of guerrilla fighters against several larger and better equipped but half-hearted Greek armies and, wonder of wonders, freed the Jews of the foreign tyranny!

This was the big miracle of *Hanukkah*. The small miracle, the burning of the lamp in the temple sanctuary after it had run out of oil when the rebels retook Jerusalem and reconsecrated the Temple, was later played up by the rabbis at the expense of the other because they did not like Maccabean politics. Simon, the only brother to survive the revolt, was made high priest. His son, John, added the kingship to this office. This violation of the separation of church and state was regarded by the rabbis as sacrilege. At the Council of Jamnia, around 90 C.E., they took their revenge by having the Books of the Maccabees rejected from the Jewish canon.

The Jews enjoyed independence until the Romans, under Pompeii, marched into Jerusalem a century later and made Palestine a tiny but strategically significant backwater of their unprecedented empire.

The relationship between the Romans and the Jews was doomed from the start. For one thing, the Jews had no desire to surrender a freedom for which they had been fighting over a thousand years. For another, the two peoples were temperamentally at odds.

The Romans were the cosmopolitan empire-builders, with a genius for engineering, administration and law. Hence, they regarded the zealous and isolationist Jews as superstitious bigots. Those Jews who attained a certain level of culture by

Graeco-Roman standards managed to impress the pagan aristocracy to no end with their high moral principles and philosophically pure monotheism. Those, however, who continued to regard the most important thing about their Jewishness to be the practices that set them apart from other peoples, and these were primarily the Palestinian Jews, excited hatred and suspicion among Roman patrician and commoner alike.

On the other hand, even those Jews who admired Graeco-Roman culture saw that the Romans had little appreciation for the realm of the spirit, and feared that Roman pragmatism would vitiate the Jewish religious ideals of holiness, justice and truth.

Even though Jews established prosperous communities throughout the Mediterranean world, Palestine, and especially Judea, continued to be their national as well as spiritual homeland. The shores of the Eastern Mediterranean likewise were of supreme strategic importance in the ancient world because they were the crossroads of Europe, Asia and Africa. Thus Palestine became the primary scene of Jewish-Roman conflict and, occasionally, accommodation. After a few false starts, the Romans for a time bent over backwards to indulge the peculiarities of this small but strategically located and inordinately productive segment of its subject population.

The Romans made two exceptions for the Jews that they did not make for any other people in the empire, and both for the same reason. First, except for occasional periods of persecution, they excused this singular people from participation in the cult of the emperor, which required no more than burning a pinch of incense before an image of the emperor, and which to the Roman world in general had no more religious significance than our pledge of allegiance has to most Americans, but to which, like the Jehovah's Witnesses to the pledge, the Jews objected on religious grounds. Second, the Romans excused the Jews from service in the Roman military, to which the subject people objected not because they were pacifists, but because it was impossible to keep dietary and Sabbath restrictions while on active duty in a Gentile army. In other words, the Romans finally decided that all they needed from the Jews was peace to keep the trade routes open and taxes to defray the cost of their military presence. Unfortunately, even the pursuit of these two modest goals proved mutually incompatible.

The Roman method of collecting taxes was primarily to blame. It worked well with those peoples who came to identify their fortunes with those of Rome, and that included almost the entire empire, but not with the Palestinian Jews. The Romans farmed out the business to locals the way some fast-food chains farm out franchises. Rome provided the backup in the way of imperial troops, but otherwise the appointed collector, who through bribes or other service had wheedled his way into the conqueror's good graces, was on his own. He was not even paid a salary. Instead, he was permitted to keep whatever he collected over and above what Rome required. Therefore in Jewish Palestine, where only renegades would take the job, the art of tax-collecting was to milk one's district for all it was worth without destroying the tax base. Of course, a man facing his last year in office would simply ignore this latter concern and grab with both hands. One can imagine how popular this system made Rome.

Thus religious sensibility, hatred of foreign oppression, fear of assimilation, and the burden of exorbitant taxation all combined to place the Palestinian Jews among the most active rebels against the Empire. A series of increasingly serious disturbances culminated in a massive organized revolt in 69 C.E., defeated decisively when the Romans retook Jerusalem in 70 and destroyed the magnificent temple whose rebuilding, begun under Herod the Great in 19 B.C.E., had been completed barely seven years before. The famous Wailing Wall, originally the western side of the foundation, is the only part of the Temple they left standing.

"That's a place very holy to Jews, isn't it?" Ariana interjected.

"Yes, and to Muslims as well," replied the Teacher. "The Shrine of the Dome of the Rock, where Muhammad is supposed to have touched down on his legendary night journey from Mecca, now stands at the site of the ancient Temple. If Christian fundamentalists, who look to the rebuilding of the Temple as a harbinger of Christ's second coming, and Jewish extremists ever persuade the Israeli government to demolish the Dome of the Rock to make way for a new Temple, there might well ensue World War III."

The Teacher gave Ariana a moment to ponder the gravity of this situation.

"Incidentally," he went on, "the monastic community of Essenes and the Christian Church in Jerusalem perished in, respectively, the prelude and aftermath to this revolt. Then again, in 132, a messianic pretender named Bar-Kochba won the adherence of the Jewish people and led them to even greater destruction. By the time the Romans mopped up the remains of Bar-Kochba's forces, they had had enough of Jewish recalcitrance and, except for a few tiny communities of scholars, expelled all Jews from Palestine,. Thus began the Great Diaspora, the Dispersion, the end of the Jewish homeland in Palestine until, eighteen centuries later, the establishment of the modern nation of Israel."

This was the substance of the Teacher's outline of the history of ancient Israel. Arriving at this point, he fell silent, as if to invite questions.

"What do you mean, 'messianic pretender?'" she asked.

"*Messiah* is a Hebrew word that means 'anointed one.' In ancient Israel, the term applied to the king and high priest, each of whom was anointed with a special oil or chrism. It was believed that along with the oil came a special blessing from God that aided in the fulfillment of regal or sacerdotal duty. Later on, in what Christian theologians call the Intertestamentary Period, the time between the last of the 'Old Testament' prophets and John the Baptist (roughly 200 B.C.E. to first century C.E.), the term came to refer to a man whom God would raise up to be his instrument of salvation. But more of that later!" he exclaimed. "Did you see a pattern in the Israelites' history?"

She thought for a moment. "Nothing but the obvious one."

"Which is?" he persisted.

"The Chosen People are like a punch-drunk fighter who keeps coming back for more and doesn't know when to quit."

"Yes," he echoed in pride and sorrow, "they keep coming back for more. Thus, to many Jews and Gentiles alike, this history is a miracle. Many little peoples rose and fell in the pressure cooker that was the ancient Middle East; but none, to my knowledge, came back from near-extinction so frequently as the Jews. If not miraculous, their history is, at the very least, unique."

"But it doesn't end with the Romans, does it?" she asked softly.

"No," he confirmed solemnly, "it does not. In fact, it gets much worse. And much more personal."

If he had been an ordinary man telling an ordinary story, she would have lain down in the soft and fragrant grass to enjoy the narrative. She knew, however, that what was coming was not to be enjoyed, so she sat bolt upright and gave him the appearance as well as the substance of complete attention.

3. The Holocaust

"You have heard of the Holocaust?" His whisper was so out of character that it stunned here like a shout.

"The slaughter of ten million innocents in the Nazi death camps," she replied, "six million of them Jews."

"And six million of them simply because they were Jews!" he exclaimed, shaking his head. She opened her mouth as if to speak, but closed it again without sound. "What is it?" he queried, ever observant.

"I have a question, but I don't know if I should ask it."

"Especially when it comes to the Holocaust," he declared, "all questions need to be asked."

"I have encountered many earthbound spirits with memories of the Holocaust. Many of them blame Christianity."

"Is that surprising?"

"No," she admitted, "but I wanted to ask if it was true. Is Christianity to blame?"

"I can only give you the facts. When you see Kristos, you can ask what he thinks."

She nodded. "But Hitler wasn't a Christian, was he?"

"No," the Teacher agreed. "Even though he was baptized a Catholic at birth, he hated Christianity, and planned to do away with it altogether after his other enemies were defeated. An important difference must be noted here, however. To Hitler, Christianity was an ideology, and to eliminate it one had only to get rid of Christian ideas."

"From what I've heard of the state of the world," Ariana interjected, "Christians have already done that themselves."

A bitter smile played about the Teacher's lips, but he merely nodded and went on. "To Hitler, Judaism was a people. To eliminate Judaism, one had to get rid of the people!"

"I see," was all Ariana could think to say.

"No, Hitler certainly was not Christian," repeated the Teacher, "and neither was National Socialism; but it was no accident that almost all of the German churches supported Hitler, and that the Papacy signed a concordat recognizing the legitimacy of his regime. Let me give you a sense of the magnitude of the problem, and then we will consider its causes. First, have you heard that so many Jews went into banking and moneylending in medieval Europe because they were greedy?"

"Yes, I've heard that."

"Well, in late antiquity, the North African Jews were the farmers who grew the grain that fed the Roman Empire. Then, in the Europe of medieval Christendom, the

Jews were forbidden to own land. They were excluded from one profession after another until, apart from manual labor, moneylending alone remained. Both Jews and Christians, you see, understood the Biblical prohibition against usury, lending money at interest, as applying to financial relations with their coreligionists but not others. Since Jews were in the minority, and since they had communities all along the trade routes from Europe to Asia, they naturally became, in the absence of other gainful employment, the bankers of medieval Christendom. Later, of course, Christians overcame their scruples when they realized they were missing out on too much of a good thing and forbade Jews in many countries to engage in banking as well. This brings me to my first point: A Jew in Christiandom has no security of profession. This means not only can one lose one's job without notice, which is something everyone faces; but one can be forbidden to practice one's profession altogether!"

"You're using present tense," she observed.

He nodded. "It happened in Nazi Germany a scant half-a-century ago. It could happen in Eastern Europe, or anywhere else for that matter, today. My second point!" he announced before she had time to question him further. "Do you know what happened in 1492?"

"Columbus sailed the ocean blue?" she giggled despite, or perhaps because of the gravity of the subject at hand.

"Yes," he smiled briefly, "that is widely known. But what is not so widely known is that in that same year his royal patrons, Ferdinand and Isabella of Spain, along with the ruler of Portugal, succeeded in overthrowing the last of the Moorish kingdoms on the Iberian Peninsula. Did you know that Spain and Portugal were mostly Muslim lands for over seven hundred years?"

She shook her head in genuine amazement.

"In fact, many Jews fled to Spain, as well as other Muslim lands farther east, to escape Christian persecution. Contrary to common Western opinion, the Muslims, as their holy book commands, were as a rule far more hospitable to Jews and Christians than Christians ever were to Muslims and Jews. As a case in point, one of the first acts of the Spanish Crown after establishing its sovereignty throughout the land was to decree that any non-Christian who did not become Christian within three months would be either exiled or imprisoned. Most of the few Moors left after the *Reconquista* knew what to expect from the Christians and emigrated to Muslim North Africa; but the choice was not so easy for the Jews. Many skilled artisans who could ply their trade elsewhere did leave. Many ironworkers of Spain, for example, went to Italy and settled around their foundries. The Italian word for foundry is *ghetto*. Many of these Spanish Jews, however, had developed great wealth in the centuries their families had been in Spain. The wealth was in the land, and therefore could not be taken into exile. Thus many Jews converted, and they and their descendants were discriminated against as *conversos* by the 'Old' Christians."

"So now Judaism begins to be a race!" interjected Ariana, another piece of the puzzle of Christian anti-Semitism falling into place.

"Yes," affirmed the Teacher. "And many of the Jews who converted continued to practice Judaism in secret. These came to be known to the Spaniards as Marrano Jews. It isn't clear whence the term derived, but it came to mean the equivalent of 'swine.' Many of these converts fell prey to the Inquisition, but that's a story I'm sure Kristos would prefer to tell. The second point, in any event, is that to be a Jew in

Christian Europe means to have no security of homeland. Every country of Europe has expelled its Jews at one time or another. Jews were forbidden to live in England, for example, from the time of the Magna Carta in the thirteenth century to the time of Oliver Cromwell in the seventeenth. They have been batted back and forth across Europe like ping-pong balls."

He paused to permit questions, but she had none. There was nothing to be asked or said.

"Now my last point," he resumed. "Have you heard of the Crusades?"

"Yes, but I'm not sure what they were," she replied. "Something about Christians trying to force their religion upon the Muslims?"

"They were fought against the Muslims," he clarified, "but they were not wars of conversion. In the eleventh century a shake-up in the Muslim world led to the closing of pilgrim routes to Palestine to European Christians. Taking this as a stain upon the honor of Christendom, the Pope called for a war to reconquer, or 'liberate,' the Holy Land, especially Jerusalem and environs, so Christians wishing to visit the site of their Lord's earthly existence would not be at the mercy of the unsympathetic infidel.

"Thus, at the Pope's request, nobles and warriors from all of Western Christendom gathered together in northern France and western Germany to free the Holy Land from the barbarous Turks. They were filled with fervor for the cause of Christendom, ready to fight and die in the service of Christ, though most of them also thought it would not be such a bad thing if they picked up a little land and plunder for themselves along the way. There was only one problem. The devilish infidels, whom they were lusting to despoil and annihilate, were many hundreds of miles and a long, dangerous and toilsome journey away. How were they going to let off a little of their fanatical steam before pressure built up to explosive proportions? The solution some of them found was to go out and slaughter defenseless and innocent European Jews.

"Admittedly, some Crusaders had just grievance against some Jews. Many a poor knight had had to borrow money at exorbitant interest to equip himself for the expedition. There was no guarantee, however, that the debtor would return and repay the debt; and the marauding Crusaders did not kill only moneylenders, but men, women and children indiscriminately, simply because they were Jews. Admittedly also, some German archbishops, who had good relations with the Jews in their archdioceses, shielded some would-be victims and prosecuted some of the offenders. The fact remains that most of the culprits got away with slaughtering up to ten thousand Jews without a word of protest from the Pope, who personally had nothing against the Jews, but did not wish to risk losing support for his Crusade. And when the Crusaders reached the Holy Land and took Jerusalem after a bitter siege, they massacred its civilian population—Jews and Muslims, old men, women and children."

"And this brings you to your third point," she said sorrowfully.

"Yes. To be a Jew in Europe is to have no security for one's very life. The massacres at the beginning of the First Crusade (which, by the way, have generally been relegated to a historical footnote) were one of the earliest instances of what came to be known by an old Russian term for 'thunderous'—*pogrom*. A pogrom could be anything from the boys getting together on a Saturday night and going down to the Jewish quarter, the ghetto, to have some fun by scaring to death some old Jewish men, raping some young Jewish girls, burning a few synagogues, and hanging some young Jewish men . . ." He seemed to lose himself in thought for a moment. "Anything from such a relatively innocent pastime to the kind of mass slaughter accompanying the First Crusade. Sometimes the violence was condemned by civil governments. Usually it was tolerated, and often actively encouraged, presumably to keep the people's minds off of the real sources of their troubles."

"I had no idea it was such a hardship to be a European Jew," she said.

"Was?" he corrected. "In many places, it still is. That is the dark side of *glasnost*. Stalin was preparing to deport all Soviet Jews to Siberia, where they would have quickly died of cold and starvation, when he died."

"That was lucky!" cried Ariana.

The Teacher nodded knowingly, as if he thought "providential" would be more apt.

"Nevertheless, the Soviets outlawed anti-Semitism and gave Jews, in theory and often in practice, equal protection under the law. With the demise of the Communist regimes, anti-Semitism is once again rearing its ugly head in Eastern Europe. The threat of renewed violence, more than anything else, fuels the emigration of Soviet Jews to Israel. And, of course, the Holocaust itself took place a scant half-century ago."

She closed her eyes, trying to fathom the magnitude of it all. When she opened them, she had but one question. "Why?"

"Why?" the Teacher echoed. "Why did it happen, or why did anti-Semitism become part and parcel of Christiandom? Why do people hate, or how did hate become the flip-side of the religion of love?"

She sighed in despair. His restatement of her question made her realize how impossible it was to answer.

"I will give you a historical explanation for Christian anti-Semitism," he resumed unexpectedly. "Later on we will explore its psychology, and perhaps then you'll find out why people hate. Given your acquaintance with Christians, how might you guess Christian anti-Semitism got started?"

She had encountered many a hate-filled earthbound spirit, and so could answer without hesitation, "With the crucifixion of Jesus."

"Yes, with the idea that the Jews were the killers of God's Son. Such a concept is of course morally absurd, even if we take the worst possible case, that all the Jews of Jesus' generation were accomplices in his death. How could such a crime cast guilt upon their children and children's children? How do you think the earthbound Gentiles would feel if they were held responsible for their ancestors' crimes? But did the Jews kill Jesus?"

"Jesus himself was a Jew," she said.

"Exactly, and all his first followers were Jews as well. According to the Christian Gospel account, Jesus was the victim of a judicial murder instigated by Caiaphas, the Jewish high priest, and aided and abetted by the Sanhedrin, the Jewish Council of Elders. According to history, however, Biblical or otherwise, who actually put Jesus to death, and for what reason?"

"The Roman governor of Judea," she replied, "Pontius Pilate, I think for sedition."

"Yes, the Romans. Very early on in Christianity, however—not in the first generation of Christians, certainly, because they were all Jews, but in the second and third generations—there was a move to shift responsibility for Jesus' death from the Romans to the Jews. One sees this especially in the last-written gospel, John. One could go through John and, unless one read carefully, go away with the impression that Jesus was not a Jew. This gospel makes a historically absurd distinction between Jesus and his followers, on the one hand, and the Jews on the other."

"If the Romans were responsible for the execution of Jesus, why did the Christians come to blame the Jews?"

"I was going to ask you that," he said in a way that made her feel uncomfortably on-the-spot.

"I don't know," she said simply.

"Where there is a crime, there is a motive," he persisted, with that ironical gleam in his eye she had come to know and dislike. "What could be the motive?"

She had no answer.

"Who were the Christians trying to convert?"

"The Jews?" she said, simply to give him an answer, but without real conviction.

"Only the first-generation of Christians, who were themselves Jews. The Jews at this later point were nothing politically, and the Gentile Christians had no personal stake in winning them over."

She suddenly saw it. "The Romans!"

"Yes, the Romans, and by that is meant all the peoples of the empire. Is it good public relations," he asked archly, "to accuse the people whom one is trying to convert of murdering the god to whose worship one is trying to convert them?"

She shook her head.

"Christian anti-Semitism originated in a face-saving device that eventually enabled Christianity to become the official ideology of the Roman Empire," he continued. "The interesting thing is that originally no one regarded the denunciation of the Jews as anything more than that. Certainly one finds the early Church patriarchs damning the Jews as 'Christ-murderers' and 'God-killers,' sometimes in extremely eloquent style; but nobody took it seriously."

"What do you mean?" she asked incredulously. "Everyone thought it was a joke?"

"No," he replied, "as an idea they took it seriously enough, and even believed it; but the peoples of the Mediterranean have always been highly sophisticated, and here they had no difficulty instinctively distinguishing the demands of faith from the realities of everyday life."

"Render unto Christianity the things that are Christianity's," she paraphrased, and they both laughed.

"They knew Jews, you see," he continued, "knew that they were a bit peculiar about religion, but otherwise hard workers and good citizens. So in church on Sunday they could well believe that the Jews had murdered Christ, but in their everyday lives they continued to rely on Reuben and Isaac and Samuel for goods and services, and even sociability and friendship."

"An ideological anti-Semitism," she encapsulated.

"Exactly, as long as one does not confuse it with that of the Nazis."

"Merely ideological," she corrected herself. "So how did it become more than that?"

"All I can do is give you my theory," he replied, and with a flourishing sweep of her arm she bade him proceed. "As I said, the peoples of the Mediterranean were too sophisticated to take the Church's official anti-Semitism seriously. One can still see that in Italy today. As a rule, the Italian people, especially in central and southern Italy, though they believe that the Jews killed Christ, are not in their day-to-day lives anti-Semitic. To illustrate my point, do you know who Mussolini was?"

She knew all the great tyrants of history. The earthbound spirits seemed so much prouder of their criminals than their saints. "The Fascist dictator of Italy during World War II," she replied. "Il Duce," she added in her best Italian accent.

"Yes, and in the 1930's and much of the 20's as well. Mussolini eventually became Hitler's closest . . . Well, 'friend' is hardly the right word. Hitler didn't really have friends."

"Crony," she supplied.

A faint smile indicated approval. "He was Hitler's closest crony. Nevertheless, despite Hitler's repeated requests and eventual demands, Mussolini would not hand over the Italian Jews to the Nazis."

"Why?" she asked. "Even if Mussolini wasn't anti-Semitic, his power depended on Hitler. Why refuse to satisfy *der Fuehrer's* little whim?"

"For two reasons. One, some of Mussolini's wealthiest backers were Jews; and, two, it would have made him even more unpopular with his own people than he already was for getting them into the war. Not until Mussolini was overthrown and the Germans marched into Italy were the Italian Jews rounded up and deported to the death camps, and then it was done directly by the Germans in the face of much Italian protest. Curiously enough, however, the Pope, Pius XII, did not say a word."

"He feared what the Germans would do to the Church," she remarked.

"Probably that's all it was," the Teacher agreed, "for popes generally have not been anti-Semitic; but recently I've heard that this same Pius XII aided Nazis to escape the war trials so they could be trained in South America, secretly of course, to take part in the battle against Soviet Communism in Eastern Europe."

"That's anti-Communism, not anti-Semitism."

"Perhaps," he mused. "Who knows? In Eastern Europe, the two have often been fellow travelers. Whatever his motives, I leave you to judge how much his silence was in keeping with the spirit of Christianity's founder, whose earthly representative he was supposed to be."

"I don't know yet," she said pensively, and then brightened. "Anyway, I accept that part of your theory. What's the rest?"

"I don't offer it for acceptance!" he said with unexpected petulance. "I want you to think about it!" Then he resumed his exposition in somewhere between a neutral and ironical tone. "What happened to the western half of the Roman Empire in the fourth, fifth, and sixth centuries?"

"It was overrun by barbarian tribes," she replied. "The Goths, Visigoths, Vandals, Franks, Lombards—mostly Germanic tribes." No one could fault her for not knowing her barbarians.

"Right," he confirmed. "As they came into the empire, they converted to Christianity. These barbarians, however, were not sophisticated like the Mediterranean peoples. When they were told that the Jews had murdered their new god, Christ, that they were the tools of Satan and the embodiment of evil, they believed it. They didn't know what a Jew was; but, when they finally encountered Jews, they saw in them, first and last, the murderers of Christ."

"So, you're saying the barbarian influence led to the development of Christian anti-Semitism."

"I'm saying that the crucial factor from a historical perspective was the conjunction of the merely ideological anti-Semitism of early Christianity with barbarian simplicity." He paused to let that sink in.

"It makes sense," she said at length, "but it's not enough."

"No, it's not," he agreed. "As I said, it is the historical perspective. We have yet to explore the psychological perspective, and I promise you that we will in good time. Confining ourselves to the historical for now, however, what conclusions can be drawn?"

"That historically Christianity is a lie," she replied with no hesitation.

"The religion that preaches love and practices hate?" he queried, and she nodded confirmation. "There's some truth to that judgment," he said, "but, also historically, it's one sided. You see, anti-Semitism became part and parcel of Christianity in those countries where the barbarian tribes settled and dominated—Spain, Germany, France, Austria, Poland, Russia, etc. It never developed in central and southern Italy, which was shielded from barbarian settlement by the Popes. Nevertheless, even though the majority of the German churches supported Hitler in most of his nefarious enterprises, they did unite in successfully protesting against his notorious "euthanasia" program for the mentally and physically disabled. There were also German Christians who embodied the genuine spirit of Christianity by, for example, hiding Jewish children even while knowing full well that, if found out, their own children would be hanged before their eyes and they themselves carted off to the death camps. It is true that France is so anti-Semitic that many of the French, who hated the Germans with a passion born of seven decades of almost constant and extremely bloody warfare, actively assisted the Nazi Gestapo in rounding up the French Jews. Nevertheless, many Frenchmen risked their lives to save Jews from Hitler, including an entire Huguenot village that hid thousands through the entire four years of German occupation, simply out of a sense of Christian duty."

"So, if you look at quantity, Christianity is the religion of hate," she remarked. "If you go by quality, it's love."

"You could put it that way. The majority of European Christians throughout history have equated loving Christ with hating Jews."

They both reflected in silence, and she felt that maybe, just maybe, he was not making things more difficult than they had to be, that the discomfort he caused in her was a necessary means to the end of understanding.

"It reminds me," she said, "of an earthbound soul I met who was saved in just the way you described. As a child he, a German Jew, was taken in by Christians. He said he could not understand—and by that he did not mean that he found it admirable and beyond his own strength, but just impossible to comprehend—how they could have risked the lives of their own children to save that of a stranger's child."

The Teacher regarded her with heightened respect. "There, in a nutshell, is an essential difference between Judaism and genuine Christianity."

"This genuine Christianity must be extraordinary," she said. "I don't think I've ever met anyone who practiced it."

He simply looked at her as if he knew far more than she about this matter. "It's not my place to say. Now we are talking about Judaism."

4. All in the Family

"Books seem to be so much more important in Western religion," she said, in the spirit of scholarly inquiry mandated by his last remark.

"Yes," he said, giving modest encouragement.

"I mean, in Hinduism you have the ancient hymns to the gods still used in rituals today, and you have lots of holy books in both Hinduism and Buddhism; but I get the feeling they are just . . ." She hesitated, groping for a word.

"Crutches?" he suggested.

"Yes!" she laughed in amazement. "How did you know? You weren't there! Or were you?"

The Teacher smiled enigmatically, but otherwise ignored the query. "Why are books so important, not only in Judaism, but all three forms of ethical monotheism?" he restated her question. "Perhaps because ethical monotheism arose out of barbaric and semi-barbaric cultures for whom writing was something strange, foreign, and therefore divine."

"Perhaps," she said disappointedly. She had come to expect from him something more profound.

"That's true of Hinduism as well," he added in deference to her disappointment, "so perhaps it's because ethical monotheism is about personal relationship with a personal God, and scripture is perceived as his messages."

"The words are preserved the way a lover might preserve letters from his beloved?"

"A dead beloved," he qualified.

"Why dead?"

"Because, while the beloved is alive, one turns not to the letters but the beloved," he explained.

"And anything the beloved says takes priority over his letters!" she exclaimed. "But that would mean that those who think the writings are the authority really believe in their hearts that God is dead!"

"Or absent, or unable to communicate in any other way. That's fundamentalism."

"Does that mean that all ethical monotheism is fundamentalist?" she asked.

"Not at all! As you no doubt will see, Islam may be regarded as essentially fundamentalist, but fundamentalism in Judaism and Christianity is a recent phenomenon, the result of special historical circumstances in which people feel unusually insecure. Christian fundamentalism is strong, especially in the United States; but Jewish fundamentalism at this point is confined mostly to a few extreme right-wing sects in Israel. Remember what I said about interpretation?"

"Then how do Jews interpret their Bible?" she asked. "Is everyone free to do it his or her own way?"

"When it comes to personal belief about the metaphysics of God and human nature, yes, everyone is pretty much free to believe what he or she wants. In that respect, Judaism is as open as Hinduism, and as unconcerned with metaphysical speculation as Buddhism. The essential question that unites all Jews is, 'How is a Jew to live?' The question of morals is paramount. All religious Jews agree that goodness comes through partnership with God. In other words, the three basic styles of Judaism split over the question of how to interpret the *Torah*, God's 'guidance' or 'law.'"

"Styles?"

"There are institutional movements that represent, and might even be said to embody, the three styles, yet do not encompass them."

"I don't understand," she said. "There's Orthodox, Conservative, and Reform. Isn't each one an organized movement? When you join, don't you join a kind of church?"

"Although there are Jews of every nation, race and clime, ethnically there are two basic groups," he replied in his typically elliptical fashion: "Ashkenazim, from central and eastern Europe; and Sephardim, from the Mediterranean. The three-fold division you mention applies to the Ashkenazim. Ashkenazi Orthodoxy is really a subset of the Rabbinical Judaism, to which most Sephardim subscribe, that began with the Pharisees in the late first century. The Temple and priesthood were gone, Christianity was on the rise, and the rabbis were circling the wagons against an increasingly hostile world. Around the year 90, they gathered together at Jamnia to fashion the Law into a vehicle for carrying the tradition through hard times."

"So, then, Rabbinical Judaism is not just obedience to rules," she remarked.

"No," he replied, "not unless it degenerates into fundamentalism; and that, on the whole, it has not yet done. The basic difference between Rabbinical or Orthodox and liberal or Reform Judaism is not that the former takes the *Torah* literally and the latter interprets it. Rabbinical Jews are as sophisticated about that issue as their Reform siblings. The difference, as both parties understand, is in principles of interpretation. Do you know what *kosher* means?"

"It applies to food, I think. It means the food is blessed by a rabbi and certified for Jewish consumption."

"Literally it means 'pure' or 'clean'," he corrected her, "but that's close enough. And what are some of the dietary restrictions associated with keeping kosher?"

"No pork, no seafood, no juicy steaks . . ."

"'You shall not eat an animal in its blood,'" he interjected.

She thought that was a disgusting way to put it, even if it was Biblical, but she held her peace. "No French cooking," she smiled. "No eating or cooking meat and dairy products together, or even cooking them in the same utensils after those utensils have been washed."

"Very good," he commended. "Now, the prohibitions against pork, seafood, and eating of blood are all straightforwardly set forth in the Torah, but it contains no general prohibition against eating or cooking meat and dairy products together. Have you read the Torah?"

"Only Genesis and Exodus," she replied. "The other books have too many lists," she added, making a face.

"Well then," he continued, "you are in a position to guess whence this rule is derived, because the passage can be found in Exodus."

"I can't guess," she protested feebly. "I haven't the slightest idea."

His silence said that he was not buying her excuse, so she searched her memory. The only passage that said anything about cooking meat and dairy products was one she had always found enigmatic in the extreme; but, in lieu of anything better, she offered it now. "'You shall not boil a kid in its mother's milk?'"

"Precisely! No doubt this commandment originally referred to some pagan sacrificial ritual."

"How did the command not to boil an animal in its own mother's milk come to mean one couldn't boil any animal in any milk?" she asked.

The Teacher looked like a comic delivering the punch-line. "By the operation of the basic principle of interpretation in Rabbinical Judaism, the 'hedge' or 'fence' around the Law. Orthodox Judaism conceives of itself as a series of concentric fortifications protecting what is holiest in all Judaism, love of God. Love is protected by justice, meaning that if you deal justly with your fellow human beings, you automatically are living in love of God. Justice is guarded by the Law . . ."

"So, if you live in obedience to the Law," Ariana interjected, "you're automatically dealing justly with men."

The Teacher smiled in acknowledgment. "And now we come to the hedge around the Law," he continued. "According to this principle, the Law is so holy that one should arrange one's life in such a way that never, under any circumstances, will one ever, even unintentionally or accidentally, be in danger of violating any one of its *mitzvot*, or obligations; and Rabbinical Judaism finds six hundred and thirteen *mitzvot* in the Books of Moses. Thus, if one never cooks or eats dairy and meat products together, one will never be in danger of boiling an animal in its mother's milk."

"It sounds a bit extreme," said Ariana.

"Yes, it does," he agreed. "It's the reason Rabbinical Judaism has no representational sculpture. If one never makes a statue of anything in nature, one will never have an idol to worship. By the same token, it's not widely known, but there were no automobiles or telephones back when Yahweh gave the Law to Moses."

She smiled at the bad joke in spite of herself.

"Their invention posed the problem of what to do with them on the Sabbath. Rabbinical Judaism's answer was to play it safe and not use them at all, because their use might constitute work."

"Now I understand," she said, "but how do Conservative and Reform Judaism differ?"

"Conservative Judaism is a middle-of-the-road affair that seeks to combine what it regards as the authentic aspects of both Orthodox and Reform Judaism."

"So, what is Reform Judaism about, then?"

"Reform Judaism began at the end of the eighteenth century, with the American and French revolutions. For the first time in history, Jews were granted full citizenship in at least two Western countries, and had to find a way to participate in secular government and still remain Jews. Their solution was Reform Judaism. It takes as its interpretive principle an idea upon which almost all religious Jews agree—the Law is intended for human welfare, not divine. God gave us the Law not for his benefit, but our own. For Rabbinical Jews the Law, like its divine legislator, is one and holy. Reform Judaism sees the Law as naturally breaking into two parts: the moral law, the Ten Commandments, the ten *sefiroth*, the ten words; and all the other rules and regulations about diet, ritual, marriage, society, etc. The moral law, prohibiting idolatry, murder, adultery, perjury, and so on, is absolute everywhere and at all times. The rest of the Law, however, is bound to a particular culture and historical period. Other cultures and historical periods may pick and choose from among these for what is of value to them."

"For example?" she queried.

"Slavery. The ancient Israelites, like most ancient peoples, had slaves, and the Torah regulates this institution. Those regulations are irrelevant in a society enlightened enough to have abolished slavery."

"Don't the Rabbinical Jews also ignore those rules?" she asked.

"In practice, of course," he replied, "but they have a much harder time making theoretical sense of doing so. And if the Temple were ever rebuilt in Jerusalem . . ."

"World War III!" she interjected.

"Possibly, since the site of the Temple is now occupied by a shrine extremely sacred to Islam. But if it were rebuilt, how could the Rabbinical Jews not reinstitute animal sacrifice? After all, that's what the Temple was for! The irony here is that Rabbinical Judaism owes its dominance to the destruction of the temple, which left the field free for the indestructible and highly portable Torah to become the single unifying force in the tradition."

"So, that's all the difference it makes?" she wondered. "Slavery and sacrifices?"

"No," he laughed, "it makes for real differences in the ordinary Jew's daily life. Take the prohibition against pork, for example. An Orthodox Jew simply does not eat pork because the Torah forbids it. Since the Reform Jew considers dietary restrictions part of the culturally conditioned portion of the law, he might reason to himself that, when Moses received the command against eating pork, people didn't know about trichinosis. They didn't know that, if pork isn't cooked properly, it can cause a deadly and highly contagious disease. By the way," he went off on one of his characteristically convoluted digressions, "did you know that the Black Plague, which wiped out two-thirds of Europe's population in the 14th century, may have passed the European Jewish settlements by because the Jews didn't eat pork? Of course, afterwards they were killed by the surviving Christians for supposedly being the demonic cause of the disease. At any rate, going back to our example, an individual Reform Jew might thus conclude that today, now that people know how to cook pork properly, it's all right to eat it."

"How convenient."

"On the other hand, he might also reason that pork, and indeed meat in general, is no good for anyone, eater or eaten, and therefore it's best to be vegetarian."

"So, Reform Judaism leaves things that matter only to the individual in the hands of the individual," she drew the obvious conclusion.

"Yes," he agreed; "but, more importantly, it regards Judaism's primary mission as bringing the moral law to the world. If a secular government is constituted in accordance with that law, with the principles of justice . . ."

"Like a democratic republic," Ariana broke in.

He nodded. ". . . then Jews may take on the rights and obligations of citizenship."

Ariana pondered. "So, according to the Reform Jews, if Judaism fulfills its mission, it disappears."

"That would seem to be the logical implication," the Teacher admitted. "At least, that's how Rabbinical and Conservative Jews see it."

"Where and when did Conservative Judaism begin?" asked Ariana, as much out of a desire for symmetry as curiosity.

"It has its intellectual antecedents in early nineteenth century Germany," he replied, apparently unperturbed by the digression, "but came into its own in the twentieth century, primarily in the United States. Conservative Jews, one might say, have adopted the philosophy of Reform Judaism and the practice of Rabbinical Judaism, and modified both. They agree with Reform Jews that Judaism should be a force for social justice and progress in the world, and thus that Rabbinical Judaism is too shut off from the world. They agree with Rabbinical Jews that Reform Jews are in danger of losing their cultural identity. They try to strike a balance between the two."

"For example?" she asked.

"They often keep kosher at home," he replied, "but will eat what's available or offered to them when in a restaurant or friend's home."

"Sounds reasonable," Ariana commented. "It seems to me that Reform Jews just want to have things easy."

"Yes," mused the Teacher. "One can argue that Jesus of Nazareth was a prototype of the Reform Jew, and look how easy he had it."

"What do you mean?" she exclaimed. "All the Orthodox and Conservative Jews I've met claim that Reform Judaism is not real Judaism! Even some Reform Jews think that way, and are ashamed of being Reform!"

"There is a common misconception that integrity is a matter of adopting and practicing rules, and that the more difficult the rules and the more rigid one's adherence, the greater one's integrity." He paused for a moment to let that sink in. "Accordingly, religion is about following religious rules, and the more strict and inflexible the rules, the more authentic the religion. However, if religion is essentially about something other than following rules, such as justice or love . . ."

"Or awakening!" she interjected.

"Yes, or awakening," he agreed. ". . . then there is nothing particularly religious about following rules."

"So you have no doubt that Reform Judaism is real Judaism?" she asked, to make sure that she had not gotten lost in the maze of his irony.

"No doubt," he affirmed. "Institutionally, it is younger than Rabbinical Judaism by over half a millennium; but in spirit it is fully as ancient, perhaps even more so. As I said before, Rabbinical Jews bitterly criticize the Reform for taking the Law, which to them is one and holy, and dividing it into the absolute moral law and the culturally relative laws. One finds Isaiah, however, the great prophet of the eighth century B.C.E., making the same distinction. Isaiah was scathing in his denunciation of the religious and political leaders of his day for being so careful to observe all the prescribed festivals and sacrifices, and neglecting the demands of justice. At its worst, Reform Judaism may be accommodation and assimilation; but at its best, it is a voice for reason and justice in the world."

5. Exodus

"That brings up something that bothers me," Ariana took the opportunity to say. "It's been bothering me since we talked about sin as the betrayal of the personal relationship with God. At first I thought it was just one of those things you had to take on faith; but just now you mentioned reason, so I thought maybe it would be kosher to ask after all."

"No pun intended," he smiled, and she smiled back.

"What about the story of the exodus from Egypt? I mean, is that history or just a story? Because if it's just a story, I get the moral, I suppose."

"Which is?"

"Don't mess with Yahweh!"

He nodded noncommittally.

"But if it's a real history," she continued, "I've got some real problems."

Again, he nodded to indicate she should proceed.

"I don't know where to begin. First of all, Moses is ordered by God to return to Egypt forty years after he ran away; but, on the way, the Lord almost kills him, until his wife circumcises their son."

"It's an enigmatic passage, no doubt about that," he agreed, "and probably came from some other source and was worked into Exodus to make a point."

"What point?"

"Figure it out. Moses is Israel's greatest prophet, yet Moses has failed to circumcise his son."

"Not even the greatest prophet is above God's law?" she hazarded.

"Yes, if God won't make an exception for Moses, how can anyone else expect special privileges?"

"But that's just the easy one," she continued. "The Israelites have fallen into slavery, but God sends Moses to lead them out of oppressive Egypt and into the Promised Land. If he really wants to free them, why does he say he will harden Pharaoh's heart and make Pharaoh resist him? Besides, isn't that turning Pharaoh into a puppet, a robot? And if I programmed a robot to commit a crime, I'd be guilty of that crime, not the robot. So why isn't God guilty of Pharaoh's sin against God?"

"You raise an important issue," he said. "That single phrase, 'the hardening of Pharaoh's heart,' has been the subject of perhaps more debate than any other in the Judaeo-Christian Bible. Undoubtedly, the author had God harden Pharaoh's heart to explain how an ordinary man could resist the Almighty."

"Why would he do that?" asked Ariana. "Because he was insecure in his own faith?"

"In a way, yes," replied the Teacher. "Most scholars agree that, even though the material in Genesis goes back further in the oral tradition, Exodus was written beforehand, probably in the court of David around 1000 B.C.E. This is the beginning of Judaism. The author of Exodus is making the astonishing claim that this tribal god of a little people in abject servitude is the almighty creator of the universe!"

"That takes a lot of chutzpah!" Ariana laughed.

The Teacher smiled. "The theme of the hardening of Pharaoh's heart reinforces the doctrine of divine omnipotence."

"It makes sense that it was merely a theological invention."

"Yes, and it is probably true, but it won't help," he declared. "The first rule of Biblical interpretation in the Jewish tradition is to take the text on its own terms, and the text undoubtedly presents itself as a history."

"How so?" she wondered.

"It is extremely careful to locate itself in historical space and time, and it talks of these events as if they were actual causes to later, present-to-the-reader effects."

"Alright," she said, "if it's history, then I don't see any way of explaining or justifying God's behavior."

"Well, suppose there is no way of understanding it. Who are we to question God?"

"My feeling was right, then," she said a little ruefully. "It's just one of those questions you aren't supposed to ask."

"You encounter such questions often?" he asked in amused curiosity.

"All the time!" she replied with some petulance. "It seems every earthbound spirit has loads of them. I put my foot in my mouth all the time."

"Perhaps you're right to do so. Certainly, there's nothing wrong with that so far as Yahweh and the Jewish Tradition are concerned. The first rule of Jewish exegesis, or interpretation of scripture, is to take the text on its own terms. The second rule is to ask the hard questions, the ethical questions, especially about God."

"Then I guess I've asked one."

"You certainly have, but let me make it even harder. What do you think Genesis means when it says that God created human beings 'in his own image?'"

"Not that Yahweh has a body?" she asked in surprise, never having considered this possibility.

"The Mormons believe that each of the three persons of the Holy Trinity has physical form, but mainstream Judaism, Christianity and Islam alike agree that God, as such, is without visible form."

"As such?"

"Simply a concession to the Christian idea of the Incarnation," he explained, "but you'll be learning about that down the line. You still haven't answered my question."

"I don't know!" she cried. "That we are created good?"

"So we lose God's image after we sin?"

She nodded.

"But if we are created in God's image, it is part of our being, not doing. Let me give you a clue. According to Genesis, it is what sets humans apart from animals."

"Reason?" she ventured.

"Reason is part of it," he assented, "but I think 'freedom of the will' gets closer to the heart of it. However, there is no need to quibble over terminology, because these two, free will and reason, are really one. There cannot be one without the other."

"How's that?" she asked, failing to see the intrinsic connection.

"Because reason involves choice and choice reason. It's as simple as that. You cannot make a choice without awareness of possibilities and the probable consequences of your actions. That's reason. You cannot reason about anything without criteria, and you choose the criteria according to which you reason. That's free will."

"And that's what it means to be created in the image of God?" she said, in awe at the idea's implications.

"It is, according to Genesis, what makes us human; but there is one other element to it, one which human beings do their best to forget."

"Responsibility," she hazarded.

"Yes, responsibility. How did you know?"

"After spending time with the earthbound, it was self-evident," she smiled sadly.

"Now," he returned to the main issue, "if one interprets God's 'hardening of Pharaoh's heart' as turning Pharaoh into his puppet or robot, one has a much greater problem than the paradox of God being guilty of sinning against himself. If the essence of Pharaoh's humanity is his creation in the image of God, and that means having free will, then when the Lord violates Pharaoh's free will, he violates Pharaoh's humanity. He commits spiritual rape."

"But didn't Pharaoh deserve it? Hadn't he hardened his own heart?"

"Even if he did deserve it," the Teacher replied, "two wrongs don't make a right."

"If it was necessary to save the world, maybe it was justified."

"The end justified the means?" he pondered. "Perhaps. But a given end can justify a given means only if the means serves the end. Only if turning Pharaoh into a puppet helped save the world could the goal of saving the world justify turning Pharaoh into a puppet."

"Of course," she said as if he had just stated the stupidly obvious, "but how can anyone judge that?"

"You are taking refuge in mystification."

"No I'm not!" she declared. "I'm just pointing out the limits of human knowledge."

"You are arguing in bad faith," he said, and the remark was all the more infuriating because his voice was full of quiet certainty.

"I am not!" she protested. "What does that mean, anyway?"

"The idea that 'hardening of the heart' means turning Pharaoh into a puppet is an interpretation, a human interpretation," he explained. "This human interpretation leads to a theological difficulty, and one invokes the limitation of human understanding to dismiss the inability of human thought to save one's very human interpretation. Religious people argue this way all the time."

"You're right," she said after a moment of reflection. "I was, and they do; but what's the alternative?"

"Honesty with oneself would be a start. Who knows, it might lead to all sorts of unforeseen, even creative, possibilities! Take the issue at hand, for example. Reason, as opposed to mystification, leads to the conclusion that, if hardening Pharaoh's heart means turning him into a puppet, God's behavior is not only ethically unjustifiable, but the very essence of evil. Human beings are evil to the extent that they try to do to other human beings what God alone conceivably could do—strip another of his or her free will. Moreover, God would be working at cross-purposes with himself."

"I still don't see that," she objected cautiously.

"Suppose I am deeply in love, and my beloved turns away from me. I kidnap her and hire a brain surgeon to go inside her head and alter her brain so that afterward she obeys my every whim without question. I have saved the relationship, haven't I?"

"That's absurd!" she cried. "You haven't saved anything! You've destroyed any possibility of ever having a relationship! Any fool can see that. You've made your beloved into a non-person. What kind of relationship can you have with a non-person?"

"Any fool can see it?" he echoed. "Any fool but God?"

After what seemed like an eternity of silence, in which she considered not the truth of what he was saying, for she had understood that immediately, but everyone's chronic inability to see what was right before their eyes, including and especially her own, he continued.

"There can be only one alternative—a different way of understanding the phrase in question."

"But what way?" she queried. "It says what it says. You yourself said we have to take the text on its own terms."

"It says what it says, to a certain point; and it says what we say, to a certain point. The coincidence of those two points indicates a valid interpretation. The question then is whether one can harden another's heart without destroying that other's free will. Consider the following situation. Suppose you've been working hard all day, or playing hard all day, or doing whatever you do all day, and when you arrive home you discover that your husband, mate, dog or whatever has prepared for you a marvelous gourmet candlelight dinner with white tablecloth, soft music, the works. You grunt hello, or maybe you don't even do that, and then go into a side room, close the door, and spend the rest of the evening watching television. Would that harden your mate's heart?"

"Yes," she said, "it certainly would."

"Did you exercise any supernatural powers, pull any metaphysical strings or push any metaphysical buttons to do so?" he persisted.

"No," she replied, "I did it just by acting a certain way in a certain situation."

"Then let us examine the situation in Exodus," he went on. "Who was Pharaoh in his own mind, as well as the minds of his people?"

"King," she replied, "king of Egypt."

"Yes," he agreed; "but, more than that, he was a god. To be more precise, he was the protector god of Egypt, who fought all of Egypt's wars and won all her victories, whether he was anywhere in the vicinity or not. Now, in Pharaoh's own mind, who was Moses?"

"A runaway Hebrew slave?"

"Nothing in the text suggests that Pharaoh knew Moses had ever lived in Egypt; and besides, he had never been a slave."

"The prophet of God?" she tried again.

"Prophet of which god?"

"Of the God," she answered testily, tired of being cross-examined. "Yahweh."

"And whose god was Yahweh?"

"The god of the Hebrews."

"And who were the Hebrews, as far as the Egyptians were concerned?"

"You know who they were!" she shouted. "Why do you keep asking me all these questions?"

"Because you, like most people, don't put two and two together. Who were the Hebrews?"

"They were slaves."

"So," he concluded, "Moses was the representative of a contemptible god of a contemptible people."

"What do you mean, 'contemptible'?"

"When one people fought another people, their protector gods fought. The winning people had the winning god. Therefore, the most powerful people had the most powerful protector god, and vice-versa. What could be more contemptible than for a protector god to let his own people fall into slavery without even giving a fight?"

He was right, she thought to herself. We don't put two and two together.

"Pharaoh is the protector god of the Egyptians," he continued. "The prophet of the weak and contemptible god of the Hebrew slaves demands their release. What would Pharaoh have to do to take this demand seriously?"

"See signs and wonders?"

"He does see signs and wonders, but he still never takes this Hebrew seriously. In a moment of weakness, perhaps, he says he will let the slaves go; but to the end he cannot swallow the bitter pill of their loss, and so leads the Egyptian army to destruction in the waters of the Red Sea."

"He would have to not take himself so seriously," she said with quiet certainty.

"Yes," said the Teacher. "Like Moses removing his sandals before the burning bush of the divine presence, he would have to step outside of his self-image. And what a self-image he had! If most of us drive an economy model, he had a Rolls-Royce. The average person's self-image is not too big, so as not to attract envy or opposition, and not too little, so it won't feel too pinched and cramped. The Pharaoh's self-image, however, was the product, not merely of his own pride and insecurity, but of the collective pride and fear of the Egyptian people, who had fashioned the greatest and most civilized empire the world had ever seen, for well over a thousand years! In the second half of the second millennium B.C.E., when Moses lived, it was starting to decline; but for many centuries it had spearheaded world civilization. The Hebrews, on the other hand, were dirty, unsophisticated barbarians. This is the burden of worldly glory that weighed Pharaoh down."

"It seems impossible for such a man to change," she said.

"Jesus, who was a Jew, did say it was easier for a camel to pass through the eye of a needle than for a rich man to enter the kingdom of God. Many commentators have said that this statement in not characteristic of Judaism, which permits the pursuit of wealth within ethical bounds, but they're missing the point. He's talking about being rich in self-image."

"What a terrible burden such 'riches' are, then!" she cried.

"Perhaps, but he also said that all things are possible with God. Even though people who buy into the pomp and glory of the roles they play are at special risk, look at how tightly the ordinary person clings to self-image and won't travel anywhere without it. Shakespeare, I believe, was right: in aristocracy we simply see ourselves writ large. This story of Pharaoh is about each and every one of us. The Lord hardened Pharaoh's heart by the way he acted in the situation. He could have come down on Pharaoh fast and hard, and that, as they say, would have been that. Instead, he comes to Pharaoh on Pharaoh's own terms, and so 'makes him stubborn' or 'hardens his heart.'"

"His own terms?"

"It's as if Yahweh were saying to Pharaoh, 'You're a god, and I'm a god. Let's dance, let's wrestle, let's have a contest.' And, as everyone knows, in any game of risk one starts out with small stakes and builds up. With every round, something sacred in Pharaoh's world is trashed. The Nile, the goddess upon whom Egypt depends for her livelihood, is turned to blood; the sun, the greatest god of Egypt, is blotted out; and Pharaoh himself, the protector of Egypt, is soundly defeated with the death of the first-born. Also with each round, the temptation for Pharaoh is like double-or-nothing. If he wins this round, all his troubles will go away. We can see that he is being backed into an emotional corner, where in the end he has only two choices which stand out stark, naked and clear. Does he forget about everything he's been taught about himself, every way he's ever thought about himself, and stand naked and vulnerable before the living God? Or does he stay within his self-image, the comfortable self-image, and be destroyed?"

"Why destroyed?" she asked.

"Because the Lord is the truth, and the self-image is a lie. When the truth appears, the lie is gone."

"But that's not fair!" exclaimed Ariana. "He didn't choose to be born Pharaoh!"

"Just as it doesn't matter to the living God what you are in the eyes of the world," he replied, "whether a rich man, street bum, criminal or saint, because he looks only to the heart; so too, in a kind of subconscious and pathetic mimicry, it does not matter to the soul lost in identification with the self-image whether it is positive or negative, beautiful or ugly. The self-image is comfortable because it is what one is used to. Jesus put it well when he said that a dog returns to its vomit."

"One's own terms," she repeated numbly.

"Yes," he confirmed with contrasting enthusiasm. "On this interpretation, far from violating Pharaoh's free will, the Lord respects it so much that he conforms to Pharaoh's own logic, the logic by which Pharaoh himself has chosen to live."

"That's a scary thought," she said.

"Yes, isn't it? It seems that most 'religious' people assume God is an objective reality, like a rock or tree, the manner of whose presence is wholly independent of themselves, rather than a personal reality experienced, as all personal realities must be experienced, through the filter of the self."

"To treat God as an object—that's idolatry," she murmured.

"Yes, that's idolatry."

"But I see why they do it," she continued. "If God comes to us on the terms we set for him . . ."

"The terms we set for life," the Teacher interjected.

"The terms we set for life," she nodded, "then the only way one could see the real and living God would be through one's own heart. One thing I've learned through all of this is that the last thing, the very last thing, a human being wants to deal with is his own heart."

"What do you think has been going on all these millions of years?" he chided gently. "Yahweh has been here all along. It is we, in our spirits, who have gone away from him."

She pondered in silence. "You said, 'On this interpretation.' Is Exodus just a piece of literature we're interpreting? I want to know if everything it describes—the plagues, the escape from Egypt, the giving of the Law on Mount Sinai, Moses' ordering the Levites to slaughter their fellow Israelites—I want to know if all that really happened, or is it made-up stories."

"That you must decide for yourself. If I answered you one way or the other, you'd still have to decide whether or not you agreed with me. All I can say is that the book itself is historical in genre; and since one of the two rules of Biblical exegesis in the Jewish Tradition is to take a text on its own terms, you cannot understand that tradition unless you interpret the book as history."

"But I don't care about the tradition!" she cried. "I want to understand Yahweh."

"Get to the heart of the tradition," he assured her, "and you will find Yahweh."

"Alright," she nodded slowly and deeply. "Alright, I will accept that. You said that the second rule of Biblical interpretation was to ask the hard questions."

"Yes," he said, as if he knew, and welcomed, what was coming.

"Then why did Yahweh have to come down on the Egyptians, or anyone else, at all?" she demanded. "Take the plagues as prime example. They must have hurt innocent people; if no one else, then babies and children. Why not reveal himself in a gentler, more loving way?"

"Love is not always gentle," he frowned, but then suddenly became inordinately, almost maniacally, excited. "An excellent question! Why, indeed, instead of turning rivers to blood and striking down the first-born, did he not heal the sick and raise the dead? If you were God, that's how you would reveal yourself, right? Unless, of course, you couldn't!"

"I don't see why he couldn't," she said. "After all, he is God."

"Suppose you are captain of a lifeboat . . ." he began, and immediately she found herself in the situation, unable to hear his further words because she was experiencing their meaning. She was skipper of a small passenger-and-cargo ship that was heading for port when a squall struck and the vessel started to capsize. Thirty people were in the water, including herself, but one of the lifeboats had been damaged in the storm, and the other could hold fifteen at most. Everyone was looking to her for direction, but at the same time everyone was scrambling for the lifeboat! It was exactly the type of situation she had always assured herself would never happen to her, but still she knew what she had to do. She ordered the strongest crew members to guard the lifeboat, putting on board only the women and children. Whatever seats remained would be apportioned to the men by lot, including both passengers and crew.

She knew that in this age of women's liberation some of the men might protest her command as sexist; but she was old-fashioned in some respects, and also knew that most would accept it out of masculine pride or love for their wives and children. She also wished she could simply order the crew to save the passengers, but she knew them well and doubted that most of them would rise so heroically to the occasion. She also wanted to sacrifice herself so that another might live, but she was the only one who could navigate by the seat of her pants, and all instruments had already been swept overboard. She had doubts and uncertainties, but she was absolutely certain of one thing: it was not only her right, but duty, to do whatever was necessary to condemn fifteen people to almost certain death in the sea so that at least fifteen might be saved. Mercifully, at this point the experience ended and she was returned to the Teacher.

"Would you now agree," he was saying, "that, if Yahweh had to sacrifice some people, even innocent people, to save his creation, he would be justified in doing so, especially since everyone otherwise would be lost?"

"I suppose he could always send the victims to heaven," she said, serious in her sarcasm.

"That's not an option here. The idea of any sort of personal afterlife did not develop in Judaism until the aforementioned Intertestamentary Period, very late in the tradition indeed. And then not personal survival, but revival, became the dominant belief."

"Revival?," she echoed. "Then you're not talking about immortality of the soul?"

"No," he said, "that was essentially a Greek idea, more specifically an Orphic and Platonic idea. When the Greeks brought their culture to Palestine, no doubt many Jews liked the idea that their lives would not end with death."

"I thought they already had an idea of an afterlife," she remarked, "in a place called Sheol."

"*Sheol*, the Hebrew equivalent of the Greek *Hades*, was simply an imaginative representation of the grave, as well as an explanation for ghosts and the appearance of the dead in dreams. The person did not live on in Sheol, only what might be called his after-image. Genesis succinctly portrays the Hebrew conception of a human being in a beautiful image: God formed the first man out of the dust of the earth and then breathed his life into him. The Hebrew word for breath is *ru'ach*. In new Testament Greek this became *pneuma*, and in Latin, *spiritus*. All three words have the same three meanings: 'breath', 'wind', and 'spirit'. So a human being is a creative integration, an organic fusion, of the spirit of God, the breath, and the dust of the earth, the flesh. When a person died, according to ancient Israelite belief, the spirit returned to God and the flesh to the earth, but the person as such ceased to exist."

"So," she deduced, "to the Hebrew way of thinking, a human being is not divisible into a body and a soul."

"Correct," he replied. "A human being is an organic whole, of which 'physical' and 'spiritual' are different aspects, two sides of the same coin. Any division between the two, other than theoretical, is death. Therefore, the only way a person could live again after death would be revival of soul and body, or resurrection of the dead."

"And this idea didn't develop until 200 B.C.E. or later?"

"Yes," he confirmed, "and then it included only the resurrection of the good to share in the kingdom of God. The wicked remained in eternal oblivion. It was left to a more loving Christianity to accessorize the idea with such luxury features as double resurrection, final judgment, and eternal damnation."

She wondered about what seemed to be his anti-Christian bias, but held her peace. "So all this means we can't use any notion of life after death, postponed reward, or anything related to these in interpreting Exodus?"

"Precisely. The issue, therefore, is whether God's treatment of the Egyptians was necessary to his work of salvation. If so, it would be justified, as a ship's captain is justified in sacrificing some so that all are not lost. If, however, there was another, less painful way, then he would not be justified. Do you agree?"

"Yes, I agree," she said, "though I don't see why an all-powerful God couldn't do anything any way he pleased."

"Do you remember what, according to the Jewish perspective, is the source of human life?" he asked.

"Relationship with God."

"Personal relationship with God. When it comes to relationship between persons, that's the only authentic kind. Moreover, according to Genesis, this personal relationship between God and humanity is the source of all life, all creation, not only human. If that relationship is broken, creation spins off into chaos and eventual oblivion. So what must God do to save his creation?"

"Reestablish personal relationship with humanity."

"And what's the first step in establishing personal relationship, whether it's a pick-up in a bar or Yahweh's self-revelation in ancient Egypt?"

"To make contact," she replied.

"To be perceived as a unique individual," he elaborated. "Without in some sense being seen by the other person as a person, how can one hope to have personal relationship?"

"But I feel Yahweh is not violent and brutal," she said earnestly. "How is he revealing himself by doing such violent and brutal deeds?"

"To understand, you must have some idea of how the ancients conceived of the world. They were, on the whole, pagan polytheists. Generally, they believed in a creative power, and many people thought of this power in personal terms, as a creator god. This god, while extremely powerful, was also usually regarded as kind and benevolent, but also very distant, and so as concerned about the lives of human beings as human beings are concerned about the lives of ants."

"Makes sense to me," she commented.

"Yes," he agreed, "this belief was simply an expression of the way the world seems to be. While most of us feel the mystery of life is good, we also feel removed, and even alienated, from it."

Ariana remembered the innumerable lifetimes she had spent, under the tutelage of Ishwara, striving mightily and in vain to overcome that alienation. The Teacher regarded her quizzically, but continued with his exposition.

"The gods to whom people prayed and sacrificed on a daily basis were the nature gods, upon whom depended their very lives. These were personifications of natural forces, such as the sun, moon, winds, trees, stars, and rivers. Since no people has a monopoly upon the powers of nature, no people had a monopoly upon these nature gods."

"That also makes sense," said Ariana.

"Yes," concurred the Teacher, "we do experience nature as a multiplicity of conflicting forces that have little regard for puny us. Other elements in ancient religion, however, were equally understandable in human terms, but not so innocuous. There are two types of gods in particular we have to consider here. The god of judgment, when there was one, punished transgressors of the moral law; and the protector god shielded the people from their enemies."

"When there was one?" she echoed. "You mean some of these pagans had no sense of morality?"

"Not at all!" he proclaimed, more than a hint of disdain in his tone. "Many people today have the strange idea that morality began with the Ten Commandments. Morality, like immorality, is as old as the human race. The meaning of Moses receiving the Law on Mt. Sinai is not that morality came from heaven to earth, but that morality went from earth to heaven. For the first time in history, human beings conceived of the divine not only as one and holy, but morally responsible. To the Greek gods, human beings were toys. To the Mesopotamian gods, they were playthings. The development of ethical monotheism was a revolution in human thought!"

He paused, but Ariana said nothing. She was simply trying to take it all in.

"Pagan polytheism may have its good points . . ."

"As in Hinduism," she interjected.

"Hinduism is *not* pagan polytheism," he said testily, but she had no idea whether he was irritated by her stupidity or her speaking out of turn. "It is mystical monism. It emphasizes the transpersonal depth dimension of being in which all is one. It arose out of pagan polytheism, but so did Judaism. Thus it's crucial to understand pagan polytheism in order to understand Hinduism or Judaism."

If that were so, Ariana wondered why this pagan polytheism had not been explained to her by Ishwara. Given the Teacher's mood, however, she thought it best to keep her question to herself. "I'm all ears," she said merely.

"As I was saying, pagan polytheism may have its goods points; but, from the Biblical perspective, the key to understanding it is the relation between the ethical god, like the Egyptian goddess of justice, Maat, and the protector god."

"Like Pharaoh."

He nodded.

"Consider this situation. Suppose you were a prominent politician against whom several death-threats had been made. Would you want a bodyguard who was constantly asking himself whether you were morally worthy of living?"

"No," she laughed, "I guess not!"

"In effect, that's what ethical monotheism does," he continued. "It combines the creator god, moral god, and protector god into one god."

"Yahweh," she said.

"Yes, Yahweh," he confirmed. "Or Allah, or even the Holy Trinity of Christianity. The important point is that life and righteousness are one, and you cannot have one without the other. That's why ethical monotheism is as radical and rare today as in ancient times, even among those who proclaim most loudly the belief in one God. Paganism, expressed in such sentiments as 'My country, right or wrong' or 'All's fair in love and war,' continues to rule the world."

She pondered. "You mean most people still worship many gods?"

"Yes," he replied, "they worship money, sex, political power, prestige, security, etc. But the important point is that they regard competition as the meaning of life: competition for survival, as the bottom line, power, as the meaning of it all, and glory, as the icing on the cake; whereas ethical monotheism holds righteousness to be more important than life itself!"

"If everyone's just in it for himself, then what's the point?" she queried. "Why does Yahweh bother? Maybe he should give up and send another flood."

"Don't mix theology with mythology," he said mildly. "And don't counsel despair. You must see what Yahweh is up against. Only then will you appreciate the heroism of his battle, the battle of justice against greed and righteousness against fear."

"Do you think he'll win?" she asked with deadly seriousness.

"I have hope."

"What does that mean?"

"I see the possibility."

She studied his face in bewilderment. Of all the heavenly figures she had encountered thus far, he seemed, paradoxically, the most ordinary and the most enigmatic.

"You still haven't shown me why Yahweh had to afflict the Egyptians," she finally said. "If for some reason he couldn't make himself known through kindness, why didn't he punish only the guilty parties?"

"If anything extraordinarily good happened to any or all of their people," he explained, "the Egyptians would have thought it the work of one of their own gods. If anything bad happened to only a segment of the society, it would have been the judgment of their moral goddess. Only if something bad happened to the entire people would they have seen beyond their pantheon to a foreign god, in this case obviously the God of the Israelites."

He let her reflect. "Paganism, then," she said at length, "is division of labor among the gods. Divide and conquer them, so that one may use them for one's own ends."

"Yes," he reiterated, "paganism is about power and the competition for power. Everyone in this story, the Hebrews as well as the Egyptians, spoke the language of power. To make contact, Yahweh had to meet them on their own terms. There's a story of how God offers to reward a great prophet for his services. The prophet asks the Lord to reveal his true nature, and God agrees. First there is a mighty thunderstorm, then a windstorm, and then an earthquake. After each of these phenomena, the prophet asks if that was the revelation of God's true nature, and the Lord says no. But then there arises a soft and gentle breeze, so soft and so gentle that, unless one were paying close attention, one wouldn't even notice it."

"And that turns out to be the revelation of the Lord's true nature?" Ariana surmised.

The Teacher nodded. "Everything else was just to get one's attention."

She was almost mesmerized by this idea. "And where there is one God, one power, there can be no competition," she said in only apparent non sequitur. "Life can't be about competition."

He smiled in profound appreciation. "Radical, isn't it? As radical and revolutionary today as it was three thousand years ago. Of course, one doesn't find full-blown ethical monotheism in Exodus, but it does make a beginning that was to culminate in the proclamation of Isaiah, one of the greatest Jewish prophets, that the Lord desires not burnt offerings and sacrifices, but justice for the oppressed and care for the poor and needy. Moreover, any ancient hearer or reader of this story would have been mystified, as the ancient Israelites were mystified, by the behavior of this jealous God. By the end of the book, it's abundantly clear that Yahweh is the only real player on the field; so why does he let his people fall into slavery in the first place? And why does he so severely judge a people whom he is liberating? The Israelites won't give themselves over to faith, not because they doubt his power, but because they mistrust his intentions. Since he doesn't fit any of the divine paradigms of the time, he is unpredictable. Indeed, it is difficult to see why anyone would invent the idea of such a god, as it brings unease and discomfort to practically all who entertain it."

She knew exactly what he meant, for even now she was wondering what terms she herself might be setting for God.

"It's not all fear and judgment," he laughed, reading her mind from her woeful expression. "In fact, not even primarily. Let me tell you a story that literally gets at the heart of the Jewish conception of the relationship between God and humanity."

6. David

"Have you heard of King David?" he asked.

"I know he was the second king of Israel," she replied, "and that in his youth he fought and killed the giant Goliath. I also remember something about Saul, who was king before him, trying to kill him, and David being saved by Saul's son, Jonathan, who loved David like a brother."

"Yes," confirmed the Teacher, "Saul displeased the Lord, so he ordered Samuel, the great prophet, to anoint David as king in Saul's place. Saul regarded David as a threat to his dynasty, so he hunted the 'rebel' like an animal. Several times Saul fell by chance into David's power, but David refused to harm the anointed of the Lord."

"It would set a bad precedent," she commented cynically.

"Perhaps," the Teacher conceded. "Or perhaps David simply respected the Lord more than his own life. To understand the story I'm about to tell you, you must know two things about David—he was an extremely passionate man, and he belonged heart and soul to God."

She took all this in, and nodded solemnly. Then he began his story.

"After Saul died in battle and David became king, he completed the work that Saul had begun. He decisively defeated the Philistines, a people of Aegean ancestry who were the Israelites' chief competitor; made Jerusalem his capital; and built himself a magnificent palace, thereby setting the monarchy, as well as his own new-born dynasty, upon a firm footing. War was still going on, but now it was offensive. The Israelite army, under Joab, was laying siege to a Syrian city a few hundred miles to the east of Jerusalem, and there was no doubt it would fall sooner or later. Otherwise, the land of Israel was at peace.

"One day, David went up to his rooftop and looked out over the city. They didn't have central air-conditioning in those days," the Teacher explained wryly, "so people took refuge from the stifling heat as well as odors of their houses, in which animals were often kept on the ground floor, by lounging on the roof-tops. There they could enjoy the cool breezes from the sea, which maintained their freshness over unbelievably long stretches of intervening land.

"David, of course, being king, had the highest rooftop in all Jerusalem, for he lived in the most magnificent dwelling, the royal palace he himself had built. As he contemplated the city he had conquered and made the capital of Israel, he must have felt pleased with himself for having persisted through such adversity to achieve so much; but he also must have felt deeply grateful to the Lord. In any event, while looking out over Jerusalem, David spied a beautiful young woman on another rooftop naked, taking a bath. As has been mentioned, David was a passionate man, and so he immediately wanted her; and what the king wanted, he usually got.

"David sent to find out who the woman was, and he discovered that her name was Bathsheba, and that she was the wife of Uriah, who was not a Jew but a Hittite, but who also was a captain in David's army away, conveniently enough, at the siege operation in the east. David then sent for Bathsheba, and she came willingly, so willingly that one might wonder whether she placed herself on that rooftop to be noticed by the king in the first place. For several weeks they enjoyed each other's charms; but then they discovered that David had gotten Bathsheba with child, and the honeymoon was over.

"The penalty in ancient Israel for adultery was death by stoning. David himself, of course, was not in any personal danger. He was, after all, king. Nor would the good citizens of Jerusalem be too disturbed by a discreet affair with a married woman, especially one whose husband was a Gentile. They must, after all, have known already, as the king was in the public eye. If the evidence of adultery on Bathsheba's part, however, became too blatant to be ignored, a mob would certainly stone her to death. Technically, perhaps, they should wait for the baby's birth; but mobs are not noted for patience or rationality, so David stood to lose not only his new love, but also his new unborn child.

"Clever man that he was, David hit upon the obvious solution—arrange for Uriah to be given furlough. What matter if the baby were born seven or eight rather than nine or ten months later? As long as Uriah's own suspicions were not aroused, no one would risk the wrath of the king by accusing Bathsheba; and, as shall be seen, Uriah was the most trusting of men.

"So Uriah came home on leave; but, instead of going in to his wife, he camped outside the palace gate. One can imagine how uneasy this made David. No doubt he wondered if someone had said something to Uriah, and if Uriah were playing for sympathy from the Israelites and plotting a palace coup in revenge. The king could not, however, send immediately for an ordinary field commander. That would severely violate protocol. What pressing need did the great king have of an ordinary field commander that he could not let him enjoy himself for a few days? So David waited, because he was a master at deception, and he knew how to control his fears as long as there was a chance of not giving the game away."

"How could David have been so good at lying if he was really as passionate as you claim?" Ariana broke in.

"That passionate people make poor liars is a common misconception that is patently untrue," the Teacher replied. "Passionate people make the best liars, because they throw themselves into whatever part they play with a passion! David demonstrated this repeatedly in his life, most notably when he took refuge from Saul in the land of the Philistines. One time he found himself utterly alone and defenseless, the helpless prisoner of a Philistine captain who regarded David as his worst enemy and had sworn, metaphorically speaking, it is to be hoped, to drink his blood. David escaped by feigning madness so convincingly that the Philistine dared not satisfy his honor at the risk of offending the gods, whose divine favor and protection fell with special power upon those whom the world today considers insane. Later on, David lived among the Philistines with his arms and men as a renegade Israelite. He massacred enemy settlements by day, leaving no survivors to tell any tales, and by night enjoyed the hospitality of an enemy warlord, whom he convinced he had been raiding Hebrew villages."

Ariana was tempted to ask what David had done to convince the enemy he was crazy, because she imagined it had to have been something outrageously disgusting. However, she decided to be nice and hold her piece. She merely nodded and indicated with a wave of her hand that he should go on.

"To return to our story, after a few days David sent for the cuckold, and again he had to wait in agonizing patience while Uriah, good soldier that he was, gave a detailed report of the military situation at the siege. At last Uriah finished, and David could get down to business. Probably putting a fatherly arm around Uriah's shoulder, he asked, by the way—it had to be 'by the way'—why was he camping out when he could be enjoying the pleasures of wife and home? After all, he would be back in the trenches soon enough.

"Uriah thanked his lord for his concern; but, in good conscience, he could not enjoy the pleasures of peace while his comrades were enduring the hardships of war. Now this was a soldierly sentiment, a noble sentiment, a patriotic sentiment—kind of stupid, but David could not order the man to sleep with his wife! The king was forced to hit upon a deeper, much darker solution.

"David wrote a letter to Joab, ordering him to make a frontal assault upon the city, and to arrange for a new signal of retreat that would be made known to all the Israelite field commanders except for—who else?—Uriah. David knew that the Hittite was too good a soldier to retreat, even if the entire Israelite army were falling back, unless he got the command; and if he did not know the signal, he would not get the command. In fact, David had such faith in Uriah's integrity that he sent the letter by Uriah's own hand, knowing that the Hittite would never think of peeking in the king's mail. Uriah carried his own death sentence back to the army with him.

"A few weeks later, David received a letter from Joab in which the latter reported that the army had assaulted the city and been repulsed, and that, 'by the way,' his servant, Uriah the Hittite, had been killed in the action. Now David had the green light. He sent for Bathsheba, took her to wife, and she gave birth to a beautiful baby boy. Everybody lived happily ever after, except for Uriah, and that did not matter because he was dead.

"Or so it would have gone, most likely, had the Lord not taken a hand in this affair. The Lord now came to Nathan, who was the greatest prophet in Israel at the time. There was no reason to think that Nathan was ignorant of the situation. All of Israel must have known what David had done to Uriah. Of course, people can know things and yet not know them, especially when there is danger in knowing. So it must have been with all Israel. One risked one's life by whispering about it, and to confront the king with his crime was tantamount to suicide! Nevertheless, that was precisely what the Lord commanded Nathan to do.

"Nathan was a good and faithful prophet, so he obeyed the Lord's command; but neither was he stupid, so he did what he could to prepare the soil into which he had to drop the bitter seed of truth. You must picture it all in your mind's eye. David was at home in his palace, happy as a clam, with his new wife and son. Of course, he had other wives and sons, but new ones are always the best. Nathan is announced, and David does not wait on protocol but goes running to greet him. One must remember, David loves the Lord, and has infinite respect for the prophet of the

Lord. He ushers Nathan into the court and says to him, 'To what do I owe the honor of this visit? Ask me whatever you desire. If it is within my power, it's yours!'

"Nathan asked David if he would take an interest in a legal affair in Nathan's own home district. There was a poor man whose sole possession was a ewe, a female sheep, but she was the most beautiful ewe in all Israel. She won all the blue ribbons at all the county fairs. She was without rival. Then there was a rich man who coveted the poor man's ewe. Rich men, of course, having so much more than everyone else, usually are content with their lot; but this rich man would stop at nothing until he got what he did not at all need but passionately desired. At first, he offered the poor man great sums of money and whole flocks of sheep in exchange for the ewe; but the poor man, who loved his ewe, would not sell at any price. So the rich man bribed the local judge, had the poor man thrown into prison on trumped-up charges, and bought the ewe at public auction. The king would immediately understand why Nathan was telling him all this—the local authorities had been corrupted, and only the king could right the wrong.

"When David heard the story he was filled with righteous indignation. 'Who is this rich man?' he cried. 'He's going to wish he had never been born! Who is he?' Nathan turned to David, looked him in the eye and said, 'You! You are the rich man! Thus says the Lord: "For the evil you have done to my servant Uriah, I am going to do evil to you. I will strip the kingdom from you and your descendants."' And then, as if to add insult to injury, he added, '"And you will see your own wives fornicating with strangers."' Finally fell the heaviest blow of all. '"And the child born of your union with Bathsheba will take ill and die!"'

"At this moment, David was faced with a forced option. He knew it, Nathan knew it, and all the courtiers present knew it—to kill or not kill Nathan. Nathan was speaking as a prophet, and the penalty for false prophecy was death. If David cared to deny the charge, he had to have Nathan put to death.

"To David's credit, it entered neither his mind nor heart to do Nathan the least harm. David loved the Lord, and had infinite respect for the prophet of the Lord; and who better than David now knew how brave and true a prophet Nathan was! Not because Nathan knew of David's crime—all Israel knew!—but because Nathan had the courage to face him with his guilt. David said simply, 'The Lord has spoken justly. The Lord must do what is right in his own eyes.'

"Nathan left, and David's new son fell ill. David went in to the sick bed. He would not eat, he would not sleep, he poured ashes on his head and tore his clothes into tatters, and he cried out to the Lord to do with David whatever he willed, only save his son! The boy died. David arose, went into his chambers, bathed, put on new clothing, and went into the banquet hall to have a royal meal. His courtiers were amazed. To them it was a complete reversal of nature. They asked him, 'Why did you mourn when your son was alive? And now that the boy is dead, why do you not mourn?' And David replied, 'While my son lived, there was a chance the Lord would repent of his judgment. Now that my son is dead, who am I to question the will of the Lord?'

"Then the Lord once again came to Nathan, and commanded him to go to the king and say, 'Thus says the Lord: "For having repented from your heart for the evil you did my servant Uriah, I have repented of my judgment against you. Though there will be troubles in your reign and in those of your descendants, I will not strip the kingdom from you. On the contrary, I will confirm it to you and your descendants as long as they walk in my way."' As if to set the divine seal upon this promise, Bathsheba again bore David a son, and this one they called Solomon, who succeeded to David's throne, and under whom Israel reached its height of power and glory as a kingdom.

"So," concluded the Teacher, pointing up the moral of his story, "Moses may have been the greatest prophet of Israel, and Solomon its greatest king; but I would say that David was its greatest mensch, its greatest human being."

"What he did to Uriah was terrible!" she exclaimed, though not in protest.

"Yes, that can't be excused," he admitted. "In fact, I would say it was the worst crime any king of Israel ever committed; and, if you look at their record, you will see many terrible crimes. David let his passion get ahead of his reason, and Uriah suffered the supreme penalty as a result. It is a sorry tale of adultery, betrayal, and murder. No, it cannot be excused. Nevertheless, one can't help wondering what Saul, David's predecessor, would have done in his place. In his youth, he would have feared Nathan and probably put Bathsheba away in an attempt to excuse and expiate his crime. In his maturity, he wouldn't have hesitated to put Nathan to death. David did neither. He knew there was nothing evil in his love for Bathsheba. What he did to Uriah was the sin, and there was nothing he could do to make it up to the victim. Saul was like the son who respects his father and tries to please him, but never understands that what his father really desires is love. David, on the contrary, is the son who can argue and fight with his father, but also joke and sing and play with him, because he loves his father and has his father's heart. The Lord in his mercy chastises David, and teaches him the lesson that he can have no lasting relationship with God if he does not show justice toward his fellow human beings. This is literally the heart of Judaism—not the following of strict rules or the wearing of funny clothes, but the heartfelt relationship with God."

7. The Left and the Right Hand

"So God forgives criminals if they love him, and rejects righteous men if they don't?" she protested. "I thought you said Judaism was about justice. I don't see the justice in that!"

"Can one love God and neglect righteousness," he rejoined, "or be truly just without loving God?"

"David neglected justice," she proclaimed, "and yet you hold him up as humanity's primary role model."

"David got ahead of himself!" the Teacher laughed, but then suddenly turned serious. "David's real test came when Nathan confronted him. Someone who loves justice does not make excuses for himself when he has done an irreparable wrong. Nor does he seek to hide from the consequences to himself."

"David may have made no excuses," she objected, "but he did try to avoid at least part of his punishment by begging for the life of his son."

"Yes," the Teacher smiled ironically, "by imploring God to do his worst to him instead. I can see I've hit a sore spot. From here on in I predict we will be covering painful and difficult ground. However, there is no other way."

"No other way for what?" she half-pouted to hide the shame she unaccountably felt.

"No other way to discover who and what you really are," he replied. "No other way to remove the cancer of the lie by which you have been living."

"What lie?" she asked, and she herself could not understand why she did so in humility rather than protest.

"That you are alright, and the world is what is awry."

"You will show me this?" she queried. "Because if you just mean to say it without showing it, then I've no time for such guilt trips."

"I and the rest," he promised. "We will show you, if you can stand the fire. And we will also give you every opportunity to retreat from the fire."

She did not ask what fire he meant, because she already was feeling its heat. Nor did she say she was ready, because to do so would have been an impertinent lie in the face of such a challenge. She knew that all she need do to indicate her reply was to stay or leave. She stayed.

"We have hit upon the fundamental question," he continued, apparently satisfied with her tacit answer: "What is good, and what evil? The basic Jewish answer to this question is to be found in the Torah. First of all, God created everything. Second, everything God created was good. Third, 'This day,' says the Lord, 'I have set before you two paths—good and evil, light and darkness, life and death. Choose which you will walk.' Time to put two and two together again," he smiled. "Do you see any problem with these propositions?"

"If God created everything and everything God created was good, whence the possibility of choosing evil?"

"Precisely. What does this imply about the Jewish conception of evil?"

"That it's self-contradictory?" she ventured, a trifle archly.

"That evil has no reality in and of itself."

"Just like Hinduism," she commented, "or Buddhism."

"No, not like either," he declared. "From the Jewish perspective, evil has no reality of its own, but that doesn't mean it's unreal. It derives its reality from the good."

"So it's parasitical?"

"Yes," he smiled joylessly, caught in the incongruity of pleasure at her correct reply with the gloom of the subject at hand, "evil is disordered good, the corruption of life. Evil feeds off the good. If evil destroyed the good, it would destroy itself, as surely as a parasite that destroys its host organism destroys its own life. As Augustine of Hippo, the great fourth-century Christian theologian, put it, sin is disordered love."

"Sounds fine in abstraction," Ariana remarked, "but I don't get the practical implications."

"What do you think about the earthbounds' penchant for going out and having a good time?" he asked.

"There's nothing wrong with that!" she replied. "In fact, I think if they did so more often, earth would be a saner place!"

"Perhaps," he mused. "But what if, in order to go out and enjoy oneself, one has to leave two small children at home alone?"

"That would be evil," she said solemnly.

"One must keep things in proper order of priority," he observed. "Otherwise, the greater is prostituted to the lesser, art and religion to money and power, and all is lost."

"But can you always tell the greater from the lesser?" she queried."And if you can't, how can you avoid the path of death?"

"The only question," he said pensively: "Good and evil."

"Yes," she asked, "how can you know good and evil?"

"Maybe one learns it as one is acculturated into human society," he suggested.

"Maybe," she replied doubtfully.

"So why don't we begin with the typical conception of good and evil to be found in the typical patriarchal society?"

"Why patriarchal?," she protested."Why not matriarchal?"

"Because all civilizations known to history have been patriarchal," he replied sensibly. "You don't have to worry about that now, however. Just think of what human society throughout history generally has accounted as 'good.'"

"Love," she replied.

"Unambiguously good," he qualified.

"Love is unambiguously good!" she rejoined.

"Not according to patriarchy. Throughout history, love has been deeply mistrusted, and never regarded as a reliable foundation for society. Love is a luxury for those who can afford it. Security, position, and wealth are the factors wise people permit to govern their lives and their society."

"I see what you mean. Truth, then," she offered.

"Yes," he approved, "no society can exist without a foundation in truth and honesty. What else?"

"Justice?"

"Yes, justice as perceived fairness. And what is the enforcement of justice?"

"Law," she said.

"And what always goes with law?"

"Order," she replied.

"So," he tallied, "we have truth, justice, law and order—what might be called the very pillars of society. Since coming here, you have experienced a simulation of all aspects of human existence. What virtues are expected of a worker?"

"Obedience," she said immediately, remembering her lives as an untouchable. "Loyalty, self-discipline . . ."

"And?" he prompted. "You may be as loyal, diligent, and compliant as possible. All these virtues will not enable you to keep your job if you lack . . .?"

"Respect?"

"Yes, but that's a part of loyalty. You're still missing something."

"I have to do the work well," she said, thinking aloud.

"Yes, productivity," he affirmed. "All these values make up what patriarchal societies traditionally have regarded as the good, and grouped under the philosophical heading of reason. Metaphorically they have been linked with light . . ."

"As in 'the light side of the force?'" she asked, remembering a popular American film.

"Yes," he smiled, evidently having seen the same film. "And they have been associated with the masculine."

"Of course," she said sardonically.

"Now that we have characterized the 'good,'" he continued cheerily, as if in inverse proportion to her petulance, "let us turn to the 'evil.'"

"That should be easy," she said sourly. "Just take the opposites!"

"You forget one thing," he warned. "We are speaking of so-called good and so-called evil. If we simply take the literal opposites, we will get the philosophical equivalent of a photographic negative, a thoroughly biased and abstract characterization of the reality behind this 'evil.'"

"I don't understand."

"What's the opposite of truth?" he queried.

"Falsehood, deception, deceit—take your pick."

"One could say deception," he said, "but secrecy or privacy would be better, because we are speaking of the kind of deception traditionally employed by women, slaves, and other dispossessed members of a society to carve out some personal space for themselves, to give themselves a measure of self-determination in a society that denies them all basic human rights."

"That's evil?"

"*So-called* evil!" he emphasized. "So let's work our way down the list. Instead of literal opposites, we are seeking existential counterparts. What is the existential counterpart of justice?"

"I don't know," she replied, floundering. "Injustice?"

"Again, that's simply the literal opposite," he admonished. "You've already said it. In fact, it was your first answer."

"Love?" she said wonderingly.

"Yes, love," he confirmed. "Justice, at least from the patriarchal standpoint, is the impersonal application of universal standards and principles. When you hear, 'If I did that for you, I'd have to do that for everyone!' that's an expression of patriarchal justice. It makes no exceptions. Love, on the contrary, recognizes the exceptional in every situation, the individual and unique in every person. For justice, every person is the same as every other person, every moment subsumed under the same principles as every other moment. For love, no two persons are the same, and neither are the demands of any two moments."

"I think I see what you mean," she said uncertainly.

"You'll come to know what I mean," he assured her, "but let's finish our list. What about law and order?"

"Chaos and anarchy?" she replied, but before he could respond she herself said, "No, I'm back to the literal opposites."

"Instinct," he said, "especially sexuality. Instinct and nature, the nature in ourselves and the nature all around us. Isn't nature the great enemy of civilization? Don't we have to instill values in our children to counteract instinct so they won't turn out to be little monsters? And don't we have to hold nature at bay for the sake of civilization? Indeed, modern society has gone a step further. It is going to do away with nature altogether. She is to be transformed into resource and playground, thoroughly at the service and under the control of the human will."

"I understand what you are saying now," Ariana sighed.

"Next comes obedience," he continued without pause.

"That's easy," she smiled. "Freedom!"

"Yes," he agreed, "or, to be more precise, self-determination. Mommy and Daddy want Jenny to be an obedient child and choose the spouse and career that they select, or at least approve; but Jenny is an ungrateful brat who marries a man or adopts a career they deem thoroughly unsuitable. After all, why can't Jenny see that Mommy and Daddy know best?"

She would have laughed, but she had encountered too many among the earthbound whose spirits were horribly twisted by just the kind of domination he was caricaturing.

"Next, what is the counterpart of loyalty and respect?"

"Thinking for yourself?" she hazarded.

"That would be a prerequisite," he agreed; "but these categories are social, not individual. Loyalty and respect have to do with how one treats others, not what one does inside one's head. Let me help you out. Suppose you and your employer are walking down the street, and he is giving you instructions about something he considers important. You are listening loyally, respectfully, when you happen upon a wino lying drunk across the pavement. Your boss steps over the derelict without missing a beat; but you stop, excuse yourself, bend down, and listen to what the wino is mumbling with as much consideration and respect as you were showing your boss a moment before. How do you think your boss would react?"

"Quite put out, I imagine," she laughed.

"From the patriarchal perspective, one owes loyalty and respect to those who deserve it," he elaborated; "namely, those in power and authority. Thus, to respect everyone is to respect no one."

"Equality," she noted.

He nodded in agreement. "And what about the counterpart of diligence or self-discipline?"

"Doing what you feel like doing!" she giggled, giddy because she was beginning to see what he meant.

"Spontaneity," he confirmed. "And, finally, productivity. If one isn't putting out or producing, one is . . . ?"

"Taking in or receiving," she pondered. "Receptivity!"

"And there we have it: privacy, love, nature and sexuality, self-determination, equality, spontaneity, and receptivity, all falling under the philosophical headings of passion and appetite, and the metaphorical rubric of darkness."

"The dark side of the force."

He nodded. "And, to top it all off, these values have been associated throughout history with the feminine. If you doubt that, take a look at the witch hunts of northern Europe. A witch was essentially a rebel against the hierarchical order ordained by God. She represented the rebellion of flesh against spirit, instinct against reason, nature against civilization. For most of the world, the major question of human existence has been how to maximize light, reason, and minimize darkness, passion, at least from a social perspective. From the standpoint of the individual, the effort has frequently been directed in the opposite direction. In the Jewish tradition, these two sides of human being are known, respectively, as the right and the left hand. But enough of this abstraction. Time for reality!"

And with those words she entered into a new experience. She had thought that perhaps she was through with these existential excursions, but this time she sank more deeply than ever; so deeply, in fact, that she forgot she had ever been anything but the husband, Aaron, who had been happily married for the proverbial seven years, but who now was explaining to his analyst, a Dr. Goldstein, that he didn't know why, his wife was as beautiful, as affectionate, as passionate a lover, and as congenial a mate as when they had tied the knot all those years ago; but his eyes had started to wander and his body was not going to be far behind. In fact, he would just about rather make love with anyone or anything than his wife. "And you're the fifth analyst I've seen!" Aaron concluded to the doctor, whose cheery look could not mask the intelligence, even wisdom, that was chiseled across his forehead and sparkled from his eyes. Aaron finally felt he had found the help he needed.

"What did the others tell you?" Dr. Goldstein asked.

"The first one asked me if I had talked about it with my wife. When she found out I hadn't, she said it was something we should work out between ourselves, and she would help if both of us came in to see her together."

"But you didn't want to do that?" the doctor inquired.

"I told her it was my problem, not my wife's, and I wasn't going to afflict her with it."

"A wise decision," Goldstein agreed. "What about the second?"

"He said that maybe I should see other women or even get a divorce."

"Promiscuity," the doctor commented.

"Or a divorce," Aaron added.

"Often divorce is just another form of promiscuity," declared Goldstein. "To employ a little ugly but useful sociological jargon, promiscuity can be either synchronic, a number of simultaneous affairs; or diachronic, what may also be called 'serial' promiscuity."

"A lot of words," Aaron responded, not certain if he had found the right analyst after all.

"Let me give you an example," Goldstein smiled, giving Aaron the feeling that he could read his client's mind. "I saw a talk show many years back—not like these fancy national ones they've got nowadays, just a local show—and the featured guest of the day was an accountant. I remember the whole thing like it was yesterday, because that show inspired me to become a psychologist."

Aaron wanted to ask the doctor to be a little less long-winded since it was costing him fifty dollars an hour, but he had a sixth sense about people. He knew an incorrigible story-teller when he saw one.

"You know how some people only work as accountants to earn their keep, while others may be glamorous movie stars or artistic geniuses but still be accountants in their souls? Well, this man was an accountant in body, soul, and spirit. You could see it in the beady eyes, the horn-rimmed glasses, the close-cropped hair, the cheap suit, the calculating and expressionless eyes, everything! But he wasn't on the show because he was an accountant, though it must have helped him keep track. It was because he had been married and divorced seventeen times! And the most curious thing about him was that he was convinced—not defensive or argumentative, just convinced—that the woman had been at fault every time."

Aaron laughed, but the laughter died in a distinct feeling of discomfort. "That's an interesting story, Dr. Goldstein, but I don't see what it has to do with me. I plan to do the right thing by my wife."

"Repression," said the doctor.

"Pardon me?" said Aaron.

"Is that what your third analyst told you?" Goldstein queried. "Do the right thing, no matter what?"

"Yes, he was a fine young man, a Christian, trying to help people serve the Lord."

Goldstein looked at Aaron with what the latter could only regard as a mocking smirk and asked, "What kind of service does the Lord need from us?"

Aaron sputtered something about living an upright life so we could be with God in heaven.

"Heaven?" Goldstein laughed. "What about right here and now? Son, you ever drive an automobile?"

Aaron felt like asking how did the good doctor think he had gotten there, but he merely nodded.

"Well," Goldstein continued, "repression is like getting in your car, turning on the ignition, shifting into gear, and then putting the pedal to the metal with one foot and braking as hard as you can with the other. What happens?"

"You burn out the engine," he murmured, seeing what the doctor was getting at.

"Now, promiscuity," Goldstein continued, "is something else altogether. It's like putting the pedal to the metal and then not steering or braking. What happens then, son?"

"You crash and burn," answered Aaron, so lost in the implications of this simple metaphor that he forgot to take offense at the condescending familiarity.

"There are two sides to every human being, just like there are two hands: passion and reason, subconscious and consciousness, instinct and awareness—it makes no difference what you call them. The point is to get them working together. I call that 'integration.'"

"Integration!" Aaron cried. "That's just what the fourth analyst told me. She said I should bring the passion back into the marriage! But when I asked her how, she just had some kinky ideas about going on vacation once a month and trying new things."

"New things?"

"You know," Aaron replied sheepishly, "in bed."

"Oh, yeah." said the doctor. "Things. But you didn't like those ideas?"

"I told her I was sure vacation would rekindle my passion—for a time. Then we'd fall back into the old routine and I'd be back where I started."

"You tried it before?" Goldstein asked, and Aaron nodded. "What about 'new things'?"

"The trouble is here," Aaron declared, placing his hand upon his heart, "not here," indicating his genitals.

"If you know that much, son," said Goldstein, "you've got half the problem licked."

"You know what's wrong?" Aaron cried, almost leaping out of his chair for joy. "You can help me?"

"Let's take it one step at a time," cautioned Goldstein. "First of all, you want to go stepping out on your wife. Do you want your wife to go stepping out on you?"

Aaron was taken aback. He hadn't asked himself that question before, and now the pain it caused him made him realize he had been much too afraid. Now, facing it, there was only one answer. "I don't think I could bear that," he whispered. Then, brightening, he rose. "So, that's it, Doctor Goldstein? Every time I get these desires, I ask myself how I would like it if my wife were thinking this way about another man?"

"Hold on!" the doctor cried, laughing and motioning Aaron to sit again. "I said that's just the beginning, the ethical base-line, so to speak, to keep you tethered so you keep your focus on the real issue and don't run from it into the arms of other women."

"I see," said Aaron. "'Genuine morality begins with empathy.'"

"What's that?"

"I don't know," Aaron replied, himself surprised at what had just passed his lips. "I must have read it somewhere." He sat down again, giving his complete attention to Goldstein.

"The next step is to ask yourself why, all other things being equal, does the passion go out of a marriage for one of the partners in the first place."

"I don't know. Maybe I just started taking Rachel for granted."

"She became an extension of yourself, maybe?"

"Yes," Aaron admitted, "I suppose she did. I suppose I began to think of us as one person, and I was the brain."

"It's about as exciting to make love to a mate one takes for granted as to masturbate," noted Goldstein.

"You're right! I hadn't seen it that way before, but you're right!"

"She's a non-person to you," the doctor continued, not mincing words, "and it's impossible to feel romantic about a non-person."

Aaron shifted uneasily in his chair, but had to admit to himself that Goldstein had hit the nail on the head. "That's right," he mumbled. "You're right."

"Now, we have to follow the thread of causality all the way to the root of the problem," Goldstein said, beginning to sound once more like a professional. "All other things being equal, why does one spouse turn another spouse into a non-person?"

"I only did it in my head, Doctor Goldstein," Aaron rapidly made excuse, "I never physically brutalized her."

"Oh, there are all sorts of ways of doing it," he remarked, "but the important question is, 'Why?'"

"I don't know," Aaron intoned as if he were praying, "I don't know. Boredom?"

The doctor settled deeper into his easy chair. "You know, some years back I saw a popular movie in which this one guy who had been all over the world and slept with all sorts of women said that affairs got to be the same old thing with a different face. The only adventure he found in sex, the only time it was different and exciting every time, was when he made love to his wife. Boredom's just a symptom."

"Then I really don't know," Aaron practically moaned.

"I think you do know, son," said Goldstein, obviously returning to his folksy familiarity to soften the force of the charge. "I think you just need someone to point it out to you."

"Alright," agreed Aaron, nodding hesitantly.

"Fear," Goldstein declared. "Fear of intimacy."

"That's all?" Aaron smiled, not knowing if he felt more disappointment or relief. "I was expecting revelation!"

"Think about your relationship," ordered Goldstein, refusing to back down. "Does what I say ring true?"

He was in too compromised a position to refuse. He thought of Rachel and how beautiful she had seemed to him at first, how much he had loved the sound of her voice. Then, gradually, he had found it difficult to talk with her or, when he did talk with her, to meet her gaze with his own. He realized that the least little thing she said or did that did not fit with the way he thought she should be made him angry, and that controlling this anger, as he invariably did, merely increased the emotional distance between them. "You're right," he finally admitted, "that's it exactly."

"You've been living in self-contradiction," Goldstein asserted, "pushing away the very intimacy you are seeking."

"But how?" Aaron cried, rising and pacing across the room. "Why do I seek intimacy with others, but refuse it to my wife?"

He could feel the doctor's narrowing gaze. "Because they're still persons to you," he observed. "Get as close to one of them as you are to your wife, and the same thing will happen. You'll turn your new mate into a non-person."

"The accountant," Aaron said.

"The accountant," Goldstein confirmed. "Or maybe you'll opt for synchronic promiscuity," he added."Get 'intimate' with a number of women at the same time, and that way you'll never have to be truly intimate with any one of them."

"What do I have to do?" Aaron pleaded.

"You've already done half of it," Goldstein declared. "Sort of. It's paradoxical. You step forward and back at the same time. You put yourself in your wife's place. That's empathy. At the same time, you allow her complete freedom to make her own decisions, even if those decision vitally affect you. That's respect. It's simple. Not easy, but simple. Start by giving her the same empathy and respect you extend to the mailman or garbage collector, and build from there."

"And that'll do it?" Aaron said doubtfully.

"That way you'll be letting her become her own person again. If my diagnosis is correct, which means if you told the truth about how wonderful your marriage was in the first place, the passion will return. At the very least, you'll discover how you really feel about her. You can't ask more from me than that, unless you want me to do your husbandly duties for you!"

The doctor guffawed at his own little joke. Aaron smiled without really hearing or caring what he had said. "Whatever you want," he laughed politely; and then, instructing the doctor to send him the bill, he rushed home to work on his marriage.

As a neutral observer might have guessed and the doctor most certainly predicted, Aaron in his eagerness made a few false starts. He treated Rachel with such exaggerated respect that for a time she openly suspected him of having an affair, and their marriage nearly crumbled. Then, of course, as soon as Aaron regained his passion for her, Rachel lost her passion for him, and she had to sign up with Goldstein to find out that she was subconsciously retaliating for Aaron's rejection of her. Eventually, however, their relationship struck upon an even keel, and it seemed to Aaron as if he were coasting through life.

That is, of course, until he reached forty. The kids were all in college, and he had more time than ever alone with Rachel, which was wonderful for both of them. His career, however, was another question. Aaron worked in research and development for a large pharmaceutical firm that was actually doing better business than usual in a recession economy, so he did not have to worry about the company folding or cutting back. Furthermore, from the lowly messenger boy on up to the chairman of the board, everyone liked and respected Aaron. The problem, just like with his marriage twelve years before, was his own dissatisfaction. The job hadn't changed. He had changed. So, even though he had not seen the good doctor in years, he decided to pay a visit to Goldstein.

Goldstein acted as if Aaron had just walked out of his office the day before. He immediately sat his erstwhile client down and questioned him closely. Work, Aaron explained to him, just wasn't enjoyable anymore. He had no complaints about compensation. Rachel and he had more money than they knew what to do with. It was the job. The problem was the job itself. It had gone from being exciting and stimulating to routine and boring; and, the crazy thing was, it had not changed at all.

"Do you remember what I said about the two sides of a person?" Goldstein queried as if they had discussed the issue only a few moments before. Even though it had been twelve years, however, Aaron did remember.

"Reason and passion," he replied.

"Right!" Goldstein affirmed. "The right and the left hand. When you're at work, which side are you on?"

"The right," Aaron replied neutrally. "Reason."

"And at home?"

Aaron could not suppress a boyish grin that undoubtedly signaled to Goldstein how well his previous work had been done. "Passion," he murmured.

"Have you ever seen a fish out of water?" Goldstein asked, and then repeated his question several times until Aaron understood that he really was asking whether Aaron had seen a fish out of water. Aaron, of course, answered in the affirmative.

"What does it do?"

"It flips back and forth." Aaron replied with alacrity, to make up for his former obtuseness.

"That's right!" the doctor agreed as if Aaron had just answered life's ultimate question. "It flip-flops back and forth—reason and passion, work and play, discipline and relaxation, day in and day out. And why does a fish flip-flop?"

At that moment Aaron felt exactly like the hypothetical fish. "Because it's out of its element," he said, talking as much about himself as the fish.

"Right, again!" Goldstein proclaimed. "Because it can't breathe! Do you know the medium of existence of the human spirit?"

"Meaning," Aaron whispered, like a man dying of thirst in the desert might whisper *water*.

"And how does one find meaning in one's life?" Goldstein mercilessly insisted.

Aaron thought for a moment, hoping against hope that Goldstein had been leading him down a spiritual "yellow brick road" and now the Emerald City would be at the end. There was, however, only the usual nothing. "I don't know," he capitulated. "That's why I've come to you."

"Ever know any artists?" asked the doctor, and to Aaron it was a sign either of his own desperation or how well he knew Goldstein that he was not at all surprised at the abrupt change in the line of his questioning.

"You mean painters?"

"I mean any artists," Goldstein clarified. "Painters, poets, dramatists, sculptors, any artists."

"No," Aaron replied thoughtfully, "I don't believe so."

"Can you imagine Shakespeare or Michelangelo or Mozart taking a vacation from his art?" Goldstein continued.

"Everybody needs a break."

"Sure," Goldstein said in irritation, as if Aaron were a dim-witted student who was always coming up with trite half-truths but never seeing the profound and whole truth. "You can't always be painting or sculpting or writing music or plays; but do such people ever set their art aside or leave it behind?"

"Only at death," Aaron admitted. Both men fell silent; but Aaron, much to his own surprise, broke the silence. "Their work is their play! Their play is their work!" he cried, beginning to wonder if he were displaying symptoms of manic-depression.

"Exactly!" Goldstein nodded, grinning broadly. "That's how every one of us should be living!"

"Impossible!" Aaron shouted. "Not all of us have the talent!"

"Sure, we can't all paint pictures or write beautiful poetry, but there is something each one of us can be creating every minute of the day."

"Ourselves," said Aaron, and immediately the situation dissolved and Ariana once again sat before the Teacher.

"All this jumping in and out of different lives is beginning to feel like Hinduism," she observed with a calm that was commendable, given the sudden transformation through which she had just passed. "Maybe Ishwara was right—it's all a dream."

"Maybe," conceded the Teacher, "but here I think 'all the world's a stage, and every man a player' would be a more apt metaphor. In any event, I presume you are starting to get the point."

"These two sides of every human being—the right and the left hands, reason and passion, masculine and feminine, have to work together," Ariana mused. "It's like the *yin* and *yang*."

The Teacher smiled. "I didn't know you knew about that. However, it's more than working together or striking a balance. Integration is a creative fusion. Is Shakespeare's *Hamlet* reason and passion merely 'working together?' Is Michelangelo's *David* or *Pieta* only a 'balance' of light and darkness, masculine boldness and feminine sensitivity?"

"You're right. 'Fusion' would be a much better term."

"This is the great dignity Yahweh has conferred upon every member of the human race," the Teacher declared, "to be a co-creator with him. He gives each one of us life, but each and every one of us creates, or fails to create, the self each becomes."

"Fails to create?," she echoed. "Don't we create ourselves even by default?"

"Creation is the fusion of discipline and passion, consciousness and subconscious," he replied. "A self, by definition, is self-created. Creation, by definition, is never automatic. Either one gives oneself to the work of integration, or one lives in disintegration."

"But how can one live in disintegration?"

"You're right," he agreed. "One can only die in disintegration, and the existential symptom of this death is despair."

"The flip-flop?"

He nodded. "People think the situation is hopeless. In reality it is always the individual who is hopeless."

"If meeting life with this creative integrity is the only alternative to despair, why do so few people do it?"

"Because," he answered, "like anything else worthwhile in life, it takes courage. Have you ever faced a blank page or canvas, an uncarved block?"

"No," she shook her head, "but I suppose I am a blank canvas."

"You're right!" he laughed. "Are you frightened?"

"Yes," she confessed. "Very."

"You have this tremendous sense of responsibility, don't you?"

"Yes," she nodded, "tremendous! Infinite! I can't tell where it begins or ends."

"There are three ways you can deal with your fear. You can shrink your responsibility to a manageable size."

"That would be a lie!" she protested.

"Of course," he agreed, "but then you would always feel as if you were doing and being exactly what and how you were supposed to do and feel."

"Self-justification is the motive for repression?" she said dubiously.

"Essentially, yes," he replied, ignoring her doubt. "And security is the motive for self-justification. To belong to a club, one must adopt the morals and values of that club. Whatever does not fit the image is disowned. One cannot, however, disown a part of oneself. One can only repress it. But it takes energy to repress a part of oneself, and the deeper that part is pushed away, the more it struggles to come to the surface."

"Sounds like Freud again."

"Of course it sounds like Freud," he declared, almost caustically, "and Jung, too. Do you think depth psychology arose out of a philosophical vacuum? Freud called this process 'neurosis'; and when the repressed conflict finally becomes so extreme that it explodes into consciousness, the result is 'psychosis.'"

"I know the third way is integration," she said, ignoring his sarcasm, "but what's the second?"

"How did you know I was saving integration for number three?" he smiled.

"Because that's how your mind works. You take two logically opposite ideas, and show how they're really two fragments of what should be an integrated whole."

"You're beginning to sound like me!" he laughed.

"Monkey-see, monkey-do. Only in this case the mimic is not the monkey."

"If you insist," be bowed. "Anyway, what you described is a form of dialectic. Yes, I am a dialectical thinker. It's the only way to bring thought into relation with real life. We don't have to go off on that tangent, however. You asked me the second way, but I've already said it."

"Promiscuity?"

"Yes, not accepting any responsibility at all. Telling oneself in oh-so-clever a fashion that infinite responsibility is no responsibility. Repression is the energy of the self fighting against itself, and promiscuity is that energy dissipated. In repression a part of the self fights another part, but in promiscuity the whole self is ignored. They are at bottom, therefore, both forms of repression in a spiritual sense. The reason they differ psychologically is that the self that is denied in promiscuity is the self that must be created."

"There you go, talking dialectically again!" she laughed.

"Repression is denial of reality," he explained, "while promiscuity is lost opportunity."

"And integration?"

"There is only one way to meet a responsibility that is infinite and absolute," he proclaimed. "With an equally infinite and absolute passion. To live with the same discipline and passion that a Mozart brings to his music or a Michelangelo to his sculpture—that is the only way to live. Every other way leads to death."

"We create ourselves," she mused. "I have heard so many earthbound spirits say that the self is a product of society."

"And have you ever asked them to show you this society? True community exists only with authentic selfhood. When people live in repression and promiscuity rather than creative integration, instead of a community of selves there arises a society of isolated individuals. Society is the collective unconsciousness, to paraphrase Jung, of all of us. We create our society by creating ourselves. Anything else is excuse."

"And one can see what a good job we are doing at creating ourselves," she added ruefully, "by looking at society."

"We?" he asked with a half-smile.

"The more I learn, the more I feel I'm a part of it all," she explained.

"For worse as well as for better?"

"Yes, even more for worse than for better. There doesn't seem to be much better."

His silence indicated he did not disagree.

"And this is what sin and salvation are all about?" she asked, as she was not sure where Yahweh came in.

"Let me put it this way: To understand the reality of sin, humans must see it from a human perspective. This philosophy provides such a perspective. Is it the best perspective possible? You must decide that for yourself after studying the field of candidates. In any event, I believe it an invaluable philosophy because it gets at the psychological truth of sin and evil. What God has joined together, humans have torn asunder. The way to life is not the mechanical obedience of rules and principles, or the abandonment of all principles, but the ultimate adventure of casting oneself and one's principles into the creative fire."

"And Jews live according to this philosophy?" she asked.

"No, most Jews don't know about it."

"I don't understand," she said irritably. "I thought you were telling me about Judaism."

"I am," he smiled mischievously. "To live according to a philosophy is to apply principles to life. That's repression. The point is to live the principle of life. This philosophy points to an attitude deep-rooted in Jewish culture. It is not itself that attitude."

"I see," she said. "And that is why Jews are so successful in life?"

"Yes," he confirmed. "You have heard that, have you—that Jews tend to excel out of all proportion to their numbers?"

"Some Gentiles, and some Jews,"she replied sardonically, "talk about nothing else."

"There is plenty of anecdotal and statistical evidence, going all the way back to the ancient Roman Empire, to corroborate the truth of this idea," he went on. "In pre-

World War II Poland, for example, ten percent of the population was Jewish, but over half the medical doctors were Jewish."

"That's quite impressive," she said, without irony.

"I have books filled with such statistics," he declared, "documenting superiority in all the indicators of worldly success—professional and social status, intelligence quotient, income . . ."

"I'll trust you for it," she interjected, "especially since my 'anecdotal' evidence agrees. I also do see what you're getting at—that a non-repressive and non-promiscuous culture will focus the natural creativity of the individual without turning it against itself."

"Yes," the Teacher nodded, "that's exactly right."

"But I still don't understand what you mean by 'repressive' and 'non-repressive.' I mean, I understand, but only abstractly. What about reality?"

She should have known that her question would have invited a new experience.

She found herself "inside" a little boy, only this time there was no real immersion of consciousness. She was able to think and feel what he thought and felt, but also to think and feel her own thoughts and feelings, as well as keep the two viewpoints separate. His parents were extremely devout and hard working, and as he grew up they exercised over him what struck her on the whole as a salutary discipline. He learned to show respect to his elders, addressing them as "sir" and "madam." He was encouraged to apply himself in school, to think about God, and to participate in religious observances. As he grew older, he was commendably divided in his career ambitions between the priesthood and soldiering, service to God and service to country.

One rainy day, when the boy was about twelve, he was reading in his room when his mother knocked and entered. She offered him a book, saying that she and his father thought it time he learned about "these things," assured him that they would be downstairs if he had any questions, and left. Anyone might have guessed what "these things" were. Anyone, that is, except the boy. He had no idea. As was his wont, he read the book slowly and thoroughly, from cover to cover. He felt shocked. Not disgust or moral indignation, on the one hand, nor excitement and titillation, on the other. Plain and simple shock. He literally had had no idea. The next day, serving mass as an altar boy at the most crowded ritual of the day, he looked around at all the married couples, unable to prevent himself from disrobing them in his imagination, and realized they had all done it.

Thus began the boy's lifelong struggle with his own sexuality. A year later, after having engaged in masturbation, the besetting vice of insecure and frustrated teenagers, for several months, he finally worked up the courage to confess his sin. The confessional seemed darker and more threatening than usual, and the boy was not brave enough to admit he had done such a thing more than once. The priest reacted as if the boy were a murderer. He never went to confession again.

Again a year passed, and the boy was growing into a young man. He had long ago abandoned his desire to be a priest, but the military still beckoned. His family moved to a new state, and he to a new school, still private but not at all Catholic. In fact, half of the student body was Jewish. He began having Jewish friends, and these friends began asking disturbing questions about war and the taking of human life to which he had no answers.

Whenever the boy went to the home of one of his Jewish friends, he felt excited and confused. His friend's parents would yell occasionally, as did his own; but then his friend would yell back, and all hell would not come down upon him. His Jewish friends called their parents, as often as not, by their first names. They were able to discuss not only politics, but religion and even sex; and even though the arguments often got heated, they never ended with the parents declaring victory because they were the parents.

The boy left home right after high school and did not go on to college. Neither did he enter the military. On the contrary, he participated in several anti-war demonstrations and then "dropped out" into the hippy counter-culture. Ariana lost touch with him just as he was about to have his first experience with a psychedelic drug.

"He seems familiar," she whispered to herself, but then she found herself looking into the Teacher's eyes. "It's you!" she cried. "Isn't it? It's you!"

"Yes, it's me," the Teacher admitted."Or rather, it was me."

"What religion were you?" she asked with intense curiosity.

"Catholic," he replied. "Roman Catholic. That hardly matters, however. The crucial point is that it was a repressive upbringing."

"It did not strike me that way," she pondered. "Sure, your parents spanked you once in a while, and punished you in other, relatively minor ways; but every child needs discipline."

"The spanking was not the problem," he declared. "Physical abuse, more often than not, is a sign of promiscuity rather than repression. One hugs or hits one's child according to mood. Neither were the rules. Real repression, psychological repression, is not about what can't be said or done, but about what one would not even think!"

"Are you saying there should be no limits?" she protested. "How can parents maintain discipline without respect for parental authority?"

"Certainly, parents must set rules for their children," he admitted, "but is the rule correct simply because the parents set it?"

"Of course not," she replied, but somebody's got to provide order, and that's the parents' job."

"I have no problem with that," said the Teacher, "assuming that the rules are for the child's own good, until the parent claims he is right simply because he's the authority. That's repression."

"But children must show their parents a certain deference," Ariana persisted. "Otherwise, chaos would reign."

"Such as, 'No talking back?'" he laughed, a note of bitterness in his voice. "Would you please tell me how you can have a personal relationship with someone if that someone can't talk back to you?"

"There has to be a balance!"

"Parents are entrusted by God with the guardianship of a precious life. It is their job to make sure that life gets everything it needs to grow, including a healthful, stable and flexible discipline; not to make it grow to their own specifications."

"What about God's specifications?" she demanded.

"Think of what you're saying!" he cried. "God has created this life. He has given it the choice to walk the way of life or death. The most that any parent can do is shelter and nourish that life until it is old enough to make that choice, and to lead by example into the way of life."

Ariana remembered her experience of Zen. "The way of creative integration?" she asked.

"Yes," he smiled, "serving God with the left hand."

"Are you a convert?" she asked, suddenly curious. "To Judaism, I mean?"

"No, I've no need to belong to any club," he laughed. "But let's not stray from the subject. The point, of which my own personal experience was but a tiny example, is that Western Christendom, which is not to be identified with authentic Christianity, is the most psychologically repressive culture the world has ever seen."

She was so shocked by the audacity of this statement she could say nothing.

"And the two elements of selfhood that are most thoroughly and systematically repressed are sexuality and selfhood," he continued.

"But that's ancient history!" she exclaimed. "Your childhood, if it really was repressive, was the last gasp of a dying era. Even the Catholic Church has changed somewhat, and the West entirely."

"Yes," he mused, "I know the West thinks it has overcome the repression of an earlier age. What is this sexual liberation, however, but the flip-side of the puritanism against which it rebels? Sex has gone from being a shameful natural function in which one may engage only for the sake of procreation, to being something one may do for pleasure; but is its spiritual significance any more appreciated today than it was two hundred years ago?"

"What is its 'spiritual significance?'" she asked pointedly, certain that he would run out of bluster when forced to come down from vague generalizations to concrete reality.

"Intimacy," he answered. "Intimacy, and the vulnerability that is its prerequisite. One's sexuality is the place where one is most vulnerable and least in control. What most people are seeking in religion is invulnerability. That's why the association of sexuality and spirituality is so taboo."

She fell silent, realizing he was not what she had thought, and wondering who and what he was. "And selfhood?" she finally managed to whisper. "I don't see how people today, with all their egotism, have trouble with that!"

"Selfhood!" he mocked. "Yes, every other ad in the 'Help Wanted' section calls for aggressive self-assertive individuals—self-assertive in the service of the company! Everyone stands up for the ego, the self-image; and every ego stands up for its family, church and nation. Show me a self that stands up for itself! Better, show me a self that has any idea what it means to be a self."

"Creative integration?"

"Creative integration."

Bits and pieces of conversations she had had with earthbound spirits were running through her mind, and something suddenly became clear. "I can see it," she said. "It's a part of me, but you've made me see it."

"Then let's go on," he suggested. Do you remember when I told you I was going to offer a psychological explanation for Christian anti-Semitism?"

She nodded.

"Do you understand the psychological concept of 'projection?'"

"Something to do with seeing what is really part of oneself in another?"

"Something like that," he replied. "Let me give you an example."

And again she found herself in a situation, and again she was in so deep that she forgot all about being Ariana.

Helmut was a Protestant leather worker in Germany about a century after the start of the Reformation. He was a good Christian who had married a good Christian woman. Together they had worked hard to build a home wherein they could raise their children to be good Christians like themselves. Helmut made sure that his family went to church at least twice a week, read the Bible at the evening meal, and lived as God and the minister commanded. His life seemed whole and complete, until a new family moved into the village.

They were dark, like gypsies, though the head of the family claimed they too were good Christians from a distant part of Germany. The father, however, wasn't the problem. It was the daughter. She was a thin, even frail-looking slip of a girl, not like the buxom wench that was his wife; but on market day she sat selling her family's vegetables in a stall next to his, and he was beginning to have images of her and himself together that a good Christian with wife and children ought not to have. In fact, it came to where he could think of nothing else; to where, if he made love to his wife, it was only to keep from arousing her suspicion, and he was able to go through with it only by imagining he was with her.

Finally, Helmut could control himself no longer. He had to have the girl. He lay in wait for her after market one night when the moon was dark, and took what he desired, with no one the wiser. After that, though no one in her family said anything, which struck him as peculiar, she no longer sat next to him at market. He still desired her, and would have taken her again, had the minister not opened his eyes. That Sunday the Reverend preached an especially powerful sermon on human weakness and demonic temptation, climaxed by a vivid description of the tortures awaiting those who did not free themselves from Satan's grasp before death marked an end to the period of earthly testing. Helmut realized that, because he himself was a good Christian, his adultery must have been the work of Satan. The girl must be in league with the devil. Right after the service, before his resolve could cool, Helmut went in to the minister's study, confessed the whole thing, and voiced his surmise that the girl was a witch. The minister, declaring how overjoyed he was to have saved another soul from the infernal powers, agreed completely and declared that not another sun would set before he had denounced the girl, and indeed her entire family, to the proper authorities. The next day the girl was not at the market, and the whole village was astir with the news of her family's arrest. Helmut did not have the stomach to attend the burnings, but he heartily thanked the minister of God for saving him from a fate literally worse than death. Only the youngest of the fallen angel's brood, a boy of eight, was spared and given to foster care. Helmut heard from the minister that he grew up singing the praises of the Lord for rescuing him from the corruption that otherwise would have been his inevitable lot. Helmut, of course, remained a good Christian husband and father to the end of his days.

"That is projection," said the Teacher as he noted the light of recognition in her eyes.

It took Ariana a few moments before she could reply. "I understand," she said hoarsely. "Helmut wouldn't own up to his own lust, so he put it all on the girl. But that was in a superstitious time. Who believes in witchcraft today? Who believed in witchcraft in Germany in the 'thirties, when Hitler came to power?"

"You are being obtuse," he said.

"Only because you're being abstruse," she rhymed, but no one was in a laughing mood.

"I was not saying that belief in witchcraft was the cause of Christian anti-Semitism," he countered; and when he put it that way, she had to admit that her own reply sounded stupid. "Projection is at its root. You're familiar with popular culture. Do you know *Forbidden Planet*?"

"Leslie Nielsen, Walter Pigeon, and . . .?"

"Yes, yes," he broke in impatiently, obviously not concerned with personalities. "A sci-fi classic of the fifties."

"A scientist is investigating some ancient and extinct civilization," she recalled, remembering also the romance between the scientist's beautiful daughter and the handsome young space captain, but thinking that the Teacher was not interested in such details either.

"Yes, a people who had reached the peak of morality, extinguishing in themselves all anger, fear, jealousy, greed, etc.; and also the ultimate in technology, a machine that could materialize thought. Think of what you wanted and it immediately appeared."

"I remember now," she nodded.

"How were they destroyed?" he continued. "That was the mystery. There was no evidence of war, disease, invasion . . ."

"Monsters from the Id," she smiled.

"Right. The negative emotions they had thought they had transcended came back to them at night in dreams. And because they were buried so deeply, they appeared as monsters. It is axiomatic that the more some aspect of oneself is repressed, the harder it fights with consciousness to be acknowledged."

"And the machine materialized their nightmares as well as their dreams," she concluded, "and destroyed them."

"It's campy, I'll admit," he too smiled, "but it does get the point across. Plain barbarism is much less brutal than a civilization that thinks itself incapable of barbarism. The barbarian knows brutality for what it is, but the civilized man always has a compelling and perfectly rational reason for committing the most horrible atrocities."

She nodded, and she was certain the solemnity in his face mirrored her own.

"Because the civilized man is more repressed," he went on, "he lives in a world more dominated by projection. If you were in a room full of civilized people and could see their projections, do you have any idea what the scene would be like?"

"A battlefield?" she ventured.

"Yes, a battlefield of warriors engaged in psyche-to-psyche combat. A projection is a weapon that can be used for offensive or defensive purposes. In fact, one might wonder whether people project because they repress, or repress in order to project. Imagine that, among these psychic warriors, there is one individual who refuses to fight, who does not engage in projection. Who would be most hurt in the struggle?"

"The one who does not defend himself," she murmured. "That would explain it. That would explain why Jesus, who was such a good man, was crucified."

The Teacher lowered his head for a moment, and when he raised it his visage was stern. "It would also explain why Jesus' alleged followers have been crucifying his own people in his name for the last two-thousand years! Take a psychologically healthy culture, at least relatively speaking, and place it in the midst of an extremely unhealthy and repressed, as well as much larger, culture, and the result is inevitable."

"The healthy become the scapegoats for the repressed," she said mournfully. "That would explain a lot of human history. It would also explain why the least popular among the earthbound spirits are the ones I most like." She smiled gratefully. "Now I understand why living in any way other than creative integration is sin. If we don't take responsibility for the life we've been given, it turns and destroys us. We become the monsters we fear. But if I own up to my deepest fear, I'm afraid you won't like it."

"The issue isn't whether I, or even you, like it," he declared.

She nodded. "I've never told this to anyone. My life was so easy and carefree, it didn't seem like I had the right. Now that I've undergone my baptism of fire," she smiled, and noted in his return smile that he understood the reference to her experiences, "and am preparing to enter combat, I can't hide from it any longer. What if God is a monster?"

8. Job

There was tremendous silence all around. The air was charged with an explosive energy the like of which she had never encountered. She thought she was about to enter another situation, but she did not change, and neither did the Teacher disappear. The wind came up, however, and in its bracing force she felt, amplified but unmistakable, that same paradoxical vibration of sweet austerity that had been introduced as "Yahweh" back when the contest began. Then, without any noticeable transition, she found herself, still with the Teacher, standing among a throng of angelic spirits. She knew, though she did not know how she knew, that the assembly had been called by the Lord God himself. The King of Heaven sat before them in indescribable glory, his closest advisors on lesser chairs arranged semi-circularly on either side. A very self-assured and extremely handsome angel was pacing before the throne, delivering what sounded like a challenge, and occasionally glaring, now at God, now at the angelic hosts, for emphasis.

"You brag about your servant, Job," he was saying to the Lord, "how he has always led an upright and holy life, championing the lowly and standing up for widows and orphans, etc., etc. I know you could go on and on. I have only one thing to say to all this: If you kick a dog, doesn't it bite? And if you feed a dog, won't it lick your hand?"

"My dear Satan," the Lord declared in a voice that struck Ariana as surprisingly mild, "Job is more than a dog." She wondered how he could let the prince of darkness speak to him in such a fashion. Come to think of it, if this proud angel were indeed the Satan of whom she had heard, he did not look dark or evil. Indeed, he shone more brightly than any other angel in the assembly.

"We don't now that!" Satan objected. "So far Job's never been kicked. You've given him everything any human could possibly desire—wealth, family, prestige, health."

"What do you propose?" said the Lord without any sign of irritation.

"That we test this paragon, this exemplar of righteousness, to see if his goodness is nothing more than the virtue of a whore. Stop favoring him. Let him see that devotion to your justice is not a means to well-being. Then we shall see if he values you at your true worth, if he loves you simply for your own sake."

"I agree," said the Lord. "Do to his family and possessions what you will, but don't touch his person."

Satan bowed to his Lord. "I would take witnesses."

"You are my most trustworthy counselor. There is no need for witnesses."

"You, of course, see all," Satan responded, though without much conviction. "These, however," he added, indicating the heavenly hosts, "will want a full account. I know I am not popular with many of them, and it would hardly be fitting for you to make report. Therefore, once again I respectfully request that you assign independent witnesses."

Immediately a light went forth from Yahweh's divine presence, embraced Ariana and the Teacher, and brought them forward before his throne.

"A man and an untried spirit, both destined for corruption?" Satan scoffed. "These are trustworthy witnesses?"

"I have chosen whom I have chosen," the Lord declared, and even Satan knew better than to openly challenge the divine fiat.

The journey to earth was swift, and even swifter was the desolation that Satan visited upon the poor man whose only crime, Ariana thought, was his fidelity to God. Satan appeared an expert at orchestrating disaster, both natural and man-made. Job was an extremely wealthy man who was blessed with a large and loving family, but in one day he lost everything. His ships at sea were lost to pirates, as were his caravans to bandits and dust storms. His flocks were stolen by marauders or devoured by wolves and lions. Worst of all, his children were banqueting in his eldest son's house when an earthquake brought the building down on their heads.

Ariana saw it all, and her heart went out to the victim. She felt rage at Satan, and even more rage at Yahweh for having given him leave to hurt one of his own most faithful followers. She wanted to do something to help Job, or at least assuage his grief; but no spirit can interfere with the Lord's workings, and Job could not see or hear his heavenly visitors. As he knelt in the dust, weighed down by his misfortune, his wife, who for some unaccountable reason had been overlooked by the angel of death, came and stood over him in silent sorrow.

"Naked did I come into this world," mourned Job, "and now naked will I leave it." Then he arose and confronted her as if she were the embodiment of his own despair. "The Lord has taken away what he himself has given," he declared with steel resolve. "May his name be blessed forever." This last phrase was spoken as if it had oft been upon his lips, and a note of expectation at the end made it clear that Job's wife habitually responded with "amen" or the equivalent. This time, however, she shook her head in silence and went off to squat among the smoking remains of their own house, which had been struck by lightning.

The return trip was at first slow. Satan, obviously put out by Job's devout resignation, was lost in sullen contemplation. Then something became clear to him, and after that he set so speedy a place that Ariana and the Teacher had difficulty keeping up. In fact, they fell behind and she took the opportunity to question him. "Is this really happening?"

"What do you think?" he replied predictably.

"I feel it is," she said, "and I feel it isn't. It reminds me of something."

"*Deja vu*?" he smiled.

"Something I've heard of," she continued, not at all amused.

"The Book of Job?" he suggested wryly.

"From the Bible, yes!" she exclaimed, as if the solution of that little mystery boded well for her fathoming of the greater mystery that was articulating itself in her soul. "So this is a dramatization?" she laughed.

"More like an adaptation," he replied, "though faithful not only in spirit, but also, except for minor details, in letter, to the original."

"Did it really happen, then?"

"What do you think?"

"How would I know?" she protested.

"How would I know?" he echoed her protest.

"But everything here . . ." she mumbled uncertainly. "You're the Teacher. Surely you know!"

"I have some idea," he responded, "but I have nothing more to go on than you."

"Then you can tell me the reason behind the Lord's behavior," she said with relief, remembering how he had explained the hardening of Pharaoh's heart and the plagues upon the Egyptians.

"If by reason, you mean excuse," he said, "I don't see any. What the Lord does to Job, betting on him as if he were a race horse, is inexcusable."

"But it's Satan doing Job harm!" she cried, unwilling to believe her ears.

"I imagine, given your intercourse with earthbound spirits, that you are familiar with the American scene?"

She nodded impatiently. "That's almost all they talk about, even if they're from the opposite side of the world. But what's that got to do with Job?"

"Suppose the director of the CIA asked the president for permission to kidnap a scientist newly appointed to a sensitive position, making the victim think his abductors were enemy agents, and then to torture him to test his loyalty. If the President gave his permission, who would bear chief responsibility for the violation of that scientist's rights?"

"God would," she sputtered. "I mean, the president. But nobody's tortured Job! As Job himself said, the Lord was merely taking back what he had given." This excuse, so persuasive when Job had uttered it, sounded lame coming from her. Nevertheless, she clung to it, as she could not bear the alternative. The Teacher did not object, but whether because she had brought him round or he was humoring her she did not have time to ascertain; for they were back in the heavenly court, and once again Satan was parading before God's throne.

"Some men," he was saying, "kill themselves if they lose their wives, their children, even their money. Others bear such losses with equanimity. Only when they themselves are in pain do they begin to question life's why's and wherefore's. Like a doting father you, my lord, forbade me to touch Job's person; but there's no room for sentiment here. Too much is at stake." Ariana wondered at the implied threat in his words and tone. "If you keep this artificial hedge of protection around this man Job, there will be no real test!"

Even though she wanted to believe that all this was just sour grapes on Satan's part, Ariana had to admit, from what she knew of the earthbound, that his argument made sense.

"I give you leave," the Lord sighed, and all the heavens groaned with his sorrow. "Do what you wish to him. Only, I will not let you end his life."

Ariana wanted to cry out against this injustice, but she felt it would have no more effect on the course of events than the warnings children who are watching a movie give the good guys that the bad guys are lying in ambush.

This time Satan so relished the prospect of Job's anguish that he sped to earth without even pretending to accommodate the slower witnesses. It was just as well. Ariana knew she had to accompany the teacher—where else was she to go?—but she was in no hurry to see Satan's handiwork.

"This can't be happening," she said to her companion as soon as they were alone.

"It isn't," he assured her. "As you yourself pointed out, it's a dramatization."

"Then it couldn't have happened!" she exclaimed.

"Keeping within the rules of Jewish exegesis," he replied in, considering the actual situation, incongruously academic style, "we must take the text on its own terms, and then ask the hard questions. Perhaps here, however, we are doing things the other way around. We have asked the hard questions, and they have led us to consider the terms of the text. To put it simply, what is the literary genre of the Book of Job? Is it history or fiction?"

"It must be history," she declared, "but I wonder if it isn't false history!"

"Why must it be history?" he asked with detached curiosity.

"Because all of the Bible is history," she replied as if he had asked a stupid question. "That's what everyone says."

"And what everyone says must be right?" he queried. "I'll admit, within the Jewish tradition itself the majority opinion has been that Job is historical, but there has always been an articulate minority who have regarded the text as a forerunner of the modern novella or short story. There is no evidence either way, of course, other than the text itself; but that is as it should be. Any work of literature carries within itself clues as to its genre, so what clues can you find?"

Ariana thought for a moment. "That heavenly court," she said.

"The one we just left?" he smiled.

"Yes," she smiled in return. "If I, who have had free run of the heavenly realms for aeons, have never come across such a court, how did the author . . . Who wrote Job, anyway?"

"Nobody knows," he replied and she was not surprised at the answer.

"Well then, how did whoever-it-was know about it?"

"Good question," he answered. "And furthermore, there the tete-a-tete between God and Satan isn't half so formal as in our little adaptation. There it's as if a journalist eavesdropped on a conversation between a nation's chief executive and one of his aides. There's nothing like it in any of the Bible's historical books. Regardless of what one may think about the supernatural events depicted in Exodus, for example, it makes sense that human beings would experience the revelation of the all-powerful God in such a numinous and awe-inspiring way. In Job, the Lord's initial appearance is too pedestrian, too matter of fact to be anything but a literary invention. The heavenly court is modeled after the court of an Oriental potentate. The king possesses absolute power, but he has advisors, upon whom he relies not only for advice, but information. What would happen to such a ruler if he did not make his counselors feel he took their advice seriously, and who made them so fearful that they spoke only what he wanted to hear?"

"That's what happened to Hitler," she said. "He lost all contact with reality."

"And so the omnipotent monarch becomes impotent. The Lord in Job is portrayed as a good king who takes his advisors seriously. He never doubts the fidelity of his servant Job, but he allows Satan to speak his mind."

"That doesn't get God off the hook!" Ariana cried. "He's supposed to be all-knowing! He doesn't need anybody to tell him what's going on!"

"No, it doesn't get God off the hook," the Teacher agreed, "but it does show that the motif is an obvious literary device. Any other clues?"

"The story, as I remember it, is too neat," she replied. "It's got a clear-cut beginning, middle, and end. Exodus is messy, like life, a chapter in an on-going history."

"You're right; and neither does Job place itself in time, unlike the histories, for whom chronology is important. Exodus picks up the story 400-odd years after the end of Genesis. Job is 'once upon a time.' Anything else?"

"Something about all these characters . . ." she mused. "You didn't show me Exodus the way you're showing me Job, but the characters in Exodus still seem more real."

"Yes, compared to the Moses and Pharaoh of Exodus, and even more so the David and Saul and Solomon of the Books of Samuel, the characters in Job are one-dimensional and flat, vehicles for a message," he said with a hint of disdain. Then he added, as if fearing to give the wrong impression, "But what a message! Even though the characters are one-dimensional, the story itself is not. As you already have seen, it deals with the most profound issue facing the human race."

"Whether God is a monster?" she queried, recalling the bulk of the human race that did not think in terms of ultimate reality as personal in nature, and therefore not only had no belief in, but also no idea of, the personal God of ethical monotheism.

"The problem of evil exists in all religious traditions," he maintained, as if reading her mind. "In mystical monism, of which Hinduism and Buddhism are prime examples, it takes the form of the question of how reality can appear to be multifarious, full of conflict, and imperfect when it is ultimately one perfect harmony."

"Maya and Brahman," she murmured, remembering.

"Or samsara and nirvana," he added. "Both sets of concepts are attempts to explain apparent multiplicity in absolute unity, seeming imperfection in absolute perfection. In Eastern religion, the problem of evil is an abstraction, because the point is not to arrive at some intellectual formula for reality, but to walk the spiritual path. In the ethical monotheism of the West, however, and particularly in the Judaeo-Christian tradition, the problem becomes more acute. Belief in a personal God forces one to take it personally."

"How can God permit evil and suffering?"

"That's the problem. If God is good but not all-powerful, then the devil or the intractability of matter can be blamed. If, as you fear, God is a monster who enjoys torturing his creatures, there is no mystery. If God is both good and all-powerful, however, why is there evil and suffering?"

"I've wondered that many times. If he's good, he desires to eliminate suffering. If he's all-powerful, he can do so. Why doesn't he?"

"Why, indeed?" echoed the Teacher, intimating that he had no easy answer.

"I thought about it a lot, but until this contest it was always like a riddle, a . . ." she sought the right word.

"An abstraction," he aided.

"Yes," she agreed. "It didn't really involve me. Now that it does, it's not only a problem. It's a pain I feel right in my heart." She looked at him, wondering how she could dare to say all those things that she had not dared say even to herself. "Does this mean I've lost my faith?"

"On the contrary," the Teacher assured her, "I would say that anyone who claims to believe in a good and all-powerful God, the God of ethical monotheism, and does not feel the problem of evil like a pain in her heart, does not take her own belief seriously. How can one live in this universe, how can one even behold this universe and, regardless of belief or disbelief, not have one's heart torn to bloody shreds simply by seeing what goes on therein?"

There was a long silence which, it appeared, he would make no effort to end. What he was saying made her uncomfortable, but absence of speech allowed certain feelings to arise between them that made her more uncomfortable still. "So, any other reasons for thinking the Book of Job fiction?" she asked, steering him back to a yet unresolved issue.

He smiled, more to himself than to her, as if he knew what she was trying to do and that she would not succeed, as if there were no sidestepping the problem of evil but, for the moment, he would humor her. She was relieved at his unusual failure to guess the true cause of her loquacity.

"One other point," he said. "You haven't read the book, so you would not know this, but the characters are not explicitly Jewish, but simply people 'of the East.' One tradition has it that they are Jews of the ancient diaspora initiated by the Assyrian and Babylonian conquests of Israel and Judah; but those books of the Bible that deal with such Jews, like Esther and Daniel, deal also with a fundamental fact of their existence, their survival and maintenance of cultural identity in a non-Jewish culture. Such is not the case in Job. No mention is made of anything particularly Jewish, such as the Abrahamic and Mosaic covenants, or the idea of the Chosen People and the Promised Land."

"So?"

"A straightforward reading of the text gives the impression that the characters are not Jews, but only pious Jews would speak as they do in the day and age in which the book was written. That makes them historical impossibilities."

"I see," she said. "But why would an author make such an obvious blunder?"

"From his point of view it wasn't a blunder. Remember how the Jewish Bible is divided into three parts? The third part is the Writings, and among those Writings is to be found the Wisdom Literature, of which Job is a part. This Wisdom Literature makes no mention of anything particularly Jewish because it was written at a time when the promise of a Jewish homeland had failed and thoughtful Jews were look-ing for something deeper, more universally human, in their tradition. The Book of Job may be an historical impossibility, but it fits right in with the program of the Wis-dom Literature."

"Is it real or not?" she wondered. "What am I to make of it all?"

"You make of it what you will," he said, looking at her with maddening compo-sure. "That's the whole point. If the book were history, God would be accountable for his bet with Satan; and frankly, I see no viable defense of his treatment of Job. On the other hand, if it's fiction, then God is no more accountable for what the character 'God' does in the book than he is for what the character 'God' does in any work of fiction."

"If it's not real," she said dismissively, "why read it?"

"Why read any literature?" he rejoined, rolling his eyes. "It may not be the literal truth, but there's truth in it; sometimes even more truth, or at least, more easily acces-sible truth, than in a history. We don't have to charge the real God with using human beings like pawns in a chess match, but as human beings we can't help feeling at times that that's exactly what God is doing. And we may not feel it's right to test love the way God tests Job, but it nevertheless makes sense to test love."

"I'm not sure what you mean," she said.

"Suppose you're a billionaire who brags about her new husband, how affection-ate, how devoted, how passionate he is, the perfect spouse! I suggest to you that he's simply after your money. Whether that raises any doubts or not, you say you will prove to me that I'm wrong. We go to your house, and you say to your husband that you've decided to give away all your money. If he'll stay with you, you'll give it to charity. If not, you'll give it to him. Is such a test ethical?"

"I don't think it wise," she smiled, "but I believe it would be ethical."

"Suppose, however, that, to see if he loved you no matter what, you bound and tortured him. Would that be ethical?"

"Not at all, even if he was a gigolo!"

"That's the situation we have in the Book of Job. If it is history, then keeping to the rules of exegesis within the Jewish tradition, I see no moral justification for God's behavior. If it's fiction, however, the issue is purely academic, because the author is simply expressing, in powerful imagery, what it often feels like to be human in this world."

"Fiction, then," she decided. "I've never heard that before, but it makes a lot of sense."

"And please note," he said. "my argument cuts both ways. If the characters of Job are patently fictional, those of the historical books obviously have a historical basis. Only a master novelist could have invented David or Saul or Samuel or Moses, and back when these books were written there were no master novelists. In fact, our modern novel owes its existence more to the realistic narrative of Biblical histories than to any other literary antecedent. Therefore, the authors of these books were setting down stories about actual human beings, however much they were changed in detail. The author of Job, on the other hand, was creating his characters to make his point."

"I thought the author's intentions were not the last word when it came to interpreting a book," she said, remembering their discussion of Exodus.

"They aren't," he agreed, "and that's equally true of Job. My rule of thumb is to seek the most profound significance the text will bear, and that is what we are about to do. But the author's intention does define the genre of the book; and, as I pointed out, proper understanding of genre is crucial for proper interpretation. Did you know that some people think, when they're watching soap operas, that they are watching real life? But if someone were about to be murdered on such a show and one thought it was real, one should call the police. God has enough for which to answer without charging him with imaginary crimes because we are too myopic to see that Job is fiction. If you aren't convinced by my arguments, however, you are of course free to continue to think of Job as history. Only, then you are stuck with an unavoidably monstrous God."

"I'm convinced," she said. "I'm just not used to the idea."

"Shall we return to the story, then?"

She rose. "But it seems so real!"

"At heart, it is real. That's why people write stories. Everything trivial in a story is unreal, so the reality of life can stand forth unencumbered."

"You don't present it as such," she smiled, "but every bit as much as Ishwara or Gotama, you're trying to lead me into a new type of awareness."

He winked confirmation. "Shall we go?"

When they arrived at Job's devastated estate, Satan, as Ariana feared, had already done his work. Job was lying in utter misery, writhing in agony. "What's he done to him?" she asked the Teacher.

"Boils. Do you know what poison ivy is?"

"Yes, I've had something like it."

"It's like poison ivy, only a hundred times worse."

She looked at the sores all over Job's body, and at the way he was trying to scratch them with broken pieces of pottery, and she realized that, even if Job were fictional, the suffering was real. Just then three men appeared, obviously Job's friends, who were much taken aback at the profound change from the self-confident man of unimpeachable integrity to the bag of bones trembling in the dust. One of them sought to embrace Job; but, when it became clear that the least touch only increased Job's agony, they waited with him in silent commiseration. Day after day went by while everyone, especially Job, awaited death, the natural surcease of his misery. Ariana's heart went out to all of them, because she knew Job had been denied even that.

"From what I've heard, Job's friends were wicked men," she finally said to the Teacher, knowing that she was neither seen nor heard by the others. "I don't see that here."

"No, you don't," he agreed. "They are as decent, as sensitive, as compassionate as you or I, perhaps even more so."

"Why would people say otherwise?"

"Why would people see otherwise?" he corrected her. "Because they like to read the Bible, or anything else for that matter, melodramatically, the good guys versus the bad guys, and to automatically identify with the good guys. Take the Christian gospels, for example. Jesus was the good guy, and everybody else, at one point or another, was a bad guy. And we all know, don't we, without the least shadow of a doubt, that if we had been there, every one of us would have gone straight to the cross and died with Jesus, wouldn't we?"

She bowed her head under the storm of his all too accurate sarcasm.

"If one reads these books melodramatically," he relented slightly, noticing her surrender, "one misses the point. They are meant to reveal something about one's own heart. One has to stop looking for self-justification, and start looking into one's own soul."

The Teacher might have gone on, but at that point Job let out a cry of anguish. He could bear it no more. His words were terrible, so terrible Ariana almost blocked out their sense. He did not curse God, not directly, but he cursed his own life, the very day of his birth; and who was the Creator but the giver of that life? Moreover, why was he cursing his entire life, why not merely that part of it where everything had gone wrong? It was impossible to miss the import. Job saw himself as the victim of some hideously cruel cosmic practical joke; and who could be the joker but the Lord of the cosmos, the one in whom he had placed an absolute trust?

In the aftershock of this explosion, Ariana turned to the Teacher. "I had always heard that Job was the model of patience. Is this adaptation following the book?"

"Almost to the letter," he assured her. "I love the Book of Job because it shows people how they read in the Bible what they expect to find, and not what's really there. The patience of Job! Ministers preach about it, Bible-study teachers extol it, but Job's patience ends here. In fact, patience is a category that no longer applies. Patience is for those who wait, and Job has nothing to await, not even death."

"What about heaven?" Ariana asked. "Surely, after all he's suffered, the Lord will admit him to heaven?"

"You forget, as far as Job is concerned, there is no heaven. If he lives on, it's through his children."

"But his children are dead!"

"Yes," he said as if he had finally gotten his point through to her, "and now he's cursing the only other thing of value to him, his life."

"He still has his wife."

"If we had arrived a bit sooner," he said with a hint of reproach at the way she had held them up,"you would have seen her bid her husband curse God and die."

"Curse God?" she echoed unbelievingly.

"Admittedly, she probably had nothing in particular against God, despite the fact that he permitted the destruction of all her children, her home, and then her husband to boot. She may have simply figured it was the best way for Job to escape his misery; for, if he cursed God, God would certainly strike him dead."

"What did Job say?" she asked, unable to restrain her curiosity.

"That we take good from the Lord, so we shouldn't complain when he sends us evil."

"He's changed," she said, unable to laugh at her own understatement.

"He's in utter despair."

Ariana looked at the horrible sight Job presented: bleeding, ulcerous skin, trembling limbs, agonized and contorted face. "This is so strange!" she cried, herself in anguish. "It's so real; and yet, it isn't real!"

"It's real, all right," declared the Teacher. "In the world one sees this sort of thing every day."

Job's friends were speaking now, so Ariana did not ask the Teacher any more questions. They were telling Job they understood how he felt, but that the wonders of God were too great for any human to question his ways.

"I know about the wonders of God as well as you," Job answered with scorn. "I know how he comes and goes unseen, how he conquers the monster of chaos to establish the order of creation, and how all is subject to his very whim. I also know how the righteous man suffers while the wicked prospers and dies peacefully in his bed, old and full of days, surrounded by his children and grandchildren. I know how the land is given over to the ruthless who brutally victimize the innocent, and this God in his heaven does nothing. I know how the flood waters swallow up the little children, and how he hears their cries unmoved. Yes, I know the wonders of God! I know that if I were to appeal to justice, he would overwhelm me with his majesty; and that, even if he were to answer my cry and give me a hearing, he would convict me out of my own mouth! But all this is between me and him. How will it stand with you if you interfere in what is not your concern?"

"That's enough!" declared Eliphaz, who seemed to be the leader of the trio of friends, all of whom were beginning to regret they had come to Job's aid. "How dare you speak against the justice of the Lord! Have you no shame? At the very least, have you no fear? Surely he will strike down those who deny his righteousness!"

Job's cackle was the closest to a laugh his tormented body could accomplish. "What have I got to lose?" he demanded. "He's already struck me down!"

"And there is your lesson!" proclaimed Bildad, another of the three. "He has already struck you down! Is this sign too difficult for you to read?"

"Why don't you read it for me," said Job, "you who know all things?"

"Come, Job, how can you fail to see?" said Zophar, the third friend. "It is divine judgment. You have sinned. What else can it be?"

"This is all backwards!" Ariana whispered to the Teacher. "This isn't the way it was told to me at all!"

"How was it told to you?" the Teacher asked in a tone that implied he knew the answer to his own question.

"That Job's friends tried to convince Job that God was unjust, but that Job refused to turn from his faith."

"They put Job's words into his friends' mouths, and the friends' words into Job's mouth."

"Yes," she said, "I guess they did. Why?"

"An important question, but we have another one to deal with before we come to that. Have you noticed that Job's friends just gave us their solution to the problem of evil? And a very elegant solution it is indeed!"

She thought for a moment. "We suffer as punishment for our sins?"

"Yes, or for testing, or discipline—the teleology of evil! Suffering always has a purpose, so it's not really evil. Now why is this so common an attitude? One finds it among religious people everywhere."

"The law of karma," Ariana recalled.

"Yes, the law of karma takes this attitude and develops its metaphysical implications to the hilt. 'What goes around comes around' is simply a popular summation. But we don't just find it in Eastern religion. People have told me that Christianity is about doing good so that God will make good things happen to you, and not breaking the rules, the Ten Commandments, so that bad things won't happen to you. It's amazing what people can convince themselves to believe! It may be true that suffering is punishment for wrongdoing, or has some other purpose, but it can't be Christianity. Otherwise, one would have to ask what Jesus did to deserve what happened to him!"

"His suffering was an exception, I think. He made a sacrifice."

"If it was," he rejoined, "then Christianity is a lie, because a basic idea of Christianity is that Christ was like us in all but sin. In any event, I'll let you hash that out with him, but we must go on. Is this attitude that suffering is punishment found only among religious people?"

"No, it's found among all sorts of people," she replied. "I remember the way the wealthy earthbound speak about the poor, with perfect conviction that they have gotten only what they deserve. Also, how the self-righteous regard the spread of AIDS as God's wrath upon homosexuals. And I remember talking with one person who made a strange confession. She said an acquaintance of hers had been killed when a truck careened through a red light and smashed into his car. When she heard the news she felt, before she was able to catch himself, that the poor victim, whose only crime had been obeying the traffic law, somehow, in a cosmic, transcendental sense, deserved it. But doesn't Judaism say as much with the idea that death came into the world by sin?"

"You let a murderer into your house and perhaps you deserve to die, but can you say the same of everyone else who dies because of your carelessness? Death and suffering are in the world because of sin, but that doesn't mean that those who suffer the most are the most sinful. Why do you think the attitude that they are is so common, though, even among fairly decent people?"

"Like Job's friends?" she said wonderingly, looking over at the four "players" who just happened to have been frozen in mid-argument while Ariana sorted things out with the Teacher.

"Like Job's friends."

"I don't know. Because it's just?"

"That undoubtedly has something to do with it," he replied, "but I think you're putting the cart before the horse. Justice isn't the reason. It's the rationalization."

"Then you tell me," she said testily, uncertain whether she simply had gotten so used to the Teacher's assumption of intellectual superiority that for some time she had failed to notice it, or that only now was it resurfacing.

"You know the answer, Ariana," he said matter-of-factly; and as he spoke, she realized she did.

"Yes, I know," she murmured. "When you're a good little boy or girl, mama and papa reward you with love and affection; and, if they don't, you're not good. When you're a good little student, your teachers reward you with good grades. When you're a good little employee, your boss rewards you with bonuses and promotions. And when you're a good little person, God rewards you by shipping you off to heaven when you die. But what if it isn't so? What if, no matter how good a little boy or girl you are, evil still befalls you? That's frightening!"

"So you see why Job's friends are certain he must have sinned," said the Teacher. "Their entire universe is at stake. If Job hasn't sinned, then the ground upon which they stand dissolves and they are adrift in chaos."

"No matter what they do, the same thing could happen to them," she added, translating into more mundane terms. "But the trick doesn't work! We know Job is innocent."

"Yes, we do, but they don't. For us, for the reader, the problem of evil is raised to an even higher power."

"Why do the good suffer?" she ventured.

"Why do the good suffer because they are good?" he completed. "Nevertheless, even we must face the question of whether Job is passing his test or has fallen from righteousness, making his affliction, in a sense, retroactively just."

Ariana was suddenly startled by Job's shrill and anguished cry. The drama had resumed. "Do you really dare to take God's part?" he asked his friends. "Do you pretend to know what he is about with me? Is he a man, that you can read his motives in his countenance? And is he helpless, that he needs such as you to come to his defense? If he were to appear before us now, I think no one would be as troubled as you! But I for my part would speak to him. I want to thrash out this business with him face to face. I don't care what he does to me, whether he calls upon the mountains to cover me or the seas to swallow me up. I still believe, despite everything, that he hears me. All I want is an explanation. All I desire is to know why!"

And, of course, Job's friends took this opportunity to reiterate the claim that Job had brought his misfortune upon himself.

The discussion settled into a tedious back-and-forth of charge and counter-charge, relieved only by the participants' gift of poetic expression. Ariana found herself listening as if she were a judge hearing a case. The argument was complicated, and much of it was by inference and innuendo; but when it worked itself out in her mind, it turned out to be surprisingly simple. Job was defending himself, of course, and prosecuting both his friends and the Lord. Job's friends were prosecuting Job and defending the Lord. After Job's initial salvo, the trio took the offensive; but Job obviously was never one to forget that the best defense is a good offense. And over all brooded the presence of an unseen power that weighed not only every word, but every speaker of every word.

Against the charge of wrongdoing, Job made the obvious defense of lack of evidence. Could they point to any iniquity on his part? He was renowned for his righteousness, and did they have any facts to sully his reputation? When had he defrauded any man, or taken advantage of the widow or the orphan? When had he failed in any point of the law ordained by God, or refused help to anyone in need?

The friends replied that Job must have committed some secret sin, perhaps some sin of the heart known only to himself and God. Job declared that there was no such sin. For example, not only had he never slept with a woman other than his wife, he had never thought about doing so. Not only had he never looked at another woman, he had never thought to look at another woman. Ariana thought that here indeed was the definitive proof that the Book of Job was fiction.

Finally, Job's friends declared that no human being could be accounted righteous before God, that we were all as worms before the Almighty. Against this line of attack, Job made another obvious defense. It might very well be true, he conceded, that no one was righteous before God; but even if that were true, why was he picked out for special treatment when so many more obviously wicked men, as he had said before, prospered through their lives and died peacefully in their beds?

Job's friends had no reply, and so each side rested its case. The air was heavy with consequence, and the gathering clouds led Ariana to believe that the Judge would not take long in arriving at a verdict. The wind came up, so she had no opportunity to discuss the case with the Teacher; but she did not see how an impartial juror could fail to vote in Job's favor.

Suddenly the wind rose to hurricane force, and they found themselves literally in the eye of the storm. Ariana involuntarily trembled, as did Job and his friends. Only the Teacher appeared calm. Then, just as she had seen him on his heavenly throne but with immeasurably magnified dimensions, the Lord appeared out of the whirlwind and aimed his remarks directly at Job.

It was possible to repeat his words, Ariana thought, at least if one had the presence of mind she herself at the moment lacked; but it was impossible to capture the precise blend of awesome majesty and withering sarcasm that informed them. In exquisitely brutal poetry, the Lord did exactly what Job had predicted. He convicted Job out of Job's own mouth and put him in his place. Ariana remembered how Krishna had forced Arjuna to his knees in fear, and Arjuna had been a mighty warrior in his prime. Now Yahweh was appearing to Job, this bag of bones lying in the dust, in a vision at least as terrifying, and telling Job to stand up like a man and match Yahweh's power. Otherwise, who was Job to question his ways?

Ariana watched the faces of the three friends while Job was taking his punishment in the only way he possibly could—groveling in the dirt. She did not see triumph in those faces, only relief, as if Job had almost convinced them that day was night and black was white, but that now "God was in his heaven and all was right with the world." Job said to Yahweh that he, a thoughtless mortal, had spoken of things beyond his ken, too wonderful for the human mind to comprehend; but now he saw the error of his ways, and begged for forgiveness. No doubt the friends regarded this turnabout as genuine repentance, but Ariana could not help feeling that he was simply bowing before a greater and irresistible power. She wished he had the strength to stand up to the tyrant; but she could not despise Job, after all he had been through, for prostrating himself before his cruel creator in abject submission. He had the right to find peace any way he could.

"You underestimate Job," broke in the Teacher, evidently reading her thoughts from the expression on her face. "Remember, the deepest meaning that the text will bear!" She opened her mouth to answer him, though she did not know what she would say, but he hushed her. "There's a bit more. We'll discuss it when it's over."

Turning her attention back to Job, she saw that the Lord was finished with him and was about to address his friends, no doubt to commend them for their piety and devotion.

"Eliphaz, Bildad, Zophar!" the Lord called, and, as each man heard his name, he prostrated himself before the numinous presence. "I am angry with you, because you have not spoken rightly of me, as has my servant Job!"

Ariana could not believe her ears. Somehow, despite the stinging rebuke of hardly a moment before, Job was exonerated. Not only that, but the Lord was going to give him a new family with daughters more beautiful and sons stronger and more upright than those he had lost, as well as twice the wealth he had before. The three friends, on the other hand, would be pardoned their sin only if Job agreed to offer sacrifice for them by his own hand. No, this made no sense. It was impossible to understand.

"Perhaps it's because he repented," said the Teacher.

"It can't be! When he repented he was doing exactly what his friends had advised all along, and yet the Lord said they spoke wrongly."

"Perhaps he meant when they accused Job of wrongdoing without any evidence," he persisted.

"That can't be, either. The Lord said they spoke wrongly of himself, of God."

"Perhaps it's just some stupid story," he concluded.

She looked at him, startled, but then realized that he had been baiting her. "Perhaps it is just some stupid story," she echoed in disgust at Yahweh, the Teacher, and the whole sorry mess they had wrapped up in so deceptively neat a package. If she had had any idea how to get out of the strange dimension of the universe to which she had been brought, she would immediately have departed. All she could do now was turn away and bury her head in her hands, something she had done often in her experiences, but now for the first time as simply herself. Unexpectedly, and totally out of what she had thought to be his character, the Teacher put an arm around her shoulders to comfort her. Even more unexpectedly, she actually did feel comforted.

"It's only a story," he observed.

"Yes, only a story; but as you told me, it happens in one way or another all the time."

"We need to talk about it."

She nodded.

"You noted the contradiction?" he asked.

"How could I miss it?"

"Many people who read the book miss it."

"Maybe it's because I wasn't reading."

"Perhaps," he agreed tentatively. "Is there any possible explanation, do you think?"

"I wouldn't know," she replied sarcastically, pushing herself away; "but I'm sure you have one."

He smiled. "You don't yet understand that all this isn't about what I think, but what you think. My task is to get you to think."

"You're certainly doing that!" she rejoined, but gratitude was not what he heard in her voice.

"Again, can you think of an explanation?" he persisted, wisely deciding to side-step her scorn.

Ariana knew that he would not let her be until he had his answer.

"Maybe God is schizoid," she replied, hoping the blasphemy would shut him up, but it only made him laugh.

"That's what Carl Jung hypothesized in *Answer to Job*. Unfortunately, we don't have that out. We can't understand ethical monotheism by opting out of its basic assumptions, one of which is that God is perfect and absolute being. Any other possibilities?"

"You said it—it's just a story."

"But you said it too—it's a story that happens all the time. And if we're going to understand this story, we have to take it on its own terms."

"You yourself said it was fiction!"

"Yes, but this contradiction is part of the story. If you eliminate it, you've got a totally different story."

"Maybe somebody added it," she persisted. "I've heard that the Bible is just a patchwork anyway. If somebody did add it, by taking it away we'd be restoring the story to its original form and meaning."

"It's possible," observed the Teacher. "In our little adaptation we've cut out parts that almost certainly didn't belong to the original; but those parts' absence or presence does not affect the story's intrinsic meaning. Furthermore, their absence does not change the book's literary structure, whereas to eliminate the ending would destroy its symmetry altogether. Finally, to turn to such 'higher' criticism"—his voice was fairly dripping with irony—"would take us out of the Jewish exegetical tradition altogether. Therefore, we must exhaust all non-invasive procedures before resorting to surgery."

"What are you talking about?" she said, sick of his erudite metaphors and allusions.

"First we have to look for an explanation," he replied with equanimity; "and, in literature, that means looking for a meaning."

"There is none, though I wouldn't put it past you to maintain that absurdity has its own kind of meaning."

"I couldn't have put it better myself!" he laughed. "But no, that wasn't what I had in mind. Job himself points the way, when he berates his friends for thinking they can defend God. Do you recall?"

She nodded slowly, remembering but not willing to admit that she had felt there was more in what Job had said at that point than she could mentally articulate at the time.

"Let's consider an analogy."

And again she found herself in an experience.

Again she was a man, this time having an argument with his wife. It was about as intense as it could be, without getting physical, over something as significant as finances or what to watch on television that evening. The man, however, simply felt that he was right, and he was tired of knuckling under merely to keep the peace. Finally, his wife burst into tears, which struck him that moment as the ultimate in emotional blackmail, and he stormed out of the house. A few hours later, after pouring his troubles into the ears of the local bartender, he returned, uncertain about where he stood now on the issue but ready to reopen communication. He rang the doorbell, because he had left in such a rage he had forgotten his keys. He did not know what he expected, but it certainly was not a beaming wife throwing her arms affectionately around him and saying, "Honey, I'm so glad you're home!" He stepped back to make sure he had the right house; and his wife, noticing his perplexity, explained that, while he was gone, three of his friends had dropped by. They could not help seeing she was upset, so she told them what had happened, and they said she had nothing to worry about because they knew him and he could not have been serious, he did not really mean it. At that moment the man was enraged anew, and was just about to light into his wife again when Ariana was returned to her own self.

"I almost felt like killing someone!" she said, amazed at discovering such an unsuspected side to herself.

"You felt like killing your friends, but in their stead you were willing to do in your wife."

"I wouldn't really have done it!" she protested.

"It happens with depressing regularity," he sighed. "Given the right conditions, the right provocation, are you really so certain that you yourself wouldn't go over the edge?"

"It was a set-up!"

"That's true," he agreed, "a set-up to make a point. Why were you so angry?"

"Because they were butting in!" she cried, experiencing the anger anew. "Even if they had been right, who were they to interpret me to my wife?"

"Who were they to insert themselves into the most intimate of human relationships!" the Teacher declared, and she nodded uncertainly at this unexpected reinforcement. "The Bible portrays the relationship between God and his children as even more intimate than that between husband and wife, so who is anyone to come between oneself and God?"

"That's what Job's friends were doing," she said with the sobriety of profound realization.

"And that's what ministers and priests do all the time," he added. "In fact, they regard it as their professional duty to explain and defend God's ways to us humans, and to make sure that we know exactly how we are supposed to think and feel about God. I call it 'conventional piety.'"

"I know exactly what you mean. I've seen it in so many earthbound spirits who were not even believers, but who had tremendous respect for 'religion'; and I've experienced it directly in the situations you've been arranging for me. The prayers in church are striking examples."

"You do understand," he said earnestly. "One stands outside the church on a Sunday morning, laughing and joking with one's friends. Then the service begins and one turns immediately solemn, taking one's seat, or perhaps, getting down on one's knees and praying with deep feelings of devotion and respect. Then, at the end of the service, it's all forgotten until next week."

"Blissfully forgotten!" she laughed.

"Fortunately forgotten. There's nothing worse than someone who's conventionally pious seven days a week."

"Like the priest or minister," she added.

"Yes," he agreed, "they get up there in their pulpits and, in the most pious and stentorian of voices, they beg the Lord, in his infinite wisdom and mercy, to overlook the sins of the faithful, to turn aside his wrath because they are genuinely striving to walk in his way. Tell me, does one speak like that to one's beloved? No, one speaks that way to a dictator, someone who has power over you and on whose good side you wish to stay. You know, I never could stand all those thee's and thou's, either. They sound so stuffy and formal. Did you know that 'thee' was once the familiar form of the second person singular in English, the equivalent of the German *du*?"

"What does that mean?" she asked.

"It means it was used only when addressing people with whom one was on terms of emotional intimacy, like one's spouse, a close friend, one's child, or God."

"That's why it's in all the prayers?"

He nodded. "It says everything about conventional piety, which is ninety-nine point nine percent of what goes by the name of religion, that it took a term of intimate address and turned it into empty formality. Or look at it from another angle. What is the hottest topic of debate when people are actually daring enough to talk about religion? What religious question is discussed over dinner and at cocktail parties more than any other?"

"Does God exist?" she ventured.

"Yes, the existence of God, or whether or not one believes in God. Is this an issue for Moses, or David or Job, or even Pharaoh and his friends, or indeed, for any other character in the Hebrew Bible?"

She shook her head.

"Why not?" he asked. "Because they have blind faith? Why do they believe in God?"

For the same reason that I believe in your reality," she replied. "They experience him."

"How many people today, even . . . no, *especially* among the 'religious,' have even a hint of a ghost of a shadow of an idea of the possibility of a personal relationship with the living God? Who even sees the possibility, let alone acknowledges it in his or her heart?"

"I've met people who say they carry Jesus in their hearts."

"It may be so," the Teacher declared, "but the acid test is whether they are themselves in relation to that presence, or whether they use it as an excuse to put on a sanctimonious front."

"The plastic smile," she laughed.

"Yes," he said seriously, "that's really a grimace that hides repressed pain. Such people are usually sensitive to the suffering in the world, and well-intentioned to boot; but intentions, in and of themselves, don't mean much when it comes to personal relationship. Suppose you were engaged to be married, and on the eve of your wedding you made a solemn vow to yourself never to have an unkind thought or feeling about your spouse. Suppose further that you kept that vow. What do you think would happen to your marriage?"

"What marriage?" she said. "There wouldn't be any marriage. It would all be a sham!"

"I agree. It would be still-born. Why?"

"Because marriage is a personal relationship," she explained with conviction, "and there would be no relationship because I wouldn't be relating to him, but to my own idea of how I should be relating to him. It gets kind of convoluted, doesn't it?" she added with a frown.

"You have no idea!" he sympathized. "And one can imagine your husband doing the most outrageous things simply to get a genuinely personal reaction out of you!"

"Children do that to their parents all the time," she observed.

"Yes," he agreed, "especially with parents who regard raising children not as personal relationship and encounter, but as duty, chore, responsibility to be done according to a formula or program."

"You are saying that this is how most humans relate to God?" The idea held a power, she sensed, much greater than that of novelty.

"What does it mean if you have to force yourself to believe something?" he asked.

"You don't really believe it."

"And if you have to force yourself to feel something?"

"You don't really feel it."

"So what of people who believe in and love God because that is what they ought to do?" he persisted.

"They don't really believe or love."

"Conventional piety is atheism," he concluded. "Those who theoretically deny God's existence are not the real atheists, but those who live in such a way that they could never experience the living God. In truth, the reality of God can be experienced only in one's own heart, and such people use religion to avoid their own hearts."

Ariana pondered his words. "So the Book of Job is really the opposite of what everyone says it is."

"Not everyone, but many people. Job is widely regarded as the exemplar of conventional piety, when in reality he attacks conventional piety with the utmost scorn. More than science or even the problem of evil, it is conventional piety that has murdered God in our time."

"Murdered God?"

"To be more precise," he amended, "murdered the presence of God in the human heart."

"Is that the same as the human soul?" she asked, not quite able to keep his terminology straight.

"Heart, soul, it doesn't matter. These are mere words. It's what they point to that counts—the infinite depth within, the very center of selfhood where thought and feeling and action aren't opposed to one another, but of a piece. It is there one encounters the living God."

"And it is there one encounters the most agonizing despair," she added.

"You're absolutely right. That's the whole point. Do you know of Elie Wiesel?"

"The Hungarian-born novelist who won the Nobel Prize?"

"Yes," he confirmed. "Elie Wiesel was the sole survivor of his extended family of sixty-odd members. He alone made it through the Nazi death camps, and years later he wrote about it in a novel titled *Night*. Once I heard him tell of a trial some inmates held. They were rabbis, and they indicted God for dereliction of duty in permitting the Holocaust. After a trial, they found God guilty, and then they bowed down in prayer."

"I don't understand."

"I'll get to that," he said with some impatience, "but let me tell you what Elie Wiesel said. He said that someday he would write a play or story about this trial, only that he would add another character, the only one who would defend God's ways, even in Auschwitz. Can you guess who that character would be?"

She shook her head decisively.

"Satan," he declared, "and here that does mean the incarnation of evil."

"I don't understand," she reiterated. "I don't understand any of this."

"To experience the reality of God, one has to be willing to face the possibility that God doesn't exist. To experience the love of God, one must be open to the possibility that God hates. Just as in any personal relationship, what one knows of the other comes through the experience of the other in one's own heart. Everything else is projection and preconception. Every time I remember Elie Wiesel saying that Satan alone would defend God, I feel a twinge inside as if it were blasphemy. The conventional piety that was ingrained in me in my youth dies hard. What, however, is the greater blasphemy, to cry out to God against the suffering of innocents that he permits in this world; or to regard that suffering, such as the slaughter of ten million in the Nazi death camps, as part of God's plan, to think that God is such a God as would plan the massacre of ten million people? As I said before, anyone who is at all alive in this world has a gaping and bleeding wound in her heart. Along comes a priest, a minister, or some self-appointed representative with a tiny adhesive bandage, and on that bandage are the words, "God's will." He puts the bandage on the gaping wound, covers it over, and smiles because now everything is better."

"What else is there?" she queried. "One needs some kind of hope just to get by."

"That isn't hope," he declared. "Yes, the Jewish tradition has always looked forward to the coming of God's kingdom, to the transformation of this world, because the only thing that can heal the wound is an experience on the same order of magnitude and with the same degree of reality as the evil that causes it. But one can't take a lease out on hope! Hope is not an insurance policy!"

"Just as I thought," Ariana mused. "You're not going to give a solution."

"To the problem of evil? The solution must come where the problem arises, in life. The Book of Job doesn't offer any solution. The Book of Job isn't about God. It's about humanity. It's about where we must stand as human beings if we are to experience the reality of life, if we are to experience the reality of God. If someone loves you, and you really feel his love and your love for him, but he treats you like dirt, what are your alternatives?"

"Let him use me as a doormat or walk away," she replied with a decisiveness that surprised her. She did not know how she knew these things, she did not think her staged experiences could have gone so deep, but she did.

"Yes, that's how most people would look at it, but think about it. If you let him walk all over you, there's no more personal relationship because there's no more person, only master and slave. If you turn away, you're turning away from your own heart."

"What am I to do, then?" she cried in anguish. "What is it you want me to do?"

"Do what Job did," he answered, not unkindly. "Do what the rabbis in Auschwitz did. Do what the Jewish people have done for three thousand years. Stand up for yourself. Denounce the injustice and oppression in no uncertain terms. Demand an accounting even from God himself, but stay in relationship. The Christians didn't invent this cross. The Jews have been carrying it for millennia. This is the hardest place to be because one is totally vulnerable, totally exposed, awaiting the revelation of the beloved, a revelation that may never come, or may not be at all what one desires when it comes. People would much rather decide everything beforehand. That's what most of their 'philosophy' and 'religion' is all about. They'd rather decide that life is a bowl of cherries or a bucket of garbage than live the mystery as it unfolds! The hardest place to be is the only place one can be an authentic human being, a genuine self."

With these words the Teacher faded from her sight, and she was left alone to confirm with her eyes what she already had intuited in her heart, that the landscape had been transformed while they were talking into a desolate wasteland, dotted with smokestacks from which arose a thick gray smoke and the stench of burning human flesh. She wanted to cry out to the Teacher, to anyone, to help her, but she knew it would do no good. She knew so much now that she had not known before, and it frightened her in a way she had never been frightened before. This fear struck at the very core of her being, leaving her helpless, desolate and alone. Then the wind came up, only this time it was not Yahweh. The vibration was a little too stately and detached. Allah, she knew, had now come to court her, and he could not have picked a more opportune moment.

CHAPTER IV.

ISLAM

1. Allah

The stirring music, at once stately and passionate, that she remembered from her introduction to Allah once again filled up the hollow places in her soul, this time in profound incongruity with the horror of her surroundings and the despair in her heart. Suddenly she realized that its strange syncopation was not produced by drums, but the hoofbeats of an approaching horse. Where there was a horse, she reasoned, might there not also be a rider? Then, at least, she would no longer be alone.

She studied the horizon in every direction for sight of what her ears told her was the fast-approaching visitor, but she did not see him until he was almost upon her. He looked like a sheik out of some Arabian fairy tale, dressed in the white robes of a desert chieftain. Yet there was something unmistakably civilized about him, as if the desert were his highway but the city his home. He rode up to her at a gallop and expertly reined in his spirited steed just a few feet from where she was standing. As he bowed, she saw that he was handsome, but even more than handsome. About him was an air of fierce masculinity that excited in her fear, admiration and desire.

"I have come to take you away from here," he announced gallantly, but without dismounting.

"I know you," she said. "You are the prophet Muhammad."

He bowed again. "And what have you heard of me?" he asked, with a half-smile that was ready to turn into mirth or disdain, depending upon the conversation's turn.

"A great deal!" she replied, without the least intimation of whether it had been favorable or insulting. "I have long found you and your movement fascinating."

Apparently realizing that she was not willing to ride off with him on the spur of this moment, Muhammad dismounted, removed his cloak, spread it before her, and asked if she would sit with him.

"Have you come here to woo me for your master?"

"My master is not a man, that he would court a woman," replied Muhammad proudly.

"I'm no ordinary woman," she declared with equal pride.

"Whether you are human," he rejoined, "or more than human, you are a creature. God is the creator. There can be no association of a creature with the creator."

"So, the Jews say Yahweh is God, and you Muslims say it is Allah," she remarked, trying to take him down a peg or two.

"*Yahweh* is a name, as *Allah* is a name. *Yahweh* means 'I am that I am'. Didn't your Teacher tell you that?"

"If he did, I don't remember," she replied warily. "And what does *Allah* mean?"

"It's simply an Arabic term for God," he replied. "In English, 'God', in Arabic, 'Allah', that is all. Arab Christians say 'Allah' as much as Arab Muslims. The God we worship is the same as that of the Jews and Christians."

"That's not what the Jews and Christians I know say," she teased, and fire leapt into Muhammad's deep black eyes.

"Alright, as you wish," he said sarcastically, rising and pacing before her. "It's not the same God. Jews worship a human God, a capricious God, a God who plays favorites and who has chosen them, for some unaccountable reason, above all the peoples of the earth. Christians worship a mongrel God, a three-in-one God, a God who is half human and only half divine. The God we worship is one, pure and holy, of perfect righteousness, who regards all men as equal . . ."

"And all women, too?"

The fire that had leapt into his eyes now leapt out at her, and for an instant she thought he was going to strike. Indeed, for an instant she wanted him to strike. His chin quivered beneath his majestic beard, and then he returned to his accustomed and inscrutable half-smile.

"Women, too," he finally replied. "Different tasks for different genders, but the faithful of either sex all go to the same glorious reward."

"Paradise!" she sighed.

"Do you mock, woman?" he asked, the hint of menace more frightening than if his voice had been saturated with it.

"Not at all," she said ingenuously. "I have heard about it, and it sounds wonderful! The Jewish idea of a kingdom of God upon earth I find attractive but unrealistic. The earth is too frail to bear so glorious a destiny. And the Christian heaven always seemed so anemic and remote. If I were a man, without a doubt I would choose a place where luscious fruit dripped from the trees and my sexual partners had none of the emotion of real women and became virgins again after every encounter."

Ariana could literally see the process by which Muhammad debated whether to humor her or cut off her head. It was all in his eyes. He chose the former strategy, and she was relieved that her own had paid off. Now he would treat her as an equal, and she could ask the questions necessary to arrive at a just evaluation of the God whom Muhammad represented. She would not make the mistake of confusing the messenger with the source, the one sent with the one sending. She was beginning to sense how literally everything was at stake here, not just for herself, but the entire world that she had never entered but was soon to be her own. She could not afford to let her ego get in the way. Muhammad would be a fantastic lover for her, but a terrible mate, and both for the same reason—they had too little in common. Muhammad wasn't the issue here, however. She had to focus on Allah.

Muhammad laughed and seated himself again. "You may ask me what you will. Allah loves an inquisitive mind, for all honest questioning inevitably leads to him. But, before we begin, are you certain you wouldn't prefer more congenial surroundings?"

This turned out to be a rhetorical question, for even as he spoke, the death camps disappeared, or rather, unaccountably transformed themselves into oases that glistened like green and blue gems in a clean, windswept desert. She and Muhammad now sat upon a raised knoll with lush vegetation next to a waterfall that should have drowned out their voices, but instead murmured in gentle accompaniment.

"Let this be your first lesson about Allah," Muhammad declared. "Where there is death, he brings life. You misunderstand about Paradise. Like the Jews, we hold that a human being is as physical as he is spiritual, and therefore ultimate bliss must consist of physical as well as spiritual enjoyment. One will have the vision of God, but also the pleasures of the earth, without any of the earth's imperfections."

She nodded, finding that she liked the idea now that, having won his respect, she could listen with an open mind.

"And, as I was saying before," he continued, "our God is not some mongrel, half-human and half-divine. He is all-knowing and all-powerful, without form and present everywhere, eternal, infinite, and absolute. Christians claim that Jesus was both human and divine, but men are weak, finite, and mortal. How can someone be weak, finite, and mortal and omnipotent, infinite, and eternal?"

"It seems impossible," she said evenly, wanting to postpone decision on this issue until she had heard the Christian side of the argument.

"Seems?" he scoffed. "It quite plainly is impossible! And there's no real evidence, except what Christians have doctored, to show that Jesus thought of himself as divine. He was, like myself, a messenger of God, and no man can be more than that."

"A messenger?" she queried, prompted by the emphasis he placed upon the term, as if it denoted some formal office.

"There are two words in Arabic signifying those through whom God transmits his will," he explained—"*rasul* and *nabi*. A *nabi* is a prophet, and there have been scores of those. A *rasul* is a special type of prophet, a messenger, and there have been but four of these in all human history."

"You are one of them?"

"I am the last messenger and the last prophet. None comes after me."

"And Jesus was another?"

"Yes, Jesus—Issa—was my immediate predecessor, and before him, David . . ."

"King David, of Israel?" she interjected.

"Yes, King David. And before him, Moses."

"Now I understand," she said, more to herself than to him.

He did not ask her what she understood, but his eyes told her that he would not go on until she had explained.

"I understand why I am meeting you before Kristos, even though you lived over half a millennium later. Christianity claims to be a continuation of Judaism. Islam claims to be a parallel tradition every bit as ancient as Judaism."

Muhammad chuckled. "That may be one reason," he conceded, "but another is that Allah, in his mercy, has granted you this opportunity to turn aside from a path that will only cause you heartache and much vexation of spirit. The Kristos you are to meet is the invention of the Christians, and therefore can only lead you astray. The real Jesus sits with God right at this moment in Paradise, and he will not return until the day of judgment."

"The day of judgment?" she echoed, feeling that this religion had been beginning to sound too good to be true.

"When all the dead are raised, and those who have proved faithful to God receive their reward, and those who have proved unfaithful likewise receive their reward."

"Paradise is the reward of the faithful?" she asked, and he nodded. "What is the reward of the unfaithful?"

"Hell, the inferno," he replied. "Eternal torment, both physical and spiritual."

"I see," she said, her disappointment evident in her voice.

"How else could it be?" he challenged. "Even Christians, whose God is supposedly nothing but love, believe in hell. There is nothing unjust about sending sinners to hell, as long as they are given ample warning. Some Christians have claimed that God sends unbaptized babies to hell, as if God cared about the hocus-pocus of some self-important priests. God looks to the heart, and he rewards those who have given themselves to his service."

"Then we are all condemned," she declared, "because no one's heart is perfect."

"It's the fantastic Christ of the Christians who demands a perfect heart," he declared. "It's Christians who condemn desire as if it were the same as fornication and adultery. But what man," he added, looking straight into her eyes, "can behold a beautiful woman and not want her? God understands the human heart better than we do, for didn't he make it? He gives us no test we cannot pass, and requires of us no task we cannot perform. To control the wayward thoughts of the mind is like seizing the wind. God looks to two things: that, in our hearts, our dedication to his service is real and not a ploy; and that we act according to his will. Within these boundaries, he wishes us to enjoy our human existence wholeheartedly and without shame."

"And how are we to know his will?" she asked.

"An excellent question!" he exclaimed with genuine enthusiasm. "We are finite creatures, lost in ignorance and swollen with pride. Like children or servants, we need discipline and guidance. As the prophet Jesus said, a kingdom divided against itself cannot stand. Both socially and individually, we are such a kingdom. Some of us look to reason for guidance, but unenlightened reason is a whore selling herself to the highest bidder; and who can enlighten reason, herself the highest of human lights, but God?"

"You sound like Ishwara," she mused.

"Islam, submission to God, is the truth in all religion," he proclaimed, "as it is in every aspect of human existence."

"So, how does God enlighten reason?" she asked.

"Reason, as you no doubt have already learned," he explained, "operates according to assumptions that reason itself cannot provide. Through his prophets, God transmits the basic laws and principles by which we humans are to live. Without God's guidance, we act according to our passions of pride, fear, and desire. With God's guidance, boundaries are placed around those passions, within which we are perfectly free to indulge and enjoy them."

"What sets a messenger apart from an ordinary prophet?" she asked, finding this religion refreshingly simple.

"A prophet brings the word of God for a particular time and place," he answered, "but a messenger brings a holy book that provides the foundation for a society dedicated to God. The modern West labors under the delusion that human existence can be divided into social and individual compartments; but the truth is that there can be no true individuality apart from society, and no true society apart from individuality. Individuals dedicated to God form a society dedicated to God. To have a law for society that does not conform to God's law is to have some other god than God."

"How can you tell who is a real prophet?" she queried. "You say you were the last of the prophets, but there are many persons claiming to be prophets in the world today."

"God gives proofs accompanying a genuine prophet," he replied, evidently relishing the opportunity to explain his faith. "Let us confine our discussion to the four messengers, for they are the only prophets of any real concern to the world today. I understand you have knowledge of the Jewish Book of Exodus?"

She nodded.

Exodus is part of the holy writings that Moses brought, the Torah. Therein are detailed the mighty works by which God signified he himself had commissioned Moses."

"The ten plagues, the parting of the Red Sea, the manna and quail in the wilderness" she cataloged. "I guess nothing could be more impressive than deeds like those."

Muhammad ignored the sarcasm in her voice. "David brought the Psalms. His mission was not accompanied by anything quite so impressive . . ."

"Fooling Uriah and stealing Bathsheba," she interjected—"that was pretty impressive!"

"That story, as it is told in the present Jewish Bible, is a lie," said Muhammad. "David did not plot Uriah's death, and he took Bathsheba to wife because it was the most effective way to extend his protection to the widow of a devoted and martyred follower."

"That interpretation would certainly make it easier to think of David as a divine messenger," she concurred, "but that's not what it says in the Bible. Where's your evidence?"

"What need of 'evidence?'" mocked Muhammad. "No messenger of God would commit adultery and murder! God would not choose such a man!"

"I see," said Ariana, uncertain whether this declaration was a sign of sanity or insanity. "Then what miracles did David perform?"

"There were a few minor things, like slaying the giant Goliath and escaping Saul in the wilderness," he replied, his eyes twinkling; "but the truly great miracle was that he united the ancient Israelites into a nation."

"Why was that a great miracle?" she wondered.

He smiled. "As a Jewish friend of mine once said, wherever you have two Jews, you have three opinions. One can see this in modern-day Israel, a tiny country of a few million people with nearly a score of political parties in its parliament. David united these people, for a season; but after the death of his wise son, Solomon, they fell apart."

"And Jesus?" she queried.

"Surely you have heard of the miracles of Jesus!"

"I've heard about what Christians regard as the miracles of Jesus," she said. "I don't know what you have to say."

"I thought you had made a study of Islam," he remarked.

"The Muslims I interviewed fell silent as soon as I mentioned Jesus," she explained.

"Unfortunately, given the history of Muslim-Christian animosity, it's a touchy subject," he admitted. "No doubt, human as we all are, they mistrusted your motives. Jesus is every whit as important a figure in Islam as in Christianity. We acknowledge him as the Jewish messiah, the anointed one ordained to rekindle the light of truth after the Jews corrupted Moses' message with their spiritual elitism."

"Elitism?"

"The proud but absurd notion that they are specially favored by God. In rejecting Jesus, they rejected God; and no one has ever demonstrated such mighty works as verification of divine commission as Jesus. He was born of a virgin . . ."

"You believe that?" she asked in surprise.

"Yes, of course," he answered, "but it does not mean that Jesus was divine. God created Adam and Eve without mother or father. Why couldn't he have created Jesus without a father? And besides, as I already have demonstrated, it is logically impossible for a man to be God."

"But can't God do the logically impossible?" she persisted. "You seem to me to be placing limits upon God if you say he can't become man."

"I've heard the argument," Muhammad frowned disdainfully, "but it's all sophistry. God can do the logically impossible, but God can be no other than God. It's like saying the ocean is limited because it can't be a pond, or the sky is limited because it can't come to an end."

She wasn't totally convinced by his metaphors, but the issue was one about which she had no clarity, so she was not disposed to argue it at this time. "And what about his other miracles—healing the sick and crippled, feeding multitudes with a few loaves and fishes, turning water into wine, walking on water, raising the dead?"

"All true," he affirmed, "except for the story of the water and wine. God forbids wine."

"But I've heard that the water in Paradise will taste like wine!" she protested.

"Yes," agreed Muhammad, "but Paradise is our reward. In this place of testing, we are to refrain from intoxicants, including wine."

"So no prophet of God would change water into wine?" she offered.

Muhammad nodded. "Jesus did not perform that miracle, but all the others, yes. And there are even more not mentioned in the Christian gospels. As a baby, Jesus could stand and talk like a man. How do you think Maryam was acquitted of the charge of adultery? Jesus explained the facts to everyone concerned."

"She conceived by the Holy Spirit?"

"Remember, we do not divide God into three!" he chided. "God ordained that children be begotten through sexual intercourse between a man and a woman. Why should it be difficult for God to make an exception to his own rule? After all, God formed Adam out of a tiny clot of blood. Do Christians claim he was divine? Behold, whether a child is born of a man and a woman or simply of a woman, God is that child's creator in any case!"

Granting the premises, his argument was convincing; but something about those premises, something she could not as yet put her finger on, bothered her. She set aside her uneasiness for the moment, however, because, for some unaccountable reason, she found herself passionately interested in this discussion about Jesus. "And what other miracles did he perform?"

"As a young boy, he formed beautiful birds out of clay," recounted Muhammad. "A passing rabbi rebuked him, for the hedge they place around the law against making graven images of God is a prohibition against all representational sculpture."

"If one never makes a statue of anything in nature," Ariana recalled, "one will never have an idol to worship."

"Yes," said Muhammad. "and it is a good rule for most men, who are impure of heart. But Jesus was pure of heart, so the birds came alive and flew away."

"I've heard that same story from Christians," she commented.

"Yes, it's in their apocryphal gospels, the ones that weren't accepted into the official canon," he admitted. "Therefore, most Christians have never heard of it. The point, however is not whether Muslims or Christians attribute more miracles to Jesus, but that by God's will such miracles can happen without God's human instrument himself being divine."

"What about the resurrection?" she asked. "Did Jesus really rise from the dead?"

"No, not from the sepulcher in Jerusalem," replied Muhammad, "but not for the reason you probably think. Some misguided Muslims hold that Jesus was nailed to the cross and then taken down before he died, as if the resurrection had to be explained away. The problem, however, is not with the resurrection, but the crucifixion."

"But if there is an undeniably historical fact about Jesus," she said, "it's that he was executed by the Romans."

"Apart from the fact that he was Jewish," he smiled.

She nodded. "Apart from that. But what's your problem with the crucifixion?"

"What does the world think of a country that permits the public humiliation of its ambassador?" he asked rhetorically.

"That it is weak and without honor," she said, giving him the expected and, indeed, only possible answer.

"So what would it mean if God permitted his messenger, his ambassador, to die a shameful and excruciating death, doubly shameful for a Jew because it is written in their Torah that cursed is he who is hanged upon a tree?"

"The unthinkable," she answered thoughtfully, "that God is weak and dishonorable."

"Yes, the unthinkable!" he concurred. "And also the unmentionable!" he added, with a note of rebuke in his voice. "To say that God would permit his messenger to die such a death is as blasphemous as to claim that a man was God!"

"And that is the greatest sin of all?" she asked ironically.

"What greater sin could there be?" he arose again in a flush of anger. "To associate a creature with the creator corrupts all that is holy! If we obliterate the boundary between God and man, who will provide the authority and discipline we humans need? If God is not God, then all is chaos!"

She was beginning to appreciate what was at stake in this Islamic version of ethical monotheism. If the individual needed discipline from outside himself, and if society needed a transcendent authority to give it order—both pretty good bets if one looked at the history of the human race—then Islam made perfectly good sense. A righteous God certainly would not leave us in the dark. The only question then would be where we were to look for his guidance. No matter what tangent she took Muhammad off on, they always came back to the order of the prophet's own exposition. She asked the next question with deepening respect for the orderliness of his mind.

"If Jesus did not die on the cross, or was not nailed there to begin with, why do so many people think he did? Why is this one of the few facts about his life upon which most non-Muslims are agreed?"

"It's simple," he replied. "Jesus could not have died so humiliating a death because he was God's messenger, yet everyone thinks he did. Clearly, this is one of God's tests. Is one to believe one's eyes or the eyes of the historical eyewitnesses, or is one to believe in the honor and power of God?"

Ariana knew this question was intended to be rhetorical, but she wondered what Muhammad would think if he knew that she took it just the opposite from how he meant it. Or perhaps he did know, and this was just his way of showing her how much of an infidel she was. She kept her thoughts to herself, however, because she was beginning to see how Islam, more than any of the other religions she had encountered thus far, looked totally different from the inside than it did from the outside. All the others had an internal principle of self-criticism. Islam was not lacking entirely in such a principle, but it did not extend to the basic assumptions of the religion itself. Hinduism was eclectic, Buddhism offered itself as a possibility for those who had come to the end of possibility, and Judaism involved wrestling with God. Islam, however, meant "submission," and that meant never questioning the authority to whom one submitted. She was in a quandary. On the one hand, the simplicity, clarity, and common sense of the religion she found attractive. On the other hand, she was repelled by the authoritarianism. Was the former to be had only at the price of the latter? When explaining his rejection of the crucifixion, Muhammad had neglected to mention the possibility that he himself had a vested interest in the issue.

If Jesus was his immediate predecessor, then the messiah's getting himself crucified set a bad precedent for a man who obviously had no intention of being a martyr. No doubt there were plenty of other elements in Muhammad's revelation that could and, from the viewpoint of an outside observer, would have to be construed as narrowly self-serving; but would that not be the case for any prophet who was not, like the popular Christian idea of Jesus, a thoroughgoing martyr? After learning the story of the young Gotama, Ariana would pick a political strongman over a life-denying ascetic any day.

"So this is the Muslim equivalent of creationism," she gibed, testing his resolve. "History, like evolution, didn't happen because it's incompatible with faith."

"Not quite," Muhammad smiled, his expression clearing as suddenly as the desert after a storm. "God put someone in Jesus' place and made him look like Jesus."

"Why would he do that?"

"As I said, for a test."

"And who substituted for Jesus?" she persisted.

"Think!" he commanded. "Who would be the most obvious candidate?"

"Judas!" she whispered, and he nodded agreement. "But what happened to Jesus? How did he die?"

"On the way to Paradise he instantaneously died and was resurrected," said Muhammad, "and he will return to preside at the final judgment."

"He will be the judge?" she asked.

"Of course not!" he exclaimed, as if she had said something absurdly stupid. "God alone is judge. He will be, let us say, the master of ceremonies." He smiled, apparently trying to make amends for his outburst.

"If Moses, David, and Jesus brought so much revelation," she asked after a moment of silence, "why were you necessary? And what marvelous and miraculous works did you perform, or God perform through you?"

"God gave man revelation," answered Muhammad, "but man mistranslated, misinterpreted, and corrupted it. The chief signs that the Jews corrupted their revelation are that they regard themselves as a chosen people, and that they rejected their messiah. The chief sign that Christians corrupted their revelation is that they took to worshiping this messiah as divine. I am mankind's final hope. The revelation I brought is the only uncorrupted version of God's will in the world today. That's my miracle. I parted no sea, healed no cripples, and raised no one from the dead. I was an ordinary man, an orphan and illiterate caravan guide, but God chose me to confound the wise and put the mighty to shame. God gave men miracles because they asked for them and he wanted to leave them no excuse. They thought that miracles would give them faith, but in reality only those who already had faith in God could recognize his messengers, and those who developed faith through miracles only perverted and twisted faith to their own ends. The miracle of the Qur'an, the message I recited, was and always will be enough. It is the miracle of the pure and undefiled word of God."

"Every religion thinks that way of its scripture," she said. "Why should anyone believe this to be true especially, or even only, of the Qur'an?" Even as she asked the question, she suspected, from the confident look on Muhammad's face, that she was going in the direction he had mapped out for her in his own head.

"If God is good, he would not leave us in this world of confusion without a clear statement of his will for us," he said, his words acquiring force from the fact that they were the expression of a thought she had had not long before.

"I've heard that argument from Christian fundamentalists as well, only they were peddling the Bible," she challenged, attempting to place this linchpin of authoritarian religion in human perspective.

"Islam is not fundamentalism!" he cried, placing his hand on the hilt of his sword. "It is obedience to the living word of God. You are free to worship God in some other fashion, but do not slander those who surrender to the path of peace."

She almost laughed at the living contradiction he embodied at that moment—the warrior speaking of the path of peace. Yet there was something compelling in the totality of both his words and stance that went beyond simple intimidation. She was not at all afraid of his sword. After all, what could he do to a spirit? She was afraid of dismissing him without fathoming the power his message held for nearly a billion earthbound spirits, a power that made Islam the fastest-growing of all the major religions. Moreover, even though he had taken no unnecessary risks in his life, she believed him a man of courage who would have said the same thing had she been an army.

"To be honest," she said with a not entirely feigned humility, "I have not read the Qur'an except in bits and pieces, and then only in translation."

"In interpretation," he corrected her.

"In interpretation," she conceded, knowing that Muslims held the Qur'an to be the Qur'an only in Arabic. Muhammad's disclaimer notwithstanding, Islam was so fundamentalist that the very language in which the revelation was written was itself part of the revelation. "Tell me why you think the Qur'an is so special?"

"First of all, there is the manner in which it was received," he explained, "as well as the manner of man to whom its transmission was entrusted. I was born in the latter part of the sixth century by the Western calendar, and for the first forty years of my life I led an ordinary existence. I worked, married, and had children. Before meeting my first wife, it is true, I was lonely, having been an orphan passed from one relative to another and then apprenticed as a caravan guide; but there was nothing that set me apart from other men. Then, when I was forty, the angel of God spoke to me and instilled the Qur'an, in its entirety, into my soul."

"You could not have been entirely ordinary to have been able to hear the angel," she smiled, and he smiled in return.

"No, not entirely," he agreed. "I had always been more interested than most in the things of God; and, in my thirties, I took to spending more and more time in the mountains, in solitude, contemplating the glory and grandeur of God. Nevertheless, though unusual, I was not unique in that respect. Perhaps a certain measure of interior quiet was necessary, but it could not have been the only reason why God ordained me. No, it must have been because I was so ordinary, untutored and unlettered. Thus, it would be evident to all that the message that came through me could not have originated with me, and no one would have an excuse before God for rejecting it."

"You could neither read nor write?" she asked, making sure she had heard him aright.

"No," he affirmed meaningfully, "I could do neither."

"Did you write the Qur'an?"

"No, I recited it, and those who followed me in the way of God wrote down what God spoke through me. *Qur'an* means 'recitation.'"

"Then what difference could your illiteracy possibly have made?" she wondered. "Does anyone claim that the followers who took dictation were divinely enabled to write?"

"Take care!" he warned. "Don't ridicule!"

"I'm sorry, but you'll have to come up with something better for me to take the Qur'an seriously. I understand and sympathize with your argument for the necessity of such a book, but I've yet to be convinced that the Qur'an is the book through which God guides us."

"Since I was illiterate," he challenged, "how did I know so much of what is in Jewish and Christian scripture? Indeed, even if I could have read Arabic, the Bible wasn't translated into Arabic in my day!"

"You were a caravan guide," she said, feeling like an interrogating detective or a cross-examining attorney. "Weren't there Christians and Jews in your caravans?"

"Yes," he admitted hesitantly.

"When you sat around the campfire under a starry desert sky, didn't your conversation ever turn to religion?"

"Many times," he also admitted, reluctantly.

"Then it seems to me that it would have been a miracle had you, a man of abiding interest in religion, not learned a great deal in your journeys about Christianity and Judaism!"

"You are a shrewd woman," he laughed. "You remind me of my own Khadija! Your arguments are sound, up to a point; but listen to the Qur'an, and then tell me if it could have been composed by the mind of mortal man!"

Muhammad recited from the Qur'an; or rather, he recited what became known as the Qur'an. She had heard such recitation before, and there was nothing particularly artful in Muhammad's voice or manner; but this time she was able to understand the words. It was as if an intimate knowledge of seventh-century Arabic had magically been instilled into her soul. The combination of sound, rhythm, rhyme, and meaning was practically overwhelming. When he spoke of the wonders of nature and the glory of God, it was as if the reality of these things were dancing in her heart. When he stopped, the air was entirely cleared between them.

"Do you see?" he asked.

"I'll admit that you are either one of the greatest poetic geniuses ever to have lived, or the amanuensis for a power too great to reside within mortal breast or head. I find the Judaeo-Christian Bible, however, equally moving in its own way."

"As well you should," he declared, "for that too originated with God. It contains so many different viewpoints, however, so many self-contradictions, that no reasonable man can avoid the conclusion that those to whom it has been entrusted have tampered with it and sullied its purity with falsehood and pride. The Qur'an, on the other hand, is self-consistent. It contains one voice and one viewpoint, that of God himself. Is there any other book in any language that comes close to being so perfect a candidate for the vehicle of God's revelation?"

She did not know every book in every language, so she felt there was no use in arguing the point; especially since she had to admit that, on the terms that Muhammad had set, of majestic beauty, self-assured authority, and unity of meaning, she knew of nothing like the Qur'an. "I understand what you are saying, and everything makes perfectly good sense. Only one thing bothers me. It bothers me a great deal."

"Be honest," he said. "God loves truth, not flattery."

"That's just it—God. In your religion, he seems so distant."

"Not at all!" Muhammad protested. "He is closer to you than you are to yourself."

"But in a distant way," she insisted.

"Even before encountering Kristos," he said scornfully, "those heathens and Jews have infected you with paradox."

"Heathens?"

"Hindus and Buddhists. They are not peoples of the book."

"I don't understand."

"If I explain it to you, will you explain your 'paradox' to me?"

She nodded.

"As I already told you, God has sent many prophets, and four messengers in particular who brought with them a holy book that formed the foundation for a society dedicated to God. When one book was corrupted by the willful mistranslation and misinterpretation of men . . ."

"Was it always willful?" she interjected?

"Of course. God would not lead astray those who sincerely seek his guidance. When a new messenger came, there were those who continued to follow what they believed to be the way of old, not admitting that that way had been lost. God holds this belief to be of some merit, so he instructs his servants to permit such misguided ones to practice their religion in peace."

"You mean Jews and Christians?" she asked.

"Yes," he said, "they are the people of the book. They are the believers in one God, however corrupt their ideas of that God have become."

"They have perfect freedom of religion in Muslim lands?"

"Yes," he reiterated. "According to the Qur'an they must pay a certain tax and not make a public display of their religion, such as the ringing of church bells or the placing of crosses on the exterior of houses of worship. If they do these things, they are free to form their own semi-autonomous sub-communities within the larger Islamic society, with their own civil, marriage, and family law, and even with jurisdiction in criminal cases that do not affect anyone but themselves. But enough of this. Your turn."

She wanted to ask him more about Muslim society, but a deal was a deal. "I thought of a metaphor. I hope it won't offend you. It's only a metaphor. I imagined what it would be like to be a slave in the court of a mighty king, a king so powerful and glorious that one could travel indefinitely without ever reaching the borders of his kingdom; and no matter where one went within that kingdom, one could feel his presence, his authority. It was so real, one could reach out and touch it. I supposed that I was the king's body servant, and that he joked with me while I helped him dress in the morning; or even that I was his concubine, and shared his bed. In such a situation, I realized, even if we were on terms of sexual intimacy, we could never have a truly personal relationship."

"What do you mean?" It was his turn to be puzzled.

"A personal relationship is between two centers of selfhood," she explained as best she could, not at all certain that he would understand. "In my metaphor, the king is the only center, and everyone and everything else revolves around him."

"And so it must be, if he is to be God," Muhammad declared, his voice a confusing and perhaps confused mixture of tolerance, scorn, passion, superiority, and self-restraint. "Would you like to discover the fate of those who seek equality with God?" he cried; and before she could reply, she found herself in a situation.

2. The Sufis

As in her last experience with Judaism, her self-awareness was not submerged beneath that of another. She remained herself, but it was a self that was becoming increasingly strange to her. In her talks with Muhammad, she discovered that she knew things she had had no idea she knew. She had told him she had made a study of Islam, but the subject had not interested her for as far back as she could remember. That must be it. What and where had she been before she could remember? What indeed did it mean to be "the spirit of the new age?" Ariana was rapidly realizing that, in being introduced to her suitors, she was also being introduced to herself.

There was little opportunity now for contemplation of this exciting but disturbing discovery. She was in the midst of a crowd, everyone sitting in rapt attention, while what evidently was some kind of prophet or holy man addressed them. At first, she wondered if she was in first-century Palestine, and if her visit to Islam had come to an end. The cut of the beards and the robes, however, did not seem quite right; and she could still feel the domineering presence of Muhammad, and beyond that, the beautiful majesty of Allah.

Usually bored by sermons, Ariana at first studied her own clothing, a plain, dark, shapeless mass of cloth; looked around at the people and speculated to herself about their occupations, family life, hopes, and dreams; and, in short, did everything to avoid listening to the speaker. At length, however, his voice sounded so profound in its simplicity that she no longer wished to shut it out. To her surprise, what he was saying was not at all tedious. Certainly, it was about God, and love, and all the subjects of what the Teacher had called "conventional piety"; but there was nothing conventional about this man's piety. He meant every word he said; and when he spoke of God, there was no doubt he was referring not just to an idea in his head, but to a reality in his experience. Indeed, it was clear that God was the reality of his experience.

"According to God's own word in the Qur'an," he proclaimed, "everything that is done is done by him. He is the only effective cause. He who holds that there are causes other than God, that God is but one cause among many, is as much an unbeliever as he who denies God's power and reality altogether. 'I' am a human being, making decisions and bearing responsibility for my actions. So the Prophet affirmed. God is the sole doer in all that is done. So the Prophet also affirmed. Some find these affirmations mutually incompatible, and so drop one in favor of the other. They may be logically contradictory in my head, however, but not so in my heart. Do I not feel that I am in God's hands at every moment? And is it not precisely because I am in God's hands that I feel myself infinitely indebted to him, absolutely responsible for any failure to obey him perfectly in all that I do? But how can I obey him, if he himself is not acting through me? How can I not obey him, if he is all-powerful and all that is bends to his will? This is only a logical absurdity if I separate myself from him; but if he is the doer in all that is done, what room is there for such separation? As it is written, he is closer to me than my jugular vein, my own life's blood. How do I know this? The truth is not merely in a book. The truth is in my heart. I am the truth!"

These words created a tremendous stir. Shouts went up from various quarters of the audience, all to the effect that al-Hallaj had blasphemed, that he had made himself one with God. So this was al-Hallaj, the great Iranian mystic, the Sufi saint! She knew of him, without knowing how she knew of him. And though she hoped her memory was at fault, she knew what happened next.

Soldiers forced their way through the crowd and arrested him. He was locked away in a dungeon to which only the most influential of his followers were ever granted access. The trial, though it lasted a long time and appeared in every way to be conducted impartially and by due process, was in reality over before it began. Evidently al-Hallaj had, in one way or another, alienated everyone who could have helped him, even if he had sought help, which he did not. The government suspected him of maintaining contacts, through his relatives and friends, with various rebel and dissident groups; and his fellow mystics, or Sufis, disowned him for preaching their secret doctrines openly and indiscriminately. After many months, the saint was sentenced to death. Al-Hallaj was tortured and crucified before a large crowd, none of whom ever forgot the way he forgave his enemies, calmly and eloquently, while his body writhed in agony. As Ariana was transported from the nightmarish scene back to the oasis, she could not help shedding tears, not only for the martyr, but also for the human race that did such terrible things to those who were its greatest benefactors.

"You should not cry," said Muhammad sternly. "He deserved it."

"What was so wrong in what he said?" she demanded. "And even if somehow he was wrong, they were only words!"

"Words move men's minds and, even more importantly, their hearts. What men feel in their hearts, they act out in their lives. Words are more powerful than armies, and their abuse more culpable than murder."

She could see the truth in what he said. "But what did al-Hallaj say that was so very wrong that he deserved to be tortured and killed? It seems to me he did nothing more than explain a few passages from the Qur'an."

"He took the step," declared Muhammad. "In pointing out the paradox, he spoke the truth; but as soon as he said he was the truth, he fell into falsehood. He was right in affirming both doctrines, that God is the only real cause of all that is, and that nevertheless we are responsible for our actions. It seems such a little distance from the affirmation of these two doctrines to the conclusion that we are merely the hands and feet of God. Such a conclusion, however, is utter blasphemy."

"Because it obliterates the distinction between God and man, creator and creation, upon which the idea of divine guidance and authority rests," she said, concluding his thought for him.

"Precisely," he smiled. "You are a true philosopher."

"Do you find that strange in a woman?" she challenged.

"You forget my beloved Khadija. Before you, she was the only genuine philosopher I ever knew. But we will talk of women later. Now we are discussing Sufism."

"Al-Hallaj was an extremely prominent Sufi, wasn't he?" she asked.

Muhammad nodded.

"What happened to them after he died?"

"They became even more esoteric. Al-Hallaj lived at the turn of the ninth and tenth centuries. Sufism has survived to this very day because his brother mystics have been far more circumspect than he. It is alright, and even praiseworthy, that a human being have profound feelings of love and devotion to God, as long as such feelings do not inspire the familiarity that leads to contempt. Through the moral purity of their lives and the fire of genuine piety in their hearts, the Sufis have been the great missionaries of Islam, its most impressive representatives; but when a devoted servant is led by his devotion to identify not only with his master's interests, but his knowledge and will as well, the servant does his master a disservice, and in extreme cases is guilty of usurpation. Not only must he be put in his place. He must be severely punished as an example to all who would follow his perfidious example."

"But al-Hallaj's love for God was so powerful, so sincere!" she protested.

"Intentions mean nothing!" he declared. "We are not able, like God, to see into the heart of a man. We must judge by actions and effects of actions, according to the guidance God has given us and in the best interests of the community of the faithful."

"So, even though al-Hallaj was condemned for blasphemy," she asked, "it's still possible that God will grant him a place in paradise?"

"We have never had the arrogance of the Christian inquisitors," he explained. "Certainly, there have been fanatics who have sought to police men's minds, but God is not responsible for how evil men twist his word to their own ends. What he demands is clear and straightforward. As long as the mystics confine their activities to secret rituals and the sentiment of poetry, they indeed form a kind of heart in Islam that energizes, though it must be ruled by the Islamic head. When the heart tries to rule the head, whether in the individual or society as a whole, God-enlightened reason must assert is authority."

3. Women

"Is that why women are subordinate to men in Islamic society?" she queried. "If the Sufis are the heart, perhaps women are to be found somewhat lower down in the general anatomy?"

"Muhammad laughed louder than she thought her crudely suggestive witticism merited. "There is a great deal of truth in what you say. It is the fashion in the modern West to speak of the equality of women . . ."

"People do more than talk about it!" she interjected.

"Perhaps, but I'm not so sure. When do you think the United States, for example, will have a woman president? Pakistan has had a woman prime minister!"

"And do you approve?" she asked.

"Her administration was rife with corruption," he answered.

"That isn't what I asked!" she cried. "Do you think God intended women to be equal with men?"

"Equality is not the issue," he declared. "Does it make sense to say that the eye is or is not equal to the hand? They have different functions, that's all; and in the end, if both have served God, both will be equally rewarded."

"So, it's alright to use women like slaves," she rejoined sarcastically, "as long as they get their 'pie in the sky by and by?'"

"You Westerners have tremendous preconceptions about Islam," he said musingly, and she was surprised she did not object at the label. She realized that in many ways she was a Westerner. "For example, many of you think that Islam was spread by the sword."

"Well, wasn't it?" she queried.

"Through Islam, the Arabs put aside their tribal rivalries and directed the restless energy of a young and vigorous people outward against the Persian and Byzantine Empires; but these conquests were political, not religious."

"I thought there was no separation between the two in Islam."

"That's not strictly true," he said. "The ideal Islamic state is not a totalitarian monolith, but an organically articulated unity arising out of the most fundamental of human relationships, those between man and woman and parent and child. Islamic law, or shari'a, as based upon the revealed will of God, does not regulate human existence in every detail, but provides boundaries within which human beings are free to build and create, enjoy and love."

"So how did this apply to the conquered peoples of the Muslim Empire?" she asked.

"It was not so much a Muslim as an Arab Empire," he replied. Western textbooks record how, in the 7th and 8th centuries, the Arabs came charging out of the desert with their scimitars waving and swept across Asia Minor and the plains of North Africa. What many of them fail to note, in the brief paragraph allotted to this 'relatively insignificant' subject, is that many of the peoples they conquered, especially the peasants, welcomed them as liberators. You see, the fact that these peasants and their overlords shared the same religion did not prevent the latter from exploiting the former. Moreover, in the Christian lands of North Africa especially, the peasants often espoused a brand of Christianity deemed heretical by the established Church, and so were persecuted as heretics as well."

"They could not win for losing," Ariana remarked sardonically.

"The last thing the Arab conquerors wanted to do was convert the locals to Islam," he continued. "If they did, they would have had to start treating them as brothers. Imagine all the problems that would arise for Israeli Jews if all the Palestinian Arabs suddenly took it into their heads to convert to Judaism!"

"I see what you mean," she said. "But, nevertheless, the people did convert, didn't they?"

"Not for several generations," he answered. "The Arabs of course could not forbid conversion, but they did discourage it. They lived apart, in their forts, which often doubled as mosques, insisting that they be regarded as a caste above and apart. They governed with relative justice and leniency, imposing far less of an economic burden upon the populace than their Christian predecessors, despite the special tax for people of the book."

"And what of people not of the book?" she insisted. "What of the Buddhists and Hindus of northern India? Gotama said that Islam, more than anything else, was responsible for the decline of Buddhism in northern India, and the deed was done with fire and sword."

"There was plenty of violence in India," he admitted—"the burning of temples and monasteries, and the putting of monks and priests to the sword; but why not? These were pagans who did not worship the one true God in any manner, but idols, statues, works made with human hands. Can such darkness be tolerated in a truly civilized society? Look at the Jews. Didn't they, on the orders of God, exterminate the heathen peoples of Palestine so they could take possession of their land? And what about Christians, with their enslavement and missionizing of aborigines all over the world?"

"Everyone doing it doesn't make it right!"

"You are a typical woman," he declared. "You won't admit what you know to be true, that human beings can't always be weaned from their foolish and self-destructive ways with gentle words and smiles. Sometimes the only way is fire and sword."

"Is that why women must be kept subordinate?" she said with muted but unmistakable sarcasm. "Because they do not understand the ways of the world?"

"That's part of it," he admitted; "but we would do well if, from the start, we recognized that we are in fundamental disagreement over the role of women in human society. You see women as interchangeable counterparts of men. I regard them as having their own special place and function."

"I do not deny that women are different from men," she corrected him. "I simply deny that this difference has any social or political relevance when it comes to the issues of responsibility and authority. You say women should not be leaders."

"God says women aren't fit for leadership," he in turn corrected her.

"You say that God says that women aren't fit for leadership," she rejoined.

"Have you come up with an alternative to the Qur'an?"

"Not on your terms, but what if I reject your terms?"

"You have already had a taste of the alternative," he said, and she knew he was referring to the desolation of Job. "When you encounter Kristos, he will teach you this lesson in full. But let us agree to disagree. Let me show you how the lot of the Muslim woman is not degrading in the way you make it out to be."

"I'm all ears," she said, but it was not only her ears that he required. Ariana found herself in a series of historical vignettes, entirely realistic, but brief and to the point, all designed to give her a sense of how Islam changed the life of women in seventh-century Arabia. She discovered something she had not hitherto realized, that Arabia at the time of Muhammad actually consisted of two cultures, a rising urban-centered civilization, of which he was a representative; and a dying nomadic, desert-based society.

As a woman of the desert, she worked hard but roamed free, not so much geographically as socially and sexually. The men traveled with the herds, foraging for pasture and water. The women, however, stayed in one place to have babies and raise them. It did not make sense to the men, then, to keep to one woman, so women were in demand because they were not in great abundance due to the fairly common practice of abandoning unwanted girl-babies in the wilderness, and the fact that warfare among the tribes, while a sport and a way of life, was waged with care not to waste precious male lives. In short, the nomadic culture of the desert was as patriarchal as the rest of the world; but a woman of energy, strength and vision could carve out for herself quite a sphere of influence and power. Both inheritance and lineage were matrilineal, which meant that the most important social relationship was that between the maternal uncle and maternal nephew, the mother's brother and her son, two people over whom a woman could have considerable, if not dominating, influence. Moreover, goddesses played almost as important a role in pre-Islamic Arabian polytheism as gods. Men were in charge generally, but an exceptional woman could make of herself an exception.

As a woman of the city, or to be more precise, a rich merchant's wife, Ariana's situation was so different she might as well have been on another continent. She had plenty of servants, so manual labor was kept to a minimum, though she saw that her poorer sisters were not so lucky in this regard. However, her husband also had plenty of wives. At the moment she was younger and more beautiful than all the rest, so she was his favorite; but she could read her own destiny in the fate of the oldest wife, who had failed to produce a son hearty enough to survive early childhood, and who therefore labored in the kitchen like a slave, fed off of scraps, and was never called to her husband's bed.

The coming of Islam obliterated these differences theoretically, and lessened them considerably in real life. The woman of the desert experienced a closing in of her horizons, while the woman of the city discovered a small but real opening of hers; but both found greater social and domestic security. Islam forbade infanticide, and commanded parents to be as conscientious in caring for daughters as sons. It limited the number of wives a man could have to four, and stipulated that all must be cared for well and equally, which meant that none could be denied a decent standard of living or conjugal rights. In effect, therefore, the poor were limited to one wife, while the rich could not use up wives and then throw them away. Divorce was still relatively easy for a man, but now a woman likewise could initiate dissolution of marriage upon serious cause, and that meant her husband's refusal of financial support or denial of conjugal rights, as well as gross physical abuse. Why were conjugal rights so important? Because a woman's honor lay in having sons, and of course she could have no sons if her husband refused to sleep with her.

In short, Islam eased the lot of the urban woman, but at the expense of the freedom of the desert woman. It gave a considerably greater measure of security to both. Perhaps the most important right it granted to women was one which many in the West, particularly married women, did not achieve until the twentieth century—the right to own property. Even if marriage involved a dowry from the bride's family, the woman retained legal title if not actual control over it, and could take it or its equivalent with her in the event of a divorce. Moreover, though it was true that a female inherited only half of what a male of the same degree of consanguinity to the deceased inherited, the man had to support his wives and unmarried sisters with his money, whereas the woman could do what she pleased with hers. In Islamic society a married woman could continue to buy and sell and, in general, conduct her own business dealings; but the authority Islam gave a husband over his wife made such independence psychologically difficult even if legally possible. One lesson Ariana learned from the experience she was certain Muhammad had not intended to teach her was that his movement, which owed so much to the encouragement and support of his first wife, Khadija, had ensured that there would be no more Khadijas in Arabian society.

When she returned to Muhammad, she voiced her opinion.

"I'll admit that, from your 'liberated' viewpoint, Islam is not an unmixed blessing for women," he conceded; "but in turn you will have to admit that the principles governing Islamic society would long since have fallen into the graveyard of academic abstraction if Muslim women themselves did not like them. Women desire security. They want men to protect and look after them. In the 'liberated' West, many women have to sell their bodies to the highest bidder to get what they need. In Islam, God guarantees security as every woman's right."

"Does he?" she challenged. "Why didn't you show me Islam today? Do you think me ignorant? What if God gives with one hand and takes away with the other? Yes, the Qur'an gives a married woman the right to own property in her own name, but it also gives her the duty to be obedient to her husband. What if, as is commonly the case today, this obedience is held to cover the manner in which she disposes of her property? How, then, is it any longer hers? And if, in divorce, the father usually is awarded custody of any children, what mother would initiate divorce?"

"Human beings are not perfect," Muhammad responded. "God frowns upon divorce, as he makes perfectly clear in his revealed word, yet he permits it due to our frailty. In divorce, the children must go somewhere. In the West, they are usually given into the keeping of the mother; in Islam, into that of the father. Would you prefer that they be cut in two?"

"No," she said ruefully.

"As far as the conflict between a wife's right to own property and her duty to obey her husband," he continued, "the spirit of God's teaching is clear. It is not like Hinduism, where the wife must obey in all things, sinful as well as lawful, and the bad karma falls upon the husband. God judges us as individuals. A wife is to obey her husband in all things lawful. If he commands her to violate God's law and she obeys, the sin is upon her head as well as his."

"What if he or society forces obedience?" she queried.

"No one can force obedience," he proclaimed. "If women are to be the spiritual equals of men, must they not be as willing to die for the cause of God?"

Ariana pondered. His answer, though thoroughly unexpected, made a certain kind of sense; but it still was not enough. "All the rights of women are guaranteed by God, you say?"

"Yes," he asserted proudly. "No man can take them away."

"And the duties as well? They too are ordained by God?"

"Of course," he replied as if it were a stupid question. "God's word is the foundation of Islamic society."

"That's where I find the problem," she said. "In the Qur'an doesn't God say that a man may physically chastise a gossipy or disobedient wife?"

"What is wrong with that?" said Muhammad. "The family is the foundation of society. Without order in the one, there will be chaos in the other. Isn't Western society today proof enough of that?"

"And I suppose you would justify granting a man the right to have sex with his wife whenever he pleases in the same way?" she challenged. "What does it say in the Qur'an? 'O man, woman is your field. Go into your field whenever you would.' "

Muhammad simply glared.

"But the biggest problem I have," she went on, deliberately ignoring his rising hostility, "is with female circumcision. Removing a girl's clitoris so she won't enjoy sex and won't be tempted to roam? How can you justify that as anything but unholy exploitation?"

"I don't," he replied coolly. "God's will is found in the Qur'an. The record of my words and deeds is in the Hadith. Neither book makes mention of this barbaric custom. It was practiced in parts of Africa and Arabia long before Islam. It is often condoned by the *'ulama*, the scholars of the law, but they are not perfect. Only God is perfect. If female circumcision is contrary to God's will, he will deal with the offenders on judgment day."

Ariana wanted to pursue the issue; but she felt Muhammad was making an effort at compromise, and it was necessary for her to do likewise if she were to learn more from him. "If Islam represented, at least on the whole, an advance for women when it began," she finally said, "today it holds women in a particular place."

"The place in which they should be held," he responded.

"That's a matter of opinion," she rejoined, but calmly.

"No, it is matter of the will of God," he said, and then smiled. "But instead of going back over that ground again, let me show you how the word of God, while clear and unambiguous, is not culturally narrow or inflexible."

"Show me?" she asked tremulously, as if getting ready for take-off.

"Explain to you!" he clarified, laughing, and she heaved a sigh of relief. Her experiences were interesting but draining, and she wanted to rest as much as possible, because she could imagine what was in store for her with Christianity.

"In Tunisia," he resumed, "a pious country dedicated to the cause of God, a man today may have no more than one wife."

"How is Tunisia pious and dedicated if it goes against the express word of God, which permits a man up to four wives?" Her voice wavered between irony and sincerity, point and counterpoint.

"Look at it this way," he said. "The Qur'an does permit a man up to four wives, but he must treat them all equally. This is usually taken to mean he must give them equal conjugal rights and financial support, but the Tunisians say it also includes equal affection. Since it is notoriously impossible for any man to give even two women an equal place in his affections at any given time, the Tunisians conclude that this was God's way of indirectly forbidding polygyny altogether."

"I like the result," she smiled, "but it sounds like rationalizing to me. What do you think?"

"I am merely the messenger," he bowed. "God says that his words have an infinite depth, and who am I to deny it?"

"Would that infinite depth someday offer a way around women's social and political subordination altogether?" she queried doubtfully.

"Again, who am I to say?" he replied. "God moves in mysterious ways. Perhaps, in a universally Islamic world, leadership as we know it will be obsolete. A society totally dedicated to God would be one of mutual cooperation rather than political and social coercion. In such a society, the peculiar virtues of women would not be confined to the home."

"What are the 'peculiar virtues' of women?" she echoed.

"Patience, sensitivity, empathy, endurance, long-suffering," he replied with alacrity, as if he understood women well. "But you know them better than I."

"Perhaps," she said, "but this ideal society you mention seems even further from realization than in the days of your ministry thirteen hundred years ago. Islam seems as splintered and at odds with itself as any other religious tradition. Would you agree with what the prophet Jesus said about judging a tree by its fruit?"

"Of course," replied Muhammad. "This saying is of the very essence of divine wisdom."

"Then," she asked, "what does the present state of the Islamic world say about Islam itself?"

4. Sunna and Shi'a

"There are many divisions within the Christian world," he began. "You have Roman Catholics and Protestants in western Europe, and the Eastern Orthodox in eastern Europe. Moreover, the Protestant Christians are splintered into thousands of sects and denominations. When it comes to Christianity, religion serves to divide rather than unite. Likewise, there are many divisions in the Islamic world, but they are primarily national, tribal, ethnic, economic, social, and political in nature. In Islam, religion does not divide but unite."

"What about the recent war between Iran and Iraq," Ariana contended, "the one that ceased only because both sides had fought each other to a standstill? Wasn't that largely a result of religious differences between the two nations?"

"Ariana, my dear," Muhammad chuckled patronizingly, "Iran is ninety-percent Shi'ite, it is true, but Iraq is fifty-percent Shi'ite."

"But Iraqi Shi'ites are the underdogs in their own country," she returned angrily, resentful not only at his lordly airs, but also at what she thought had to be his willful misrepresentation of the facts, something she remembered noticing while reading the Qur'an as well, though she did not remember in what circumstances she had read it. "They have no control over the government."

"You may be right," he conceded, "but the larger issue, the decisive issue, remains. Are the admittedly tremendous tensions and hostilities among the various nations and factions of the Islamic world religious or political in essence? Is Islam an originating or exacerbating cause of disunity, or is it perhaps the only force that prevents the Islamic world from degenerating into chaos altogether?"

"I suppose only history itself will answer that question," Ariana mused.

"Nevertheless," he said energetically, "we may find it profitable to explore the issue. Let us look at the major division in the Islamic world, the one you already so astutely have pointed out. Eighty-five percent of the Muslim world is Sunni, and fifteen percent is Shi'ite."

"What do the terms mean?"

"Sunna means 'path,' and refers to the path taken by me as the model for all of the faithful. Shi'ite means 'partisan,' and refers to the partisans or followers of 'Ali, my son-in-law, and his heirs."

"Now I'm more confused than ever!" she laughed.

He shifted from a sitting to a reclining position, settling his head comfortably in the branches of a velvet-soft bush. She was tempted to offer him her lap as a headrest, but the stakes were too high for mere dalliance. She had to be absolutely certain of her choice before she offered encouragement to any one of her suitors. Besides, Muhammad was not a suitor, only Allah's representative, though he himself had declared it blasphemy to think of Allah marrying, even metaphorically. Would marriage to Muhammad, then, be "marriage" to Allah? Muhammad certainly gave that impression; but she dared not question him on this matter, lest he suspect she was as interested as she actually was.

"I shall explain," he said dreamily, as if looking forward to telling the story. "After my death, the Muslim community was faced with the first of many tests from God—how to determine who should lead them after me, and what should be the nature of my successor's authority."

"You've spoken very little about yourself," Ariana observed.

"I am of no importance," he said. "God alone is great."

"But how am I to understand the problem if I do not comprehend its origin?" she teased.

"As you wish," he declared, and immediately there unfolded before her, as if in a dream, the drama of Muhammad's life. It was the story of a man orphaned at an early age, and therefore inured to hardship and loneliness from his youth. He also learned early to bear responsibility, and this he did with grace and competence. These qualities, plus a facility with language and dialect, led to a promising career as a caravan guide. His big break came when, in his mid-twenties, he caught the fancy of one of his rich clients and married her. Khadija was an older woman, a widow, whose wealth opened up new possibilities in Muhammad's life. His character was a profound blend of the practical and the mystical, and the satisfaction of worldly needs enabled the former quality to recede and the latter to come to the fore. Over the years, as the love between them, always strong, continued to deepen, Muhammad spent more and more of his time in the mountains surrounding Mecca (his home town and the chief city of Arabia) and less and less time dealing with business. Fortunately, Khadija not only was understanding of his spirituality, but supported and encouraged it. On that fateful night in 612 when he gave utterance to the first sura, or chapter, of the Qur'an, she was the first to believe in and follow him.

The new prophet's message of monotheism, justice, and final judgment soon brought him into conflict with the wealthy and powerful merchants of Mecca. Unless they themselves initiate it, such men always regard change as threat. Moreover, though Muhammad was of a respectable tribe and had an influential protector in his uncle, Abu Talib, he was of a minor branch of that tribe and himself of no property or consequence. Who was this upstart to tell them how to conduct their lives? Finally, and most importantly, Mecca was the religious as well as economic hub of Arabian society; for located in its environs was the Shrine of the Ka'ba which, in addition to the sacred Ka'ba stone, a shiny black rock unlike any other mineral in the area, housed altars to practically all the deities worshiped by the polytheistic Arabs, who formed the majority of the population of the desert peninsula, the remainder consisting of a few tribes of Christians and Jews. Every year tribesmen from hundreds of miles around made pilgrimage to Mecca, and spent good money in the process. If Arab polytheism died, the pilgrimage would come to an end, and so would the profits.

For all these reasons, Muhammad eventually was forced out of Mecca. In 622, three years after his beloved Khadija died, he fled with most of his followers to Yathrib, several hundred miles to the north. Eventually Yathrib became known as the "City of the Prophet," or simply "the City"—Medina. As she watched, it seemed like such a minor transition, involving tiny groups of people, that it took her some moments to realize that this was what later was to be known as the *Hijrah*, the "flight," that is Islam's equivalent to the Jewish exodus. The Muslim calendar dates from this point, she knew, this time not mysteriously at all, but because her Muslim friends among the earthbound had often spoken of it. She understood now that the event was great not because of its scale in terms of numbers, but because it marked the formation of the first Islamic state, the nucleus for all later developments; for Muhammad had been invited to Medina not because he was a prophet, but because the city was suffering the death throes of tribal culture.

The desert tribes were governed not by a codified system of laws, but by a code of honor whose central tenet was blood revenge, much like the code by which inner city gangs live in present-day America. If someone killed a member of your tribe, you were duty-bound to kill a member of the offender's tribe, and so on. The desert vastness prevented this custom from degenerating into a round-robin of mutual destruction. Indeed, in the desert it played a positive role, encouraging the tribes to stick to their own territory, and ensuring that the constant tribal raiding remained sport rather than war. The object of this raiding was to steal from and humiliate one's enemy, not to kill him, for nobody wanted a blood feud. In the cities, however, it threatened to undo the very fabric of society. The only way around it was to find a mediator without local tribal affiliation. Muhammad, with his reputation for honesty and sagacity, combined with the animosity of his fellow Meccans, made him a natural candidate for the job. The people of Yathrib needed a judge, and Muhammad needed a new home.

Once in Medina, Muhammad quickly consolidated his power, which gained him additional enemies. In particular, the Jewish tribes of the city came to resent what they considered the pretension of this false prophet. Muhammad raided Meccan caravans, and the Meccans retaliated with attacks upon Medina. After repelling one such incursion, the Prophet discovered that one of these Jewish tribes had been in league with the enemy. He summarily beheaded all eight hundred of the tribe's adult males, and sold the women and children into slavery. This, however, proved to be the darkest moment in a rule marked by wisdom, moderation, and generosity toward both friend and vanquished foe.

Eight years after fleeing his native city, Muhammad returned in triumph. Concerted opposition had dissolved, partly due to his military successes, but also to the fact that he, or rather, God, had made Mecca the spiritual center of the new religion; so the pilgrimage could go on as before, with a new meaning but the same profits. Tribes from all over the peninsula declared their allegiance to the cause of God. When Muhammad died just two years after reentry to Mecca, he was temporal as well as spiritual ruler of all Arabia.

"Thus the pattern was set by God," Muhammad was saying as the historical vision faded, "and it was up to my followers to adhere to it after my death. Genuine Islam is neither a religion nor a belief. It is a way of life that embraces every dimension of human existence, social, political, and economic as well as religious. Otherwise, human beings succumb to the kind of fragmentation and social disintegration from which the modern West suffers, perhaps terminally."

"One finds no social fragmentation in the Islamic world?" she queried.

"Again, one most certainly does," he replied, "but Islam is a mighty force working to counter it. To continue my illustration, when I died my followers were faced with the task of maintaining a society dedicated to God in the face of venality, apostasy, betrayal, and simple human greed. The first issue demanding resolution was that of succession to my political authority. *Sunna* came to be the name given to the majority who agreed that the leader should be he who, regardless of ancestry, demonstrated the greatest fitness for the position according to popular consensus. The minority held that authority should be passed down through my blood line, beginning with my son-in-law, 'Ali. The issue was settled for a time at the battle of Karbala, in western Iraq in 680, when a Sunni army surprised and massacred my grandson, Husain, and his bodyguard, who carried the Shi'ite banner; but it has continued to crop up throughout Islamic history."

"It's simply a matter of succession to political authority?"

"Not simply," Muhammad said. "Very little in life is ever simple. Each group has developed its own religious style, and from the beginning the dispute was not merely over who should hold authority, but what the nature of that authority should be. The Sunnis hold that the Qur'an itself is all the spiritual authority society needs; and Muhammad's *Kalif*, deputy or successor, was a political rather than religious figure. Abu Bakr, the first Kalif, reigned only two years, but he set the tone for the Sunna ever since. He was my closest and ablest follower, truly a man of strength, courage, and inviolable integrity. He took seriously my saying that all believers are equal like the teeth of a comb, and God's saying that there would be no prophet after me. He never claimed any religious authority. His task was to protect and lead the faithful politically and militarily. The Shi'ites, on the other hand, revered the leader who followed in my blood-line as *Imam*, who was neither prophet nor messenger, but who was held to be divinely inspired in giving the authoritative interpretation and application of the Qur'an."

"That is quite a difference!" Ariana exclaimed. "The Imam sounds like a pope and emperor rolled into one."

"In theory, yes," he said, "but never in practice. Since all my sons died in child-hood, the first Imam was 'Ali ibn Abu Talib, my cousin and son-in-law."

"Your daughter, Fatima," Ariana interjected wryly, "being a woman, was unfit for leadership."

Muhammad ignored the barb. "'Ali, though a wonderfully bright and coura-geous comrade, proved too generous and trusting a leader. He was also named fourth Kalif, but refused to take revenge upon his enemies and was murdered by his own men. His elder son, Hasan, my elder grandson, became the second Imam, but abdicated out of fear of his enemies. My younger grandson, however, favored his mother . . ."

"Who favored her father?" Ariana interjected.

Muhammad smiled. "Husayn was an able, dedicated, and courageous leader. He and a party of seventy followers were massacred by an army of one-thousand Sun-nis at Karbala half-a-century after my own death. And so it went. Though for a time Shi'ite dynasties controlled Egypt and environs, the vast majority of Muslims have always been Sunni."

"So, the Imams were mostly rulers in name only," Ariana drew the logical con-clusion. "Is that who the Iranians believed Ayatollah Khomeini to be?" she asked. "One of these great Imams?"

"Now it becomes even more complex!" Muhammad laughed. "Neither Kalif nor Imam exists today."

"But I've heard Muslims call fellow Muslims *imam*," she protested, "though it didn't seem they meant anything so grand as what you just described."

"The term is used in a variety of ways," he explained, "as is the English equiva-lent, 'leader.' In Sunni Islam it refers merely to whoever leads prayers in the mosque, and perhaps gives a sermon on Friday afternoon. The Sunni imam is something like a Christian Protestant minister, the 'first among equals' with no inherent spiritual authority. In Shi'ite Islam, besides referring to the great leaders of early Shi'ism, the term has also come to be applied to leaders of local Shi'ite congregations, something like a cross between a Roman Catholic pastor and bishop."

"Then who was Khomeini?" Ariana persisted.

"A member of the clerical hierarchy of Iranian Shi'ism," he replied.

"It sounds just like a church." she observed.

"It is a church," he confirmed. "You see, in Islam the *umma*, the community of all Muslims throughout the world, is most important; but after that comes the *'ulama.'* In Sunni Islam the *'ulama'* consists of scholars who write learned commentaries upon the Qur'an, and whose authority, while considerable, is intellectual rather than spiritual."

"Like college professors," she said.

"Yes, like college professors," he agreed. "In a religiously egalitarian society, rea-son alone can create genuine consensus. Behavior alone is regulated, because the free commerce of ideas is essential to rational discussion."

"As long as the Qur'an itself is not questioned," said Ariana.

"Of course!" declared Muhammad. "We are not like the Jews, who pridefully take it upon themselves to wrestle with God! The Shi'a, on the other hand, since it is based upon authority, has always been more accommodating to socially irresponsible mystics. With someone else in charge, moreover, one is free to let oneself go. Some Shi'ite mosques are famous for the outbursts of emotion during prayers."

"But you said there is no Imam today," Ariana pointed out.

"No, but there is a clerical hierarchy," he reminded her.

"Why is there no Imam today?" she asked.

"Most Shi'ites today believe that the succession of my authority held for twelve generations," he replied, "but then the twelfth Imam disappeared."

"And the rest?"

"A minority traces the descent through a different line," he said, "and holds a different man, six or seven generations removed, to have been the final Imam, the one to have disappeared."

"What do you mean, 'disappeared?'" she asked, inferring from the inflection he had given the word that he referred to something other than death.

"Just that," he smiled, evidently more relaxed now that he was talking neither of God nor of his own mission, but of the vicissitudes of his followers. "He went into a mystical place, and from there he guides the faithful through the Shi'ite 'ulama, the clerical hierarchy."

"So," she said, "the mullahs, lesser imams, and ayatollahs get their authority from the last Imam?"

"Precisely."

"When did he 'disappear,'" she asked, "and is he to stay in this mystical place forever?"

"As I said, there is disagreement upon this point," Muhammad replied, "but the majority hold that the last Imam went into occultation late in the ninth century. The Shi'ites believe that he will return shortly before judgment day as the *Mahdi*, the 'guided one', to lead the faithful in one final *jihad* against the infidels and establish Islam's sovereignty throughout the world."

"*Jihad?*"

"*Jihad* is any effort over and above what is strictly required on behalf of the faith," he explained. "The greatest jihad is to fight and, if need be, die for the faith. Thus the term is often erroneously translated as 'holy war.'"

"How else would you distinguish between that and other types of jihad?" she queried.

"I suppose the phrase has its uses," he unexpectedly conceded. Ariana was discovering how much of a political realist Muhammad was. "Nevertheless," he continued, "it is not the barbaric custom so many Westerners make it out to be. It is a war in defense, not only of the faith, but social justice as well."

"That sounds pretty much like the Christian definition of a just war," Ariana commented.

"Yes," Muhammad agreed.

"But there's more to it, isn't there?" she probed.

"Yes," he avowed. "One who dies while on jihad is guaranteed Paradise!"

"Fanaticism!" Ariana cried, before she could catch herself. She expected Muhammad to explode in anger. On the contrary, he only looked saddened.

"The concept has been abused," he said darkly, "leading to fratricidal strife. Ayatollah Khomeini, leader of the Iranian Shi'a, proclaimed the war against Iraq a holy war. Iranians fought it with corresponding ferocity. Iranian mothers sent their young sons joyously off to battle, knowing they would never see them again . . ."

"How could they know that?" Ariana interjected.

"Because these boys did not serve as soldiers," he explained. "They were nine, ten, and eleven years old. They served as cannon fodder. For example, these boys cleared mine fields with their own bodies so that the regular troops could pass unharmed! But their mothers sent them off with joy, in many cases, because they thought they were sending their sons to Paradise!"

"And they weren't?" Ariana asked.

Muhammad sorrowfully shook his head. "That is in God's hands," he said, "but I do not see how a war between brothers can be anything but unholy!"

"Is that why Saddam Hussein didn't return the favor?" she queried.

Muhammad looked puzzled.

"Is that why he didn't proclaim the battle against Iran a holy war?" she clarified.

Muhammad smiled. "He did and he didn't," he said. "He used the rhetoric, but no one took him seriously, including himself."

"Because it was against fellow Muslims?" she asked.

"That," he replied, "and because he has no authority to declare a jihad. For example, in the recent Gulf War, when Saddam Hussein called upon Muslims everywhere to rise up in a holy war against the United States and her allies, Westerners could have spared themselves a great deal of hysteria had they sought to understand the differences between Sunni and Shi'ite Islam. As it was, they saw Hussein as another Khomeini. The Iranian Shi'ites regarded Khomeini as their spiritual as well as political leader. Thus, in their minds what he called a holy war was a holy war, a true jihad. Hussein, on the contrary, has no spiritual authority. In Sunni Islam, which makes up eighty-five percent of the Islamic population in the world, no one individual has the authority to call a jihad. For there to be a true jihad in Sunni Islam, all the forty-odd Muslim nations of the world would have to come together, agree that the faith was threatened, and join in active alliance to defend it, something that in Islam's present political disunity is almost unthinkable."

"Almost?" she echoed.

"There have been two genuine jihads in the history of Sunni Islam," Muhammad explained. "The first was the original war of Arab conquest that enabled Islam to be. The second was the war against the Christian Crusaders, but only after they massacred the women and children of Jerusalem."

"Yes, I've heard of that," said Ariana sorrowfully. "Jews and Muslims both died."

Muhammad nodded. "There is only one event I could imagine setting off a holy war in Sunni Islam today," he continued. "That would be the demolition of the Dome of the Rock in Jerusalem to make way for the rebuilding of the Jewish Temple."

Ariana recalled what the Teacher had said. "A holy war," she murmured, "and World War III!"

"Quite possibly," said Muhammad.

"Then why did Hussein call for a holy war?" Ariana asked in bewilderment.

"No doubt to play upon Western fears," he replied, "to make them see in him a dangerous religious fanatic who could command Muslim loyalty far beyond the borders of his own country, and therefore who had better be placated rather than conquered."

"It worked," she said.

"Yes, in large measure it did," he agreed, "but only with the West. Apart from a few fanatical extremists who look for any opportunity to stir up resentment against the West, no Muslims took Hussein seriously on this issue, as he undoubtedly did not expect them to. After all, Iraq had just finished one war and was about to engage in another with, respectively, the two most Muslim of Muslim polities: Iran, whose state religion is Shi'ite Islam, and Saudi Arabia, the archetypal Sunni land whose very constitution is the shari'a, the system of Qur'anic law. How could either of these conflicts be a jihad? Contrast the fanatical heroism of the Iranian soldiers in their war against Iraq with the defeatism of the ordinary Iraqi soldier in the Gulf War."

"There were the Republican Guards," Ariana noted. "They gave a good account of themselves."

"They are devoted to Hussein, not Islam," Muhammad scoffed, "and that only because he brainwashes them at a young age and buys their services at exorbitant cost."

"The difference, then," Ariana summed up after a long interval of reflection to be sure she had gotten it straight, "is that, in Sunni Islam, the entire community of Muslim nations must participate or no holy war is possible; whereas, in Shi'ite Islam, the word of one man is enough?"

"It is possible for one man to set the Shi'ite world aflame," he said, "but hierarchical position alone is not enough. Given the fluidity of political dealings in the Islamic world, only someone with the charisma of a Khomeini could have forged so strong a unity of church and state, and then only in the country of his jurisdiction. The Lebanese and Iraqi Shi'ites have their own ayatollahs to whom they pay heed."

"So, only in Iran are the Shi'ites the dominant majority," Ariana observed, "and so, only in Iran was an Ayatollah Khomeini possible."

He nodded.

"What about the Kalifs?" she asked. "What happened to them?"

Ariana felt him emotionally wince.

"The office of Kalif was supposed to be filled by the ablest man in the umma," he explained, "but it soon came to be seized by whoever had the military might and turned into a hereditary office. Dynastic wars were fought over the *Kalifa*! By the time of the First World War, it had become so meaningless that the Arab Sunnis fought in alliance with the British against the last Kalif, the Sultan of the Ottoman Empire. After defeating the Turks, the British and French dissolved the office, mercifully, I think."

"And do Sunnis also await the coming of a savior, a Mahdi?" she queried.

"In theory, yes" Muhammad replied, "but the belief has much less significance to them than to their Shi'ite brothers. Ironically, the one known to Western historians as the Mahdi, Muhammad Ahmed, was Sunni. In the 1880's, he led an army of Berber tribesmen out of the Sudanese desert and threatened the British hold upon the Suez, before dying of a mysterious disease. Perhaps such a one will arise again and unite all of Islam. Only God knows the direction in which he is leading his people."

"Again, you speak of Islam as if it were one," she challenged, "but you just now described a division that has led, and continues to lead, to much bloodshed and war."

"Bloodshed and war are the way of this world," rejoined Muhammad. "The question is whether Islam is its cause."

"Then tell me," she baited, "which is the true Islam, the Sunna or the Shi'a?"

"Again," he answered, "you assume that the differences between them are religious, whereas I am showing you that they are primarily political."

"You are showing me that the religious and the political are so bound up together in the Islamic world that it is impossible to disentangle them!" she protested.

"Only for the unsympathetic observer," he said pointedly. "Take another example from the recent war in the Gulf. Shortly after Saddam Hussein invaded Kuwait, the American government announced that it did not plan to assassinate Hussein because it feared making a martyr out of him. There is no ideal of martyrdom in Sunni Islam! Martyrdom is a Shi'ite ideal, going back to the assassination of 'Ali, the massacre at Karbala, the legends of the martyrdoms of most of the other Imams, and the fact that the Shi'ites have been the underdogs in the Muslim world. In the Sunni world men aim at success, and nothing argues God's favor like success."

"And why is that?" she asked.

"Because God said that, if I were taken and destroyed by my enemies, I would be no messenger of God."

"Ha!" she cried. "I was right! You had no intention of being a martyr!"

"You yet fail to understand," he said evenly. "All that is in God's hands. He had no intention of me being a martyr. In any event, the only way the Americans can prove that Hussein is not favored by God is to remove him from power. If they had done so in the Gulf War, he would have been forgotten the next day."

"So, the American government was being stupid?" Ariana asked, not finding this hard to believe, since she had heard this sentiment expressed frequently by earth-bound Americans and non-Americans alike.

"Or disingenuous," he replied. "Perhaps the Americans mistrusted Iran more than Iraq, and wanted to keep their former ally in power as a buffer. In any case, they brought a deep stain upon their honor."

"You think they should have followed through and destroyed Hussein?" she exclaimed. "Are you taking sides?"

"Not at all!" he laughed. "American secularism is the foe of my people, the enemy of God. One can, however, recognize when an enemy fights with honor. The Americans pledged themselves to the cause of the Iraqi Kurds and Shi'ites, and betrayed their pledge when it became politically inconvenient. Even if the best interests of Islam might have been served by that betrayal—and I do not say they were or they weren't—it can bring nothing but shame upon the United States." He stared into the trackless desert. "But I digress. Surely, now you can see how Islam is not the cause of violence in the Middle East. If anything, it is as the proverbial oil poured upon troubled waters."

Ariana shook her head. "No, I'm afraid I still don't see."

"Nations go to war for political and economic reasons!" he shouted with exasperation as he jumped to his feet. "Religion is used as the excuse, but how much of that excuse can plausibly be traced back to the Qur'an? If all Muslims lived by the precepts of God, there would be one Islamic state governed in justice and peace, and wars would be fought only against outsiders in self-defense."

"If there were only one Islam," she countered, "whose would it be—the Sunna or the Shi'a?"

"Men are given the principles of government," he declared. "They must work them out for themselves. I will, however, say this. No one can stand between the true believer and the word of God. On the other hand, genuine Islam always embodies itself in an Islamic state."

"So you see truth on both sides?"

"I see differences in religious style, not in religious substance," he replied, sitting down and resuming his former calm. "The Sunni style is egalitarian and rational, whereas the Shi'ite style is hierarchical and emotional. However, both groups follow the shari'a, both go on pilgrimage together, and both fulfill the duties prescribed by God. This is what it means to be a Muslim, a servant of God. If they would but focus on these things, all differences would fade into insignificance."

5. The Five Pillars

Ariana considered Muhammad's argument and found much merit in it, but something still bothered her. "You are saying that, unlike Christendom, there are no serious religious divisions in the world of Islam. Am I right?"

He nodded emphatically.

"Then what of the debate al-Hallaj mentioned over freedom of the will?"

"He also said it was much ado over nothing," Muhammad replied.

"One could say the same about the disagreements among Christians," she countered. "Men kill over nothing."

"He was speaking of the Mutazilites, a sect that arose in the ninth century and declined in the tenth. They were the rationalists of their day. Never popular, they tried to force their ideas upon the community of the faithful. For all their reason, they did not understand that ideas conquer through their own virtue, and never by force. Force merely clears the way at times," he added, forestalling her objection, "for an idea's fair and just consideration."

"Are there no rationalists in the Muslim world today who object to the idea that humans are puppets of an omnipotent God?"

"Let me tell you a story that will illustrate the infamous fatalism of Islam," he smiled ironically. "A sorcerer of Alexandria became so accomplished in his art that he conceived of a plan to cheat death. Through his necromancy, he discovered the day and time he was destined by God to die. A half-hour before his appointed doom, he whisked himself off on his magic carpet to Baghdad, some eight-hundred miles away, saying to himself that, when his spirit-servant, his *djinn*, told the angel of death that his master had left only moments before, he would never think to look for his victim in so distant a place. A quarter-hour before the appointed time, the angel of death knocked on the sorcerer's door. The servant, being good friends with the angel, chatted for a few minutes, and then informed him that his master had left but a short time before without saying where he was going. Did he wish him to give his master a message upon his return? The angel declined, saying that he himself would see the sorcerer shortly, as they had an appointment in Baghdad in just a few minutes."

"One can't escape the predestined time of one's death," she concluded.

"Exactly," he affirmed. "Rationalists, who confuse reason with intellect, think this belief must lead to despair. On the contrary, if one knows that the moment of one's death is foreordained by God, one no longer need worry about death. One is free to live. Islam is not about death. It is about life. Have you heard of the Five Pillars?"

She nodded.

"They are the best illustration of what I am saying."

"Why are they called 'pillars?'" Ariana asked, genuinely curious. "No one, Muslim or non-Muslim, has ever been able to explain that to me."

"It is really very simple," Muhammad smiled broadly, evidently pleased with the question. "What we are building is the *Dar al-Islam*, the dwelling place of those who live in submission to God, a home of justice and peace. The foundation of that dwelling place is the Qur'an, the word and will of God; but the pillars hold up the roof and enable there to be a protected space. You have heard that in Islam there is no separation of church and state. That is not precisely true as, except for the Shi'a, there is no church in Islam; and, in Iran, even under Khomeini, the church administration is distinct from that of the state. The truth is that the shari'a, the system of law derived from the Qur'an, provides the framework within which the community of Islam can thrive and grow. What that law forbids, the state should forbid; and what that law encourages, the state should encourage. There are but five exceptions to this rule—the Pillars. They are religiously required, but legally only encouraged."

"If they are so important, why not require them?" she asked, confused.

"Because the community of Islam is formed by the free allegiance of each of its members," he replied. "The Five Pillars are the ways in which each individual gives that allegiance."

"I see." Again Ariana was struck by how much sense Islam made. "I have heard a great deal about them, and I know what they are, but I'm not certain what makes each of them distinctively Muslim. I don't know what they mean. Would you please explain?"

The smile with which he greeted this question showed that he would be genuinely happy to do so. "In the modern West religion has become a hobby, to play at if it pleases one and to drop if it does not. Islam makes demands of its followers, concrete demands that may at times be difficult, but are never impossible, to fulfill. The first of these is the *shahada*, the profession of faith." He closed his eyes and in the lilting assonance of Arabic proclaimed that there was no god but God, and Muhammad was his messenger. "You already know the meaning of this proclamation; but you should also know that, to become a Muslim, you need not study a catechism or be certified as fit by a rabbi or priest. You need not make a contribution to a synagogue or church, or even be circumcised or baptized. All you need do is proclaim this declaration of faith from your heart in the presence of two adult male Muslim witnesses." He paused, as if in invitation. "If you do, God wipes your slate clean and you make a new start, free of sin," he added, reinforcing the invitation.

"How convenient," she commented, "just like Christian baptism."

It was amazing how quickly a storm could come up on a sunny face. "It's not a sacrament!" he cried. "There can be no cheating of God. In late antiquity and the early middle ages, kings and princes of Christiandom often put off baptism until their death beds so they could have the pleasures of leading a sinful life and the security of dying a blessed death. According to the God of Islam, one who postpones conversion to gain such advantage is as guilty of sin as one who converts to gain worldly advantage without truly believing in his heart. To lie to God is as great a sin as associating a creature with God, because one lies only to those whom one thinks one can deceive. To think that one can deceive God is to deny that God is God."

She was not sure that he was being fair to Christianity, but she saw the justice in what he was saying about Islam.

"And the second pillar," he continued, "devotion or *salat*, reminds the Muslim of the allegiance to God he has declared five times in every day."

Ariana laughed. "Is that why Muslims say, 'Blessed is he who converts to Islam in the morning and dies before noon?' Because then he is assured paradise without having to pray?"

Muhammad half-smiled at the jest. "Men are weak. They are lucky that God is merciful. Prayer is not onerous if one gives oneself to it completely. Life is only boring if one holds oneself back."

Ariana was startled by this reminiscence of Zen. "Didn't Allah originally order Muslims to pray forty times a day?"

"He was emphasizing the importance of prayer, that is all," said Muhammad. "Otherwise, he would not have agreed to three."

"Three?"

"The two extra are our gift to him," Muhammad smiled.

"I thought one was never to question God's will," she persisted, "but in the Qur'an it is you who change God's mind."

"I did no such thing!" he maintained. "In the Judaeo-Christian Book of Exodus, after the children of Israel worship the golden calf, God says he will wipe them off the face of the earth and raise a new people from Moses' own loins. Moses rebukes the Lord as if he were a naughty child, and he relents. Now I ask you, would either God or a prophet of God behave in such a fashion? You ask for evidence that the revelation given to the Christians and the Jews has been corrupted. It's self-evident! I did not question God's will. I asked to ascertain God's will, for the number forty was obviously symbolic."

"So, parts of God's word may be taken symbolically?" she said.

"Of course," he replied. "All language is symbolic, but that does not prevent it from having plain and unambiguous sense. If you are sitting in a crowded theater and someone shouts, 'Fire!', you do not argue with your neighbor over possible interpretations."

She had to admit that he had a point. "Prayer in Judaism and Christianity is talking person-to-person with God," she said. "One can go over one's problems and ask for favors as a little child would of her mother or father. If such an assumption of personal intimacy is blasphemous in orthodox Islam, what is Muslim prayer all about?"

"I have already said," he replied impatiently. "One renews one's allegiance to the cause of God. Thus, unlike Christian prayer, which as you say is personal communion with God, prayer in Islam is most virtuous when offered in public assembly. All sorts of masters claim our obedience every day, so we must remind ourselves to whom we owe ultimate obedience."

"Everything goes to God," Ariana mused. "Isn't that just another way of rationalizing everything going to oneself?"

"It can be," Muhammad admitted. "Like everything else in human nature, Islam does not condemn the desire to possess and enjoy, but it places boundaries that prevent that desire from becoming inhuman and all-consuming. There has been bitter argument in the Muslim world over whether Islam is most compatible with a socialist or capitalist economic system. Islam is neither socialist nor capitalist because, unlike the dehumanized West and East, it does not place economics before human life. And it escapes such degradation because it does not place human life before divine command. It is all a question of priorities."

Ariana remembered Judaism's concept of evil. What Muhammad was saying was making too much sense, and she fought against being overwhelmed. "Sounds nice," she commented, as coolly as she could manage. "Nice and abstract."

"There is nothing abstract about Islam," Muhammad proclaimed. "In Christianity, God is supposedly incarnate in a man. In Islam, God's will is incarnate in his word, the Qur'an. All that is required of the human race is set out clearly and unambiguously in words of power and embodied in commandment, law and custom. Hence, when it comes to dealing with poverty, we have the *zakat*, the alms-tax."

"I thought you said the pillars were voluntary," said Ariana.

"'Alms-tax' is a bit misleading," he explained. "In the great Islamic empires of the medieval period, the zakat was collected forcibly by the state. Since the political fragmentation of the Islamic world, the zakat has not been mandated by law."

"I perceive a contradiction here," she observed. "When Islam was at its height, people were forced to pay the zakat. When the Muslim world disintegrated, the zakat became legally voluntary, though still, if I get this right, religiously obligatory." He nodded. "Yet you say that it should be voluntary?"

"This is a matter of some debate in the Muslim world today, which," he added admonishingly, "divided rather than disintegrated. Sometimes God teaches us the truth in strange ways. If God has broken Islam, it can only be to reform it more perfectly."

"So, progress in understanding God's ways is possible," she said.

Muhammad bowed piously. "The word of God is infinite in depth. But to return to the zakat, the customary amount is one-fortieth of one's capital holdings in coin, crops and cattle. Nowadays, most Muslims simply give one-fortieth of their annual income. Of course, if one is poor, one pays nothing."

"And all this money goes to the needy?" she asked.

"It is permissible to use it for the defense and propagation of the faith," he replied, "and, of course, part must go to pay the salaries of those who collect and administer it, but it is customary to use the bulk of it to help the less fortunate. God says that a true Muslim does not close his eyes at night as long as one of his brothers lacks bread or a place to sleep."

"The zakat may only be used to help Muslims?" she queried.

"You must understand the structure of the society in which the custom originated," he said. "In the East, religion defines community, as it did in the pre-modern West. In the Islamic empires, Christians and Jews literally formed sub-societies with their own domestic laws, customs and traditions. Each community took care of its own. A Muslim living in a pluralistic society like the United States gives to charity without regard for the religion of the beneficiary. Nevertheless, the Muslim's first duty is toward the faithful."

"Charity begins at home," she commented.

"Precisely," he agreed. "But Islam does more than require aid to the needy. The modern West is filled with people who regard the poor as animals—one should be kind to them within the limits of convenience, but they belong to a different world. Islam demands solidarity of all God's people, rich and poor. Partly for this reason, and partly to remember who is the true giver of all good things, a faithful Muslim fasts in the time and season appointed. This is called *saum*."

"I don't understand," Ariana said. "How does fasting make for social solidarity?"

"The beginning of all genuine unity in a society is empathy," he explained. "Only if one places oneself in the shoes of another can one understand the other's interests as one understands one's own. Many people in the West have never gone a day without eating, and many go many days without eating. The rich cannot understand the poor without themselves knowing hunger. The fast of Ramadan, the fourth pillar of the house of Islam, ensures commonality in understanding the human condition."

"Ramadan?" she echoed.

"A month in the lunar calendar of Islam," he said. "Since the lunar year is eleven days shorter than the solar year, Ramadan creeps backward through the seasons from year to year. This fast is significant because, throughout the month of thirty days, a faithful Muslim will not eat or drink anything, and indeed will not even allow tobacco smoke to pass his lips, during the daylight hours. In winter, the time may be short, but in summer daylight may last as long as sixteen hours."

"Why don't people simply take a holiday," Ariana asked, "or, at the very least, sleep in the day and work at night?"

"Some do," he answered, "but most cannot. Most Muslims are farm workers, and the crops do not wait upon human convenience. They must be tended in their own times and seasons, and work in the open field requires daylight. The truly interesting point"—he frowned as he drew out the word "interesting"—"is that the poor and ordinary Muslims, for whom fasting is often a great hardship, observe Ramadan far more faithfully than the rich, for whom it would be at worst a minor inconvenience. God will requite each man according to his works."

"Fasting is a good work?" she asked. "I thought you said that, apart from the Sufi mystics, there is no ascetic ideal in Islam."

"There is no virtue in fasting for its own sake," he declared, "only in fasting in obedience to God."

"Then why does God command us to fast?" she persisted.

"What man can know the mind of God?" he replied, throwing up his hands. "But I have already given you plenty of reasons—empathy with the poor, remembering God, learning obedience to God. Forgive me, Ariana, if I ask, what counts for you as a reason."

"You're right," she smiled ruefully. "I'm sorry. Even after experiencing it myself, I just have never been able to understand why people fast!"

"I cannot tell you why all people fast," he bowed graciously. "I can only say why Muslims fast."

For a lingering moment she looked into his eyes, and there saw so paradoxical and powerful a combination of pride, humility, authority, self-discipline, strength, sensitivity, spirituality and sensuality that she was at a loss to understand how she felt about him. She did know that his religion made a good deal of sense, not only on its own terms, but from what she knew of earthbound spirits. Part of her wanted to surrender right then and there, but another part feared too hasty a commitment. All the evidence had to be in before she could come to a decision, and there was one more from whom she was to hear, the most familiar but also to her the most enigmatic—the founder of the religion whose sign was the cross.

As if reading her mind, Muhammad broke the silence by saying, "Soon you will encounter Kristos. You will hear much of how Christianity is the religion of love. Please note two things. First, this religion of love has spawned the most violent and fanatically intolerant tradition the world has ever seen. Second, Islam does not lack an ideal of universal love. It may be tempered with a greater realism, but it is unmistakably there. The first two pillars, the declaration of faith and prayer, root one in allegiance to God; but the next two, the alms-tax and Ramadan fast, direct the faithful to work for the benefit of their brothers and sisters. The fifth pillar, the most glorious of all, illustrates how human solidarity is utterly dependent upon obedience to God. I speak of the pilgrimage to Mecca, the *hajj*."

"It certainly is a grand event," Ariana admitted. "Every year, I have heard, between one and two million people attend."

"Yes, it's marvelous how God works, is it not?" Muhammad beamed. "Modern air travel, charter flights, and the generosity of Muslim governments and individuals have turned what formerly, at its height, was an affair involving no more than 60,000 souls into an overwhelming expression of Muslim brotherhood."

"And a logistical nightmare, I imagine!" Ariana laughed.

"Not so much as one might expect," Muhammad smiled. "Every year the Saudi government works wonders, but all their efforts would avail not at all were it not for the spirit of peace and cooperation that fills the pilgrims themselves. Once in a lifetime an able-bodied Muslim is supposed to make the greater pilgrimage to Mecca . . ."

"The greater pilgrimage?" she echoed.

"A Muslim may of course visit Mecca at any time, and that would be a lesser pilgrimage. The greater pilgrimage, however, happens only once each lunar year, in the twelfth month of that year, and is a supremely communal event. Muslims from every quarter of the globe come together in the holiest city of Islam in remembrance and worship of God. I will not bore you with the details. Suffice it to say that the Shrine of the Ka'ba, where the father of all monotheists, Abraham, himself set up a house of worship, is central to the proceedings, and that they last for some eleven days. What you need is to taste the spirit of the hajj."

And, with that, she sank into another experience.

Again she kept her identity, but found herself inside the being of a young man, a black man, who had just been thrown into prison for running numbers and dealing drugs. A visitor, also male and black, was explaining to him how a movement called the "Nation of Islam" wished to help him. At first, the convict wanted nothing to do with religion; but, as he listened, pieces of the puzzle that was his own life began to fall into place. The visitor declared that Islam was the religion of the black race, a natural religion for natural men. Christianity was so unnatural a religion because the white race was not created by God, but was a horde of demons manufactured by an evil sorcerer. The Nation of Islam, or the "Black Muslims," as they were known to outsiders, were led by Elijah Muhammad, who presented a shining example of black power and black pride to his fallen brothers and sisters. The black race, the only truly human race, had to raise itself up. For this reason, the Nation sponsored all sorts of community programs to aid single mothers, help the orphaned and abandoned children, and get convicts and drug addicts to take responsibility for themselves by realizing their own black manhood.

The young convict, whose name, she gathered from the conversation, was Malcolm Little, joined the movement and changed his name to Malcolm X in recognition of the fact that a black slave got his surname from his master, and therefore that surname was a badge of slavery and shame. A man of great intelligence, energy, and charisma, Malcolm rose rapidly in the movement until Elijah Muhammad himself was grooming him as his successor. Then he started to take the "Islam" in "Nation of Islam" more seriously than Elijah Muhammad had intended, and the two men grew apart. The climax came when Malcolm went on pilgrimage to Mecca.

When the young African-American arrived in Mecca, he was astounded. He had expected to see only blacks, but instead he found himself coming together with people of all races, nationalities, and socioeconomic strata, all wearing the same simple white garments to worship the one true God in brotherhood and peace. When he returned to the United States, Malcolm turned away from Elijah Muhammad and started a genuinely Islamic movement among black Americans that grew by leaps and bounds. At this point, Ariana's consciousness was returned to Muhammad and the blissful oasis. Mercifully, she told herself, because she knew how the story ended. In 1965, Malcolm was gunned down, no one knows for certain by whom, though many believe on orders of Elijah Muhammad. His movement, however, lived on and assimilated all but one branch of the Nation of Islam, bringing black American Muslims into the mainstream Muslim world.

"In the story of that young American warrior and martyr," Muhammad said as soon as he noted the light of recognition in her eyes, "is to be found the essence of the Hajj and the essence of Islam: one world under one law serving one God in peace, brotherhood, justice, and love."

Ariana did not know if she found this vision glorious or frightening. Probably, she said to herself, both. She became so lost in thought that she failed to notice when

Muhammad left or her next visitor, Kristos, appeared. All she knew was that there was a tension, an edge in the air much like what she had felt throughout Yahweh's visit, only this time sharper and more threatening. She was about to announce that she had made up her mind, that she had no need to explore Christianity; but then her eyes became prisoners of his gaze, and she knew she had to see this thing through to the end.

CHAPTER V.

CHRISTIANITY

1. The Logic of Love

His eyes held hers and, more than with any of the others she had encountered thus far, she felt that he could see through to the bottom of her soul. Because of this, she was afraid to speak or even feel a thing. Then he smiled a winsome smile, and fear turned to relief. There was no need to play a part or keep up appearances with a man one could not deceive.

"It's funny," she said. "I've looked forward to meeting you more than anyone else; but, now that you're here, I don't know what to say."

"Let's keep it simple," he suggested in a plain and direct voice. "What would you like to know about me, and what don't you understand?"

"I don't really have any questions," she faltered. "I mean, I have questions, but I don't really know what they are! Are you God?" she blurted out, before she could catch herself.

"Let's get one thing straight," he replied in amusement. "Whatever else I may be, I am a man. Treat me with the same respect you would show any other human being, no more and no less, and we'll get along fine."

She heaved a sigh of relief. "But are you God?" she smiled.

"If I said yes, would you believe me?" he asked, returning her smile; only, by the time it got back to her, she was already frowning again.

"I don't know," she said seriously. Then, brightening, she added, "Would you want me to?"

"You're very quick," he laughed gently. "Why don't we circle around to that issue? Did you know that the first Christians did not believe that I was divine?"

"No?" she said. "Then why did they call themselves 'Christians?'"

"They didn't," he replied. "The term was coined in Antioch several decades after my death."

"What did they believe, then?" she asked, finding it easy, emotionally as well as intellectually, to follow his lead.

"As you well know," he answered, "I was a Jew, and the first Christians were Jews who believed that I was the messiah. *Kristos* is the Greek translation of that term."

"'The anointed one,'" she said.

"I see that my good friend, the Teacher, has already covered this ground," he laughed. "Almost everything he said about the Jewish conception of God, human existence, revelation, and salvation may be taken as a given in Christianity. Christianity arose out of Judaism in much the same way that Buddhism arose out of Hinduism, but with one crucial exception: I was born, lived, and died a Jew. Gotama Buddha may be held to have repudiated his Hinduism when he rejected the Vedas and the caste system. I never repudiated Judaism."

"Not even when you believed yourself to be God?" she queried, and he burst into laughter.

"You don't give up!" he finally managed to say.

"And you don't give in," she countered.

"Alright," he surrendered, "suppose for the sake of argument that I did and do believe myself divine. Ancient Judaism rejected the idea of a man becoming God, but it did not address the issue of God becoming man."

"Because it didn't think of it!" she declared. "As soon a it did think of it, it rejected it!"

"No," he corrected, "as soon as it thought of it, it split into Judaism and Christianity."

"Would you call the breaking off of a tiny faction a 'split?'"

"Historically and sociologically, no," he conceded; "but philosophically and theologically, the question is still up for grabs."

"So, the first Christians were Jews who believed you were the messiah, the man by whom God's kingdom would come to earth," she said, realizing that he wasn't going to give away anything until he believed her ready.

"Yes, that's clear from the Christian New Testament," he confirmed. "When my disciples did not understand what I was saying about going down to Jerusalem to die, it wasn't because they were stupid. They really believed I was the messiah, and the messiah was not supposed to die. He was supposed to usher in the kingdom of God, in which there would be no more death."

"When you did die . . . Or did you?" she caught herself. "Muhammad said Judas took your place on the cross."

"I died," he answered her, and the reality of his death was so profoundly evident in his eyes that she was ashamed she had even appeared to make light of it.

"When you died," she continued more seriously, "they must have been confused."

"They were torn apart inside!" he exclaimed. "I don't merely mean from their personal affection for me. They were faced with a choice, and nothing is more upsetting to people than to be faced with a fundamental choice. They had to decide whether to adhere to the conception of the messiah that was so deeply rooted in Jewish belief and hope, or to redefine that conception in light of their experience of me. Those who took the former course continued to be Jews, plain and simple. Those who chose the latter became Jews of a particular sect that went against the mainstream. In other words, they became the first Christians."

"How did they redefine the idea of the messiah?" Ariana asked with intense curiosity.

"At first, as little as possible. If you read the New Testament—the gospels, the apostolic letters, even the Book of Revelation—you will see that the earliest Christians expected me to return in their own generation and then bring in the Kingdom of God."

"So in effect they kept the traditional idea of the messiah, but simply broke it into two parts," she summed up, and he nodded in confirmation. "But you didn't come back," she continued. "At least, you haven't yet."

"When I didn't return as expected, the redefinition went further," he continued, "and resulted in the distinctive doctrines of Christianity—the Holy Trinity, the Incarnation, and the Atonement."

"Distinctive?" she echoed.

"Christianity, like Judaism and Islam, is a form of ethical monotheism," he explained. "Belief in one, personal, all-powerful and loving God is as central to it as to Judaism and Islam. It does, however, have other beliefs that set it apart from Judaism and Islam."

"I see," she said, hesitating for a moment, but then taking his openness as an invitation to broach the difficult issues. "What do you think of these 'doctrines?'"

"I do not think they should be doctrines," he declared straightforwardly, not at all discomfited by the question. "A doctrine one believes because one is supposed to. I agree with Job—if you have to be honest about anything in life, it is what you think and feel about God."

"What do you think and feel about God?" she asked pointedly. "Do you think these distinctive ideas, whether doctrines or not, are true?"

"What do you think?" he returned.

She was tempted to play the game of "I asked you first!," but she felt that he was not merely avoiding her question, that he would not have requested her answer if it were not somehow crucial to his own.

"I've heard about them, but I don't really understand them," she said. "I've talked about them with all sorts of earthbound spirits, including popes, theologians, 'born-again' Christians, Protestant ministers—I don't know to whom I haven't spoken! They could always tell me what the idea was, but never what it meant. Take the idea of the Holy Trinity, for example. I know that it's about there being three persons in one God—the Father, Son, and Holy Spirit. I even know that the original Greek term for 'person' here was *hypostasis*, or 'entity.' What I don't know is why anybody would believe such a thing!"

"Why do you think?" he asked again.

Ariana reflected. "The best I've been able to come up with is that each 'person' is God in a different role. As Father, he is creator, as Son, redeemer, and, as Holy Spirit, sanctifier. But why anyone would say it that way, that God is three persons in one God, is beyond me."

"Your idea is interesting," he said, "and it was actually taught by a man named Sabellius, but it was rejected as the 'Sabellian' or 'modalist' heresy by the early Church."

"Do you think Christians were right to reject it?" she asked mischievously.

"I do," he replied with unexpected directness. "The idea of the Holy Trinity is about the nature of God's being, not his action."

"Then each 'person' is an aspect of God," she suggested. "The Father is God's will, the Son is God's intellect, and the Spirit is God's memory."

"You've been reading your Augustine," he laughed, and she flushed. "No, no, that's not a bad thing!" he assured her.

"I was trying to impress you," she said ruefully. "I was passing the idea off as my own."

"Wherever the idea came from," he said, dismissing her offense, "I've always had one problem with it. No," he caught himself, "two problems. The interpretation makes the Trinity an appearance rather than a reality, something God is from our various perspectives rather than in himself. I also wonder, if each person is merely an aspect, what prevents there being a hundred or a million persons in one God, as would be the case in Hinduism."

"Then I take my original stand—the whole idea doesn't make any sense!" Ariana declared, thinking that maybe those Jehovah's Witnesses who said the concept of the Holy Trinity can't be found in the Bible were right.

"I'm not so sure," Kristos mused, so convincingly that she almost believed he didn't know what he was going to say next. "When I listed the distinctive ideas of Christianity, did you notice anything missing?"

"Let's see," she said, wondering if he noticed that she was mimicking his manner. "You mentioned the Holy Trinity, the Incarnation, and the Atonement. What about baptism?"

"That's not exactly an idea. It's a ritual, and such initiation rituals are found in one form or another in any religious tradition. I'll give you a clue. It's what I consider the most fundamental idea of Christianity."

"Distinctive and fundamental," she summarized. "I don't know."

"God is love," he said.

"But many religions hold that God is love!" she protested. "You said that yourself about both Islam and Judaism."

"I said these religions affirm that God is loving. I did not say they held to the idea that God is love."

"What's the difference?" she queried, beginning to think that Kristos was going to be every bit as exasperating as her other suitors.

"In Eastern religion, one can say that God is love," he explained; "but, of course, 'God' there is not personal, and love is like the cosmic glue that holds the universe together. In the West, love is irreducibly personal. In fact, one could say that love is personal relationship. To the extent that one opens and remains faithful to genuinely personal intimacy, one loves."

She nodded to show him that she both followed and agreed thus far.

"In Judaism, then," he went on, "one can say that God is loving, because God has personal relationship with human beings and angels, both personal beings. In Islam one may say likewise, if one holds the master-servant relationship to be in some sense personal. Only in Christianity, however, can God be love, because only for Christianity is there personal relationship in God. What is the number of relationship?"

"Two?" she ventured.

"Three," he corrected her. "There are the two persons in relationship, and then the relationship itself."

"I don't understand," she said, though somewhere inside she felt that she did.

He dismissed her plea of ignorance. "We all know this. Haven't you ever experienced that agonizing moment in a relationship when what your partner demanded and what the relationship demanded were diametrically opposed? And to be in relationship with someone who has no awareness of the reality of the relationship is living hell."

This last he said with profound conviction, and there was no doubt from the look in his eyes that he was speaking from experience. It was strange to think that to be God meant to be in the living hell of unacknowledged relationship. Strange, but she could see how, if God is love, it was also true.

"Alright," she assented, "three is the number of relationship. So?"

"If love is the essence of personal relationship," he concluded, "then only for Christianity can God be love, for only for Christianity is there personal relationship in God. The Father is in relationship with the Son, and the Holy Spirit is the relationship itself."

"I see what you mean," she said tentatively, "but I'm not sure that explains the doctrine."

"It depends on what you mean by explanation," he declared. "Ultimately, the Holy Trinity can't be explained, not because it is some ineffable mystery, but because it is a basic assumption, or rather, a theological corollary to the basic assumption of Christianity, that God is love. As I'm sure you've learned by now, basic assumptions can't be explained because they are that by which all else is explained."

"If the fundamental belief of Christianity is that God is love," she queried, "then why didn't you mention it when you ticked off the distinctive ideas of Christianity?"

"That is a problem, isn't it?" he smiled sadly. "Not for me, but for those who would follow me. Curious, isn't it, that Christians have fought among themselves tooth and nail over the meaning of the Holy Trinity, the Incarnation, and the Atonement, as well as a host of lesser issues, but have neglected to explore the doctrinal significance of the one idea without which Christianity makes absolutely no sense, in heaven as well as on earth? Take the doctrine of the Incarnation. There was more quarreling in the early Church over the business of me being fully God and fully man than over any other idea."

"Really," she remarked, remembering Muhammad's scorn for the idea. "Among Christians themselves?"

"Yes," he said, "just about every alternative was proposed and gained a following. In the second century, the Docetists held that I only seemed to have a physical body, and therefore that I did not really suffer and die. In the third and fourth centuries, the teaching of a certain Alexandrian bishop named Arius, that I was not divine by nature but merely God's adopted son . . .'"

"The Jehovah's Witnesses!" she interjected.

"Yes, they are a survival of Arianism," he confirmed. "This teaching swept through the Church, at first under imperial patronage in the east; but later, in the west, even after it was condemned by the bishops, many barbarian tribes coming into the Roman Empire converted originally to Arian Christianity."

He spoke coldly, impersonally, as if he could not put his heart into what he was saying because none of it went to the heart of the matter.

"Finally came the Monophysites," he said, "who, except for the Coptic, Syrian and Armenian Churches, are now mostly dead and gone, but whose spirit lives on in much of popular Christianity. They held that I was a divine mind in a human body."

"Isn't that what you meant by 'Incarnation?'" she asked with surprise.

"Not at all," he replied, "though it's a common misconception. The orthodox idea was expressed in three different formulae, each countering one of these heresies. Against Docetism, the Church maintained that I am fully God and fully man; against Arianism, that I am two natures, divine and human, in one person; and, against Monophysitism, that I am like all other human beings in everything but sin."

"Heresies?" she echoed, fascinated by the term.

"Sooner or later, all these movements were condemned by the Church and repressed," he explained. "Heresy is wrong belief."

"What's wrong for one may be right for another," she observed.

"To affirm the basic logic of Christianity against its corruptors is necessary," he declared, "but to coerce individuals in any way to accept that logic is utterly self-contradictory."

"You lost me!" she laughed.

"Remember when Muhammad explained to you how the idea that God became man is absurd?" he asked.

She nodded. "That would be difficult to forget."

"And do you remember when Gotama explained how logic varies with varying assumptions?" he went on.

"You mean, how we see reality determines how we think?" she asked. "I believe Ishwara said something about that, too."

"Put the two together," he said.

Ariana thought for a moment. "Something is absurd because that's the way someone sees it."

"Yes, something is absurd only within a given logic," he affirmed. "Within what logic is the idea of God becoming man absurd?"

"I know what the question means," she replied, "but I haven't the faintest idea how to answer it."

"All those terms Muhammad used to distinguish God from humanity—omnipotent and weak, infinite and finite, eternal and mortal—with what are they all concerned?"

It came to her as in a flash. "Power—who has it, who doesn't have it, what kind of power one has or doesn't have."

"In all three forms of ethical monotheism," he continued, "God's justice, power, and love are affirmed; but each differs from the rest in asserting the logical primacy of different characteristics. Judaism is the logic of justice. Islam is the logic of power, or, to be more precise, the logic of obedience to divine authority."

"So Christianity is the logic of love," she whispered, to herself more than to him.

"Muhammad was absolutely right," he declared. "If God's being is understood primarily as power, then the Incarnation is indeed absurd. If God is love, however, it makes perfectly good sense."

"How so?" she queried.

"Let me tell you a story from my favorite philosopher, Kierkegaard," he replied, and she laughed.

"What's so amusing?" he half-smiled.

"Oh, I don't know!" she managed to say. "It just seems funny, you having a favorite philosopher!"

"Remember," he chided gently, "human in all but sin."

"But doesn't that make you superhuman?" she objected, suddenly serious.

"In no form of ethical monotheism is sin seen as an absolute necessity of human existence," he replied. "At most, to be human one needs the possibility of sin. I had that possibility, or else, how could I have been tempted? But do you want to hear my story or not?"

"Oh, yes!" she clapped her hands. "I love stories!"

"It's not really a story," he said, and then laughed at her feigned look of extreme disappointment.

"More of a parable?" she inquired ironically.

"In a way," he said. "Actually, more of a riddle, but it fits right in with the metaphor you used to characterize the relationship between God and humanity in Islam."

Ariana did not bother to ask how he knew. "The great king?"

"Yes, the great king. Kierkegaard puts it this way . . ."

"Before you tell the story," she interjected, "would you mind telling me something about Kierkegaard, like who is he?"

"He was a nineteenth-century Danish philosopher and theologian," he answered with alacrity, "one of the founders of existentialism. He was practically ignored in his lifetime, because that was the age of optimism, and he told a lot of unpleasant truths; but he came into his own in the twentieth century."

"I can guess why," she said, "but what's existentialism?"

"A way of seeing," he replied. "Existentialists may be theists, atheists, agnostics, or what have you, but they all have one thing in common. They try to understand life not from the spectator's viewpoint, but from within, from the standpoint of living it."

"Zen," Ariana remarked.

"Yes, Zen is existential." He paused, as if to see if she had any more questions on that side-issue. "You want to hear the riddle?"

She nodded.

"Suppose you were a great king," he asked, "and fell in love with a peasant girl. What would you have to do to win the girl's love?"

"Not much!" she declared, remembering her own lifetimes in poverty. "Any girl would be overjoyed to marry the king!"

"I didn't say 'win her hand'," he admonished. "I said, 'win her love.'"

"What's the difference?" she gibed.

"If you don't know the difference," he said sternly, "then I have nothing more to say to you."

"Alright, I know the difference!" she confessed. "If he swept her off her feet, dazzled her with his regal glory, he'd never be sure that she loved him for himself."

"She'd never have the choice," he corrected her. "She'd never see him."

"So, he'd have to leave his throne," she resumed. "He'd have to come to her as an ordinary man."

Kristos smiled in agreement. "When it comes to love, power and authority are not only no advantage. They are positive disadvantages. The king must win the girl's love on his own merits. Afterwards he may reveal his royalty and lift her out of her poverty."

"I understand your parable," she said, "but I still don't see how an infinite and all-powerful God can be a weak and finite man."

"Only in love," he declared. "If God is defined as power, the idea of God becoming man is absurd; but if God is defined as love, then what love demands, love makes possible."

"As with the Mahayana bodhisattwa!" she cried.

He nodded. "Kierkegaard's story of the king and the peasant girl is in line with the apostle Paul's theme of *kenosis*—God empties himself of his power and glory so he can enter into authentic personal relationship with humanity. The insight of genuine Christianity, however, is even more profound. God becoming man is not the abdication of power, but the expression of the only real power, the power of love. The cross is the revelation of true omnipotence. According to the logic of love, divinity and humanity are mutually complementary: God becomes human so that humanity may participate in the divine life."

"And according to the logic of justice?" she queried.

"That's the paradox of justice," he replied—"what it demands, it cannot fulfill. What justice promises, love alone can deliver. If Judaism is about coming into personal relationship with God, then Christianity is its logical development. In Judaism, the whole idea of revelation is based upon the assumption that humans can't go to God, so God must come to them. And how else could God come to them in a fully personal way but as himself a human being?"

"So, you really do believe you are God," she said.

"I forgave sins, didn't I?", he responded. "I did not teach like the scribes, the academics of first-century Judaism, with their foot-note mentality. Neither did I preach like a prophet, saying, 'Thus says the Lord!' I spoke on my own authority."

"And what is that authority?" she queried.

He suddenly looked severe. "The authority of love."

"That's quite a claim," she murmured, realizing that she was more bothered by it than by the idea that he was God. "Can you back it up?"

He looked long and deeply into her eyes.

"Are you trying to hypnotize me?" she laughed, to hide her discomfort.

"Do you really want to know the answer to your question?" he asked meaningfully.

"Is there any way around it?" she asked.

"No," he agreed, "there isn't, but you had to realize that before you could understand the answer."

"I do realize it," she said, "so tell me the answer."

"I can't tell you the answer," he replied. "I can only show it to you, but you have to have the patience to see it. It will take some doing."

"If that's so," Ariana returned more bravely than she actually felt, "then let's get started."

2. The Good News

"We begin with the Christian gospels," he announced.

"What do we need them for?" she protested. "If you're really the Christ, you must know the story of your own life. Why do we need secondhand reports?"

"Because those reports, along with the rest of the Bible, document the human race's experience of the living God," he answered. "The truth of that experience is to be found not merely in who and what I say I am, nor in what human beings say I am, but in the encounter between God and man, humanity and divinity, that happened in my life and the lives of those I touched. If God is love, then truth is the truth of relationship."

"Is that why you called the Holy Spirit the spirit of truth?" she asked.

"You are perceptive," he smiled. "Very perceptive. Or look at it another way. You want to know the real facts of my life, but facts are facts only when seen as such. What one counts as fact depends upon one's way of seeing. And beyond that undeniable insight of Eastern philosophy, there is the existential truth that how one sees is conditioned by one's basic value."

"Whether that be obedience, justice, or love," she added.

"Right again," he nodded. "Thus, it would avail you naught to receive additional facts about my life if you persist in the delusion that such knowledge would make a fundamental difference in your understanding of life itself. On the contrary, the understanding of life you bring to the gospels will determine what you make of them."

"Just as in Judaism," she smiled.

"As I said, I see no real break between authentic Judaism and genuine Christianity," he reiterated.

"So it's all relative?" she asked. "What you put in determines what you get out?"

"In a way," he replied. "However, you will find that, if you bring a certain understanding to the gospels, it will unlock their meaning and point you on the way to life."

"What understanding is that?" she queried, knowing but dreading what his answer would be.

"The understanding of love!" he proclaimed.

"We keep going around in circles!" she cried. "Love, love, love! Everything ends up at love, and then we start again with the same old question: what is love?"

"That's why we need the gospels," he said calmly. "All 'Christians' today 'know' that I am God, and they think that's the final word on everything. Can you tell me what it means for a man to be God?"

"I used to think I knew, but now I'm totally confused!" she laughed.

"So are they," he said. "Human beings don't know what it is to be God. They only know what it is to be human. If they wish to know my divinity, they have to look at my humanity. My humanity, according to genuine Christianity, is the revelation of the truth of divinity!"

"I understand what you're saying," she said petulantly, "but I still don't see why you can't give me the straight story."

"If I told you, would you believe me?" he challenged.

"It depends," she replied.

"Upon what?" he persisted.

"I'm not sure," she said. "I think maybe upon whether what you say fits my picture of Jesus."

"And where did you get that picture?" he queried.

"From the gospels," she admitted sheepishly.

"To change your perception of me, then," he concluded triumphantly, "I have to change your perception of the gospels."

"So that's where we'll begin," she smiled impishly, "just as I've been saying all the time."

"Just as you've been saying all the time," he mimicked gently, "but you didn't know it. Do you know what the word 'gospel' means?"

"Life story?" she hazarded.

"No," he said, "though that's a natural guess, as most Christians today assume that I had no life apart from what is in the gospels. 'Gospel', however, means 'good news', and the Christian Gospel is the proclamation that God's salvation has come through me. The gospels were never intended to be biographies. They say a great deal about me because I am the instrument of salvation, but only as it concerns my mission. Thus they focus on my public ministry, and two of the gospels contain legendary stories about my birth. Otherwise, except for an incident in the Jerusalem Temple when I was twelve, they say nothing about my early life."

"Isn't that strange?" she asked.

"Lots of people have found it strange," he smiled. "Books have been written about my secret life in India and Egypt. Perhaps, with all the talk today about visitors from outer space, someone will get really imaginative and have me kidnapped and replaced by an alien. There is no real mystery, however. I was merely an ordinary Galilean boy growing up in an ordinary Galilean town. People take note only of the extraordinary."

"And people didn't take note of you until you started performing miracles?" Ariana wondered. "Or did you? Did you really perform miracles?"

"Yes," he said simply.

"I have no problem believing you because I'm a free spirit," she remarked; "but, if I were earthbound, I wouldn't know what to think. After all, look at the gospels, since that's what you want to do. There are four of them. Four. And each one paints a different picture. In Matthew you're a Jewish rabbi, in Mark you're a wonder-worker, in Luke you're the son of God, and in John you're practically God the Son!"

"That's putting it succinctly!" Kristos laughed.

"I'll admit, she continued, "the Synoptic gospels aren't anywhere as different from one another as all three are from John; but still, in one place you say whoever isn't against me is for me, and in another whoever isn't for me is against me."

"Those were different situations," his eyes twinkled.

"Maybe," she said, ignoring the amusement in his voice, "but that doesn't explain geographical discrepancies among the gospels; or were there four different Palestines as well?"

"Parallel universes?" he suggested.

"And time, too," she went on. "In the Synoptics, your public ministry lasts a year. In John, it lasts three years. Time warp?"

His smile became more infuriatingly knowing, egging her on.

"And the biggest, most inexplicable difference of all!" she announced. "In the Synoptics—Matthew, Mark and Luke—you come off as a real human being who feels weary, put-upon, and misunderstood; who gets angry, and experiences anguish and despair. In John, you're like the Christ of medieval iconography—the seven foot-tall, super-cool, laid-back dude with the radiant aura and the simply divine bedside manner!"

She said these words with increasing rancor, but they only had the effect of making him practically roll on the ground with laughter. "You've made a real study of all this," he said, when he finally caught his breath.

"Not really," she relented somewhat. "An ex-Catholic priest, an extremely learned and disenchanted theologian, once bent my ear. I have to say that a lot of what he told me made a lot of sense."

"Such as?"

"Such as the way the Catholic Church throughout the Middle Ages made it impossible for anyone but learned churchmen to read the Bible. The Church would not allow it to be translated into the languages ordinary people understood; so whenever it was read in services, it was always in Latin. Even the average parish priest knew barely enough Latin to stumble through the mass, certainly not enough to make any real sense of the scriptures. Everyone got their revelation homogenized, pasteurized, and harmonized with the party line."

"That criticism could also be leveled at the Eastern Orthodox Church, where the sacred language was Greek rather than Latin," he observed. "But it was a wise strategy, don't you think?" he added, and she had a hard time detecting the irony in his voice that she could see in his eyes. "It preserved the unity of Christendom."

"That's right," she confirmed, oblivious to the apparent role-reversal, "but at the price of repression and tyranny. By the time of the sixteenth-century Protestant Reformation, spiritual hunger had driven the peoples of Western Christendom to the adventures of world exploration and domination, on the one hand, and the reading of the Bible, on the other. The holy book was translated into every language of Europe, and it was basic Protestant teaching that a believer did not need a church hierarchy to interpret the Bible rightly. All he needed was the aid of the Holy Spirit."

"And that would inevitably be there if one had genuine faith," added Kristos.

Ariana suddenly realized that she had been lecturing to someone who must know the subject far better than she. "I'm sorry," she said.

"For what?" he returned with unmistakable sincerity. "Your thumbnail sketch of the history of the Bible's role in Christianity was excellent. There's only one problem. It's incomplete." He gestured an invitation to go on.

"Well," she continued with renewed confidence, "this Protestant idea, that everyone should read the Bible and each would be guided to the proper conclusions by the Holy Spirit, sounds nice, but it opened a real Pandora's box. Hundreds of Protestant sects arose, many of them claiming, like the Catholic Church from which they were spawned, to hold the one true interpretation of the faith. This led to endless quarrels, controversies, and religious persecutions, culminating, in 1618, in the Thirty Years' War. This war enjoys the dubious distinction of being the first in modern European history to be more destructive to the civilian population than to the soldiers who fought it."

"Yes, that war," said Kristos pensively, as if he knew the subject well. "The Germans could no more imagine a religiously divided Germany than a politically united one."

"The Europeans could no more imagine a religiously divided Europe than a politically united one!" she amplified.

"Yes," he acknowledged, "and, when it was over, Germany was devastated, and both sides merely agreed to disagree."

"Whoever ruled determined the religion of those he ruled," interjected Ariana. "So much for religious freedom!"

"That was the principle of the Peace of Westphalia," he admitted, "with some qualifications; but the hold of religious orthodoxy upon men's minds was broken."

"Yes," she said sardonically, "freedom of religion only became an idea in Western Civilization when religion ceased to have objective significance!"

"Yes," he agreed sadly, "by the end of the 18th century, the thinking people of the West had had enough. They turned away from religion for their sense of reality and looked to natural science."

"The Age of Enlightenment," said Ariana.

"The age of schizophrenia," he said bitterly. "From this point on, what the individual held to be the ultimate meaning of life ceased to have any influence upon how he lived his life!"

"So," Ariana marveled, "you think the solution is to return to the Age of Faith?"

"There never was an age of faith," he replied, even more bitterly. "No, this insanity was always there, buried deep in the human psyche. Unless it is brought into the light, it can never be healed. But more of that later," he added, brightening. "On with your story! What of the Bible in all this?"

"As you wish!" she bowed. "The critics and historians of the Age of Enlightenment tore the Bible apart! The Bible went from being the most revered to the most despised book in Western culture, from the book that was above criticism to the book for which no criticism was severe enough."

"What you point out is but one example of a widely observed phenomenon," he remarked. "The ancient Greeks called it *enantiodromia*—extremes pass over into their opposites."

"Absolute cold burns, and total silence deafens," she noted. "I can see it, but the ex-priest who told me all about it couldn't see it. He didn't want anything more to do with Catholicism or Christianity. He was thinking of becoming a Buddhist."

"Certainly a much more peaceful tradition," Kristos smiled wanly, "but, perhaps, not so exciting. However, this ex-priest, though he seems to have had much insight into the Christian tradition, isn't here. Is there anything else in the Bible you find disturbing?"

"I've already discussed much of the Old Testament with the Teacher," she responded. "I know this isn't what you asked, exactly, but there was one other thing the priest mentioned . . ."

"If it's an issue for you," Kristos interjected, "that's all that counts."

Ariana smiled gratefully. "There's a passage, I think he said it was in Matthew, where Jesus . . . I mean, where you say . . ."

"To say 'Jesus' is fine," he reassured her. "Not only are you not required to believe that I am God. You are entitled to doubt whether I am he."

She smiled, and then went on. "Jesus tells Simon, his chief disciple, 'You are Peter'—meaning 'rock', I guess . . ."

"Yes, *petros* in Greek," he confirmed. "This is in the sixteenth chapter."

"'You are Peter,'" she continued, "'and upon this rock I will build my church.' He said that the Greek word for 'church' here is *ekklesia*, and that it appears only one other place in all the gospels, and that is in the eighteenth chapter of Matthew, twice in one verse. Now, as he put it, the Catholic Church has gotten tons of mileage out of this single verse in Matthew. It is the basis of the Church's entire theory of papal authority, the pope being the spiritual successor of St. Peter. He thought it very unlikely that Jesus actually said this, and I agree. What do you think?"

"Personally," he said, "the only authority I acknowledge is that of love, and each of us knows that for himself in his own heart."

"Then how did this passage get into the Bible?" she asked.

"It was added," he explained. "That's also how the obviously spurious prohibition against women speaking in the *ekklesia*, the community of the faithful, was added to Paul's First Letter To the Corinthians."

"Why 'obviously?'" Ariana asked.

"Not only does it break up the flow of exposition," he replied, "but, in the same letter, Paul tells women they should cover their heads when they prophesy in the *ekklesia*!"

"Yes," she said, remembering. "Gotama said Buddhist monks justified excluding women from the monasteries by adding such interpolations to Buddhist scripture when, in order to preserve them, they recopied the sacred scrolls."

"To be fair," said Kristos, "such additions were not necessarily intentional. A scribe might put a note of his own in the margin, and a later scribe might unwittingly incorporate that note into the text."

"Perhaps," Ariana mused. "But there's something else that's always bothered me, and no one else has been able to understand. I even tried bringing it up with that priest . . ."

"If nobody understands it," interjected Kristos, "chances are nobody's willing to understand it!"

She looked into his eyes and felt, without any particular reason for doing so, that he would understand.

"All the gospel writers, in numerous places, say, or even have Jesus say, that he said and did such and such to fulfill prophecy, to fulfill scripture."

"Yes," observed Kristos, "God has this master plan of salvation, this magnificent drama, and he's told the prophets of the Old Testament portions of the script, especially parts of the messiah's role. Jesus is saying and doing what the messiah is supposed to say and do, and that proves he is the savior."

"Exactly!" she cried. "But what kind of an explanation of the meaning of a play's line is that, merely to say that it's in the script?"

"No explanation at all," he agreed.

"But there's something else about it," she pondered. "I've never been able to put my finger on it."

"It makes you feel dead inside?" he asked.

She nodded vigorously, hardly able to believe her ears.

"Me, too," he said. "After all, even if drama is scripted and rehearsed down to the finest detail, doesn't it depend for its very meaning upon its reference to real life in which real people have to make real decisions without benefit of a script?"

Again, she could only nod, she could not speak.

"So what if this, from the Christian viewpoint the most momentous event in history, the coming of God into the world as man, is just part of some script, with God as author, director, and irresistible prompter? Then, from that same Christian viewpoint, life itself is meaningless and dead, and this drama of salvation has no reality to it—no real passion, life, or death, and no real encounter with God!"

Ariana was dumbfounded. He had not read her mind. He had seen into her heart!

"What bothers you most about the Bible?" he probed.

"To tell you the truth," she replied after reflecting, "it's none of the things I've already mentioned. It's the way Christians use it today. The mainstream Protestants pretty much toe the academic line. Whatever is fashionable in Biblical scholarship is fashionable in your standard Lutheran or Methodist church. Then there are the Fundamentalists. They're much worse. I suppose they take the Bible more seriously, but they try to force their ideas on people. I just don't feel comfortable with any of it. Maybe if they were up front about what they're doing, like the Muslims, I could respect them even if I decided it wasn't for me; but they're not. They talk about Christian freedom, and everything they do they do out of love. By definition. It's really scary. By the time I make it to earth, I wonder if they'll have taken over!"

"Yes," he said sadly, "the best argument against the truth of Christianity has always been Christians themselves. Do you think fundamentalists are what Christianity is all about?" he asked in full seriousness.

"I don't know," she replied. "Like I said, they seem to take the Bible more seriously than other types of Christians."

"Perhaps," he said mysteriously. "Let's forget about them for the moment. Suppose you were a police officer called to the scene of an accident, and you took down statements from four eyewitnesses. As a joke, or maybe because you forget, you turn these depositions in to your superior without any indication of exactly when and where the accident occurred. Merely looking over the reports themselves, what might your superior conclude?"

"That there were four different accidents. If what I hear from the earthbound is accurate,"—he laughed at her irony—"even eyewitness accounts of an event almost never agree in exact detail."

"Why, then, should one expect the gospels to agree in every detail," he said, pointing up the "moral" of his story, "whether they were themselves written by eyewitnesses or simply based on hand-me-down accounts? Or take another analogy. Do you know what a blind date is?"

"Something no one will confess to but everybody's been on?" she laughed.

"Precisely!" he replied, and for the first time she understood what she found so disturbing about him. He had the intelligence of the Teacher, the gentleness of Gotama, and the passion of Ishwara, all integrated into a personality with a seemingly infinite depth. "You're getting to be more earthbound than the earthbound."

"I'm learning from the best!" she replied, herself surprised at the bitterness lurking in this supreme irony.

He studied her, evidently regarding this rejoinder as some sort of sign, but not at all offended. "You're right, I am more earthbound than the earthbound."

"I didn't mean just you," she said hastily. "I meant all my suitors."

"A strange manner of courtship, isn't it?" he commented, and at that moment there was something about the gentle irony in his voice that caused her to realize she had fallen in love with him. "But what you say is true," he continued. "We all love the earth and the things of the earth, but especially me. That's why I will do anything rather than let it go the way of destruction."

She remained silent. Too much was coming clear to her too fast. As if he sensed the reason for her discomfort, he rose to stretch his legs and then settled down in a more distant place. His voice became more friendly and less intimate, and he turned the conversation back to his incipient analogy.

"Suppose four friends fix you up with a blind date, but they give it a twist. Each gives you an account of the man in question, and you have to use those accounts to pick him out of a crowd. How would you read them?"

"I'm not sure what you mean."

"First of all, what would you think if all the accounts agreed in every particular? Would that make you think them reliable?"

"That would make me think I was being set up!" she replied. "If each friend gives her independent and honest opinion of the man, there are bound to be differences."

"Significant differences?" he queried.

"Probably," she replied, "just as with eyewitness accounts of the traffic accident."

"How would you deal with those differences?"

She thought for a moment. "I think I'd look for what all the accounts had in common."

"And you'd dismiss the differences?"

She thought some more. "I'm not sure," she finally said, and then, after another pause, added, "I don't think I'd dismiss them. I think I would try to figure out why they were there. Maybe one of my friends says he's a nice guy because she's always wanted me to marry. Maybe another friend says he can't be trusted because she doesn't want me spending time with a boyfriend instead of her. There are all sorts of possibilities."

"Yes, there are," he agreed. "How would you sort them all out?"

"I don't know that I could," she smiled, wondering if he would catch her meaning. "I'd probably pick out the wrong guy and end up marrying him instead."

He smiled in return, but tentatively, and she wondered if she were being too elliptical. Then she realized that she could not be more straightforward because she herself did not understand her own feelings.

"Academic theology is in the same boat," he said, evidently thinking the only safe course was to stick to business. "In the Age of Enlightenment, for example, many 'free thinkers' pointed out the various discrepancies and contradictions among the four gospels. In the nineteenth century, theologians composed a number of 'lives of Jesus' in which they sought to harmonize the gospel stories without leaving anything out from any gospel. None of these was convincing so, in the first part of the twentieth century, the majority of academic theologians, spurred on by Albert Schweitzer's *Quest For the Historical Jesus*, concluded that we have little, if any, historically reliable information about Jesus of Nazareth. In fact, some concluded that Jesus never really existed!"

"You speak as if he were not you," she observed.

"I didn't want to confuse the issue," he said.

"No chance of you not doing that!" she laughed. "But I get your point. Anyone would expect to find differences in portraits of the same person by different people, but critics regarded differences as evidence of tampering. Your analogies make it clear how foolish that criticism was."

"As foolish as the opposite approach," he said. "Let's go back to your prospective blind date. No matter how much you thought about it, would you ever consider saying to yourself that, because these accounts were written by friends whom you trust, you believe every word without question, no matter how many discrepancies there may seem to be?"

"No, I would never think to do that," she said immediately.

"Why not?" he queried.

"Because I know my friends!" she laughed.

"Is that all?" he persisted.

Now she had to think for a moment. "Because then I couldn't read them at all. They would make no sense because I would have forbidden myself to think about them. I would have made it impossible for myself to make sense out of them."

"I agree wholeheartedly," he declared, "but isn't that how fundamentalists approach the Bible? You say they take the Bible more seriously, but I say they don't take it seriously at all, for to take it seriously is, above all, to read it on its own terms. If the Bible is inspired in some way, isn't it curious that God caused or allowed it to contain four accounts of my ministry? Muhammad was right. From a fundamentalist perspective, Islam makes a lot more sense. It is logical to believe in the literal truth of the Qur'an, because the Qur'an has one unified message; but to believe in the literal meaning of the Bible is absurd, because there is no one unified message or viewpoint. There are common concerns, but a great variety of perspectives. If God somehow inspired it, why would he leave it that way?"

"Maybe so we would be forced to think for ourselves," she mused.

"Maybe so you would have to arrive at your own conclusions, which is exactly what fundamentalism forbids," he concluded with unexpected bitterness.

She reflected, and then smiled. "If you were the one going on the blind date, how would you figure out what the woman was like?"

He returned her smile. "I would read each account slowly, meditatively, getting a picture of the person in my mind. When I came upon discrepancies, I would neither dismiss them nor try to force them into some artificial harmony, but strive to find perspectives from which they resolved themselves by taking into account all the reasons they might be there, including the authors' respective motives and viewpoints. Eventually, I believe, I'd have a sense of the real person who inspired these accounts, but who can't be reduced to one or even all of them. I could even go back and critically evaluate the details of each account in light of the intuition all the accounts have given me."

"Sounds vague and subjective," she remarked.

"That's what fundamentalist and academic theologians say," he said evenly, "but I think it's common sense. Suppose you are a spy, and you have five minutes alone with the enemy's top-secret device, but you can't touch it because it's wired to an alarm. You have to gather as much information as possible with a camera. What do you do?"

"Take as many different pictures from as many angles as possible," she answered.

"You return to headquarters and turn the film in to the lab so they can construct a mock-up," he continued. "What would you think if the reply came back that they could do nothing with your pictures because they were all different?"

She smiled. "That they were idiots."

"Until recently, and in some ways still, that has been the position of academic theology," he said. "On the other hand, what if you received your developed pictures in glossy prints arranged in a tasteful collage, and were told that that was the reproduction of the enemy's device?"

"Fundamentalism!" she laughed.

"Each gospel is a two-dimensional picture," he said. "Is it vague and subjective to realize that a picture is not the multi-dimensional reality of which it is a picture? Is it fidelity to the picture to forget that it is a picture, to think it is the reality?"

"That makes sense," she said. "That makes a lot of sense, but I can see why nobody reads the gospels your way."

"Why not?"

"Because people want safe, mechanical solutions to all the mysteries in life."

"And why is that?"

"Does there have to be a 'why' for everything?" she complained. "Don't we ever come to the end of the why's?"

"Yes, but we have to make sure it is the end," he rejoined. "Otherwise, our thought is rationalization, a tissue of self-deception and meaningless abstraction."

"How can you know if you've done that?" she cried, exasperated.

"You have to decide for yourself," he answered.

"Well them, I think I've done it!" she declared.

"Let's see if I can give you a 'why' that takes you deeper," he said. "Academic theology and fundamentalism are intellectual opposites, but they have one thing in common. They seek an interpretation of the Bible that would be valid for anyone, and therefore that anyone could understand. What they both fail to comprehend is that, in real life, formal validity means nothing and truth is everything. The reason they don't understand this simple truth is because it implies that the quality of one's understanding of the Bible, like the quality of one's understanding of anything, depends upon the quality of one's own selfhood."

"Is this spiritual elitism?" she challenged.

"In a way," he said, "but it's an elite anyone can join, because the quality of one's selfhood depends upon the quality of one's choices in life. If you choose to live on the surface, your understanding of the Bible will be superficial. If you choose to live mechanically, it will be mechanical and ideological. If you choose to live in fear, you will participate in religious authoritarianism. Only if you choose to courageously enter the depth of your own experience will you find the depth of the Bible's meaning."

"I get it," she said ruefully. "I'm sorry I hit out, but now I think I understand. Fundamentalists take a book that is meant to open up one's experience to life's mystery, and make it a substitute for experience. It becomes a banner instead of a book, the emblem of an exclusive club."

He nodded. "And if you belong to the club, you go to heaven. If not, to hell. Thought-provoking, isn't it?"

"But how did this purchasing of one's own salvation at the price of another's damnation ever become part of a religion whose founder said, 'He who would be my disciple must take up his cross and follow me?'"

"Everything about Christianity can be understood from the perspective of love," declared Kristos. "Apart from love, it is entirely opaque."

"Even its history?" she challenged.

"Especially its history," he maintained."Love has a most paradoxical quality. Do you know the literal meaning of 'sin?'"

"'Missing the mark,' I believe the ex-priest told me."

"In love," he continued, "to miss by an inch is worse than missing by a mile. One would do better not to love at all than not to go all the way with love. It's as with a microbe—if it is outside the body, it is harmless; but if it gains entry, it can kill. Love is one's entry into the soul, the heart, the center of another. One can do incalculable harm to the beloved if one mixes love with self-interest, fear, or the will to power."

"The history of Christianity!" she said with the shock of recognition.

"Yes." he affirmed, "Christians do not understand Christianity because, like most people in the world, they think and live according to the logic of power, while Christianity is the logic of love. Thus, from the very beginning, even among my own disciples, they have done untold harm because they did not, they would not accept the absolute necessity to be perfect in love."

"So, the religion of love became the most violent and fanatical of all," said Ariana. "Wouldn't it have been safer, as Muhammad suggested, to have done without?"

"You will have the opportunity to consider that option in some depth," he smiled knowingly, "but I personally see no real choice. Without love, there is no life."

Ariana felt like biting her lip, a habit she detested, especially in spirits, who had no physical excuse. "We either attain perfect love or destroy ourselves?"

"You do understand," he bowed, "but do you truly appreciate what is at stake here?"

"I'd be foolish to say I did," she replied humbly. "Please show me."

3. Fully Man

And immediately she found herself in, or rather, observing, another experience. The scene was the interior of a simple mud-brick, one-story dwelling, the home of poor people. She did not know how she knew him, he did not look or even feel exactly like Kristos, but she knew it was he. Jesus was sitting at the table, evidently the guest of honor. It was a fairly small gathering, consisting only of a handful of his most faithful disciples and the host family. Suddenly the door opened, ever so slowly, and this seemed to disturb the intimate assembly far more than if the intruder had broken in violently.

It turned out to be a woman, fairly young but worn by childbearing and housekeeping, or perhaps simply by worry. She wore finer clothes than the rest, and also had a habitual self-assurance that contrasted, charmingly, Ariana thought, with the humility with which she approached Jesus. The charm, however, seemed to be wasted upon the diners, because they looked upon her with undisguised hostility and contempt. The woman ignored their animosity. From the moment she entered the one-room home, her eyes fixed upon Jesus and him alone.

The master nodded his permission for her to speak. She explained in a few words that her daughter was possessed by an evil spirit, and she begged him to heal her.

Ariana was surprised to see that Jesus did not grant her request immediately, but appeared to be deliberating. Finally, he said to her, "It is not right that the bread reserved for the children of the kingdom be given to dogs." Before Ariana was able to fathom the significance of this remark, the woman replied, "Yes, rabbi, but the dogs may eat of the crumbs that fall from the master's table." As Jesus told the woman that she could go, her daughter was healed, Ariana realized that he had called her a dog.

"How could you!" she cried as soon as the experience came to an end.

"How could I what?" he asked ingenuously.

"How could you call that poor woman a dog?" she demanded.

"So you do believe I am the real Jesus?" he said with irritating irrelevance.

"Not if you say things like that!" she cried.

"The story is in the Gospel," he said. "In fact, it's in two of the gospels, Mark and Matthew. I prefer Mark's account—it's less melodramatic."

"Why did you call her a dog?" she persisted, increasingly angry at his apparent levity.

"'Dog' was a common term of contempt first-century Palestinian Jews used of Gentiles," he explained, without explaining. "The woman was a Gentile. I, my disciples, and the family we were visiting were all Jews."

"Are you saying you were a bigot?" she demanded, hardly able to believe what she was hearing. "Are you saying you are a bigot?"

"That is what you must decide," he replied seriously. "It would not be a particularly original interpretation. There are plenty of fundamentalist Christians, especially those affiliated with the neo-Nazis and Ku Klux Klan, who see it that way, and who use this story to validate their own irrational hate."

"But you healed the woman's daughter!" she exclaimed, arguing with herself. "That means you were showing everybody that you came to all peoples, not just the Jews."

"So many say," he replied, "but the reasoning's not too convincing."

"Why not?" she objected. "It makes sense to me."

"Did you ever hear an argument among the earthbound between a liberal of the American North and a conservative of the American South?"

She nodded. She had heard such an argument not too long ago, and now she had little doubt that Kristos had had a hand in arranging it. The Southerner was saying to the Northerner that "you damn Yankees think you know how to take care of our Negroes better than we do. You come down here with your fancy ideas of equality and freedom and voting rights, and all you do is set them to thinking they're better than they are; and, naturally, the higher they rise, the farther they fall. We take care of our own. As long as they keep in their place and do the labor that's their God-given lot in life, we take care of our own."

"Well," said Kristos, returning her to the present, "when Jesus called the Gentile woman a dog, couldn't he have been putting her in her place? When she replied that the dogs eat the crumbs from the master's table, couldn't she simply have been showing him that she knew her place? When Jesus told her that her daughter was healed, couldn't he have been 'taking care of our own' by giving her a few crumbs?"

She ignored the demonstration of his power to read her thoughts verbatim. "Why did the Jews hate the Gentiles so?" she asked.

"Not all of them did," he replied. "Many admired the Graeco-Roman culture and sought to make it their own. Most Palestinian Jews, however, blamed any and all Gentiles for the ill fortune of the Chosen People, for making them feel like aliens in their own land. The same sort of sentiment fueled the popular revolution in Iran that overthrew the Shah and brought Khomeini to power. A traditional way of life was threatened. The Jews feared assimilation into the dominant Gentile culture. Their very survival as a people was at stake."

"So they were the underdogs," Ariana observed.

"Yes, but it doesn't matter," he said. "In their minds, they were chosen by God to rule over the Gentiles in his coming kingdom. If Jesus were the harbinger of that kingdom, then in my put-down of the Gentile woman they would naturally see an anticipation of their own ascendance."

"Are you justifying what you did?" she exclaimed.

"Not at all," he replied simply. "I never justify what I do. But I am trying to get you to see that, when it comes to understanding what I'm about, there are no easy answers."

"Isn't love an easy answer?" she said sarcastically.

"In one sense, yes," he smiled. "Easy as opposed to complicated. But, if you oppose easy to difficult, love is the hardest answer of all."

"The hardest and the simplest," she pondered.

"Yes," he echoed, "the hardest and the simplest."

"But love doesn't seem to be any kind of an answer here," she said.

"It could be," he responded, "but only if we find it more directly elsewhere in the gospels. Let's leave the story for a moment, and look at what Jesus demanded of his disciples."

"If you demanded anything, it couldn't be love," she declared. "Love doesn't demand."

"On the contrary, love demands everything!" he proclaimed. "Love is the most demanding master of all!"

"Then you and I have different ideas of love!" she said.

"Perhaps," he mused, "but first let me clarify mine. When the Son of Man returns, the dead will be raised, and he will send his angels to every corner of the Earth to gather in all humanity. They will separate everyone into two groups, as shepherds separate the sheep from the goats, and he will direct them to put one at his right hand and the other at his left. Then he will turn to those at his right and say to them, 'Well done, good and faithful servants, enter into your reward! Because when I was hungry, you gave me to eat; when I was thirsty, you gave me to drink; when I was naked, you clothed me; when I was imprisoned, you visited me; and when I was sick, you ministered to me.' And then they will reply, 'Lord, when did we see you hungry, thirsty, naked, sick, imprisoned?' And he will say to them, 'As long as you did this to the least of my brothers and sisters, you did it to me.'"

As he spoke, nothing changed outwardly, but she felt that everything he described was actually happening. "And you don't attach any riders, do you?" she murmured. "One doesn't have to love and get baptized, or love and join a church, or love and learn the secret handshake, or even love and believe in you or God. All that is required is love."

Again, he did not respond outwardly, but she felt he assented to what she had said. "Then," he continued, "the Son of Man will turn to those on his left and say to them, 'Depart from me, you wicked and unprofitable servants, you have no place in my kingdom. For when I was hungry, you gave me nothing to eat; when I was thirsty, you gave me nothing to drink; when I was naked, you didn't clothe me; when I was imprisoned, you didn't visit me; and when I was sick, you didn't minister to me.' And they will say to him, 'Lord, when did we see you hungry, thirsty, naked, sick, imprisoned?' And he will say to them, 'As long as you failed to do this to the least of my brothers and sisters, you failed to do it to me.'"

"And," Ariana added, "you can just imagine the goats complaining, 'Lord, if we had only known it was you! We love you, sweet Jesus, we love you! If we had only known you were that twelve-year old hooker on the street-corner, or that wino puking his guts out in the gutter, or that bag-lady freezing to death because there was no room in the shelter, or that drug addict going cold-turkey in central lock-up. If we had only known they were you!'"

"And by saying that," he smiled sadly, "they show how they are still missing the point. The kingdom of heaven is not about loving God or Jesus, nor even about loving others for the sake of God or Jesus. It's about love. God is love, or, as the evangelist John also said in his letters, 'He who loves, knows God'—not 'He who loves God, knows God,' but 'He who loves, knows God.' The knowledge of God is in the heart, not the head."

"I can understand that," said Ariana, "but I can't understand how you can speak of judgment and love in the same breath. How can a God of love send anyone to hell?"

"I agree," said Kristos. "The only one worthy of eternal damnation would be someone who would condemn someone else to eternal damnation. It all goes back to something about which the Teacher spoke with you—reaching people on their own terms. Most people live in fear of the world. Fear of hell counterbalances fear of the world. When two opposing fears are equal, it doesn't matter which way one goes, as far as fear is concerned."

"So it's just psychology?" she queried.

"Don't belittle psychological necessity," he replied. "It's the law that even God must take into account, if he wishes to enter into relationship with those who have become its abject slaves. But there is another reason, a more direct truth to this business of hellfire and damnation. It emphasizes how everything is at stake in each person's choices at every moment of life."

"That's a lot of responsibility!"

"Yes," he nodded. "Nevertheless, that's what Christianity demands. That's the demand that I am. Many people think Christianity is about God understanding that humans are weak and imperfect, and so forgiving them their sins. That's not what I say. I say, 'Be perfect, even as your heavenly father is perfect.' I say, 'Those who would be my disciples must take up their crosses and follow me!'"

Ariana turned and stared off into the featureless distance, wondering when and why the oasis had disappeared. "Muhammad was right," she said. "It's all too much for a human being to bear."

"I might agree," he said, "but do we have any other way? If love is what it's all about, then it's all or nothing, perfection or destruction."

She turned to him abruptly with a look that demanded an explanation.

"Love is not something you can play at," he declared. "Love isn't something you work towards. As I said before, to miss in love by a little is worse than missing by a mile, for love gives one entrance into the heart, the inner sanctum of the beloved. If one perverts love to one's own ends, ends that are not of love, one can warp the beloved's very soul. Parents and spouses do this to their children and mates all the time, and then they use the love they bear their victims as an excuse. If one loves without taking upon oneself the absolute responsibility of love, then it were better never to love at all."

"Then we should give up on love altogether!" she cried.

"Yes," he said, suddenly quiet, "but what else is there? Love is the very essence of life!"

"So says Christianity," said Ariana.

"So says Christianity," he echoed. "And so says your own heart."

She was too confused about her heart to even begin to argue with him on that score. She rose, feeling suffocated by him in this desert of endless nothingness, and paced restlessly about, much as Muhammad had finally done in her own presence. Ariana wondered if she had made the Prophet of Allah feel as Kristos was now making her feel. "If love is the meaning of it all," she asked with feigned nonchalance, "what's all this business about faith and belief?"

And immediately she was in another experience.

She was a widow, a lonely member of a crowd who had come to see the wonder-worker, Jesus of Nazareth. She had expected great things, and she had not been disappointed. This seemingly ordinary man, whom some said had been a shepherd and others a carpenter, had made the blind see and the lame walk, and even cured leprosy. Wonder of wonders, in the evening when everyone was hungry and no one had much of anything to eat, he fed the entire crowd with what they said were the few loaves and fishes a little boy's mother had packed for him! She herself had not been close enough to actually witness this miracle, but she could not doubt the sincerity with which everyone who claimed they had seen attested to it.

As the sun sank bloodily into the Sea of Galilee, a number of the Nazarene's followers piled into a fishing craft and set off in the direction of Capernaum. The holy man, however, stayed behind; so she and the rest of the crowd settled down on the patches of mossy green that dotted the rocky shore, all in great hope and expectation of what tomorrow would bring.

That night she had a strange dream. The Nazarene arose in the middle of the night and stood for a long time looking out over the lake. Suddenly the wind came up, and there was no doubt that one of the violent storms for which the Sea of Galilee was famous was about to descend upon them. Everyone sought what shelter they could under the rocks and shrubs, and snatched a few hours of miserable sleep in the damp and cold. All this seemed real, and when she awoke in the morning there had been a storm; but she knew it had to have been a dream, because at that point the Nazarene set off on foot across the water!

Then she had another dream. A man wearing strange clothes was talking to her. He was in a box, and at times he seemed smaller, and at other times larger, than a normal human being. He was telling her that she must believe in the Lord Jesus, the Son of God, who came into the world two thousand years ago and died on the cross in atonement for our sins so that we might live forever with him in heaven. She remembered that the holy man who had walked on the water was named "Jesus" and wondered if the two were connected. It was such a common name, however, that she doubted it.

Then she awoke again, and this time arose from her makeshift bed. The pastel hues of an after-storm sunrise did little to allay the consternation of the crowd when they discovered the holy man was gone. But where? He could not have crept away on foot, for he was surrounded and someone would have noticed it. The only possible avenue of escape was the water, but no boat that had been there when night fell was missing when day broke. Then the widow remembered her dream, and wondered if it really had been a dream. In any event, she said to her neighbors that his followers, more likely than not, had gone to Capernaum, and he had never been known to leave them for long. Word quickly got around, and soon everyone was clamoring aboard the remainder of the fishing fleet and sailing for Capernaum. Luckily, the sea was as smooth as silk after the storm, or the boats would certainly have capsized, overloaded as they were with the eager and needy.

When they reached the other side of the lake, a keen-eyed boy spotted the Nazarene with his disciples, lounging on a tiny knoll not too far from shore. They were breakfasting. By that time everyone knew of the widow's dream, so they pushed her forward to confront the holy man. She was determined to ask why he had abandoned them; but, when she came up to him, she managed only a demure, "Rabbi, how did you get here?" Less intimidated voices raised her question to the intensity of a challenge; and, deriving confidence from them, she repeated her question, only this time with insistent defiance.

"You only come after me because I fed you yesterday," he declared, ignoring the question. "You are too concerned with what you can get out of me."

"What should we be concerned with?" she challenged. "We have nothing! What should we be concerned with?"

Not at all perturbed, he looked straight into her eyes; and, for some strange reason, she felt certain, no matter how impossible it might be, that he was looking into the eyes of every other living soul on that beach. "You should do the work of the One who sent me."

"And what is that work?" she found herself whispering, even though she feared to hear the answer.

"To believe in me," he proclaimed, "for I am your salvation."

At that moment, the rest of her dream came back to her. "It's not the same," she said to herself. "It's not at all the same!"

When she returned to the wilderness setting of her tryst with Kristos, she did not feel so desolate. "It wasn't the same," she was saying to him. "It wasn't at all the same."

"That's exactly the point," he replied, evidently pleased.

"When you confronted me just now, asking for my belief," she explained, more to herself than him, "it was a call to recognize you for who you are."

"It was a call to personal relationship," he added, "for true relationship is possible only when one relates to the other in the fullness of that other's reality."

"Yes," she agreed excitedly, "but the evangelist's demanding belief in you, third person rather than first, was just the opposite. He was asking me to give assent to some abstract proposition. You were confronting me in your concrete personhood, whereas he was confronting me with a name, the most abstract thing about a person. A name doesn't mean anything unless one knows the person. Otherwise, it's just a name."

He nodded. "Starting as early as Paul, Christians spoke of believing on the name of Jesus. In fact, Paul says that whoever confesses Jesus as Lord must be of God. Jesus, on the other hand, says just the opposite: 'Not all who cry, "Lord, Lord!" will be saved, but he who does the will of my heavenly Father!'"

"Believing in the name of Jesus!" she laughed, feeling as if she had just been released from a curse.

"Yes," he also laughed, "as if there were something magical, mystical and holy about the name! Certainly, 'Jesus' is the Greek form of the diminutive of the Hebrew 'Yeshua,' which does mean 'God's salvation'; but the name 'Jesus' was as common in first-century Palestine as 'Jimmy,' 'Teddy,' or 'Bobby' in 1950's America! In fact, according to Matthew's gospel, Bar-abbas, the thief whom the crowd chose to save rather than Jesus, was himself named Jesus, Jesus Bar-abbas. That means, 'Jesus, son of the father.' Isn't that a much better name for the messiah than 'Jesus, son of Joseph,' or even 'Jesus, son of Mary,' which would imply that Jesus was a bastard whose father was unknown, if it's about a name? But it's not about a name! It's about the first-person encounter with the living reality!"

Ariana reflected for a moment. "But how is confrontation with you the same as the demand to love?" she asked. "If Christianity is about nothing but love, that's how it would have to be for this business about believing in you to have any place, first person or third, in real Christianity. Whereas, the tiny minority of Christians who have tried to live perfect love, like the *Fratricelli*, the little brothers who sought to follow St. Francis' rule of simplicity and poverty after his death, have been persecuted by the majority, for whom Christianity is about holding the right belief. The Fratricelli were mostly burned at the stake! For most Christians, love is an ideal that never can be attained, and so faith is what really counts."

"Let's go back to the story of the Gentile woman," he suggested, "the one Jesus called a dog."

"If you hadn't suggested it, I would have demanded it," she said severely.

And, of course, she found herself back in that miserable excuse for a home on the edge of Gentile territory in first-century Palestine, only this time she wasn't a spectator. She was the Gentile woman herself! Giving her daughter into the care of friends, she had spent all day following the trail of the reputed miracle worker, who evidently was trying to get away to rest. It did not matter. Her daughter was more important than anyone's rest, the holy man's or her own.

When she caught up with him, she was taken aback. She had anticipated hostility from his followers, for they were reputedly average and nondescript; but to be called a dog by Jesus himself was an unmitigated shock. His words set off a chain of inner reactions so complex in their interconnections and so far-reaching in their implications that it was as if she lived a thousand lives in that short moment before she responded. She remembered what the elders of his own people had said, that he was a prince of demons who cast out demons through the power of Satan himself! No matter how desperate she was to help her daughter, no holy man would call another human being a dog, no matter how much hate his people bore hers. She could not trust her daughter to such a man, for under his care the illness might become worse. Then she wondered if perhaps she was a dog and deserved to be rejected in contempt. After all, if he was a holy man, he might know how she had often joined in the general derision her friends and neighbors directed toward the Jews. Perhaps she did not deserve his help. But no, it was for her daughter, not herself, that she had come to him; and every spiritual teacher she had ever heard, Jew or Gentile, had proclaimed that hate could not be defeated with hate. No matter how she interpreted his words, whether as justified rebuke or unholy bigotry, there was no reason for her to stay. He had refused to help her daughter, and if he were as unholy as his words implied, he could have no help to give.

Something, however, kept her from turning away—not something in his voice or facial expression, nor even in his unfathomable eyes, but something about him that she could feel only in her own heart. She remembered her dead husband and how, when they were courting, they found themselves playing a game of trading insults. The worse the insults, the more certain she was of his love. It was as if the rejection on his lips forced her to feel the reality of his love in her heart. The holy man's words struck her like that now. She could not have imagined it, nor could it be the product of wishful thinking, for nothing could have been further from expectation or even hope. She did not even know the man! Nevertheless, he had started the circle of intimacy and invited her to complete it. Looking into those eyes in which whole universes, it seemed, could lose themselves, she felt he would never take advantage of that intimacy, that he was worthy of her absolute trust. Then she said the fateful words, "Yes, rabbi, but the dogs eat of the crumbs that fall from the master's table," and the circle was complete. She was complete, her heart was complete; and, as he bid her farewell, she felt that neither he nor her daughter would ever be lonely again.

"I understand," she said as she returned, the feeling of intimacy not at all fading.

"Yes, you do," he agreed, "but only half of it."

He smiled at her, and then she found herself ripped from her new-found communion with him like a babe from the womb. She was back in first-century Palestine, in the mud-brick house, only this time she was one of his followers. When the woman came in, he rose to push her away, back into the Gentile world from which she had come so unceremoniously and without invitation. The rabbi, however, gave him the look he had come to know so well that said, "Don't interfere." Upon hearing the master's words, he was glad he had heeded the unspoken command, for it was the first time Jesus had made unambiguously clear exactly on whose side he stood. Now his followers could be absolutely certain that he was the messiah, come to overthrow Israel's oppressors and bring justice where it was long overdue. Then something strange seemed to be happening. The woman neither threw herself at his feet in abject desperation, nor turned on her heel in pride and walked away. She stood there, and Jesus stood there, and he, his follower, felt as if the two of them were an immeasurable distance away. He had never felt lonelier in his life.

When Ariana returned, she carried the anger of betrayal as she had carried the warmth of their former intimacy, and her anger was all the greater because of that intimacy. "How dare you play such mind games?" she demanded bitterly. "What gives you the right?"

He looked at her solemnly, not at all disconcerted. "The only thing that gives anyone the right to do anything," he responded. "Love."

"How was that love?" she cried, laughing scornfully. "If you flayed me alive, I would count that pleasure in comparison!"

"It was the same thing Jesus did when you were the Gentile woman," he reminded her. "Then you welcomed it with joy."

"But then it included me!" she protested. "This time it did not!"

"This time you did not include yourself," he said. "Do you remember: 'As long as you do this to the least of my brothers and sisters . . .?'"

The point hit home, and she bowed her head in shame. Then, returning to her former defiance, she cried, "But why couldn't you have just explained it, especially when your words would be so open to misunderstanding by later generations?"

"I'm not concerned with later generations," he said with an intensity that found its way, like a laser beam, into her heart. "If I am with you always, there are no 'later' generations!"

"But what of the Church, then, and the transmission of your word down through the centuries?" she softened.

"Those who look for me in history find nothing but confusion and thoroughgoing ambiguity," he explained, his own passion abating in measure with hers. "Like the Gentile woman in the story, you can find my reality only through your own heart."

"But why didn't you simply explain it?" she reiterated, though her question was now a plea rather than a challenge.

He smiled. "Imagine if, like a preacher or teacher, I had turned to the audience and said, 'I suppose you think I shouldn't help this woman because she is a Gentile. But God made a covenant with Noah as well as with Abraham, not just with the Chosen People but the whole human race. Salvation comes through the Jews, but to all who, by the uprightness of their lives, reveal that they are faithful children of God. Therefore, this woman is as deserving of my aid as any daughter of Israel.'"

"That's beautiful!" she exclaimed.

"It may be beautiful," he said, "but, if I had said it that way, what effect would it have had?"

"I can only judge from my own experience just now," she replied, "but I think it would have made me see the light."

"And if you had 'seen the light,'" he persisted, "what would have become of your darkness? Be honest. If I had said something like that, would you have even admitted to yourself the possibility that I was addressing your hate, your bigotry? Wouldn't you have thought I was speaking to everyone else but you?"

"It's possible," she answered, realizing that he could read her like the proverbial open book.

"I admit, it's not the only possibility," he said, "but it's the likeliest, given how my followers had made me their unquestioned authority figure."

"You're talking about repression, aren't you?" Ariana said.

"Yes," he confirmed, "playing it psychologically safe."

"But," she went on, "by confirming their feelings of bigotry and hate, however ironically . . ."

"They were blind to the irony because of their hate," he interjected.

"Which means they ambushed themselves," she concluded. "I ambushed myself."

"Don't be too hard on yourself," he smiled. "That was a make-believe you."

"Yes, but it must have been made out of something inside me that's real," she insisted.

"All human possibilities exist within each one of us," he declared. "That's the purpose of this contest, to show you all those possibilities."

She allowed his words to echo in her heart, and there they rang true.

"You made us see ourselves," she said, feeling better.

"And then you were faced with the choice," he declared: "Do you hate me for making you feel so uncomfortable with yourself, or do you take responsibility for your own dirt?"

"Projection," she murmured, "or creative integration."

"Sin," he translated, "or love."

"But you didn't always operate that way!" she countered, but with humility. "You performed miracles! The people who saw those miracles knew who you were without any deep soul-searching."

"Did they?" he replied. "If I did not know that the human capacity for self-deception was well nigh infinite, I would wonder how you could ask that question after your experience by the water. Do you know of John the Baptist?"

Ariana nodded. "He proclaimed you to be the messiah."

He nodded. "After John was thrown into prison by Herod Antipas for denouncing him and his new wife as adulterers . . ."

"She had divorced his brother and married her uncle, wasn't it?" interjected Ariana.

"Something like that," said Kristos. "Anyway, as you can well imagine, John suffered from fits of despondency, since he was facing almost certain death, and he began to have second thoughts about me. So John sent two of his disciples to ask if I were truly the one everyone was awaiting, or were they to expect another. I replied that they should report to John what they saw: the lame walked, the blind could see, and the poor were comforted with the message of salvation."

"That's exactly what I was saying!" Ariana exclaimed. "You're pointing to the miracles as proof of your messiahship!"

"You would be right, if that were all," he replied. "but then I added something that struck everyone as peculiar. I pointed out all the wonderful things I was doing, and then I said, 'And blessed is he who takes no offense at me.'" Kristos turned away and sat with head bowed for what seemed the longest time. Then he turned back to her and said, "People aren't convinced by signs and wonders, but by whatever satisfies their hunger. I am the bread of heaven, but who is willing to partake of the nourishment I offer? I come as a sign of offense!"

And then she found herself in another experience.

It was a dusty land on a day when the sun's fire scarred one's very soul. She was a he, more precisely, a very important he—Caiaphas, the high priest of his people. The Sanhedrin, the Council of Elders who had little official power in an Israel governed by pagan Rome, but which alone maintained the integrity of the cultural tradition, had met to consider what to do about a rabble-rouser whose capacity for troublemaking was increasing at the same rate as his influence over the people. Some had spoken in the man's defense, and Caiaphas had weighed their arguments carefully, knowing that the course of action be contemplated would, if carried out, weigh heavily upon him and the rest of the assembly as long as they all should live. Finally, it was Caiaphas' duty to sum up and take the vote.

Caiaphas thanked the various members who had spoken, but declared that the real issue was not the man's guilt or innocence. The real issue, and the only one about which they need concern themselves, was the survival of the nation. Whether this man's soul was black as hell or white as the linen vestments of the priests, he was creating a disturbance; and any prolonged disturbance could have but one outcome—suppression by Rome. The Romans did not care for petty sectarian distinctions. If they heard that the people were proclaiming him king, they would come down hard not only upon this man Jesus and his followers, but everyone. What would anyone think, he asked them, of a statesman who sacrificed his entire people simply to save the life of one man, however innocent that man might be? There was no doubt what they had to do. Better one man die than the whole nation perish.

When Ariana returned, she said to Kristos, "I always thought of Caiaphas as jealous and power-hungry, but now I see that he only did what most people would have done in his place."

"Yes," agreed Kristos, "that's the point—what most people would have done in his place. We have just penetrated the most superficial dimension of human existence, the political. Shall we peel away the next layer?"

And immediately she was in another experience. This time she lived not in the hot and dusty land around Jerusalem, but in the better watered and more temperate Galilee to the north. She was, nevertheless, poor—not so poor that she had to wander and beg, but poor enough to occasionally think she would be better off doing so.

She heard of the wonder-worker, Jesus of Nazareth, and went off with her children in search of him. She was so impressed by his healing powers, as well as by his beautiful words of comfort and hope, that she took to following him, and so ended up a wanderer after all. Placing her children with relatives for a spell, she gave up everything else to be in the presence of him who would usher in God's kingdom and put an end once and for all to poverty, disease, war, famine, and death.

But he did not do it. She knew he could do it because she had seen him feed thousands from practically nothing, and even raise people from the dead. As the powers-that-be closed in on him, she decided she would give him one more chance. He was going to Jerusalem for the Passover, and she would follow him. If he did not set things in motion then, she would turn away.

The pilgrimage began well. Jesus commandeered an ass and made a triumphal, messianic entry into Jerusalem in self-conscious fulfillment of the ancient prophecies. This was a declaration of war upon his enemies, and soon the battle would have to be joined.

Next, Jesus visited the temple, and was so offended by the sight of buying, selling, and most importantly, cheating within the sacred edifice that, in a fury of which few thought him capable, he drove the perpetrators out with a whip of cords and overturned their tables, sending their coins ringing on the marble floors straight into the waiting palms of hangers-on like herself. From that promising beginning on, however, it was all downhill. Jesus refused to demonstrate any of those powers he had manifested so readily in the hills and meadows of Galilee. The people of Jerusalem dismissed him as a charlatan, but she and the rest who had followed him knew he was much worse. If he had been only a fake, she would have returned home poorer and wiser, but certainly not bitter; for the world was filled with con-men, and if you couldn't spot them you deserved what you got. She, however, and all the rest who believed in him, knew he could deliver. They had seen him do it. They had heard him promise to deliver, even saying that the poor and dispossessed would inherit the earth. Now, however, he was going back on that promise, refusing to make it good. When she found herself in the crowd before the Roman governor's palace the day Pilate had to decide Jesus' fate, she did not need to be bribed to scream for his crucifixion.

When she returned to Kristos, she had difficulty meeting his eyes. "How many more layers are there?" she said curtly.

"One more."

"Who will I be for that one," she asked sarcastically, "the soldier who drove the nails into your palms?"

"Actually, the nails went into my wrists," he said, holding her gaze as only he could. "There's no need to be anyone or go anywhere now, because we've come to the essential issue, the one that applies to each individual in every place and time— why is love itself so offensive? Why do people hate and fear love more than anything else?"

"I wasn't aware that they did," she said petulantly. "What do you mean, anyway? You've talked about love without end, but what is love, anyway?"

"You've just seen the two sides of it," he answered, "but perhaps you need to see them both brought together."

This time she did not go anywhere. The scene seemed to spring up around them. Darkness fell, and in the darkness she could hear Kristos sobbing. He was not play-acting. It was for real. He prayed to his heavenly father to let the bitter cup pass; and, as he did so, she saw a man with absolutely no psychological defenses against the storm of fury and hate about to break upon him. He had no desire to suffer, no desire to die. He had nothing to prove to anyone, least of all to himself. He did not know what anyone would gain by his death, any more than he knew what anyone had gained by his life. He trembled like a leaf in the wind.

When at last the soldiers came, Ariana, despite her knowledge of history, expected Kristos to flee. No doubt he was so traumatized by his former experience, she thought without realizing the anomaly in the idea, that he could not go through it again. She did not understand until it was all over that this was the first time, and that it would always be the first time for one such as he, no matter how often he had to go through it.

Kristos, of course, went with the soldiers; and even though he never stopped trembling, neither did he seek to escape. When he was beaten, mocked, whipped, and crucified, he felt with full force the fear, anger, bitterness, and despair that anyone would have felt in his place, only with an added dimension of depth. If he had repressed his fear, she saw, he would not have been able to go forward in courage. If he had hidden from his hate, he would not have been able to forgive his enemies even as they ridiculed him in his final agony. And if he had not confronted his doubt and resentment, he would not have been able to turn into a prayer that cry of most profound despair, "My God, why have you abandoned me?"

When the grisly scene faded and she was alone with Kristos once again, she knew the answer to her own question. "The two sides of love are total vulnerability and absolute courage."

He nodded. "Yes, and the human race, it seems, has conveniently split itself psychologically along the biological fault line of gender to avoid these two sides coming together. Take courage. Who is supposed to get up when something goes bump in the night, or stand up to the bully, or risk death in defense of home and country?"

"The man," she said, "at least traditionally."

"And it's relatively easy," he continued, "to fight and even die in a war, for example, if one is emotionally invulnerable, if one is wearing emotional armor. After all, isn't military training designed to disconnect the soldier from his feelings, so he will obey without reference to them?"

"Again, repression."

"Again, repression," he affirmed. "You have heard of the Vietnam War, I presume?"

She nodded. "Yes, I have many friends from America among the earthbound. Sometimes I feel certain that's where I'm heading." She was hoping for some sign of confirmation, but his face was a study in inscrutability.

"Why was the Vietnam War the most traumatic ever fought by American servicemen?" he asked.

"Because they lacked support on the home front," she replied.

"There was support on the home front," he disagreed, "just as there was opposition; but, to one degree or another, that's been true of every war fought by the United States."

"Because it was the first war the United States ever lost?" she ventured.

"That's not quite true," he said, "but even if it were, strategic defeat, like strategic victory, is always in the postscript. The ordinary soldier takes his defeats and victories one day at a time."

"I give up," she said, genuinely curious about what he had to say.

"Have you ever noticed how the most macho male always has a streak of sentimentality?" he asked. "The big biker with his little old lady of a mother, and Adolf Hitler with his dog, Blondi? No one can wear emotional armor all the time. It drives one literally insane. Vietnam differed from the rest of America's wars in that there was no front line and no rear, only an omnipresent battlefield situation. Vietnamese children handed GIs hollowed-out melons with live grenades inside! If a soldier dealt with fear by wearing emotional armor, as most soldiers do, there was no opportunity to remove it. That makes one crazy."

"And that is how men enable themselves to be so 'courageous,'" Ariana added. "It never seemed quite real."

"But the other side is no more real," Kristos resumed. "Who is sensitive and open and emotionally vulnerable and empathetic and all the things you women accuse us men of not being, and usually rightly?"

"Women," she said, deigning to state the obvious.

"But it's easy to be emotionally vulnerable if there's no risk," he declared, "if no courage is required—as easy as being courageous if you are emotionally invulnerable. Real love is the conjunction of the two; or rather, the original unity from which the two have schizophrenically split."

"But I still don't understand why love should be offensive," Ariana said. "Why wouldn't the insane welcome their healing?"

"Do you remember how, according to the Gospel, I spoke of the sin against the Holy Spirit?" he asked.

"I have heard something like that," she replied.

"I called it blasphemy against the Holy Spirit," he said, "as well as the unforgivable sin."

"Now I remember!" she cried. "I used to wonder if God were sitting up in his heaven one day, listing all the deeds that were forbidden to humans as sin, when, to make the game of life more interesting, he decided to make one of those sins unforgivable, like loading one of the pistol's chambers in Russian Roulette."

Ariana suddenly felt as if she were the bullet in that chamber. When she stopped spinning, she was once more a he, and her self-awareness was thoroughly submerged.

She was Nicodemus, the Pharisee who came to Jesus in the night lest word get out that he, a man of substance and reputation, was associating with a renegade. Just that morning he had been among a deputation appointed by the Sanhedrin to remonstrate with the misguided teacher. One of their number had offered the opinion that the Galilean was possessed by evil spirits, perhaps the devil himself, in

Jesus' own hearing, and reaction had been swift. The holy man had called them poisonous snakes and hypocrites, white-washed tombs that were clean and sparkling on the outside but within were filled with dead men's bones and all manner of unclean filth! He had declared that they had committed the unforgivable sin against the Spirit of the Holy One! He and his colleagues were the moral pillars of the community. What could Jesus have meant?

Now he was being admitted into private audience with the man, and he saw from the prophet's look that preamble was unnecessary. Nicodemus needed merely to allude to the morning's incident, and Jesus was ready with an explanation. In language filled with analogies and allusions that only a learned man like Nicodemus himself would understand, Jesus reminded his visitor that God's spirit dwelt within every human being, as to be a human being was to be dust of the earth filled with the divine breath of life. He and his colleagues were not hypocrites in the usual sense of playing a part for others, but in the more terrible sense of playing a part for themselves. The worst form of deception was self-deception. To forgive sin was to overlook it, to behave as if it had never been. All other sin could be forgiven, because in all other sin one either was moving toward God, in which case one had simply stumbled and would pick oneself up and keep going; or one was moving away from God, and some day one would reach the dead-end of despair, turn around, and see how things really stood. In the sin of self-deception, however, the denial of the witness of one's own heart, one stagnated, holed up behind pride and fear, bristling with defenses against love itself. God could not overlook this situation or bypass those defenses. The walls had to be torn down. The sin was unforgivable, but not the sinner. The sin could not be forgiven for the sake of the sinner.

After taking all this in, Nicodemus was impressed. His only difficulty was that Jesus had not explained this last point, the distinction between the sin and the sinner, when excoriating the notables. Jesus said that they must have mercy upon others before they could feel God's mercy in their own hearts.

As Ariana returned to herself, she remembered the words of the Christ of Revelation: "I would you blew hot or cold, because then I could touch and heal you. Because you are lukewarm, I will vomit you out of my mouth."

"So hell is for the lukewarm," she said as Kristos' eyes met hers.

"Hell is being lukewarm," he corrected. "There is nothing more repulsive to life. Hypocrisy must be stripped of its defenses. That is the battle I fight, the struggle to which I call all who hear my voice, the voice of love."

She could no longer laugh at this claim. "And the cross—that's your weapon?"

"The cross represents total vulnerability and absolute courage. It symbolizes the peace that surpasses understanding. There is nothing people fear more."

"Why should people fear peace?" she asked, knowing what he said was true but not understanding why.

"Because they want an excuse," he explained. "When love makes its absolute demand in their hearts, they want to be able to tell themselves that there is a limit beyond which they will not in good conscience have to go, beyond which they will be able to say, to themselves and everyone else, that they have done all that can reasonably be expected of them, that they have given all they have to give. Love, however, accepts no excuse."

"Where's the peace in that?" she queried.

"None, except for those for whom love is all-in-all," he declared. "The good news that I bring, the good news that I am, is only good news for those who desire to love, because I am love's pledge that those who give themselves to love will always have the strength to meet love's demand."

"Yes, I have met those types," she said caustically. "They always have sweet Jesus in their hearts, heaven on their minds, and damnation for everyone else on their lips."

"That's just another form of emotional armor," he said. "To endure sword and fire for the sake of a heavenly reward is a kind of peace, but it certainly doesn't surpass understanding. The annals of history are filled with examples of such religious fanaticism. The peace I bring, the peace I am, does not banish fear or doubt or despair, but lives in the midst of them. This peace comes through the faith that, no matter what one's own strength, love will give one strength to take each step that love demands. This peace comes through the knowledge that, no matter how many voices cry out in the world for one's obedience or allegiance, whether of parents, relatives, teacher's, employers, rulers, or what-have-you, the voice of love demands one's absolute devotion and total obedience."

"And so to follow that voice of love," Ariana observed, "is to come into conflict with parents and teachers and employers and the rest!"

Kristos' face looked paradoxically gentle and stern. "Yes, conflict with anyone who seeks to set up his or her own little kingdom in opposition to the kingdom of love."

"Now I understand why love is so offensive," she declared. "Now I see why people are so afraid of love." Then, feeling an unfathomable sorrow well up from within, she murmured, "Now I understand why they crucified you, and why you suffered so much. Why you still suffer! You are what everybody needs and nobody wants."

At these words, the look on his face matched the sadness in her heart, and she wanted to embrace him, even kiss him, and let her tears wash away their mutual pain. His sorrow revealed to her that he truly was love, because pride would take joy in being everyone's secret desire, but love would feel the agony of the beloved's denial of her own need. This realization made her want to embrace him, but at the same time made it impossible to do so. Who was she to embrace perfect love? Furthermore, what good was perfect love if it had to remain on that most unreachable of pedestals, the cross? Love and hate warred in her heart. She felt within that struggle, however, a seed germinating with a promise more real than anything she had experienced in Zen. "So, the cross is everyone's koan," she finally smiled. "The cross is the way to life."

He returned her smile, pleased with her understanding.

4. Fully God

"I'm not sure how that works," she said, and both smiles faded. "I don't understand what the death of one particular man two-thousand years ago, even if he was God and rose from the dead, has to do with me or anyone else more than the death of any other man."

As she spoke the sky grew darker, but the horizon lit up with flashes like lightning. Instinctively, she turned away to watch the spectacle, and when she turned back the Teacher was sitting in Kristos' place.

"Time for another reality check?" Ariana gibed.

"Not precisely," he replied exactly as if they were resuming a conversation that had been interrupted but a moment before. "Kristos has presented himself to you. Now you must figure him out for yourself. He realizes, however, how difficult that can be. From the last question you directed toward him, it's obvious you have far to go. Therefore he mercifully has appointed me to clarify a few points."

"Why can't he clarify them?"

"After they are clarified, you'll know why," he answered cheerily, as if enjoying her discomfort.

"But there's so much I . . ." she began, and then realized the Teacher was the last person in the universe to whom she wished to bare her soul.

"There was so much you still wanted to tell him," he completed her sentence. "Don't worry," he said sympathetically. "Before this contest is over you'll be seeing Kristos again. Right now we have to deal with your question. Would you mind restating it?"

She had no desire to repeat the words that had driven Kristos away, but she knew the Teacher would give her no rest until she complied. She also knew, somewhere deep inside, that the only way to bring him back, if there was one, was to follow her doubts and difficulties, even if they only led to a bitter end. "What does the death of one man two thousand years ago," she reiterated slowly and painfully, "even if he was God, have to do with you, me, anyone or anything today?"

He studied her as if she were a mathematical problem proving itself particularly difficult to solve. "You want to know how it works," he said at last.

"How what works?"

"The Atonement, the Christian doctrine of the Atonement—the idea that through Christ, or Kristos, if you will, God saves the world."

"Why are you here?" she asked. "Why you?"

"To explain."

"But why you?" she repeated more forcefully. "I thought you were Jewish now! Why are you explaining Christianity to me?"

"*He* was Jewish," the Teacher declared. "As for me, you don't have to worry over me, only over what I say. Of course, if you'd rather give up . . ." He raised his eyebrows suggestively.

This was a tempting proposition, but out of the question. Going back was out of the question, but so was staying where she was, which was nowhere. The only possibility was forward. If faith was going on when love demanded it, she wondered what going on when necessity required it should be called. Perhaps desperation. "I'm ready," she said, composing herself. "Explain."

"What have you heard?" he asked, and she was too tired to protest his little mind games.

"That he died for our sins."

"Why was it necessary for him to die for our sins?" he pressed her.

"I never thought about it," she said, after thinking about it. "All I know is that Kristos . . ."

"Christ," he corrected her.

"What's the difference?" she demanded, exasperated.

"Linguistically, only that between Greek and English," he replied, "but psychologically it is necessary because the Kristos you met may not be the genuine Christ."

More mind games! "I have no doubt that he is!" she exploded.

"Really?" he said, mocking irony in his voice. "You should."

"Why?"

"Because all the evidence isn't in."

"As far as I'm concerned, it is!" she declared, surprising herself with her own vehemence. "But, in the interest of maintaining peace and harmony,"—her voice was every bit as sarcastic as his own—"I'll humor you. All I know is that Christ is supposed to have been some sort of perfect sacrifice who took our well-deserved punishment upon himself so that our sins might be forgiven, but it's never made sense to me."

"Why not?" he asked, seeming genuinely interested.

"I don't know," she answered. "Does one always have to have a reason for everything?"

"The idea you're talking about," he said, ignoring her gibe, "is called the Substitution Theory of Atonement. It has its roots in the New Testament, especially in the Letter to the Hebrews and some of the writings of Paul; but do you remember Anselm of Canterbury?"

"The Ontological Argument," she replied promptly and succinctly.

"You have remarkable retention," he observed, she suspected, with double intent, but both his face and voice gave nothing away. "Anselm was primarily a theologian, and he systematized the Substitution Theory of Atonement in a little book called *Cur Deus Homo—Why God Became Man*. Would you like to hear what he had to say?"

With an abrupt gesture, she indicated that he should proceed.

"Anselm says that God is perfect love, and within that perfect love, part of the very idea of it, is perfect justice. Sin, which by definition is offense against God, just as crime by definition is offense against society, cannot be forgiven until divine justice is satisfied. Anselm goes on to say that the severity of an offense is measured, not simply by its objective character, but also by the quality of the one against whom the offense is committed. For example, even though premeditated murder is premeditated murder, we all feel that to murder a child, even if the weapon is the same and is employed the same way in each case, is worse than murdering an adult. Or again, a lie is a lie, but to lie to someone who loves and trusts us is worse, all other things being equal, than to lie to a stranger. Do you understand Anselm's first point?"

She nodded with genuine interest.

"Anselm next declares that we all have sinned against God."

"You mean, 'original sin?'" she asked.

"Anselm's idea doesn't depend upon that superstitious doctrine of inherited taint," he declared. "All that is necessary is that all human beings have in fact, not by nature as the doctrine of original sin absurdly implies, sinned."

"That's an undeniable proposition if I ever heard one," she commented.

"Not necessarily, but you'll find that out later," he said. "In any event, Anselm says that we all have sinned, and that a sin against perfect love, however minor objectively, is infinite."

"What's an infinite sin?" she queried.

"A sin for which only a perfect sacrifice can make restitution," he said.

"And what is restitution?" she persisted. "The idea has never made sense to me."

"It may have never made sense to you," the Teacher replied, "but it is enshrined in the legal and penal systems of every nation in the world. A crime is, by definition, an offense against society, and offense is a moral debt. Punishment is the way society collects that debt. Prisons are not primarily places where criminals are reformed, or even places that protect society from criminals the way a cage protects us from a wild animal. If prisons were either places of protection or rehabilitation, criminals would not be set free until they were reformed and/or no longer dangerous. A prison is a place where a criminal pays his or her debt to society. Society may forgive a portion or even all of the debt—that's parole, commutation, and pardon. Society may accept a species of currency other than or in combination with punishment, such as community service or good behavior leading to parole. However, as a rule, society demands restitution. Once restitution is made in full, then the criminal is set free, regardless of his probable future conduct."

Ariana felt like the whole idea of atonement was starting to come down to earth. "So you're saying that, in sinning against perfect love, which is what we do in all our sin, we've done something so terrible that we've racked up a sentence of eternal punishment without parole."

"Yes," he confirmed, "we've dug ourselves a pit from which we can't escape."

"And that's where Kristos . . . I mean, Christ, comes in?"

"By associating himself with our humanity," the Teacher explained, "he takes our sins upon his shoulders, carries them to the cross, and there makes restitution through his perfect sacrifice."

"Why is it perfect?" she wondered.

"Because it is spotless," he said. "He is the only human being without sin, and therefore the only human being who can make restitution for sin."

"A paradox!" She smiled for the first time since the Teacher had reappeared. "What happens then?"

"Divine justice has been satisfied," he answered, "so divine forgiveness may come into play. Sin closed the gates of heaven. Christ's sacrifice opens them again."

"So we all get to go to heaven after all!" she laughed and clapped her hands. "Kristos said there was no hell!"

"Not exactly," the Teacher qualified.

"How 'not exactly?'" Ariana echoed, instantly suspicious.

"The 'how' of it depends upon to whom one speaks," he replied. "You see, this Substitution Theory developed in Western Christendom, where Roman legalism joined with Jewish moralism and pagan ritualism to produce Roman Catholicism. It therefore is held by that church, as well as by the majority of its Protestant offspring. Protestants and Catholics agree that God offers us the free gift of salvation through Christ. The theological formula is salvation by grace. However, they disagree over what individuals must do to avail themselves of that gift."

"I don't get it," she protested. "You say it's a free gift, but then it sounds like they set conditions."

"That's what Protestants say about Catholic theology," he replied, "so they maintain that one receives the free gift simply by believing in it, by faith. Let me try my hand at a little parable to get you to understand the Catholic position."

Ariana groaned, but if not in good then at least improving humor. "I'm all ears," she said perkily, wondering at the transformation in her mood.

"Imagine a rich man invites all the homeless, all the street people of his city to a huge banquet, but under one condition. So that the party is enjoyable for all concerned, he wants everyone to clean up first. He therefore hires experts in personal hygiene and makes facilities and new clothes available to his guests so they can make themselves presentable. They can't even pay for their own soap, and they don't have to. The rich man takes care of everything. All they need do is participate in the process."

"And that's the Catholic Church?" she asked.

"Yes," he replied, "in its own mind. For the Catholics, there are two essential preconditions the individual must fulfill in order to receive the gift of salvation: faith, and cleansing of the soul through the sacraments—baptism, whereby one joins the communion of the faithful; confirmation, whereby later in life one reaffirms that commitment; penance or the rite of reconciliation, whereby one receives forgiveness for sin; the eucharist, the central sacrament, the mystical reenactment of Christ's atoning sacrifice; matrimony, whereby a man and woman become one flesh; holy orders, if one becomes a priest; and the anointing of the sick. Through participation in the sacramental life of the church, one's soul is purified and made fit for residency in heaven."

"It makes good sense," she said, feeling her own impurity. "Why did the Protestants object? Don't they have sacraments?"

"Yes," he said, "usually at least two: Baptism and the Lord's Supper, the equivalent of the Catholic Eucharist. However, the Protestants hold that the only saving element in a sacrament is the faith that informs it."

"And that's all that led to the Protestant Reformation?" she asked dubiously.

"No," he responded. "In fact, this Protestant theology of faith was fueled by clerical abuses within the Catholic Church. By the sixteenth century, much of its sacramental process of purification had become purely formal and even mechanical, and churchmen often behaved as if their services were for hire. Institutions are notorious dens of corruption, especially those which claim divine charter. In order to circumvent the possibility of institutional corruption, the Protestants eliminated the ecclesiastical middleman and taught a direct relationship with God through faith."

"That makes sense to me too," she said, smiling at her own ambivalence. "I suppose both sides have a part of the truth. But aren't Protestants tempted by the ease of that relationship? If you get to heaven just by faith, can't you believe and then do whatever you please?"

"What you're talking about is the danger of antinomianism," he said.

"Anti what?"

"*Nomos* is 'law' in classical Greek," he explained, "and so antinomianism is the rejection of law—to paraphrase Augustine, 'Believe and do what you will.' There were one or two antinomian sects in early Protestantism, but they died out early, or more precisely, were suppressed by their fellow Protestants, because human beings for the most part value security over pleasure, and law and its enforcement seem the surest way of achieving security in a world full of outlaws. The proof that the Catholic criticism is wide of the mark in this controversy over faith and good works is that the everyday morality of Protestants has tended to be even more rigorous than that of Catholics."

"Because Catholics always have a second chance," she speculated, "like confession and purgatory?"

"That seems the most logical explanation," he concurred. "Such distinctions, however, are relatively incidental. The major difference between Protestantism and Catholicism lies in ecclesiology, the theory of the nature and role of the church. In Catholicism, the church is the hierarchical and centralized mediator between God and humanity, carrying on Christ's work on earth by ensuring the purity of the faith and the proper administration of the sacraments. The priest is a magical, mystical, *manna* personality through whom one receives God's grace. In Protestantism, in theory, at least, God does his work directly, and the church is simply a community for inspiring and encouraging faith, and the Protestant minister the first among equals who inspires and strengthens faith, primarily through preaching."

"In theory, you said?"

"Humans being what they are," he smiled, "the institution sometimes becomes more important than it should, even in Protestantism."

Ariana reflected. "This means that, according to Catholics, you have to be Catholic to go to heaven, and, according to Protestants, you have to be Christian, or at least, any other kind of Christian but Catholic."

"Yes," the Teacher laughed pleasantly. "That's what I like about your mind—it's perfectly logical. In an age when such exclusivist sentiments are unfashionable, Catholic and Protestant theologians alike have turned cartwheels to find ways of soft-pedaling the doctrine of eternal damnation, but never very successfully because, as you point out, exclusivism is built into both their theological systems."

"But I don't see why it has to be," she said, encouraged by his commendation. "They share the Substitution Theory of Atonement. Why don't they just stop there?"

"Just say everyone is going to heaven?" he queried. "Then they could no longer explain the evil in this world as a test of righteousness and faith."

"The problem of evil," she intoned.

"In ethical monotheism, there's no getting away from it," he maintained. "But while we're still on the subject," he added, and she could tell from the edge in his voice and the glint in his eye that this was like one of King David's "by the way's" in his conversation with Uriah, "do you still feel that the Substitution Theory makes no sense?"

"Actually, no," she said. "Now it seems to make a lot of sense."

"Do you mind if I offer a few criticisms?"

"A few?"

"Three, to be precise."

"Be my guest," she said, irritated at the way he had once again set her up for a fall, but exhilarated at the possibility that there were depths here he would show her how to fathom.

"Let's start out with an analogy," the Teacher said. "Let's say you have a brother, and your brother murders your parents and is apprehended, tried, convicted, and condemned to death. All appeals have been exhausted, and the governor has refused to commute the sentence or pardon the offender. Your brother is going to die. You go to the judge, the governor, or whoever has the authority, and beg him to let your brother spend the rest of his life in prison if he is a danger to society, but to let you die in his place. What would any governor, judge, or tribunal on earth say to such a proposal?"

She wondered why he always had to make his "parables" so gruesome. "No one would accept such an offer."

"Why not?"

"Because it would not be just!" she declared. "Punishment has to fall on the guilty, not the innocent."

"I agree," he said, "but doesn't the Substitution Theory of Atonement make punishment fall upon the innocent? In fact, doesn't it require that the punished one be innocent for his sacrifice to be perfect?"

"But don't they explain that by saying it's a mystery?" she countered. After all, we're talking about God!"

"God's justice may be greater than human justice," he rejoined, "but are we to assume that it's less? Furthermore, look at the logic of what you are saying. Human beings come up with a theological interpretation that, granted, is rooted in Biblical imagery, but the Bible allows a variety of theories, not all of which are theologically compatible. Then, when the theory in question proves self-contradictory . . ."

"How 'self-contradictory?'" she interjected.

"The theory is based on an ideal of justice that the theory itself contradicts. When that becomes clear, its proponents claim what is in effect the status of divine revelation for their all-too-human attempt to understand the ways of God."

"Can they be blamed for that?" she protested. "You make it sound as if it were their fault!"

"We shall see," he said in his infuriatingly know-it-all tone. "In any case, whether or not the theory itself is blameworthy, its proponents are certainly to be censured for claiming that it is above criticism. I don't feel sorry for them, as you evidently do. They are intellectual and spiritual imperialists, the blind taking it upon themselves to lead the blind!"

"What's your second theory?" she asked, a bit humbled by this last speech.

"Would you mind another analogy?" he asked.

"As long as it's not as gory as the last one," she half-smiled.

"That depends on how you look at it," he returned seriously. "Suppose someone you love hurts you very deeply, betrays you, and then comes begging your forgiveness. You say to him that you will forgive him, but that someone first must pay for what he's done. Is that love?"

"No," she said glumly, feeling that Christianity, which had been within her grasp scant moments before, was now slipping away again, perhaps never to return. "Love is unconditional."

"But isn't that what the Substitution Theory has God doing," he asked rhetorically, "placing conditions upon love? My second criticism, therefore, is that, not only is the Substitution Theory illogical, but it is also unchristian, because it places some abstract notion of justice before love in God, and the fundamental idea of Christianity is that God is love."

"And your third criticism?" she asked, feeling like the condemned murderer in the Teacher's first analogy.

"My third criticism is not the most compelling, from a strictly logical point of view. Logically, the charge of self-contradiction is always the most damning; but from a religious viewpoint, a spiritual viewpoint, and, most crucially, a simply human viewpoint, I think it by far the most serious. Couldn't one just imagine, as have critics of Christianity down through the centuries, that human beings, in the fear and anxiety with which they live every day of their lives, had invented an implacable God, a God for whom the greatest of human efforts would never be good enough, and then, equally subconsciously, had invented a perfect sacrifice that would satisfy that insatiable God? The Substitution Theory is spiritual bookkeeping, pure and simple. On one side is the infinite debit, sin, and on the other the infinite credit, Christ's sacrifice. Everything balances out, and one has peace of mind."

"What's wrong with that?" she wondered.

"We can debate that question," he rejoined, more forcefully than she thought her innocent inquiry merited; "but whether it's right or wrong, it not only is illogical and unchristian. It's positively antichristian, because it deflects and defuses Christ's challenge of love, the challenge that Christ is, and transforms that challenge into the ultimate escape trip. Everything goes on over our heads in some heavenly court of appeals. Of course, Christ does die on earth, but executions always take place near dumping grounds. It's all about whether we go to heaven when we die, not how we live here and now. The Substitution Theory of Atonement, therefore, creates a vacuum in human existence where the challenge of divine love, the divine challenge of love, should be. In practice, the Christian churches and sects have filled that vacuum, more often than not, with their own repressive and reactionary social and political agendas."

"Isn't that a bit extreme?" she cried.

"Perhaps, but so were the Crusades, the Inquisition, the witch hunts and the Holocaust!" he exclaimed. "As I pointed out previously, Christianity enjoys the doubtful distinction of being the most violently intolerant of the world's major religious traditions. How did the religion of love spawn so many ideologies of fear, despair, and hate?"

"I don't understand," Ariana interjected at the end of a question that was plainly meant to be rhetorical. "What ideologies?"

"Christianity itself has become an ideology," he declared, "but, in addition, you have National Socialism, Marxist Communism, and several lesser sectarian creeds that are further degenerations. Remember what Kristos told you—the closer one comes to loving, without being perfect in one's love, the more destructive that love will be."

"But isn't it all just plain human weakness?" she protested, but without her previous force.

"From a certain viewpoint, no doubt," he replied; "but from a Christian viewpoint, it's sin, and indeed, to date the ultimate refinement of sin."

"Will you explain yourself?" she demanded in frustration.

"In the Gospel story one can see all the ways in which humans defend themselves against love," he responded. "First comes boredom and indifference. We see this today as well. People don't have to be concerned with Christ because they are Jewish, Buddhist, or Muslim; or people don't have to be concerned with Christ because they are already Christian. Pride would stop right there, saying to itself that, if the world doesn't care about me, I don't care about the world. Not so love, so up goes the second line of defense—laughter and ridicule. Nothing is more comical to a world governed by power than the spectacle of perfect love. This too doesn't stop love, because love fears nothing but failure to love. So love passes through what seem to be our final defenses: anger, intimidation, violence, and death. The message in Christ's resurrection is that love is not stopped even by death. Death seems the ultimate defense, but there is one more that is far more sophisticated than anything going before—worship." The Teacher drew himself up, struck a dramatic pose, and declared, with a touch of what seemed to be an accent from the American South, "'I fall at the feet of Jesus and embrace the cross upon which he died, so that I don't have to die on my own cross!'" Then he continued in his own voice, "What safer place to hide from the challenge of love that Christ is than in Christianity itself! For if I believe in the Lord Jesus, and love the Lord Jesus, who could accuse me of betraying what Jesus is all about?"

"So, Christianity is an absurdity no matter how you look at it," she finally managed to whisper. "What can I say? You've proved your point, and then some. But so what? Absurdity seems to be a plus in religion!" She tried to sound nonchalant, but both heart and voice were all too evidently breaking.

"You misunderstand me entirely," he said softly. "I am not saying that Christianity is absurd from every point of view. I am saying that what generally passes for Christianity is absurd from the standpoint of genuine Christianity, and vice-versa."

"And what is genuine Christianity?" she cried. "I feel like we keep going in circles!"

"What Kristos taught you."

His answer engendered a certain warmth in her heart, and she wondered if it was from self-delusion or hope. She wondered if perhaps they weren't the same thing. Nevertheless, she still felt like she was on a theological treadmill, going faster and faster but not gaining any ground. "But he didn't explain what it all has to do with saving the world!" she protested in a hoarse whisper. "Sure, he talked about love, but so have hundreds of others. What is he but one more prophet of a dying god?"

"I agree," said the Teacher. "If Christ were merely a prophet or teacher, Christianity would be absurd. He has to be something more."

"What?" Ariana asked, her voice both plea and demand.

"There is another way of understanding the saving work of Christ," he replied, "a way embodied in much of the liturgy and theology of Eastern Orthodox Christianity."

"Eastern Orthodoxy?" she echoed, pained and humbled again by her own ignorance.

"I see a historical digression is in order," he smiled with what to her was an unmistakable hint of condescension. "The story goes back to the very beginning of the Christian Church. For the first three-hundred years of its existence, Christianity was outlawed in the Roman Empire, chiefly because Christians refused to participate in the state cult of emperor-worship."

"Sounds like a real totalitarian state," she observed.

"Not really," he said. "There was as much freedom of religion in the Roman Empire as, for example, in the Western democracies today, and in some ways even more. The West has little tolerance for genuine religious diversity, so mainstream religious practices of whatever faith or denomination contain mostly the same elements. Throughout the Roman Empire flourished every manner of religious practice, such as self-castration in devotion to Cybele, the mother goddess, or sacrifice of bulls in worship of Mithras. Can you imagine what would happen to a religious sect that performed such rituals in the modern West?"

"It would be featured on a nationally syndicated talk-show," she quipped, and, to her surprise, he laughed with genuine amusement.

"Only if a movie star converted to it," he rejoined. "Otherwise, the sect would be cited for violation of a score of criminal and civil statutes and hounded out of existence. The point is that Roman persecution of Christianity was not religious, but political, at least from the Roman standpoint. The Christians were considered, at the very least, disturbers of the peace, and at worst, traitors to the empire, and therefore to civilization itself. Much of the work of converting that empire lay in convincing its rulers and administrators that Christians, despite their refusal to perform a ritual that was nothing more to most Romans than the pledge of allegiance to most Americans, were good citizens, and thus that Christianity was good for the empire. The early Church, therefore, focused on building a particularly close relationship with the ruling class; and a movement that had originated among a superstitious and barbaric people in a backwater of the empire eventually conquered the Roman world from the top down."

"Really?" she queried. "I thought Christianity started out as a grass-roots movement among the poor and then gradually worked its way into the upper levels of Roman society!"

"So, for some reason, do most people today," he answered. "In reality, from the very beginning Christian missionaries, as the Biblical Acts of the Apostles makes clear, quite cleverly targeted the important people of Roman society—patricians, wealthy merchants, monarchs, government administrators, and most significantly, members of the imperial family. When Theodosius declared Christianity the state religion of the empire in 385, less than half its population was Christian, and most of the remaining pagans were peasants. In fact, the terms *pagan* and *heathen* literally mean 'country people'! Nevertheless, at the emperor's command, everyone had to convert."

"So much for religious freedom," Ariana remarked sardonically.

The Teacher's sad smile was eerily reminiscent of that of Kristos. "This meant," he went on, "that paganism continued to thrive just beneath the religious surface. Many temples became Christian churches, and many gods and goddesses became Christian saints."

"I had no idea!" cried Ariana.

The Teacher nodded vigorously. "In the 1960's and 70's, Popes John XXIII and Paul VI threw scores of such spurious saints out of the Catholic roster of saints. And many pagan holidays became Christian holy days, most notably Christmas. I suppose there's a one-in-three hundred and sixty-five chance that Jesus of Nazareth was born on December 25th, but nobody knows. The reason Christmas is celebrated then is because it was the time of the greatest festival in the ancient world, the Saturnalia, the winter solstice . . ."

"The death and rebirth of the sun," she interjected.

He nodded again. "And what of these pagan survivals could not be assimilated to the up-and-coming Christianity persisted as folk practices and beliefs until, with the Roman Catholic Inquisition and the Protestant witch-hunts at the end of the Middle Ages, they were rooted out with fire and sword!"

"I know about the witch-hunts," said Ariana thoughtfully, "but what exactly was the Inquisition?"

"In due time," said the Teacher, "but now we must return to the early Church."

"Yes, I suppose that would be wise," agreed Ariana, "as long as you promise not to forget."

The Teacher's look said there was no way he could forget.

"This desire to convert the Roman Empire would explain the hierarchical structure of the Church from early times," she commented, once again sure of her knowledge but not sure where it came from. "When you seek to win the devotion of another, you naturally pattern yourself after that other."

The Teacher smiled, as if at a promising pupil. "Despite the hierarchy," he said, "the Church did remain decentralized. In the second and third centuries it developed an episcopal structure, dividing itself into dioceses along Roman administrative lines. Each bishop was accounted supreme spiritual authority in his diocese; but, whenever anything involving the entire Church had to be settled, the bishops came together in a council. These councils literally hammered out both the institutional form and doctrinal substance of Christianity in late antiquity and the early Middle Ages. You see, the theory behind the conciliar method was that, when all the bishops agreed on a particular issue, it could be by nothing other than the inspiration of the Holy Spirit."

"Consensus was required?" she asked in mild amazement.

"Nothing less than absolute unanimity," he replied.

"Then the triumph of Christianity must have been miraculous!" she laughed. "Only by miracle could these councils ever have gotten anything done!"

"By miracle and the aid of the emperor," he said.

"I thought Christianity was persecuted by the emperors until 385," she observed.

"Constantine legalized Christianity around 312," he corrected.

"How did the church survive this persecution," she wondered, "let alone grow into a complex institution that spanned the empire geographically and socially?"

"The persecution was not constant," he explained; "and, though it often was spectacular, with Christians ignited as human torches and thrown to the wild beasts in the arena for the entertainment of the masses, no more than ten thousand Christians died for their faith in those first three hundred years of the new movement's existence. Some historians estimate that as many as three hundred thousand people were executed as witches in the three centuries of the Protestant witch-hunts."

"That's quite a difference," she remarked sadly.

"Yes," he said sympathetically. "At any rate, throughout this period, as you astutely noted, the Church grew in prestige and influence, until only an idealistic emperor like Julian the Apostate, the last imperial pagan, could fail to see the advantages it offered the ruler who wished to impose ideological unity upon an empire fractured by a variety of economic, political and sociological forces. That's why Constantine patronized Christianity and Theodosius made it the state religion of the empire. At that point, one may say, Christianity had arrived, and from that point the fortunes of the empire and the Church were indissolubly joined. The emperors knew this; and so, when factionalism threatened to disrupt Church administration, they took as active an interest as in keeping the secular peace. The Church councils saw a lot of filibuster and power-playing. If one side didn't get its way, it might very well walk out and form its own council, sometimes going so far as to excommunicate the opposition. The emperors provided a moderating and unifying influence, at least in the East. Therefore the Church hierarchy in the East became dependent, in fact as well as in theory, upon the secular authority, and this is a noteworthy feature of Eastern Orthodoxy to this day."

"What about the West?" Ariana asked, feeling as if she had missed something.

"The stage was set for the split between East and West by Diocletian, who came to power in 284, and who was the last Roman Emperor to persecute Christianity, if one doesn't count the brief and mild opposition from Julian the Apostate around 360. Diocletian decided the the empire had become too vast and complex for one man to rule directly, so he divided it administratively into two parts. An associate emperor governed the western provinces, while Diocletian himself took the eastern half and retained supreme authority."

"Why did the highest power take the East?" she queried. "I thought Rome, the capital, was in the West!"

"It was," he explained, "but it was no longer the capital. The East was smaller, but also more easily defensible. It was also much richer, which no doubt was the deciding factor. Constantine, who succeeded Diocletian, built his capital on the site of the ancient city of Byzantium, and renamed it Constantinople."

"Modest, wasn't he?" she quipped, and he gave a hint of a smile.

"That's why the Eastern half of the Roman Empire," he continued, "which out-lasted the empire in the West by nearly a thousand years, is known to history as the Byzantine Empire."

"You seem to be telling this story backwards," she complained. "How did the Western half fall?"

"You already know," he teased.

"The barbarians!" she cried.

"Correct," he said. "As the barbarian tribes trickled and then poured into the empire, the imperial administration was first strained, then neutralized, and finally destroyed. The elimination of imperial authority in the West left a two-fold vacuum, political and religious. The political vacuum was filled by the barbarians themselves, who became the aristocracy of medieval Europe. The religious vacuum was filled by the bishop of Rome, the pope."

"By one man?" she marveled.

"By one office," he explained, "filled at this time by a succession of very able and ambitious men. Rome was by legend the site of the martyrdoms of the apostles Peter and Paul, and of course was the chief city of the empire in its ancient heyday, so the bishop of Rome naturally enjoyed great prestige in the early Church. Furthermore, various bishops of Rome, through wise and even heroic diplomacy, had held the Western Church together when the imperial government had disintegrated. Many of the pope's fellow bishops in the West, therefore, felt they owed their very survival to him and thus readily acceded to his claims of more and more authority. The Eastern bishops, on the other hand, were not at all ready to shift from an episcopacy to a centralized Church. The dispute over papal authority came to a head in 1054, when the Pope gave the Eastern bishops an ultimatum: either they accept his sovereignty over the entire Church, or he would excommunicate them."

"He had the power?" she asked.

"He claimed the power," he replied. "The Eastern bishops responded by excommunicating the pope. Their mutual excommunication was officially mutually revoked in 1965, but the Great Schism between East and West continues to this day."

"Schism?" she echoed.

"The Roman Catholic Church never held the Eastern Orthodox Church to be heretical, as it did the Protestants," he replied. "According to Rome, the Protestants had perverted the true faith and shut themselves out of heaven, whereas the Ortho-dox continued in a valid form of the true faith, but without the benefit of the guidance of Christ's designated vicegerent."

"Protestants automatically go to hell, but not the Eastern Orthodox?" she summarized.

"Until the current Catholic ecumenism," he confirmed, "that was the attitude. Nowadays, it seems, provision graciously has been made for Protestants as well."

"So it was just a split over Church politics," she said.

"Essentially," he agreed, "but there were tragicomical complications."

"What do you mean?" she queried, feeling exasperation arise once more, but tempered by genuine curiosity.

"Let's start with the comical," he answered. "In 381, the Council of Constantinople formulated a statement of Christian doctrine now known as the Nicene Creed, because not until 451 did the Church adopt it at the council of Nicea. Nicea was in the East, and almost all the bishops attending were from the East, but the bishop of Rome was represented and the decision was accepted as binding by the entire Church. The creed said that the Holy Spirit proceeded from the Father with the Son; but the Western version came to include a variation, that the Holy Spirit proceeded from the Father and the Son. This difference engendered the famous Filioque Controversy, a source of much ill-will between East and West."

"Why do you call it comical?" she challenged. "And what does *filioque* mean, anyway?"

"'And with the son,'" he replied. "It's comical because this hot dispute over what both parties deemed a crucial point of doctrine originated, it seems, in a copyist's error. The Nicene Creed was transmitted to the bishop of Rome in Greek, and then a papal scribe made a copy before translating it into Latin so the original could be kept safe in the Vatican archives. It appears that he either made a simple error or the ink smudged, and incorporated that error into his translation, which was sent to the bishops of the West, most of whom knew no Greek."

"Now I see what you mean by comical," Ariana said with a frown. "If that's the funny part, though, I don't know if I want to hear the tragic."

"Do you remember the Crusades?" he asked.

She nodded. "Western Christendom's attempt to retake the Holy Land from the Turks."

"The first three Crusades met with varying degrees of initial success," said the Teacher, "but all ultimately failed, partly because the Crusaders fought more among themselves than with the enemy. In 1198, therefore, the Pope called for a fourth Crusade. To make a complex story simple, the Crusaders struck a deal with the Venetians by which they would pay for sea-passage to Palestine by first stopping off at Constantinople. The Byzantine emperor and the Venetians were at loggerheads over trade issues, and the dispute was badly hurting business for the island city. By taking Constantinople, the Venetians could solve their problem and the Crusaders could reunite Christiandom."

"Very neat," Ariana observed, "and very ruthless."

"It gets worse," he warned. "Constantinople was at that time perhaps the most magnificent city in the world, with gold, silver and precious gems in visible abundance throughout its palaces, cathedrals, libraries, stadia, and theaters. Paris and London were as yet provincial villages in comparison, and Rome had fallen into ruins. The Russians converted to Eastern Orthodoxy because of Constantinople. They were first approached by Roman Catholic missionaries, but decided to check out the option they had heard about to the southeast before making a decision. When the Russian envoys arrived at the Byzantine capital, they thought they had died and gone to heaven!"

"Don't tell me, let me guess," she said. "Constantinople was too tempting a plum for the Crusaders to resist."

"Obviously," he replied. "But the point isn't simply that they picked it, but how they picked it. Originally the Venetians planned a coup d'tat, installing one of their number with some degree of kinship to the Byzantine imperial line in the place of the former emperor. He would submit the Byzantine treasury to Western use, and everyone would be assured of an excellent yield on a high-risk investment. The coup eventually failed, however, due to popular opposition; and besides, even if it hadn't, when the Crusaders laid eyes on Constantinople, it was only a matter of time before they reached out and took what they so hotly desired. For three fateful days in 1204 they pillaged and burned the city and raped and murdered their fellow Christians, who found no refuge even before the sacred altars of God. Finally, the dead were piled so high and stank so badly that the invaders themselves couldn't stand the horror, so they withdrew with their plunder from the city proper. The Latin kingdom they set up petered out within a century, but the damage had been done."

"They never made it to the Holy Land?" she asked wonderingly.

"No," he declared, "and, with this Sack of Constantinople, they set a seal of blood upon the Great Schism. So it remains to this day."

"It's too bad that Christianity is so divided," Ariana said sincerely.

"In this case, I'm not so sure," replied the Teacher, "especially if reunion would mean assimilation to the theological and liturgical ways of the West."

"You mean the Substitution Theory of Atonement?" she asked.

"Yes, and the Roman mass that goes with it," he answered. "As I said before, the mass is defined theologically as a mystical reenactment of Christ's substitutionary sacrifice. The Eastern celebration of the eucharist is quite different. There's no magical moment when the bread and wine suddenly become the body and blood of Christ. Rather, God is held to be already present in a special way throughout all his creation through Christ. Therefore, his presence isn't effected, but revealed. At the outset, the bread and wine are hidden away from the congregation and gradually brought nearer until, at the culmination of the service, they are placed in full and glorious view upon the altar."

"You say a different theology goes with this?" she asked, feeling a renewal of hope.

"Yes," he affirmed, "and that difference is crucial to what I consider to be the only viable alternative to the Substitution Theory. I call it the Ontological Theory of Atonement."

"Ontological?" she echoed. "The word sounds familiar, but I can't remember what it means."

"I think Ishwara, of all people, explained it to you," he smiled. "However, to refresh your memory, *ontos* is Greek for 'being,' so ontology is the logic, science, or meaning of being. I call my theory ontological because it states that Christ, by his life, death, and resurrection, effects a real change in the structure of being."

"Your theory?" she exclaimed. "I thought it was from Eastern Orthodoxy."

"In part," he said, "In part, of course, it stems from the gospels, especially John. Part of it also comes from Irenaeus, a second century father of the Church who originated the concept of 'recapitulation.'"

"What comes from the gospels?" she asked, seizing the chance to discuss Kristos again.

"In John's Gospel," he replied, "there is beautiful imagery suggesting that we participate in the life of God through Christ, that the life of God flows to us through

Christ. Jesus says that he is the vine and we the branches, and that the branches abide in the vine through love. He calls himself the bread of life. He says that he comes so we may have life, and have it more abundantly!"

Ariana felt thrilled by the resonance of these words.

"In Eastern Orthodox theology is found the concept of divinization. Divinization means that, in and through Christ, all of creation is taken up into the life of God. We enter a sacred marriage between the divine and the human that can never be broken. Like any true marriage, any marriage of the heart, if one enters into it with love and trust, it will be heaven. If one approaches it in fear and pride, it will be hell. Heaven and hell aren't places God sends us when we die. One is in heaven or hell depending upon how one lives this eternal marriage with God!"

"And recapitulation?" Ariana asked, after a moment's meditation.

"Recapitulation means that, in his life and death, Christ touches base with every essential aspect of human existence as it actually is in this broken and sinful world, including pain, despair, and death. In and through Christ, God enters into total empathy with his creation, with us as that creation made conscious of itself. Empathy is love's power. Through empathy, love gives the beloved the opportunity to be transformed into love. That doesn't mean that love is blind. Love not only sees, but suffers, everything in the beloved that is not of love. But, by embracing the beloved in total empathy, love enables the beloved to become love. And love is the only thing in all the universe which, the more one becomes, the more one becomes oneself. And, if one fails to live in love, one is a caricature of oneself!"

Ariana felt entranced.

"Put these three themes of participation, divinization, and recapitulation together," the Teacher concluded, "and you have my theory: by becoming man, God makes a real rather than quasi-legal connection with us, and thereby brings the power of divine love into the world. In Christ, God isn't clearing the way for a forgiveness that he gave before we ever asked. Rather, he is reestablishing the personal relationship with us lost through our own betrayal, and thereby overcoming the power of evil, conquering sin, sickness, suffering, and death."

"Sounds simple," she said, "and wonderful."

"Right on both counts," he agreed, "and please note that this theory is not subject to the same criticisms as the Substitution Theory. It's not self-contradictory, it places love before all in God, and it has direct implications for how we live—when we love, we participate in the saving work of Christ. That work will never be complete until each and every one of us lives in perfect love!"

"Simple and wonderful," she reiterated, "but I don't see how it works. I also don't see why it's necessary. If God is love, I can see how maybe he needs to become human to enter into a love relationship with human beings; but why does he need to die?" As she said this, she realized she must have been echoing the sentiments of many who knew Kristos.

"There are two answers to that question," he replied. "One is that Christ's death wasn't planned by God. Love simply is crucified in this world. The other is that, unless Christ does suffer and die, unless he experiences the full spectrum of human experience, he can neither understand nor empathize with humanity. Where there is no understanding or empathy, there is no love."

"Which answer is yours?" she queried.

"Both," he said promptly. "The same necessity is to be found in each. What we do to ourselves, God allows us to do to him."

"It still sounds abstract," she maintained.

"It did to me for the longest time as well," he admitted. "You see, I was raised a Catholic, so all I ever knew was the Substitution Theory. It never seemed quite right to me. Then, when I went to graduate school, I discovered theological bits and pieces that eventually coalesced into the Ontological Theory. I knew that, if Christianity had any real meaning, it had to be in this theory; but that meaning remained distant and theoretical. It wasn't until years later, after I added some lessons from my own and others' experience, that the whole idea finally hit home."

"What experience?" she asked, genuinely curious.

"You see," he answered, "it wasn't until I thought deeply about the transformative power of love as I'd seen it in my own life, as well as our human resistance to that power, that the theory connected fully for me with reality. This connection came through my experience with autism."

"I know a little about that," she said. "It's when someone is emotionally turned in on himself. Were you autistic?" she queried, only half-joking.

"No!" he laughed. "At least, not clinically. And it's something like what you say, though not quite so simple. The term *autistic* was used originally to designate children who were extremely withdrawn emotionally, and that seems to be the symptom that all individuals so labeled today have in common; but it's quite possible the cause of the disorder varies from case to case. There is evidence in some instances that emotional withdrawal is a response to the inability to process sense-data, to make perceptual sense of a jumbled and confused world, and that this inability is organic, not merely psychological. This is all a fancy way of saying that the experts have almost as little understanding of autism today as they did when it was first 'discovered' in the 1940's."

"I don't think they would agree," she remarked.

"Probably not," he admitted. "They used to ascribe it to early infancy trauma, but now everyone recognizes that it is present at birth. At least they no longer blame it on the mother. But the acid test is their ability to help such people, and the general attitude is that autism is a genetic disorder, and therefore incurable until we discover how to fix the relevant genes. In the meantime, while a great deal can be done to help the mildly autistic lead ordinary lives, severe autism remains without foreseeable remedy. Indeed, as severe autism tends to worsen with age, the experts count it a victory if they can merely hold the line!"

"Wasn't there a popular movie about autism?" she asked.

"Yes," he replied, "*Rain Man*, and for Hollywood it was fairly realistic; but it did not show the darker side of autism, how violent some autistic individuals can became, not only toward themselves, but others."

"Is that from your experience?" she asked.

"At one time I worked with autistic adults," he said, "and yes, that's from my experience. But the film also didn't show the bright and hopeful side either, though it made some tentative steps in that direction. Would you like to see?"

Before Ariana could say yea or nay, she found herself viewing another situation. A happy family, consisting of handsome and intelligent parents and two bright and beautiful little girls, decided to have a third child, and this turned out to all appearances to be a healthy boy. When the boy was about what Ariana would have guessed was a year old, however, the mother noticed that he was neither as active nor as emotionally responsive as her previous babies. She and her husband took him to a number of doctors and specialists; and, though a variety of diagnoses were offered, the one that eventually made the most sense was autism. The little boy showed all the symptoms except peevishness and outbursts of rage, but the parents theorized that he was a placid child because they had never sought to force him to be like other children. They had always accepted him as he was and recognized his right to his own peculiarities.

In any event, the couple took full responsibility for their son. They read everything they could find about autism, and sought far and wide for professional help. Most of the schools and clinics they found followed a philosophy called 'behaviorism', which Ariana thought as appalling as did the parents, both in theory and practice. Children were treated like complex and mysterious machines. To fix the machines, one had to find the right buttons to push or adjustments to make. The technique was tricked up in all sorts of fancy scientific jargon, like operant conditioning and positive and negative reinforcement, and it presented itself as the cutting edge of truly scientific clinical psychology in the twentieth century; but, as far as Ariana could tell, it was the same old reward-and-punishment method that parents had been using on their children, with less than spectacular results, for thousands of years.

This particular couple, however, knew they could not make their son more human by dehumanizing him.

The boy's parents did find one or two places with a less mechanical approach, but these would not take him until he was at least a year older, and by then they thought it might be too late.

So the family, including the girls but especially the mother, worked with the boy on their own; and they began by doing the one thing that many experts had warned them against. The boy, like all autistic children, engaged in repetitive motions like rocking back and forth, clapping, etc. This particular child, especially, would spend hours spinning plates and saucers on the floor. The family members started to imitate him. When he made funny gestures or rocked, they would follow suit. One time they even had a living room full of friends and neighbors down on the floor spinning dinnerware!

The experts regarded such mimicry as not only unhelpful, but positively harmful. They were supposed to be positive role models. They were not supposed to imitate the boy, but he to imitate them. Nevertheless, the parents continued with this course of action because they understood that one can be a role model only for someone in the same perceptual, conceptual, and emotional universe. The whole problem was that their son was trapped in his own world. If he was happy in that world, they did not wish to force him out of it. They simply wanted to give him the option of entering the world of human relationship. To do that, they had to reach him in his world. By imitating his "rituals," they showed they loved and accepted him as he was, and gave him the opportunity to love and respect them as they were. By stepping inside his skin, they came to understand the perceptual, intellectual, and emotional roadblocks that prevented his free intercourse with the larger world, and then they systematically worked to remove those roadblocks.

The task was extremely taxing and difficult. Not only did they have to bear with the open disapproval of the experts, but also the fears and uncertainties of their own hearts. The boy made steady progress, and everyone thought the hardest part was over, but then he slipped back into a more extreme state of withdrawal than before. In other words, often their work seemed like wasted effort, one step forward and two back. Gradually, however, the boy came out of his autism, and anyone meeting him today would never know he had suffered from such an extreme disorder. They would discover in him nothing more, and nothing less, than a sensitive, intelligent, and unusually but not abnormally pensive young man.

When Ariana returned to the Teacher's company, her attitude toward him had changed. He had worked with people like the autistic boy, and he could appreciate the depth of their problems as well as the dignity of their humanity. "That was a beautiful story," she said solemnly.

"A true story," the Teacher added. "Perhaps the most instructive part, however, is not in the story itself. When a documentary about that family's experience was shown at the school where I worked, everyone on the staff, as I remember, declared that the boy could not have been severely autistic."

"Why?" Ariana exclaimed.

The Teacher smiled. "Because autism is incurable."

"I see," she said. "I mean, I don't see. Actually, I do and I don't!"

"My feelings exactly," he said. "There were people in that room with masters degrees and even doctorates in special education or psychology. Some had over twelve years of experience. How could they admit that this family, without experience or expertise, had cured an autistic child when they themselves had never put so much as a dent in anyone's severe autism?"

"Still, he was autistic and they did cure him," she maintained.

"Absolutely!" he affirmed.

"And they did it with love," she added. "Is that your point?"

"I don't know if that family was Christian, Jewish, atheist, or what have you," he said. "To my way of thinking, in what they did for their son they were genuine disciples of Christ. They loved the one most in need, and they followed the way love leads. Most people think that to live love and to live lovingly are the same thing, whereas the two are often opposites."

"I don't understand," said Ariana.

"Most people think that to live love is to lovingly run along the tracks laid down by one's culture," he explained. "If you want to be spiritual, become a monk. If you want to help people, become a trained helping professional. Love doesn't run along any tracks. It always strikes out on its own. Love is, and always has been, the only real pioneer, the only real adventure! Those parents were not rebels. They listened to what the experts had to say, but they made their decisions in the crucible of their own hearts!"

Ariana pondered. "I see," she said at length, "but how does this story clarify the Ontological Theory of Atonement? Isn't that why you told it?"

"In relation to the God of love, the God who is love," he said, "we sinners are all spiritually autistic, though through our own fault. We are trapped in the loveless world we have created for ourselves. We can't escape that world to reach God's world, which is love, so God must come into our world if there is to be any hope at all. And the process of reestablishing relationship with us is at least as long and difficult, cosmically speaking, as it was for that family and their little boy."

"And we can always refuse," she noted.

"Yes," the Teacher agreed, "we can always refuse. In fact, until we give ourselves completely to love, we are refusing."

Ariana pondered this last statement. She had a glimmer of what he meant, but her mind was too tired to continue. She rose, stretched, and looked around. The conversation had been so engrossing that she had hardly noticed the changes. The sky had been dark to begin with, but now it had become as black as the earth's night. The flashes off in the distance had continued throughout the discussion, but now she noticed that they had drawn nearer and grown in intensity. For some reason, she felt completely detached from the strange happenings around them, so her curiosity had an abstract quality about it when she asked the Teacher what all the lightning and thunder was about.

"It's a war," he explained.

"What war?" she queried. "Between whom?"

"The war you are about to enter," he said seriously.

"I don't understand," she returned, a knot of anxiety suddenly forming within her.

"Really?" he said, equal parts of irony and sincerity in his voice. "They said this would happen, though I found it difficult to believe. In any event, we have prepared a play that should bring home to you the nature and gravity of the conflict in which you are about to become a participant."

"Who are 'we?'" she demanded. "Who are 'they?'"

"That's not important," he replied. "Call them my colleagues, if you will. What's important now is that you enjoy the show. It should be quite an experience, seeing that you are now ready to be a thoroughly empathetic spectator. You will, in a very real sense, 'become' the play, and it will become you. When it's all over, we'll talk again."

Before she could think to say anything, a curtain appeared, the kind that hangs before a stage. As the curtain went up, the Teacher shouted as he receded into the distance, "Oh, by the way, the play is called *The Grand Inquisitor*, after the story by Fyodor Dostoevsky, of which it is an adaptation. The playwright has taken some liberties with the text, but we will leave you to judge how much his poetic license enhances the spirit of the original."

And then he was gone, before she had a chance to say that she had never read the original. She had no doubt, however, about who had written the stage version; but, as it turned out, it did not matter. The play began. When it was over, her universe was changed.

5. The Grand Inquisitor

ACT I. *A plainly furnished drawing room in Russia, circa 1877. Ivan, a professional man in his late twenties, sits on a worn but expensive sofa reading, but not with much attention. His gaze keeps wandering to the window; but, when he looks out, one can not help feeling he sees something millions of miles away. There is a knock at the door, and he rises abstractedly to answer it. Before he has gone more than a few paces, however, Alyosha, a younger man approaching twenty, enters. He is Ivan's brother, and is dressed in a simple robe with a wooden cross hanging around his neck. He is preparing to become a monk.*

IVAN Alyosha! To what do I owe the honor?

ALYOSHA I heard what you said. Dmitri told me what you said.

IVAN About our father?

ALYOSHA No, about God.

IVAN Oh, about God! And what did our dear brother say that I said about God?

ALYOSHA That if God did exist, it would be necessary to murder him!

IVAN And that upsets you?

ALYOSHA (*sitting wearily*) You know it upsets me. I'm worried about you, Ivan.

IVAN I thought you didn't worry about anything. I thought you simply enjoyed the life dear God has given you, playing with your bratty friends or attaining to holiness with your spiritual director.

ALYOSHA Do you hate me, Ivan?

IVAN On the contrary, and I'm sorry if I gave you the impression I did. However, I do hate people worrying about me, especially people I love.

ALYOSHA And God isn't one of those people? I fear for you, Ivan. You have no one. Without God, your world must be so cold. You must feel utterly alone.

IVAN   If that's the way it is, then that's the way it must be. But I
                really am touched by your concern; so, if you don't fear that I'll
                corrupt your pure and eternal soul, I'll give you an explanation.

ALYOSHA   (*extremely attentive*) Please do!

IVAN   Let me tell you a story. Once upon a time, there was a little girl
                of five who soiled her bedclothes at night. Her parents were quite
                upset by this habit, so they did everything they could think to
                stop it. They intimidated her, beat her, sent her to bed without
                supper—nothing worked. Finally, one night they were so fed up
                that they smeared her with her own feces, in her eyes and in her
                mouth, and locked her in the outhouse for the rest of the wintry
                autumn night. Now tell me, little brother, how could anyone
                listen to the whimpering of that little girl and not help? How
                could God listen and do nothing? Where was God?

ALYOSHA   (*hoarsely*) Yes, I know there is evil and suffering in this world.

IVAN   Not all suffering bothers me. You and I know that adults, venal
                and jaded as they are, fully deserve every bit of it they get. It's the
                suffering of children I don't understand, and I never will, because
                it is absolutely impossible for a good God who has the power to
                prevent the suffering of innocents not to do so.

ALYOSHA   (*whispering*) It is the darkest mystery.

IVAN   Perhaps I should tell another story. Once upon another time a
                nobleman, a retired general in fact, went hunting early in the
                morning with his friends. They came upon a peasant woman
                gathering firewood while her nine-year-old son threw stones
                innocently into the forest. The dogs surprised the pair so
                abruptly that the boy accidentally lamed the general's favorite
                hound, which had to be put out of its misery. This so infuriated
                the general that he ordered his servants to strip the lad before his
                mother's eyes, and then set the dogs upon him. Again, brother,
                I ask you, where was God?

ALYOSHA   (*bows his head and says nothing*)

IVAN   Still no answer? Perhaps the third time, as they say, really is the
                charm. Once upon a third time, then—never mind if it was in the
                present, past or future—an unwed mother's little girl chattered
                constantly; and her lover, who had converted the woman to some
                pseudo-Christian cult, convinced her that her daughter was

possessed by demons. Again, the couple did everything imaginable to stop the child—intimidation, beating, denial of sustenance. The litany of barbarities by which adults seek to control their children remains depressingly the same down through the ages. Nothing worked. And, do you know, Alyosha, to me the most poignant feature of the story is that, while the little girl knew she was doing something wrong because her mama was mad at her, she never understood what it was! Finally, the couple decided an exorcism was in order. They sprinkled some 'holy water' on the child, stuffed her into the oven and then lit it. Curiously enough, though the woman lived in an apartment house and plenty of people heard the screams, the most anyone did was summon the police. By the time the authorities arrived, the girl was cinders. They found the couple sitting at the kitchen table mumbling some sort of prayer, evidently in a semi-catatonic trance.

ALYOSHA   (*burying his face in his hands*) Where was God?

IVAN   Bravo, brother, you anticipate my very question! Where indeed was God?

ALYOSHA   (*opening his eyes, sees the cross, grasps it, and holds it up to Ivan triumphantly*) There! God is there!

IVAN   On the cross? Oh yes, you are absolutely right! God is love and created us to love. We cannot love if we cannot hate, cannot create if we cannot destroy. We choose. In a world where we have chosen hate and destruction, there is but one place God could be—on the cross with our victims.

ALYOSHA   (*nodding vigorously*) You understand! (placing his hands on Ivan's shoulders) You really do understand!

IVAN   Of course. But it's not good enough. It can never be good enough.

ALYOSHA   The cross isn't good enough? But, Ivan, what more can God do?

IVAN   Nothing. That's the tragedy. There's nothing God can do.

ALYOSHA   (*murmuring*) I don't understand.

IVAN   Do you remember the Inquisition? We learned about it as boys.

ALYOSHA   Yes, but you can't blame Christ for that.

IVAN   And do you know, I actually did a project on it in law school? It was called "Rules of Evidence"—a study of how a judicial system would degenerate into tyranny without them.

ALYOSHA   Tyranny, yes. The Roman Catholic pope asserts his absolute authority.

IVAN   Do you know the theory behind the Inquisition?

ALYOSHA   What is there to know? "Power corrupts, and absolute power corrupts absolutely."

IVAN   We are into famous quotes now, the kind everyone remembers without remembering who said them? Well then, how about, "Better that nine guilty men go free than one suffer unjust condemnation."

ALYOSHA   I like that. Who said it?

IVAN   An American judge, Oliver Wendell Holmes. It's got something to do with the American theory of government. The idea behind the Inquisition, however, was just the opposite: better that nine innocent people suffer unjust condemnation rather than one guilty person go free.

ALYOSHA   That doesn't surprise me. And what were they guilty of, anyway?

IVAN   You're missing the point, brother! It's the idea, the idea behind the Inquisition, that you have to appreciate. *(Ivan rises and pours himself and Alyosha each a brandy at the sideboard. When Alyosha declines, Ivan downs them both.)* It began in the thirteenth century. The pope instituted Inquisitional tribunals in every country of Western Christendom. The Inquisition's first great triumph was the suppression of the Albigensians in southern France. Philip the Fair used the Inquisition to destroy the Knights Templars and plunder their estate, and of course later it became an instrument of policy for the Spanish Crown. But we'll get to that. The idea, Alyosha, the idea! If your limb were gangrenous, what would you do?

ALYOSHA   If the doctor could not stem the infection, I'd have him cut it off.

IVAN   Of course. Otherwise, you'd die. Any doctor would be sure to take some healthy tissue as well, to insure that all the infection was removed. As I'm sure you know, if only a tiny bit remains, it goes straight to the heart and kills you. What about a plague? If a plague breaks out in a city, what must the authorities do?

ALYOSHA   It's their responsibility to seal off the town so that the contagion will not spread.

IVAN   Of course, even if the majority of the populace is healthy at the time, and sealing them in with the sick condemns them to nearly certain death. Otherwise, the plague may wipe out many cities.

ALYOSHA   (*impatiently*) What's your point?

IVAN   I think you already know my point, little brother. The Catholic idea—and we Eastern Orthodox too little appreciate it—is that heresy, the corruption of the true faith taught by the Church, is an infection in the mystical body of Christ. It is a plague that must be contained and eliminated, even at the cost of innocent life.

ALYOSHA   It's mind control, pure and simple!

IVAN   You are too intolerant, Alyosha, too unwilling to entertain a different point of view. Perhaps you yourself think the Romans are heretics! But the consistency of the idea is what is so impressive. Look at what's at stake! The Church is necessary for salvation. Without the Church, Christ might as well never have died for us, because the Church alone can make us fit to enjoy heavenly bliss. What matters the death of the body, if it ensures the salvation of the soul?

ALYOSHA   You really believe all that? Perhaps that's it! You wish to convert to Catholicism!

IVAN   If it were all that simple . . . What's truly amazing is how few victims it took to keep the rank-and-file in line! The Protestants, with their witch hunts, executed tens and perhaps hundreds of thousands of people. No exact figures are available, of course, but it seems that the Spanish Inquisition, which was the institution at its most ferocious, killed only a few thousand, and the entire Inquisition no more than ten thousand!

ALYOSHA   (*in indignation*) It's not a matter of mathematics!

IVAN   Of course not, if one is speaking morally; but I was talking about the idea! It seems they really do understand how the masses work, and how to control them with maximum efficiency. Today's would-be dictators could learn a lot from them. Let me explain to you how it all worked.

ALYOSHA   I already know.

IVAN   But you don't know the details, and the truth of anything is always in the details. According to Christianity, isn't that why God incarnates into the world in the first place? To take care of the details?

ALYOSHA   I'm listening.

IVAN   For reasons I've already explained, the Inquisition followed rules of evidence that were in effect in civil courts of the time only in cases of high treason. Hearsay evidence was the rule rather than the exception, and there was no writ of habeas corpus. One could be held indefinitely without being charged. The accused did not have the right to be faced by his accuser. Thus, if one coveted one's neighbor's land or wife, one could get him out of the way by denouncing him to the Inquisition.

ALYOSHA   So anyone suspected was already condemned. This is no great idea! It's merely the anxiety and paranoia that always lurk in the hearts of tyrants.

IVAN   That's not strictly true, historically. If the accused had enough pull with the civil authorities, and if they in turn were important enough to ignore the Inquisition, the tribunal would be helpless. As I've already intimated, the Inquisition was strongest where the state used it for its own ends. Neither is it true ideologically, because everything was done for the spiritual benefit of all concerned, including the accused.

ALYOSHA   That's absurd!

IVAN   Not if one accepts the idea! If purity of faith is essential to salvation, then heresy must be stamped out at all cost. Better innocent people suffer physically than everyone die spiritually.

Better to play it safe by assuming the accused are guilty than to risk leaving any of the lethal infection.

ALYOSHA   If that was the idea, why not just summarily execute the accused, and save everyone a lot of pain and bother?

IVAN   You disappoint me, brother! Heresy is a spiritual infection. The heretical tendency had to be snuffed out, not the heretic. Just as a doctor will do everything to save an infected limb short of risking the life of the patient, or do everything to save a patient stricken by plague short of risking the spread of the contagion, so too the inquisitors did everything they could to save the accused.

ALYOSHA   By maiming and torturing him?

IVAN   Yes, even by that. This was called "being put to the process." The torture was administered by the ecclesiastics who staffed the tribunals, usually Dominicans and Franciscans, because they were highly trained in theology and therefore knew what constituted heresy and what did not better than the heretics themselves. But you misjudge these men if you think them sadists. The salvation of the accused could only be assured through full and contrite confession. They were exceedingly patient in extracting such confession, spending not only months but years in gentle interrogation of the prisoner. Only when all else failed, and usually it did not, would they resort to torture. There were a variety of possibilities, Alyosha, so please follow closely.

ALYOSHA   (*pacing impatiently*) Is this really necessary?

IVAN   The details, brother, don't forget the details! (*At this point the stage opens, leaving Ivan on stage left and Alyosha stage right, where they remain until the end. As if behind a screen, shadows enact the gruesome business of torture while Ivan continues.*) Let's first take the case of the open and defiant heretic, who most likely would have been a Protestant, or one of the forerunners of the Reformation.

ALYOSHA   Why not a Jew?

IVAN   "Heresy" is the corruption of the true faith, so the Inquisition only dealt with avowed Christians. Plenty of Jews and some Muslims died in the Inquisition, but that was because they had gotten themselves baptized so as to be permitted to stay in Spain. They therefore were secret rather than defiant heretics. Though, come to think of it, I suppose the son of such a family, baptized at birth, might have been so proud of his cultural antecedents as to proclaim himself a Jew and so fall under the category. But you divert me from my train of thought. The defiant heretic who remained defiant throughout the torture would be condemned. The defiant heretic who repented under torture and then 'relapsed', or went back on his confession, would likewise be condemned. The defiant heretic who repented and maintained his repentance would be forgiven.

ALYOSHA   And the forgiven would be set free and the condemned executed?

IVAN   Not quite that simple. The only case in which the accused would simply be freed after torture—without double jeopardy, mind you—would be that of a suspect heretic who maintained innocence throughout.

ALYOSHA   Suspect?

IVAN   Alleged. Claiming to be innocent at the outset. If the suspect heretic confessed during the process, he would be forgiven, as long as he did not go back on his confession later. If he did, he would be condemned as a relapsed heretic.

ALYOSHA   So, whatever the accused said under torture was the truth!

IVAN   That was the assumption.

ALYOSHA   And what happened to them all?

IVAN   The forgiven were given a variety of penances, depending upon the severity of the offense. They ranged from the payment of a fine or several years in a monastic order to life imprisonment or deportation to a penal colony.

ALYOSHA   How merciful!

IVAN   (*smiling*) As merciful as a God who sends the repentant to Purgatory.

ALYOSHA   And the condemned?

IVAN   The Church held it unfitting for monks dedicated to God to execute the condemned, so they were "relaxed" or turned over to the "secular arm," the civil authority, with a recommendation of mercy.

ALYOSHA   (*laughing sardonically*) It was alright for churchmen to torture prisoners, and for prisoners to die under torture, but it wasn't good form to finish the job they'd started!

IVAN   Yes, but again, you miss the idea! The recommendation of mercy was pure fiction, or, if you will, pure irony. If the civil authority in question did not have the condemned executed . . .

ALYOSHA   Burned at the stake!

IVAN   That was the usual method, but barbaric only in the abstract. Except for the occasional malefactor, like Joan of Arc, who really deserved a roasting . . .

ALYOSHA   Why did she deserve it?

IVAN   She defeated in battle the English who engineered her condemnation, of course! However, she was an exception. As a rule, the condemned heretic was drugged or strangled to unconsciousness before being burned. But as I was saying, if the king, duke, earl, prince, mayor, or whoever did not execute those entrusted to his care and was not strong enough to defy the Inquisition, he himself would be arrested as a suspect heretic.

ALYOSHA   But what was the point of such pretense? Surely everyone saw through it!

IVAN   That's just the point! It wasn't mere pretense. It was literary artistry lifted from the pages of holy scripture and made socially, historically, and existentially incarnate. As pretense, everyone saw through it; but, as fiction, everyone believed it.

ALYOSHA   Now you sound crazy!

IVAN   (*soberly*) That's a consummation devoutly to be wished. I am not crazy, but to further paraphrase the noble Bard, there's madness in my method.

ALYOSHA   (*burying his face in his hands*) I think your method is to drive me crazy! I don't understand.

IVAN   Would you like to hear a story that will help you understand?

ALYOSHA   (*raising his head and looking full of compassionate concern for his brother*) Yes, very much so.

Again, the scene of the auto-da-fe' is enacted by shadow figures.

IVAN   The day before my story opens there has been a tremendous auto-da-fe'. Do you know the term?

ALYOSHA   Portuguese for "act of faith." It referred to the burning of heretics.

IVAN   Not precisely. The common notion is what you say; but the auto da fe', with its paradoxical air of festive solemnity, involved only the public reading of sentences. The executions, as I said, were purely civil affairs. Nevertheless, since my story is set in Spain, and since there the executions often followed so hard upon formal condemnation as to make such legal distinctions invisible to the untrained eye, I will exercise my poetic license as author to get to the event's essential significance.

ALYOSHA   Author?

IVAN   Oh yes, I was not explicit on that point. This is my story.

ALYOSHA   Then perhaps I may read it, or you may read it to me.

IVAN   I've never written it down! I carry it in my head. I've always admired poetry, and envied anyone who could write it. This is my very own prose poem. (*proudly*) You are my first audience!

ALYOSHA   (*meaningfully*) I see.

IVAN   Anyway, the day before the story opens there has been a massive auto da fe' in the town square.

ALYOSHA   Any particular town?

IVAN   I have always pictured my story taking place in the city of Seville, where the days are hot and languid and the nights warm and breathless, and where the scent of jasmine and carnation perfumes the heavy air.

ALYOSHA   You are a poet.

IVAN   (*smiling at the compliment*) It is, of course, the sixteenth century, the time of the Reconquista and Counter Reformation, when the pope, at the behest of the Spanish Crown, appointed a Grand Inquisitor with special powers to root out opposition and infidelity to the Holy Catholic Church in Spain. When the pope discovered how brutally devoted to his mission this Inquisitor was, however, he abolished the office. By then, of course, it was too late. Spain was strong enough to continue its Inquisitional proceedings without the papal blessing.

Throughout preparations have been going on in the shadow play. Now the king and queen arrive, as well as the Cardinal Inquisitor, and the crowd enthusiastically cheers.

ALYOSHA   I didn't know that.

IVAN   Another popular misconception. The pope has been much vilified in our Church, but often he has been the puppet of greater powers. Often he has been a weak, ordinary sort trying to fill shoes no man can.

ALYOSHA   That's the evil in it—the pretense.

IVAN   As you will, brother, I see there's no changing you. And I wouldn't want you to change, really. Anyway, the king and queen weren't about to let go of their invaluable ally in suppressing dissent against the established order. The pope's command was ignored. The day before the story proper begins, one hundred heretics were burned at the stake *ad majoram gloriam Dei*.

ALYOSHA   "To the greater glory of God."

IVAN   They taught you some Latin, eh? Know thine enemy? The function was a perfect success. The royal couple attended in all their regalia, and the the Grand Inquisitor himself, the one who had the last word on who lived and died, presided in his gorgeous cardinal's robes. Have you ever seen a cardinal of the Roman Catholic Church dressed in his formal robes?

ALYOSHA   I've seen paintings. A beautiful crimson.

IVAN   And the king and queen were there as well. Like public executions everywhere, it was a great party, a time of feasting and frolic. Only this was even better. Not only did the audience get to satisfy its bloodlust, but it did so, as we said, for the greater glory of God.

ALYOSHA   The best of both worlds.

IVAN   (*approvingly*) Precisely! A hundred heretics were burned at the stake. The smoke of charred flesh mingled with that of sacred incense in an aroma pleasing to God and edifying to humanity. Now you see my idea.

ALYOSHA   I see it, but I don't see why you choose it over the God of love. I don't see that at all.

IVAN   I don't choose one over the other. I'm like the donkey in the philosopher's tale who starves to death because he's equidistantly between two piles of hay. For lack of a reason to choose one idea over the other, I despair.

ALYOSHA   That's what I don't understand! How could you think there's even a contest?

IVAN   There's a contest, alright! Shall we begin my story?

ALYOSHA   If the answer lies therein, by all means!

ACT II. *The shadows dissipate, and in their place are full-blooded men and women. The scene is a serene hubbub of buying and selling—market day in Seville. As before, Ivan and Alyosha are in the wings.*

IVAN   The day before was Sunday, dedicated to the Lord, on which a hundred heretics were burned at the stake. Now it's Monday, market day, and the same people who had come from miles and miles around to watch yesterday's fun have returned to Seville on the serious business of earning a living.

Enter KRISTOS stage right, with the crowd.

IVAN   Then, out of a dream, as it were, *he* came again to grace their city.

CRIPPLED

BEGGAR   (*to* KRISTOS) Help me, sir, give me a few coppers!

KRISTOS *touches the man, and he is healed. Someone else notices the miracle, and begs likewise to be healed. Soon a procession has formed, moving through the square with Kristos at the head. He goes slowly, healing whomever is placed in his path. The procession steadily grows in size and volume.*

IVAN   The people are overjoyed! Their God walks among them again! This isn't the second coming, only a little visit incognito; but still, they all know who he is. That would be the best part of my poem if I were ever to write it, how all know in their hearts it is the Christ.

This procession meets a funeral procession. A little girl has died, and the mother trails the open coffin in tears. KRISTOS *bends down and whispers something to the figure of the dead little girl, and she opens her eyes and sits up in her coffin. Helping hands from the crowd assist her in stepping out, and everyone goes wild with joy and adulation. Enter* CARDINAL INQUISITOR, *or simply the* CARDINAL, *stage right. He eyes* KRISTOS, *who by this time has crisscrossed in procession to stage left.*

IVAN   What do you think of the Cardinal Inquisitor?

ALYOSHA   No cardinal's robes today. A sinister figure, if ever there was one.

IVAN   Sinister? Saintly, I would say! He's not one of your voluptuary cardinals or pleasure-loving popes of the pre-Reformation Church. He represents the lean, mean Counter-Reformation Church, ready to take on Protestantism. He's an ascetic, a holy man! The Roman Catholic roster of saints is filled with figures like him. He only wears his official robes when his office requires. He's probably worn that thread-bare cassock for years. No doubt he washes it, wrings it out, and hangs it up each night so he can put it on the next day. He's over ninety, but still vigorous and ramrod straight. His ring is his only insignia of office, but of course everyone knows who he is. Here's a man who has mastered every passion, stilled every desire, overcome all fear . . .

ALYOSHA   Who are they?

The Cardinal Inquisitor's Guard, a handful of soldiers, enter and languidly arrange themselves in at-ease formation to the Cardinal's rear.

IVAN	His guard.

ALYOSHA	If he's overcome all fear, why does he need a guard?

IVAN	They aren't there to protect him, obviously, but to do his bidding, to arrest whom he bids them arrest. As I was saying, the roster of saints of the Roman Catholic Church is filled with men such as he. He has no life of his own, all of his energy is poured night and day into his work.

The CARDINAL INQUISITOR *frowns and points at* KRISTOS, *and his Guard rushes forward and surrounds him, the crowd clearing out of the way. The soldiers march the prisoner away in the direction of the Cardinal's palace, now visible in the distance. The crowd gathers around the* CARDINAL. *At first it seems they intend him harm, but then they kneel for his blessing. All characters are then frozen, as in a tableau.*

ALYOSHA	Impossible!

IVAN	Quite possible.

ALYOSHA	But you said they all know in their hearts he is their God!

IVAN	Yes, and I stand by that characterization absolutely.

ALYOSHA	Then it's absolutely absurd!

IVAN	I see you've been infected by modern mechanistic psychologies more than you thought.

ALYOSHA	Is it fear? Are they simply cowed into submission? Are they afraid of what the Inquisitor can do to them?

IVAN	Now who's being absurd! My dear Alyosha, they are a potential mob. Every man in that crowd has a weapon, every nobleman a sword, every peasant a knife. They could easily dispatch the Guard. And if, by some stretch of the imagination, you think they might be afraid of the Guard, once the soldiers are out of the way, they can have their way with the venerable Cardinal, and who can say them nay?

ALYOSHA	What about the authorities? Would they do nothing? What about the legal consequences?

IVAN   Brother, think! What could the authorities do, prosecute an entire province? The most they could do would be to string up a few ringleaders. What mob cares about that?

ALYOSHA   Then it is absurd!

IVAN   Not at all! Remember when we were children, and you were caught playing with that boy Reuben?

ALYOSHA   I wasn't "caught." We had just met. There was something about him, Ivan! He would have been my best friend.

IVAN   This was mother's one time, wasn't it?

ALYOSHA   I don't blame her. He was Jewish, and . . .

IVAN   Blame her! You are the one to blame, if anyone! You've never been afraid of anything, yet you feared her. And it wasn't the thrashing papa would have given you had she told him. You were afraid of her!

ALYOSHA   She was our mother! How could I disobey her?

IVAN   The voice of authority.

ALYOSHA   But she loved us! Certainly I defied papa, but papa never loved us.

IVAN   All the worse, to use love as an excuse not to love!

ALYOSHA   (*bowing his head*) You're right. No matter what it's foundation, hers was still my voice of authority.

IVAN   Then are these sheep so hard to understand? For ninety-nine-point-nine percent of the human race, when the knowledge of the heart comes into conflict with the voice of authority, fear wins over love hands down!

ACT III. *The dungeon of the Cardinal Inquisitor's Palace. Throughout, the prisoner, KRIS-TOS, holds center stage, with the CARDINAL circling around him. ALYOSHA and IVAN are still in the wings.*

CARDINAL   Tell me, is it really you?

KRISTOS *opens his mouth as if to speak.*

CARDINAL   No, don't speak! Don't say anything! You haven't the right to add to or subtract from anything you said or did fifteen hundred years ago. You gave us the keys to your kingdom, and how can you interfere now? You valued human freedom so highly that you came and gave everyone the choice, nothing more and nothing less. You can't change anything now without giving the lie to all you stood for then, and you are notorious for the extremes to which you will go for the sake of truth.

ALYOSHA   What does he mean by "the choice"?

IVAN   That's the chief part of what he has to talk about. Hush, and listen.

CARDINAL   I was one of your saints, your spiritual heroes. I took up my cross and followed you into the wilderness of freedom, where one is utterly alone and not even God is present.

ALYOSHA   What is he talking about? God is present everywhere!

IVAN   You don't understand, brother? That surprises me. To be created in God's image, to have freedom like God, is also to be alone like God, to bear God-like responsibility. Conventional piety aside, if one grants the hypothesis of free will, the wilderness of responsibility follows axiomatically.

CARDINAL   I overcame bondage to my fears and passions. I won my freedom. But then, I turned around and came to my senses. I saw that, for every individual who had the courage and strength to carry the cross of freedom, there were a hundred, a thousand, a hundred thousand who were too weak. For every saint and hero who heeded your call to be perfect, there were millions and hundreds of millions who did not have the possibility of perfection in them. And I also saw that you, who would be humanity's greatest benefactor, had become its worst criminal. You, who would bestow upon the world its holiest blessing, had instead inflicted the most terrible of curses.

ALYOSHA   What in heaven's name is he talking about? Is he mad?

IVAN   Is it that hard to see? Of course, you never had to experience it directly; but with object lessons all around you, one may be pardoned for assuming you would understand.

ALYOSHA   What?

IVAN   (*in deep earnestness*) Have you never heard tell of a son who wanted to please his father more than anything, but his father's expectations were so high that he failed miserably and suffered that failure the rest of his life?

ALYOSHA   (*meaningfully*) Yes, of course, but what's that got to do with Christ?

IVAN   Hush! Listen.

CARDINAL   They love you! They really do love you, but you asked of them too much. You asked them to be perfect! Yes, of course, you and I know that love must be perfect to be real love. We also know that only love gives meaning to life. But you didn't ask dumb animals to be perfect! Why ask them? Of course, there will always be the extraordinary few who heed your call; but if you don't care for the sniveling and contemptible many, who will? That is what we have taken upon ourselves to do. Of course, you alone could have made the illusion perfect, but we have corrected your work to the extent that we are able.

ALYOSHA   What can he mean? How does one correct perfection?

IVAN   An astute observation, Alyosha. This is just the old man's ironical way of saying that he and his colleagues have given the human race an alternative. But it really is a correction from his point of view, when you think about it. To demand the impossible of a little child or a dumb animal is the worst cruelty.

ALYOSHA   But we are neither children nor animals!

IVAN   History might take issue with you there. But listen, he's ready to go on!

CARDINAL   You should have heeded the word of that dread spirit of nothingness and self-destruction when he exhorted you in the wilderness. My God, if ever divine inspiration begot true wisdom, it was that day!

ALYOSHA   He's speaking of the temptation! He means Satan!

IVAN   Of course. My poem has a Biblical as well as historical basis. After Jesus is baptized by John, he's dragged into the desert by the Holy Spirit, and there he fasts for forty days. Afterwards, the gospel writers say in their marvelous gift for stating the obvious, he was hungry. But hush! See who comes.

Enter SATAN.

CARDINAL   You should have listened! What he told you was simple, but infinitely profound. He instructed you in the care of your own creation. But you would not listen. Love would not listen. Love is too proud!

SATAN   (*to* KRISTOS) Jesus, if you are truly the messiah, the one who is to usher in God's kingdom of joy and peace and love, why don't you turn these stones here into bread? If you are the messiah, surely you can do it!

KRISTOS   I'm hungry, but my heavenly father will satisfy my hunger when it pleases him.

SATAN   Not for you, Rabbi! Do you think my opinion of you so small? But now that you know the agony of human hunger, how can you refuse to alleviate it?

KRISTOS   Humanity does not live by bread alone, but by the breath that comes from the mouth of God.

SATAN   Show me that breath, that spirit! Take any human being and make him God for a day, and one of the first things he'd do would be to eliminate human hunger, the root of most human suffering. Why don't you?

KRISTOS   Humanity has but one absolute need.

SATAN   Humanity has many needs, and bread is one of the most absolute!

KRISTOS   There is but one need—not to eat, not to drink, not to sleep, not even to be loved, because God already loves each and every one of us. The one thing needful is to love.

CARDINAL   (*to* KRISTOS, *as* SATAN *backs away*) You self-deluded, arrogant fool! He offered you the power of seduction, and you refused. The physical comfort that human beings spend most of their lives either pursuing, enjoying, or pining after, you belittled!

ALYOSHA   (*shaking his head*) It's not enough.

IVAN   No, there's more to come; but still, it's quite a lot! What do you think the modern preoccupation with science and technology is all about? Soon the human race won't have to look to God for miracles. It will create its own. Human beings want to change everything but themselves. The conditions in which they live and the nature they've been given are to blame, not themselves. You're right, though, it's not enough. The comfort of the body means nothing if the soul is not at peace with itself.

A crack of thunder and flash of lightning mark the transition from desert to Temple.

SATAN   (*to* KRISTOS) Do you recognize this city?

KRISTOS   I've never seen it from this height before, but it's Jerusalem.

SATAN   A city I know you love. And do you know where you are standing?

KRISTOS   At the very pinnacle of the Temple.

SATAN   Most beloved of edifices in your most beloved of cities! Why don't you throw yourself down, because it is written in the holy book, "The Lord will send his angels, lest his anointed one dash his feet against a stone." Or don't you believe the prophecy? Don't you believe the angels will come to save you?

KRISTOS   It is also written in the scriptures, "You shall not tempt the Lord your God."

SATAN   You don't really believe you're the messiah. Anyone can play games. How do you expect people to take you seriously? If you jump and fall, at least everyone will think you really meant what you said, even if you were crazy. And if the angels do come, then the spiritual leaders of all the people, gathered together in the Temple precincts below, will proclaim your power and glory throughout the land. If you don't jump, however, what is anyone to conclude but that you are bluffing?

KRISTOS   Suppose, my friend, that I do jump. What do you think that will prove?

SATAN   At the very least, that you truly are the messiah, and perhaps even God himself.

KRISTOS   It would prove that I was powerful, yes, or that I had connections in high places; but would it prove that I am love? Since the love in the human heart alone can bear witness to the love that I am, all it would prove is that I haven't the first clue what all this is really about.

CARDINAL   (*mimicking*) Nothing can "prove" love! (returns to normal) But what if something could? Human beings are incapable of love! Again you reject the wisdom of one whose feet you are unworthy to kiss! Men will risk everything, even life itself, to be at peace with themselves; but they need someone to constantly assure them that everything is alright. They need clear guidelines established by recognized authority, by the following of which they can convince themselves that they have done the best they could, all that could reasonably be expected of them. You refused men the blessing of inner peace, preferring to establish in them the restlessness of an implacable love. Do you think that, by destroying our mystery, another will not be hallowed in its place?

Thunder and lightning. The CARDINAL INQUISITOR, KRISTOS, *and* SATAN *freeze. Enter* TEACHER *on raised platform, center upstage.*

ALYOSHA   What's he talking about, another mystery?

TEACHER   What he says is true.

ALYOSHA   (*startled*) Who are you?

TEACHER   A window into the future. That business about human beings making miracles their own business was absolutely true. In my day and age, they will think themselves the lords and masters of the universe!

IVAN   (*to* TEACHER) Interesting, very interesting.

TEACHER   You know who I am?

IVAN   It does not matter. Your epiphany means my story will have a life of its own.

TEACHER   Most definitely.

IVAN   You are the expression of that life!

TEACHER   (*spreading his arms*) As are we all. But this business of mystery is even more interesting. You live in an age of transition, and perhaps you can't see it, but less and less will people be going to priests and ministers to have their consciences cleared.

ALYOSHA   (*with genuine interest as well as irony*) Who will hold the keys to the kingdom in the future?

TEACHER   Experts. Let me give you a few examples. In my own time the rule will be birth in the hospital, as it is for the middle and upper classes of Europe in your day. Birth at home, however, will become not only a rarity, but also an oddity.

IVAN   But isn't the hospital a more enlightened setting for a passage fraught with so much risk?

TEACHER   That's a matter of opinion. However, I don't wish to argue the relative merits of giving birth at home or in the hospital. I merely wish to use the issue to illustrate a point. Believe it or not, I've been something of a renegade in my time, and I've been involved in several home births. Naturally I've talked with plenty of people about the subject, and I always remember the couples who say they think that home is the best place to have a baby, but they'd feel so guilty if something went wrong. I always ask them why they'd feel guilty if something went wrong at home but not in the hospital, where things go wrong so often they have a special term for attendant-induced complications—iatrogenic; and they invariably reply that then they would have done everything they could.

IVAN   But they would!

ALYOSHA   Ivan, you need to study your own lesson. They would be equally responsible no matter where they had their child.

TEACHER   Or take another example. Violence in my time and place . . .

ALYOSHA   America?

TEACHER   Impossible to mistake, eh? Violence, street violence, is a way of life in many parts of our cities, and no place is entirely free of it. Now, suppose you were walking down the street and you came upon a gang beating up a defenseless individual. What would you do?

ALYOSHA   Place myself between the victimizers and their victim and let their blows fall upon me.

IVAN   I would take the less heroic but wiser and, I believe, more effective course—pull out my revolver.

TEACHER   The police in our day not only advise, but tell us it is our duty as good citizens not to intervene!

ALYOSHA   Impossible!

IVAN   Shameful, but logical. How easily we let ourselves be absolved from our humanity.

TEACHER   As in the incident of the little girl exorcised in the oven. The neighbors were only following expert counsel.

IVAN   So it was you! I wondered whence that story came. I also wondered why no one did anything more than call the police, but now it makes perfectly good sense. In your time, people have divorced themselves from their consciences to such a degree that duty demands nothing more than obeying the experts. "I absolve you from your sins . . ."

More thunder and lightening. The CARDINAL, KRISTOS, *and* SATAN *are still frozen, but now they are on a high mountain overlooking a vast plain dotted with diverse cities representing the kingdoms of the world.*

ALYOSHA   Now he's going to deliver.

TEACHER   Yes. Up until now, Satan has been offering bogus goods, trying to get something for nothing, because nothing with which he's tempted Jesus has been within his power to give. The confidence game has failed. Now he's got to barter with his own currency.

IVAN   (*pleased that his audience understands*) But Jesus has been equally cagey. Now, with reality on the line, the messiah's mettle will be put to the genuine test.

SATAN   Look around you, Jesus. What do you see?

KRISTOS   All the kingdoms of this world.

SATAN   If you kneel down and swear allegiance to their lord and master, I will give them all to you.

SATAN *waits, but* KRISTOS *calmly maintains his stance.*

SATAN   Perhaps you don't believe me.

KRISTOS   I believe you. The kings and rulers of the earth claim to hold their authority in my name, but I freely confess that they are no vassals of mine. Your disciples serve power, mine love. It's clear who owns the kingdoms of this world.

SATAN   Think of how much good you could do were you to unite your cross with Caesar's sword! Human beings are sheep. They will have someone to rule over them no matter what. Should it not be someone who does so for their own good?

KRISTOS   Depart, Satan! For it is written, "The Lord your God shall you worship, and him only shall you serve." Love alone shall you worship, and love only shall you serve.

There is one final resounding crash of thunder and blinding flash of lightning. When it is over, SATAN *and the* TEACHER *have disappeared, and the* CARDINAL INQUISITOR *and* KRISTOS *are back in the cell.*

CARDINAL   (*to* KRISTOS) Do you understand now why I hate you? One cannot have one's cake and eat it too, but you could at least have made their illusion perfect. They are like children lost in a trackless waste. Whoever looks like he knows where he is going they follow, even if it's into an abyss! I know for sheep such as these there will never be any other place to go, but at least you could have alleviated their suffering and eased their fears along their meaningless sojourn from nothing to nothing. Now you have left it in our hands, and we have done what we could. For their own sakes we have lied and governed and terrorized, all in your name. We have betrayed you in your own name, but you are guilty of the deeper treason. You demanded faith without seeing, and therefore left the blind to lead the blind. You offered us hope but, save to the heroic few capable of following you, gave us despair. You loved us, all of us, but that love was at the same time a stern and impossible demand. Your gift of grace took everything, but our rule of law gives everything. Instead of demanding faith, we give miracle, a miracle so independent of the vagaries of sense that belief itself creates it. Instead of hope, we display the mystery of a morality accommodating to human weakness and greed. Finally, out of pity for our charges, we strictly subordinate love to authority, knowing that the firm and steady hand is always, in the final analysis, the kinder.

ALYOSHA   He's truly a hero to you.

IVAN   Is that so impossible for you to understand?

ALYOSHA   He's not a hero. He has no tragic secret. He's an atheist, that's all.

IVAN   You're right, you've guessed his secret, he doesn't believe in God; but isn't that tragic, to understand God yet not to believe in him? Isn't that heroic, to care for Christ's flock when the shepherd has died in one's soul?

ALYOSHA   He doesn't have to do it.

IVAN   Just so! He doesn't have to do it. But he does. Why?

ALYOSHA   For power. Simply for power.

IVAN   There is nothing simple about any of this, brother, except for you, if you really mean what you're saying. I don't believe you do. If I did, I wouldn't make another intelligent remark to you again. Power? He acts out of compassion, or pity if you will, the same pity that would lead you or I to put a wounded animal out of its misery.

ALYOSHA   Human beings aren't animals!

IVAN   No? Well, some of them, I'll grant you that. You, for example, are as far from being an animal as heaven is distant from earth!

ALYOSHA   (*good naturedly*) Despite my stupidity.

IVAN   (*making as if he wants to embrace him*) Forgive me, little brother, but you were being disingenuous, and it doesn't suit you. You know as well as I what history proves.

ALYOSHA   History proves only what people have done, not what they are capable of doing.

IVAN   (*to audience*) The eye of history sees into the souls of men, and there it finds such cruel, weak, and irrational creatures that it can do no more than relegate the human race to the dustbin of failed evolutionary experiments. What is a human being but a self-contradiction between the illusion of freedom and the pinch of necessity, too comical to be called tragic and too painful to bear repeating?

ALYOSHA   (*to audience*) The soul may belong to history, but the heart belongs to love. Your vision may seem to you, in your cold, intellectual way, frightening and magnificent; but you actually find it comforting. The truly awesome view of human existence can be seen only by the heart. The eyes of knowledge see a tragically flawed species, but the eyes of love always and forever see only individuals—men, women, and yes, children—who choose to do such terrible things to themselves and others when they could have done otherwise. Love neither pities nor despises them, as your fine Cardinal, your Grand Inquisitor does. It calls them to account. And it does so without self-righteousness—a silent reproach, simply by being love.

IVAN   This, my dear brother, is the choice.

ALYOSHA   This is what you meant to show me?

IVAN	Yes. There's no going above, below, around, or beyond this choice. One can think down to it, but one cannot think through it, because the very way one thinks about this choice is determined by how one already has made it.
ALYOSHA	It's not just a choice between being religious or non-religious, Christian or non-Christian, is it?
IVAN	No, it's a choice facing every individual at every moment of every day: Is one governed by miracle, mystery, and authority, or does one sacrifice oneself to love?
ALYOSHA	I'll admit, more people are on your side than Christ's.
IVAN	(*smiling*) Not Christ's side, your side; for those who choose miracle, mystery, and authority have their own Christ. And not my side, but the Grand Inquisitor's, for I fall somewhere in the middle.
ALYOSHA	(*amazed*) But I thought your entire point was that there is no middle ground!
IVAN	Precisely. That is why I said "fall" instead of "stand."
ALYOSHA	(*somberly*) Your poem is the most powerful attack upon, as well as the most glorious defense of, genuine Christianity, the Christianity of love, ever conceived.
IVAN	(*bowing like an author who has earned his praise*) Your humble servant. But hush, it's not over!
CARDINAL	(*to* KRISTOS) You give the human race the agony of freedom. We bestow the tranquility of illusion. Which would they prefer? To prove to you that we are the elect of their souls, tomorrow I shall order them to burn you at the stake; and the same mob that today was shouting for joy and kissing your feet in adoration, will heap up burning embers all around you and cry out for your blood. Do you doubt it?

The CARDINAL INQUISITOR *gives* KRISTOS *the opportunity to speak, but the latter only looks at him in inscrutable silence.*

CARDINAL	Speak, damn you! Tomorrow you die, but now I have said my piece, and wish to know your reply. Speak! I don't care how

violent your denunciation, how terrible your condemnation may be. I have a clear conscience. In your majesty you may damn me to hell, but in my integrity I defy you. Speak!

KRISTOS *kisses the* CARDINAL *and gives him a brotherly embrace.*

CARDINAL   (*recoiling and unlocking a side door with his own keys, and then pointing to the exit*) Get out! Get out, and never come back!

KRISTOS *studies the* CARDINAL INQUISITOR *with a look of profound compassion, then leaves. The lights on stage dim into blackness as* IVAN *pronounces the Grand Inquisitor's epitaph.*

IVAN   He held his ground, but the kiss forever seared his heart.

For a moment, everything is dark and silent like a church, with spotlights on the pensive brothers still in their respective wings. Then the lights come up on the stage proper, and the scene is the drawing room where Ivan and Alyosha initiated their conversation. The brothers take seats in natural positions, as if that is how they've been talking throughout.

ALYOSHA   I have to go.

IVAN   A pressing engagement with a young lady?

ALYOSHA   (*smiling, as if he is used to such teasing from Ivan*) Father Zossima wants to see me.

IVAN   Oh yes, the pressing affairs of the spirit!

ALYOSHA   (*rising*) You've given me much to think about, brother.

IVAN   Don't let it drive you crazy.

ALYOSHA   Do you really believe there's no hope?

IVAN   I choose to believe there's no hope.

ALYOSHA   Why?

IVAN   Because hope is the easy way out.

ALYOSHA   There you are wrong brother. There your magnificent intellect fails you. Despair is easy. Despair is like sinking into a comfortable feather bed of the spirit. One simply lies back and sighs, no longer responsible for anything because nothing can be done. Hope is the hardest thing imaginable. Hope is holding open the possibility, no matter how dark and impossible everything becomes, that love will win out. Thus, hope leaves no excuse for not giving oneself to life in love!

IVAN   (*musing*) Well, then, let it be because I hate more than anything the thought of being a fool.

ALYOSHA   But if love can conquer fear, in anyone and anything, wouldn't you be a fool not to give yourself entirely to love?

IVAN   Ah, but then no one would care, because folly would be the order of the day!

ALYOSHA   But in the end your own Inquisitor is split! He's at war with himself, whereas Christ is whole and at one with himself. Love alone can heal our wounds.

IVAN   I agree absolutely! Love alone can heal, if healing is possible. But love is like a homeopathic remedy that so exacerbates the symptoms that it kills the vast majority of patients before it cures them. Love raises the stakes to an infinite degree on the mere chance that somehow and someday it will have its way. Love is a fool's bet, and I choose not to be a fool.

ALYOSHA   (*smiling*) And I glory in being a fool.

IVAN   Touche'! A victim of my own art.

ALYOSHA   Brother, you know I mean it.

IVAN   So did Christ.

The brothers look into each other's eyes, the full spectrum of emotions over which their meeting has ranged flickering swiftly but recognizably across their faces. Lights dim to darkness. **The End.**

CHAPTER VI.

THE WAR

When the play ended, Ariana sat comfortably in the darkness, allowing portions of the drama to replay in her mind. The light slowly increased to twilight, but not beyond, and she was once again aware of the flashes and explosions of battle, this time even nearer. Then, without her knowing exactly when he had returned, she found herself looking into the Teacher's eyes.

"You wrote that play?" she asked in respectful awe.

"To Dostoevsky goes all the credit, and to me all the blame," he smiled.

"I've read *The Brothers Karamazov*," she said. "In fact, it's one of my favorites. A lot in that play came from you, and not all of it was bad," she said in what she hoped was evidently ironical understatement.

For the first time the Teacher seemed almost shy. "Do you understand now about the war?" he asked, changing the subject.

"I understand that there is a war, and that it has something to do with love," she replied. "I'm not sure I understand what side I'm on, or even what the sides are."

"There is the side of truth," he said, "and there is the side of love."

"Truth and love?" she cried. "You say truth and love are at war with each other? I can't see that. I won't see that. Truth and love are allies, not enemies, if they aren't the same thing."

"Then," he amended, "let us rather say, 'the love of truth versus the truth of love.'"

"Mere word-play."

"Perhaps," he allowed. "Perhaps that's all it is. Tell me this: Are you ready to fight in that war?" He gestured around toward the enveloping storm.

"How can I be ready?" she protested. "I'm not even sure what it's about!"

"But if you were sure," he persisted, "would you be ready to fight and die?"

"For a good cause," she replied firmly, searching her own heart.

"This is not only the best cause," he declared. "It's the only cause."

And then she found herself in the most terrifying situation yet. She had witnessed Kristos' crucifixion from practically every angle but that of the victim himself. Now she learned first-hand what he went through. She and Kristos were one.

His was the will, and she could only imagine how much worse the fear and pain would have been for a spirit bound to and embedded in the world of humanity; but she did get a taste, a glimmer of the intensity of his suffering, from the moment when Judas betrayed him to the final agonizing heave of resignation on the cross; and that was enough to make her feel fortunate that the experience was not real, at least for her, that she was not and never could be he. As she returned to what she now regarded as her haven in the eye of the storm, she vowed that she would never put herself at risk as he had done, God or no God.

"Many people think that Jesus had an easier time going to his death because he knew he was God," the Teacher was saying. "Some argue that a divine Christ could not, as a consequence, ever be fully human."

"I used to think that way," she murmured, "but now I know that's not so. If anything, knowing he was God made him suffer more. To know you are God and then find yourself hanging helplessly in utter agony, while all around the crowd laughs and jeers . . ." Her voice trailed off into the mists of recollection.

"You said you could die for a good cause," he resumed. "Did Jesus die for a good cause?"

"Of course!" she declared. "What could be a greater cause than love?"

"I'm not asking you if the cause his death served was good," he persisted, "but if he died for a good cause."

"I don't see the difference!"

"Is love a cause," he queried, "or is love what makes a cause a cause?"

She began to see what he was getting at, but still it was not clear. "I think, if you explained a bit more, I might understand."

"Suppose we are in a room full of people," he said, "and I hold a pistol to the head of one of them and ask if two plus two equals four. He says yes, and I pull the trigger. The next person says no, and I also pull the trigger, declaring that she didn't really mean it. I go around the room, and by the time I come to you, everyone else is dead. Do you think you might be doubting whether two plus two did equal four?"

She tried to imagine the situation as he described it and suddenly she got it. "Certainly," she said. "There is no certainty."

"It exists only in the heads of professional peddlers of knowledge," he affirmed. "You find it in classrooms, business offices, research laboratories, think tanks, but you don't find it in real life. In real life, the only truth for which one is willing to live or die is the truth in which one invests oneself. That self-investment is love."

"I understand what all that means," she said after reflection; "but, then again, I don't understand at all. Is it all subjective then, all relative? Doesn't it matter what cause you choose?"

"Not the cause you choose," he declared. "What matters is the cause you are."

She was so confused she rose and looked out, trembling, at the monotonous violence on the horizon.

"Did you enjoy the acting?" he asked cheerily.

She wondered if this were the same man who earlier had mercilessly interrogated her. Twice since the play this 'educator,' who habitually rode every issue to death, had changed subjects, once out of . . . shyness? And the other out of . . . consideration?

Despite the increasing warmth she felt between them, she put herself on guard. "I thought it was wonderful," she replied with feigned but, she hoped, convincing nonchalance. "Even the academic was believable! Well, almost."

"What makes an actor convincing?" he picked up on her lead. "How does one come across as believable?"

"The actor must believe he is the character," she replied. "He must become the character."

"So, if I'm playing an axe-murderer I go out into the audience and chop people up?" he queried.

"No!" she laughed at the incongruous image of the Teacher committing mayhem for art's sake. "You also have to remember that you're just acting."

"In other words, I have to be schizoid," he rejoined.

"Yes," she said after some thought, "in a controlled sort of way."

"What is the key to producing this controlled schizophrenia?" he persisted.

"Imagination?" she hazarded.

"Again, necessary but not sufficient," he said.

"Knowledge?" she ventured. "Understanding of the character?"

"If that were it," he grinned, "literature professors would be the greatest thespians!"

"I give up," she said.

"What is the key to making a character come alive?" he reiterated. "In theater-talk, it's called 'playing to the objective.' Take a simple example. You are a police detective hunting a serial killer. As far as the drama is concerned, that's your super-objective throughout the play—what you're after in everything you do. You've been working hard on the case, but then you decide to take a break and go home to rest. Your super-objective recedes into the background, and a secondary objective—to go home to rest so you can be fresh when you renew the chase—has taken its place. That's called a beat, a change in immediate objective. An actor has to break his role down into beats in order to get the dramatic rhythm of the character. On your way home you pass a fast-food joint and, realizing you're hungry, decide to stop for a bite. That's another beat. Your super-objective is pushed back even further, and your secondary objective becomes part of the backdrop of your awareness as well. As you pull into the restaurant's lot, you spy the bad guy pulling out. Another beat. Your secondary and tertiary objectives, rest and food, are forgotten. The super-objective is once again immediate. You take off after the bad guy."

"I get the picture," she said, doing her best to imitate the manner of a hard-boiled cop.

He smiled. "By the way, one can also think of the super-objective in terms of value. The super-objective is what the character is after in everything that he does. The basic value is what the character won't surrender no matter what the threat or promise. When one is acting, it's best to think in terms of objective, because that's intentional and specific. When analyzing the meaning of a play, value works best because it's general and opens up multiple levels of meaning; but these are simply two ways of talking about the same thing. Now, why is playing to the objective the only way an actor can make a character come alive?"

"Because it makes the characterization clear and definite," she replied, so proud at the speed with which she was picking up this basic acting lesson that she forgot to wonder why he was giving it.

"That's the technical reason," he agreed. "What's the philosophical reason?"

"I'm beginning to think I'm a technical sort of person," she said. "Every time you get philosophical, you lose me."

"The answer is a lot simpler than you think."

"Because it's the way we really are?" she blurted out, certain she had replied stupidly.

"Exactly!" he affirmed. "Because it's the way we really are! One can't go out on stage and act happy or sad or angry without being taken for a ham, because people don't decide to be happy or sad or angry. You are happy when you want something and you get it. You are sad when you want something and you don't get it. You get angry when you're after something and someone or something gets in your way. This is the way real people are! That's why drama often seems so much more real than 'real life.' In 'real life,' people live with the illusion that they are occupying some kind of value-free territory or neutral space. We call that neutral space 'ordinary reality' or 'everyday life,' and all our institutions are set up to foster this illusion. They are staffed by experts who, by definition, are value-neutral professionals who are governed by objective reason. Look at our classrooms! One leaves one's personality at the door and becomes a disembodied intellect coolly and rationally listening, judging, and assimilating according to objective, value-free criteria. But it's a lie. There is no neutral space, no objective territory. Life forces one to make choices, and every choice implies values. People don't want to take responsibility for making what literally are life-and-death decisions, so they establish the supposedly convenient fiction of a psychologically neutral space. Genuine drama undermines and destroys this delusion. It strips its characters down to the core."

"As life strips us," she observed.

"You do get it!" he exclaimed.

"And that is what this contest, this courtship is all about? " she asked. "I'm to choose my basic value?"

"Something like that," he said. "But right now you think you have five possibilities. In reality there are only two."

"Is this the war you've been talking about?" she queried. Do the various religions line up on either side?"

"Not exactly," he said. "The war cuts across traditional religious lines, as it does those of family, club, nation, or what have you. In reality, there are but two fundamental values. At this very moment, you are choosing one or the other."

"Shades of the Grand Inquisitor!" she laughed, trying to shake off the feeling of dark oppression his words, even more than the inevitably approaching conflict, had brought upon her.

He smiled, kindly but briefly. "Shall I explain?"

She nodded, slowly and uncertainly. "Please do."

He reached out his hand, and together they flew, like Peter Pan and Wendy or Scrooge and the Ghost of Christmas Past, down and away to a lonely beach with magnificent surf on a brilliant day so perfect that clouds softened the sun's intensity without dimming its glory. A handful of college students frolicked and lazed upon the sand and in the water. She knew this was the real thing because some of them drank beer and smoked cigarettes, items one never saw in the spirit realms, even among the earthbound.

Then Ariana had the shock of her eternal existence. What made it so jolting was that she had no sense, no premonition that it was coming. The Teacher landed them in the midst of a group of four, two young men and two young women, and one of them was Ariana herself! She would have cried out, but feared creating a disturbance.

"Don't worry," the Teacher said, putting a comforting arm around her shoulder, "they can't hear you."

And then she realized she could not hear them. "It's me!" she whispered. He merely nodded, and his brevity told her everything.

"It's really me!" she whispered even more stridently.

"Listen!" he commanded.

She could see they were talking, but the harder she tried to make out their words, the more garbled they became.

"No!" the Teacher exclaimed. "Listen with your inner ear."

She sank as deeply within herself as possible without closing her eyes and, wonder of wonders, she understood, not every word, precisely, but the gist of it all. It seemed Ariana's double wanted to read a paper by one of her teachers; and her boyfriend, evidently afraid of the influence this professor had upon her, resisted. When she made it clear that she was going to read it aloud whether he listened or not, he resigned himself to the inevitable, looking as if he were used to it. Amazingly enough, once she began the reading there were no interruptions. On the contrary, the paper drew into its magic orb the four or five other students lounging about nearby. Obviously, they all knew Ariana's double and probably thought of her as their trendsetter. Ariana was not being conceited when noting her double had the brightest spirit of the group; nor was she hallucinating when she saw that, while everyone but one young man, not the boyfriend, darkened as the reading progressed, Ariana's double became even brighter.

1. Objectification

We face a choice. In everything we do, we face a choice. No matter what we are doing or not doing, we cannot get away from that choice. To understand that choice is to understand what it means to be human. To hide from that choice is to hide from one's own humanity. To live with that choice? That is what this little paper is all about.

Since the choice is what life is about, and since life is about love, the choice is about love. The choice is to love or not to love. With that statement, everything has been said, and yet also, given humanity's insouciance, nothing.

What is love's opposite? How does one betray love? Here, as elsewhere in life, the *via negativa* may be more revealing than the *via positiva*. Discovering what is not love may be the key to understanding what love is, especially since the former seems so much more in evidence than the latter.

A variety of terms point to the opposite of love: hate, indifference, brutality, jealousy, greed, lust, and the psychological roots of all the rest, pride and fear. We do not need another word added to the list, but a term that sums up the essence of lovelessness. I propose "objectification."

"Objectification" sounds complicated as well as ugly, but it really is very simple. To live in objectification is to live in such a way that the fundamental business of life is relating self, as subject "in here," to the world, as objective order "out there." In here are thoughts and feelings; and out there are things and facts and forces, and relations between things and facts and forces. It does not matter whether one thinks of the objective order in religious terms, as created and governed by a God; or in scientific terms, as the effect of the blind working of natural law; or in social, political, and economic terms; or, as with most people, a confused mishmash of all of these. The important point is that oneself, in one's subjectivity, stands over and against the world in its objectivity. The relation between the two is what life is all about. Thus, objectification and subjectivism always go hand-in-hand, and one is always the flip side of the other.

This relation between subject and objective order, self and world, is never neutral or value-free because the world out there presents a double face to me in here. On the one hand, it holds danger. Just about anyone or anything in that world could squelch me in an instant. On the other hand, it contains things that give me sustenance and pleasure. Thus, the objective order is both threat and promise. What I seek, in my relation to the world, is survival and security, pleasure and fulfillment. In a word, happiness. A basic value is something one seeks in all one does and never surrenders no matter what. Happiness is the basic value of anyone living in objectification. In other words, I seek power, because power is, by definition, the ability to protect oneself and one's own, and to get what one wants. The basic values of one living in objectification are security and pleasure. Power is the means of realization.

Of course, there may be other ways to cut the cake, but it seems to me that there are seven fundamental modes of objectification, distinct ways in which power is sought and used, as well as in which the balance is struck between pleasure and security. These are control, conformity, rebellion, revolution, criminality, moral idealism, and nihilism.

Control

Control is the keynote of all modes of objectification, which is simply another way of saying that power is what objectification is all about. In his magnificent and self-repudiated ontological masterpiece, *Being and Nothingness*, Jean-Paul Sartre says that every human being seeks to be God. I would agree if one added the crucial modification, every human being living in objectification. Control is the most desirable mode of all. Do not most people think of God as the being who can have things however he wants them, and whom no one and nothing can harm? Most people spend their lives trying to be as much like this God as possible.

The key word here, of course, is "possible." Why are people more fascinated by a Hitler or Napoleon than by a Jesus Christ or Gandhi? I do not say they admire Hitler or Napoleon more, but most people certainly find such malefactors more fascinating.

It cannot merely be on account of their power, because Napoleon on St. Helena or Hitler in his Berlin bunker is as fascinating as Napoleon crowned emperor or Hitler worshipped as "the Leader" (der Fuehrer). What makes them fascinating (and I would not use the word so many times could I think of a suitable equivalent) is the fact that they risked all to win all, they bid for the supreme control that everyone else in objectification desires but practically no one has the unthinkable daring to pursue. In fantasy, the world is projected wish-fulfillment; but, in reality, the world is an ant heap, and one ant who tries to climb to the top is pulled down by all the rest.

Conformity

Much safer is the mode of conformity. There is little bitty me in here, and out there is a great big monster of a world, a horrifying machine ready to chew me up and spit me out. What better way to avoid the danger than to become a part of that world, a cog in that machine? The machine will never destroy itself (so one tells oneself!), and from henceforth one is identified with its awesome power.

Therefore, as their dominant mode of being in objectification, most people opt for conformity, because most people value security over pleasure. One may have security without pleasure, and still the possibility of having pleasure; but one can have neither the possibility nor reality of pleasure without security.

So the argument runs, and it is convincing up to a point; but no one can live without pleasure. Since pleasure is the experience of meaning, and the meaning of objectification is power, in the final analysis total conformity is impossible. One cannot live in objectification without some sense of power.

Take a typical laborer for example, someone who works on the assembly line. While on the job everything he does is choreographed by some engineer he has never seen in order to service a machine. When not on the job, he conforms to society's laws, union and club rules, expectations of peers, and the dictates of common courtesy. So when he gets home, by God, he is going to be king of his castle! And if his wife and children will not accept his tyranny, then maybe he will kick the dog. Anyone who lives year in and year out without any sense of power will one day do something to reclaim his or her lost sense of self. It may be something creative, something stepping outside of objectification altogether. After all, Jesus did say that the meek will inherit the earth. Today, however, more likely than not, it may be buying a shotgun and blasting to hell a dozen or more people, family or strangers, before turning the gun on oneself. People in the despair of impotence will literally do anything for a single moment of power.

These two, control and conformity, are the primary modes of objectification. Control sounds the keynote and conformity sets the parameters. As a rule, people who live in objectification control when they think they can and conform when they think they must. In objectification, an individual is divided into an objective function, defined by his role in the objective order, and a subjective personality, defined by variables to which the objective order is essentially indifferent. In our society today these variables include, within certain limits, how one dresses and wears one's hair, the type of car one drives, one's choice of profession, and even one's religion. Personality is defined by how one strikes the balance between control and conformity in the various aspects of one's life. One may dress flashily and be politically conservative. One may take risks in one's profession but not in one's domestic life. If one analyzes an individual living in objectification, one will invariably find that power and conformity, pleasure and security, debit and credit tend toward balance. A daring individual runs up huge debts before paying up. A prudent individual keeps the psychological checkbook perfectly balanced. A disturbed individual fails to maintain the balance. In objectification, sanity is always some kind of balance.

The five other modes of objectification are so many permutations of control and conformity spanning the breadth and depth of human existence, yet so distinctive in their own right as to be worthy of independent definition.

Rebellion

Rebellion is the most paradoxical mode of all. One may think that rebellion takes one out of objectification altogether, because it is the opposite of conformity and has nothing to do with control. Here, however, we run up against, if not the dialectical character of life, at least that of our conceptions of life. The basic issue in objectification is that of self-definition. One simply cannot be oneself, one must define oneself. In other words, where does one fit in the objective order? What is one's place in the world?

The rebel's self-definition is wholly negative. He or she has no place in the world. Therefore, he or she has no place. The premise is a gateway beyond objectification. The conclusion places rebellion squarely within objectification. If to have no place in the objective order is to have no place, then the objective order is everything. It is absolute. Even in rebellion, the rebel acknowledges the deity of the objective order. Rebellion therefore is weak, as any stance based upon a purely negative value must be weak. It is simply the reverse side of conformity. Consider the purest form of rebellion, adolescent rebellion.

It matters not to an adolescent rebel the nature of the authority against which he rebels. It simply has to be authority. One can imagine controlling an adolescent rebel by commanding him to do the opposite of what one wants him to do! Nerddom is the flip side of rebellion. The adolescent rebel rebels against the expectations of authority in order to conform to the expectations of peers. The nerd rebels against the expectations of peers in order to conform to those of authority. If adolescent rebels do not destroy themselves, then eventually they come to terms with the powers-that-be. As all parents of adolescents know, rebellion is always a phase.

Revolution

Revolution is something else altogether. In fact, it is rebellion's opposite. The rebel hates the established order, but has such implicit respect for its absolute power that he finds no rest apart from its embrace. The revolutionary, on the other hand, feels such scant respect for the established order that he sets out, often alone at first but eventually in conspiracy with fellow revolutionaries, to destroy the old and create the new. That is why revolutions are invariably chaotic. The period between the fall of the defunct objective order and the rise of the new and improved objective order is without objective order, at least in that aspect of existence to which the revolution pertains. This mode of being falls well within objectification, of course, because the revolutionary seeks to exchange one objective order for another, not to do away with objective order altogether. His focus is upon changing external conditions rather than himself.

This is not to say that rebellion may not pass with the greatest ease into revolution. Psychologically, it is a well-documented fact that opposites are often closer than equivalents and similarities. In fact, as in a game of "Chutes and Ladders," at any time an individual may find himself sliding from one mode of objectification to another. Objectification is the realm of unconsciousness, and, in the imagination, before one knows it a dictator may become a slave, a rebel a revolutionary, and a criminal a saint. Possibility, however, is not reality. One cannot, in actuality, be at one and the same time dictator and slave, rebel and revolutionary, criminal and saint. One may appear to be all these things and more to those living in objectification, which is governed by appearance, but that point must be reserved for later.

Criminality

The essence of criminality is simple. A criminal is a businessman who breaks the rules. Why does an individual cheat at cards, for example? The answer is obvious— to maximize profits. Business is about maximizing profits. Why are criminals, like businessmen, socially and politically conservative, and why do they tend to support law-and-order candidates? For one thing, there is no percentage in cheating if everyone else cheats; and, for another, because to change the established order is to change the rules of the game at which they have learned to cheat consummately. Learning to cheat at a new game with new rules takes time; and time, as every good businessman knows, is money.

Thus, criminals only support a revolution when they figure no more profits are to be had from the present objective order and/or they can get in on the ground floor of the new objective order and milk it for all it is worth. When criminals do support a revolution, moreover, they always believe they will end up controlling it, rather than the starry-eyed idealists who started it, because criminals believe themselves to be the most realistic of men. They are wrong. Criminals are the least realistic, the least real and the most superficial of men, because they live in out-and-out self-contradiction.

One is a superficial person to the extent that one blithely accepts one's own self-contradictions. There are essentially three ways of doing so: 1. Self-righteousness: "I don't have any self-contradictions!" 2. Sophistication: "I have all these charming self-contradictions. Aren't I cute?" 3. Criminality.

The essence of criminality is expecting everyone else to obey the rules to which one makes oneself an exception. This is blatant self-contradiction.

Our culture is obsessed with the mystery of the criminal mind. If one checks the television listings for any given week, one will find at least twenty shows dedicated to exploring the mystery of the criminal mind. The term, "criminal mind," however, is a contradiction in terms. To the extent that one refuses to wrestle with one's self-contradictions, one has no mind. Perhaps we are so obsessed with this bogus mystery of the criminal mind because we instinctively feel that, if we find some profound meaning in criminality, we can justify to ourselves our own self-contradictions!

Moral Idealism

To the superficial observer, moral idealism may appear to have little influence in human affairs. Indeed, one could argue that we make so much of it when we find it because its occurrence is so rare. To reason in this way, however, is like arguing that, because there are so few mathematicians, mathematics has little influence upon how humans actually live. Moral idealism is literally the mathematics, or if you will, the logic, of objectified personal relationships. It subordinates the concreteness of such relationships to the universality of principle. Moral principles have as much force in the personal realm as mathematics and logic in the realm of technological and scientific abstraction. Justice is as axiomatic in the social sphere as the Law of the Excluded Middle, A or not-A, in the sphere of thought.

Ethical relativists point to widespread differences in morals from culture to culture to refute the logical character of the moral law; but, apart from the fact that those differences are hardly so widespread as relativists would have us believe, there is a simple explanation. As with any other type of principle, the simpler the moral principle, the more widespread its recognition. The fundamental theorems of calculus are as axiomatic as those of elementary arithmetic, but very few people have the intellectual sophistication to understand them; and what one does not understand, one cannot employ. The prohibition of murder, the wanton destruction of a person, is a moral constant in every society. Less universal is the recognition of the equality of all human beings as persons, regardless of race or gender, though this is equally axiomatic. That one should respect one's neighbor's property is a principle also found at work in every society, though the definition of "property" varies from culture to culture. That one should respect the ecological balance of the world without whose existence the very idea of property is meaningless, however, is a principle that requires a higher degree of moral sophistication than the modern West has thus far evinced. In our culture, technological genius and moral idiocy seem to be perfectly compatible. Indeed, at times they appear to be one and the same. Someday we may attain to the ethical genius of the native American, if that genius survives our depredations.

The essential point is that, no matter how often we betray and ignore the moral law, it still has an absolute hold upon us, and this the ethical relativist cannot explain. Somewhere inside themselves even criminals know that they are living in self-contradiction, upholding a law they themselves do not obey. When people do wrong, they go through endless gyrations to convince themselves they are doing right. Failing that, they suffer guilt. Why?

To violate the moral law is an act of self-contradiction, and therefore self-negation. The spirit knows no greater agony. This is the nature of conscience, of authentic moral guilt. It may be overlaid by self-interest and social conditioning. In the sheer hurly-burly of everyday life, moral idealism seems impotent. The currents of righteousness run deep, however, and carve out channels along which the river of history necessarily flows.

Nevertheless, though moral idealism is the most powerful mode of objectification considered thus far, it is as schizoid as the rest. Morality divides the self into that which is subject to moral regulation and that which is a matter of individual preference, and the fundamental moral question is where to draw the line between the two. However lofty and exalted it may appear, moral idealism is simply the striking of a balance between control and conformity in the dimension of interpersonal relations.

Nihilism

Nihilism is the most paradoxical mode of objectification and, from the viewpoint of all the other modes, the most frightening to contemplate. As Nietzsche's Zarathustra sounds the eternal "yes," the nihilist answers with an absolute "no." Nihilism says of everything we have discussed thus far and everything we have yet to discuss, "What does it matter?"

Nihilism is the attitude, philosophy, or belief that there is nothing of intrinsic value or inherent worth in life. So, I may decide to become a Mahatma Gandhi or Martin Luther King, on the one hand, or a Joseph Stalin or Adolf Hitler, on the other. It is merely a matter of personal taste.

We live in an extremely nihilistic age. Witness the popularity of films like *Pulp Fiction* and *Natural-Born Killers*, the former of which has spawned its own cult. Likewise, our preoccupation with economics. A great book is a bestseller, a great film grosses so-many million at the box office, and a great painting fetches thirty million at auction. The value of anything is whatever price it commands on the open market. What do people do today when they arrive at an unusual spiritual insight? They find the most profitable way to merchandise it!

The most dangerous forms of nihilism, however, are those which profess to be anti-nihilistic. In the medieval and early-modern periods, there were the Inquisition and the witch-hunts. In the first half of the twentieth century arose the totalitarian ideologies of National Socialism and Stalinist Communism. Nowadays, we have fundamentalism.

Such phenomena are nihilistic because they substitute an abstract system of ideas for the living truth of the human heart. The resolution of every moral dilemma is to cut the Gordian knot by appealing to authority, whether it be the Church, the party, or the holy book. We have no reliable understanding of right and wrong in our own hearts.

When nihilism is up-front and honest about itself, when it does not indulge in ideological masquerade, it harbors a profound truth, which is that objectification is nothing but a tissue of hypocrisy pandering to fear and despair. Nevertheless, nihilism continues to worship at the altar of objectification in a backhanded way, because it implicitly equates objectification with life. Nihilism declares that objectification is meaningless, therefore life is meaningless.

That is why, when one watches a nihilistic film, one experiences extreme ambivalence. One does not know whether to laugh or cry, so one ends up giving an occasional nervous chuckle. The "heroes" are tearing down the pretense and self-importance of the objective order, and that is good. At the same time, however, they are tearing down life. They destroy indiscriminately. Nihilism, the avowed enemy of hypocrisy, is therefore the ultimate hypocrisy, the ultimate weakness, and the ultimate evil. It is metaphysical rebellion, rebellion against life!

In the face of such hypocritical and uncompromising resistance to life, Plato's refutation of relativism, or intellectual nihilism, sounds curiously hollow. Plato said that the statement, "There is no truth," is self-refuting, because it denies its own truth. Likewise, one may say to the nihilist, "What does your 'What does it matter?' matter?"; but self-refutation cuts both ways. Nihilism can be refuted with its own principle, but it can only be refuted with its own principle! If one fights fire with fire, one is bound to get burned.

Better to look for the truth in nihilism. Nihilism regards itself as the end of all meaning, but why not see it, with Nietzsche, as the beginning of meaning? Nihilism recognizes that freedom transcends all possibility by its very power to refuse to realize any or all possibilities. Nihilism is the penultimate wisdom. It recognizes there is no meaning in power. Nietzsche's mistake was to think that power could create meaning. In reality, power and meaning are antithetical. A universe of power is *ipso facto* meaningless, and a universe of meaning is not concerned with power.

The universe of power, of objectification, is therefore meaningless; or, to put it in objectification's own terms, all "meanings" in objectification are relative to human ends. Security and pleasure, and their proper balance, happiness, are the goals that bestow meaning upon the human enterprise. Therefore, the more security and the more pleasure, the more meaning. Such is the moral calculus of utilitarianism, the dominant ethical theory of our day, and everyone believes it with a will. Yet everyone also knows that all the security and pleasure in the world do not add up to meaning. A curious paradox, no? Curious, yes, but falling well outside the official version, the public version, the we-can-take-it-for-granted version of human existence. According to the official version, the goal of human existence is to maximize pleasure and security. Therefore, the god of objectification is the maximizer of pleasure and security. This god is knowledge.

Here we arrive at another curious paradox, likewise beneath official notice. Power is the meaning of objectification (a meaningless meaning, as has already been shown). The god of power, as Hitler well understood, is will. Will is an individual category. You have your will, I have mine. A collective will, despite Rousseau and other poets of nationalism, is a contradiction in terms. Knowledge, on the other hand, as modern science has demonstrated beyond doubt, is a collective category. Knowledge that does not submit itself to a collective process of critical review and constructive development is opinion, and, in its more virulent forms, fanaticism. Therefore, the god of power is at odds with the god of objectification; and, in the long run, as Hitler discovered in his lonely bunker in Berlin when he committed suicide, the act of ultimate impotence, knowledge wins out over will. By deeming his own genius greater than the strategic wisdom and technological prowess of his enemies, Hitler doomed himself to defeat. The irony here is that knowledge itself has made the long run problematic, if not obsolete. A madman with his finger on the nuclear trigger can redress the balance and grant will, as well as the nihilism that is will's reduction to absurdity, its long-sought victory.

That knowledge is the god of objectification is obvious from history. In medieval Christendom, the nobles embodied will and power, but the priests represented the ultimate reality, God. When reality is beyond human control, the better part of wisdom is conformity to the will of the God who controls it. The Church alone knew how to conform to God's will, and therefore the Church dominated life in the Middle Ages. Today humanity has taken control for itself. Science and technology are the credo and praxis of this new revolution, a revolution that perhaps would have died in its infancy, from sheer fright at its own audacity, did it not seem that humanity had burned all its bridges and had no other direction in which to go.

Is there another direction? Is there a point to all this vilification of objectification? What else is there? What else can there be? The answer is love.

But, of course, there is love in objectification. How can love be opposed to objectification, the "either" to objectification's "or," when there is love in objectification?

Yes, one finds love in objectification, but not love as absolute reality, which is the only love worthy of the name. A simple example: You are starting out in life, finishing your education and beginning your career, when you fall profoundly, if not irrevocably, in love. You have experienced infatuation, and this is something else, something so intense that you fear you cannot stay in the relationship and have much left over for school and career. The love is all or nothing in its demand upon your soul. You go to your parents and ask their advice. Wait, they say, there will be plenty of time for love, one must first build a foundation in life. You go to your guidance counselor for more advice. Wait, the professional says, there will be plenty of time for love. Finally, you go to your beloved and say, let's break it off, there will be plenty of time for love.

No one ever betrays love. Everyone merely postpones love. If love is the reality of life, however, what is one postponing it for? If love is the reality of life, what other foundation is there?

In objectification, one substitutes for love the foundation of career. Career is the safest and most comfortable niche one can attain in the objective order. To have a career, one must be goal-oriented. Being goal-oriented is regarded as a great virtue in our culture, but it really is just a heroic-sounding word for having tunnel-vision. One's goal becomes everything, and life itself nothing.

When you cut yourself off from life, however, life cuts itself off from you. The inevitable result of goal-orientation is alienation.

Alienation is not merely a feeling of loneliness or despair, though such feelings often accompany it. It is literal disconnection from reality.

A friend of mine was in the hospital carrying her second child. Heavy labor was commencing. She was lying on her left side, the side usually best for the fetus, when she had an intuition that something was wrong with the baby. She rolled over to her right side, and then felt the baby was fine. The nurse asked her what she was doing, so she explained. To humor her, the nurse hooked her up to the fetal monitor and discovered that, indeed, when she was on her left side, the baby's heart was racing, a sign of fetal distress. When she was on her right side, there was no sign of fetal distress. Then the nurse laughed and said, "What a funny coincidence!"

It had to be a coincidence, because everybody knows that pregnant women, especially women in labor, are irrational. Their hormones are shooting all over the place. They are completely out of touch with reality. Right?

In truth, no one is more in touch with reality than a pregnant woman! Our culture, however, does not allow for the idea of a direct, intrinsic, immediate and individual connection with reality. We regard the very idea of such a connection as superstitious and weird, because we operate with the "billiard-ball" model of a person. We are all billiard balls, each stuck inside his own skin. Occasionally, we run up against other billiard balls, and that registers upon our "sensors," our senses; but we cannot even trust our sense-data until it is run through the knowledge-mill of science. In fact, in our culture we have reached the ultimate in alienation, because what counts as real in our culture is only what registers on a machine!

So, what becomes of love in objectification? If one gives less than all to love, love ceases to be love. It becomes a feeling, competing with other feelings. It becomes sentimentality.

There are two kinds of sentimentality, weak and strong.

Weak sentimentality is the feeling one might have for one's pet or automobile. It is love devoid of self-investment, love without risk. In weak sentimentality one seeks the feeling of love without any giving of oneself.

Strong sentimentality involves investment of self, but only within a self-defined magic circle of love. This magic circle may include only oneself. That is what is called egotism. It may include only the other. That is what is called altruism. What is often mistaken for romantic love draws the circle around lover and beloved—"We two against the world!" One can draw the circle around one's family. In its extreme form, that is the "Godfather-Syndrome." One can draw it around one's class—classism, one's nation—nationalism, one's religion—religious fanaticism, one's race—racism. One can even draw it around the entire human race.

I once saw footage documenting a noble medical experiment in the service of humanity. Researchers were, methodically and automatedly, bashing in the heads of apes. The animals were not killed outright, and no anesthetic was administered, because the scientists were studying the neurological effects of various head wounds in order to develop more effective treatment of brain-injured humans. And if the brutal sacrifice of all those dumb creatures ultimately saves just one human life, it is all worth it! And if it were my child or my parent or my spouse whose life were at stake, I would not be so critical of the use of animals in medical research! Sometimes we have to be brutal in order to avoid being sentimental.

Or so people generally assume. The psychologists who studied the Nazi war criminals at Nuremberg, however, discovered that, not only were these malefactors brutal, but also sentimental, and the greater the brutality, the greater the sentimentality. Brutality and sentimentality go hand-in-hand. They could not well explain why; but, if one thinks in terms of objectification, the answer is obvious. Sentimentality is the warmth on the inside of the magic circle, while brutality is the frigidity without.

Sentimentality is love that draws a magic circle. Those within the magic circle are objects of love. Those on the outside are objects of indifference. Indifference is the worst form of brutality. When you hate, at least the object of your hate exists for you. When you are indifferent, the object of your indifference may as well not exist.

Thus, there is no middle ground between love and objectification. If you do not love all the way, if you put a limit to your love, then somewhere in your life you are living in the brutality of indifference. Ultimately, there is only Christ or Hitler.

The essential problem here was expressed by Christ: "He who seeks to save his life shall lose it." Love cannot be had for the asking or the taking. Love can only be had for the giving. It is not a commodity that can be purchased. It cannot be packaged for individual or group consumption. We do not consume love. If we give ourselves to it, love consumes us. If we do not give ourselves to love, it leaves us out in the cold. Objectification, as already stated, is the realm of alienation. Here I am trapped inside myself, and an entire universe is out there. "Out there," by definition, is where I am not comfortable, where I am not at home. Only in love can one feel at home because love, like the slow and humble turtle, carries its own home with it wherever it goes. Love is its own home, because all love needs is to love.

The objectified self, on the other hand, needs security and pleasure, both forms of connection with the objectified world. These forms of connection are poor, ephemeral and untrustworthy substitutes for the absolute relationship, the total involvement, the passionate engagement of love. Nevertheless, since the objectified self fears such total involvement, it must make do with the bogus and ersatz, which explains why sentimentality and superficiality go hand in hand. It also explains why knowledge is so venerated in a society as sentimental as our own. Only through knowledge, so it seems, can the objectified self make reliable connection with the objective order. Knowledge, however, does not overcome alienation. On the contrary, it turns alienation into a tragic virtue, the price of intelligence. It is another curious paradox of objectification that its exalted intellect is always fruitlessly striving, like Sisyphus, to eliminate the alienation it wears as its badge of greatness. The hungry baby cries, but the alienated self rationalizes.

Love does not alienate. It embeds one in the texture of life. Just as a good movie has texture and a B-movie has no texture, so a life lived in love has texture, while a life lived in objectification has none.

We all know this texture of life. We discover it through personal relationship, which is what love is all about. There is no greater agony, for example, than to be in an intimate personal relationship with someone who has no feel for the texture of that relationship. It is like being rubbed all over with a low grade of emotional sandpaper!

If love is the reality of life, if God is love, then all of life is about personal relationship, and therefore all of life has texture. This is what we see in many aboriginal world-views, like those of the Native Americans. You have the rock people; the standing people, the trees; the two-legged people, bears and humans; the four-legged people; the creeping and crawling people; etc. Even the sun, moon, wind and stars are personal entities. Thus, all of life is personal relationship, and all of reality is spiritually textured. We, however, from the superior height of our alienation, have the arrogance to regard such an understanding of life as primitive and irrational! We have exiled ourselves so far from our home that home itself has become the place where we feel least at home. "If the light within you be darkness, how great is that darkness!"

It is time to turn on that light! One could go on and on defining and refining the concept of objectification. Perhaps one could even develop an entire ontology and psychology of objectification, and as a result earn a professorship at a major university. The task, however, is a relatively trivial one, because objectification is an abstraction, and an abstraction naturally can be defined with great precision and analytical complexity because, after all, one is creating it as one goes along. Indeed, objectification is not merely an abstraction, but abstraction itself. Therefore, to dwell upon objectification is to dwell upon abstraction, when the point is to step out of the artificial light of abstraction into the light, warmth, and fire of reality.

Love is that reality.

Love cannot be defined.

Love cannot be defined because it is reality.

Numerous people today, not only scholars and philosophers, but the famous "ordinary person" as well (whom I have yet to meet, though I have met many people trying to fit the part), regard such statements as intellectual cop-outs. Try defining color to a person born blind, however, or sound to a person born deaf, and you will see what I mean. "Color" and "sound" are concepts, but they derive their meaning not from human invention, but reference to features of human experience. If one's experience lacks those features, one cannot understand those concepts. So it is with love, except that love, in the proper sense, is not a feature of human experience, but of human possibility. One does not need to experience love to understand it. One only has to acknowledge its possibility.

This leads to an interesting paradox, one of the curious paradoxes of love. In human experience, the possibility of something is generally derived from its reality. It is or has been, we reason, so it is possible. If something is not and never has been, therefore, one cannot know if it is possible. Love, however, derives its reality from its possibility. On love's own terms, even if love did not and never had existed, it would still be the reality of life. Love is life's reality because it is its only real possibility. All other possibilities, which I have grouped under the category, "objectification," lead to death. Love alone yields life.

Love, therefore, cannot be defined; but one can point to it, and almost anything may serve as a guide post.

Take the popular detective, martial art, or war film. Admittedly, the leading man in such a film is almost always emotionally constipated; but still, something in him causes anyone willing to leave the critical faculty at the theater's door to identify with him as the hero. One does not need the hero pointed out, nor does one need to know much, if anything, about the cultural vocabulary of the movie. People say values are culturally relative, but a hero is a hero universally, or not a hero at all. A hero is a hero not to the Eastern, the Western, the American, the Russian, the Japanese, the Arab, or the African, but the human heart.

What makes a hero a hero?

One may say power, but that would make Hitler a hero. One may say that Hitler was a hero, but only to those to whose pride and fear he pandered. Self-interest always obscures the values of the heart, which is why our human race's true heroes often emerge into the light of history only after they embrace the oblivion of death. When they cannot bother us anymore, we see them as they are. Propaganda plays upon fear and pride. Art ruthlessly strips away all fear and pride until the naked heart stands revealed.

The popular adventure film attempts to trade upon the advantages of both propaganda and art, so it is an excellent genre in which to distinguish between them. So again, even in such hybrid, Hollywood hot-house creations, what makes a hero a hero?

Win or lose, the hero always does the right thing. The hero serves life. If the hero singlehandedly slaughters four hundred enemy soldiers, those soldiers are vermin corrupting life. Is this art serving propaganda or propaganda serving art? An interesting question, but not directly relevant to the issue at hand. The point is that, within the world of the film, however fantastic that world may be, the hero is the good guy, the servant of life.

To serve life, however, righteousness alone is not enough. A typical character in the popular adventure film is the strait-laced foil, sometimes the hero's sidekick and sometimes his rival, who is on the side of righteousness but insists upon going by the book. This character always comes across as a nerd. The hero, in contrast, does not care what rules are broken or red tape cut to get the villains. A genuine hero serves life from the passion of the heart. What makes the typical adventure film so popular and so phony is the illusion that one can live from the passion of the heart and be emotionally invulnerable. The heroes of such films never have to wrestle with that most dangerous enemy of all—oneself. They never have to fight the most harrowing battle of all, that with self-deception. They never have to suffer the worst agony of all, the death of cherished illusions. People will climb treacherous cliffs, hunt ferocious beasts, and even fight and die in war to avoid the task of changing the self. To refuse that task is the most profound cowardice. To accept that task is genuine heroism. To perform that task is love.

In other words, in objectification one may be consciously selfless because one is subconsciously selfish, i.e. the kind of person who controls others by never doing anything for oneself; or one may be consciously selfish because one is subconsciously selfless, i.e., lacking in spiritual substance; but love is concerned with being a self, i.e. taking responsibility for one's fundamental choices, one's basic value.

Vulnerability and courage, the passion of the heart and the service of life, are all aspects of love. One can be a self only in relation to other selves. Love and love alone recognizes that selfhood is relative and absolute at one and the same time. Thus love alone recognizes that selfhood is a sacred right and categorical duty, the right and the duty to love. Love does not seek pleasure, security, or power. Love seeks to give of itself in love.

The god of objectification is knowledge, because knowledge alone gives power. Knowledge takes the multiplicity of the phenomenal world and reduces it to a system, a model of reality. A system, by definition, has one perspective, and therefore is one-dimensional. This statement may sound stupid to those familiar with multidimensional mathematical or mechanical systems, but such systems are only multidimensional in a trivial sense. They are systems because they bring several dimensions into systematic coordination, reducing them to the single perspective of the system. One perspective yields one functional dimension. All other dimensions are functions of its functioning.

By reducing the world to one dimension and the self to one perspective, objectification seeks to reduce all selves to one self, one knower before one system of knowledge. In objectification, individuality consists of personal specialization within that system, on the one hand, and the subjective flotsam and jetsam for which the scientific method has no use or place, on the other. Love, on the contrary, recognizes the infinite multidimensionality of perspective, and so the infinite diversity of selves. At the same time, it holds that all are embraced by one reality, the reality of relationship, the reality of love.

Objectification's reality is a system. Love's reality is a family. Knowledge restricts what counts as reality, accepting only what can be brought into the unity of its perspective. The understanding of love opens to encounter and relationship wherever the possibility presents itself; and love does not prejudge that possibility. Knowledge is duplicitous, renouncing control in order to create the system without which there can be no control. Love is paradoxical, making the absolute demand that sets the heart free. Knowledge asks many questions but listens only to selected answers. Love listens to all but asks only one question—what does love demand here and now? And the here-and-now of love is totally different from the here-and-now of objectification. Objectification reaches the universal by transcending the particular. Love realizes the absolute in the moment and situation of love.

People who live in objectification experience the here-and-now as an isolated point in space and time, a prison from which they need to escape. People who live in objectification are never here and now. One can see it in their eyes. They are always where they have to be next, or where they would rather be. Since objectification flees life's depth, it has no alternative but to spread out on life's surface, like a fungus.

Hence for objectification universality is an end in itself, not only in the realm of knowledge, but in all aspects of existence. For objectification, there is great virtue in dressing, thinking, feeling, walking and talking like everyone else, in being "normal," "fashionable," "with-it." People who feel isolated try to overcome that feeling by getting in touch with the universal, e.g. by finding out what's happening in the world. There are people who know everything about what happens in the world and nothing about what happens in their own hearts! And where is it really happening for people who live in objectification? Wherever the most people are making the biggest noise, such as wars and revolutions; or wherever you have a celebrity.

A celebrity is a universal person. That's a contradiction in terms, there is no such thing as a universal person, but nevertheless that is what a celebrity is. A celebrity is an empty space, a cipher into which one can project oneself and feel vicariously in touch with the universal. That is why the art of interviewing a celebrity is to ask the most innocuous, insipid, inane and idiotic questions imaginable; and the art of being a celebrity is to give the most innocuous, insipid, inane and idiotic answers possible; for the moment a celebrity becomes a real person, he ceases to be a celebrity.

Love, on the other hand, seeks nothing but the here-and-now. Love finds its connection with life through the depth of the here-and-now. As far as love is concerned, if you cannot give it and get it in the here-and-now—and, dear reader, I do mean *you*, and I do mean *here*, and I do mean *now*—you cannot give it or get it anywhere!

Love is about understanding, not knowledge, about responsibility, not control. Love literally stands under, or holds up, life, as if it were a baby in love's arms. Love does not care what others say or do. It will risk anything, suffer anything, rather than let the baby fall.

Between love and objectification there can be no compromise. Love compromises everything but itself. Objectification is the compromising of love. Love is life's real possibility. Objectification is abstraction posing as reality. Love and objectification, therefore, are at war. From love's standpoint, objectification is sin and insanity. From the viewpoint of objectification, love is the worst criminality. Each undermines the other, and each cannot abide the other. Objectification fights love with repression. Love fights objectification with liberation, setting the heart free to love

All this business about love being life's reality because it is life's only possibility may strike one as sophistry. If love is in mighty conflict with objectification, one might argue, it is a most peculiar conflict, because objectification appears to have swept the field. If love is the reality of life, why is it in so little evidence? Isn't love a pipe dream, an unrealizable ideal? And if so, then isn't objectification not sin or insanity, but simply the tragic way things are?

If love is the reality of life, and if objectification is the repression of love, then in the realm of objectification love exists in projection, because projection accompanies repression as darkness the closing of one's eyes.

When one represses something because one feels it is dark and evil, one projects it in negative and destructive form. When one represses something because one feels it is good, only too good and one does not wish to be responsible for it, one projects it as an ideal. An ideal is the ultimate excuse, because by definition it can never be attained. Where is the projection of shining love in this dark and loveless world? It stares one in the face every day. One sees it on television, in the cinema, at the theater. One reads it in novels and hears it on the radio. It is to be found in art.

Art is essential to love. When one engages in art, whether creating or experiencing it, one's little objectified ego is set aside, and one can experience the free play of one's heart, explore life's intrinsic meaning, and then go out and live accordingly. In objectification, however, art becomes entertainment.

A simple experiment will bring this point home. Imagine it is late at night, and you have put aside all the cares and worries of the day. You are watching television, an episode of *Miami Vice* to be exact, and you allow nothing to get in the way of losing yourself in the film. The story concerns an undercover police detective, Sonny Crockett, whose best friend, Robby Kahn, is the son of a racketeer. The detective does not know this, because his friend changed his name from Kahnada to Kahn out of shame at his father's profession long before they met. Now Robby has a newborn son of his own and asks Crockett to stand as godfather. Out of sheer coincidence, by the way, Kahnada and his partner, Johnny Doss, happen to be under investigation by the detective's own unit for illegal gambling. In television, at least, it truly is a small world!

To make matters worse, Robby, though ashamed of his father, has not severed all connection with him. When he returned from the war, he borrowed money from the partners to finance a nightclub that, ironically, is much like the nightclub the partners own and employ as cover, though Robby's club is legitimate. The gangsters use the loan as a leash, the father hoping for reconciliation and the partner fearing betrayal.

Into this situation comes a young woman from New York, fleeing with her baby from an abusive husband. She lands a job as a cocktail waitress at the partners' establishment, but is let go after her first shift because she proves skittish under the pawing of the patrons and spills a tray full of drinks, and because the head of the wait-staff thinks a single mother will be more trouble as an employee than she is worth. Penniless and with a child to raise in an unknown city, the woman is on the verge of despair when a stand-up comic who is a friend of the partners promises to set things right. He takes her and her baby up to a combination office and bedroom the partners are letting him use, and assures her that he will get her job back. She believes him because, after all, they are in the special room; and she is grateful, but not as grateful as he thinks she should be. So, when he is putting the moves on her, she kills him in self-defense with a steak knife. Now even more frightened and alone, she hurriedly grabs some papers lying about to line her carrying basket, and takes her baby into hiding. How could she know that those papers are gambling sheets that, if they fall into the hands of the authorities, will put the partners away for many a year to come! The partners, however, are not concerned with motive but action. They put out a contract on the woman and, since the safety of innocent bystanders is not a priority for hit men, her baby is in danger as well.

Eventually Crockett discovers who Robby's father is, and forces him to admit that he knows where the woman is and when the hit is going down. He begs his friend to reveal her whereabouts, and his friend in turn gives all the reasons why he cannot.

First, he says that he cannot sacrifice his father, his own flesh-and-blood, for the sake of a total stranger. This may strike some as a weak opening, even a gambit; but I once knew a girl who had seen this very show, and she told me that she completely identified with the son at that point, because she herself could never do anything to hurt her father. I asked her, not even to save an innocent person? She said no. Not even if he were about to murder a little baby? She was in tears at that point, but she reaffirmed that she could never do anything to hurt her father. Here, however, the sentiment rings hollow. Robby means to say that he will let this woman and her baby die, Crockett reminds him, to save his scum-bag of a father of whom he is so proud that he changed his name? On to the next line of defense.

For the first time since he returned from Vietnam, says Robby, he can hold his head up like a man. He has a family, a business, he belongs to a church, he pays his own way, he has respect. Now he is to risk losing all that to save a stranger?

Crockett replies that all those things mean nothing if, when he looks at himself in the mirror in the morning, he cannot live with what he sees. That is the measure of real manhood, of authentic humanity.

Next our friend comes to the line of self-defense. If he does what the detective demands, if he helps save the woman, they will kill him. What has gone before has made it clear that, while his father would not hurt him, his partner most definitely would.

Crockett points out that, when he and his friend were in Vietnam, they did not massacre innocent people or throw prisoners out of helicopters (a common method of interrogation—two suspect Viet Cong go up, one goes out, and the other is more than willing to talk, then he goes out too, to leave no witnesses), no matter what the higher-ups threatened. (As a historical footnote, the higher-ups were in a position to put a man or unit in a position where he or it would be cut to pieces.) They did the right thing no matter what the danger or cost. That is what being human is all about.

Finally, Robby comes to the ultimate defense, the one that would touch anybody: If he helps save this woman and her baby, they will hurt his baby, they will kill his newborn son. And again, his father would not do it, but his father's partner would not hesitate.

Crockett takes his friend by the shoulders, looks into his eyes, and says that, if he does not help save this innocent woman and her child, he will never be able to really look at his own child again!

This is the crucial moment. You have been sitting back, absorbed in the unfolding drama, and at this point your feelings of sympathetic participation are at a fever pitch. Which side are those feelings on?

If you do not allow self-interest to intervene, if you pretend that right now you are not a silent contestant in a philosophical debate, if you allow yourself to forget yourself entirely, then the answer cannot be in doubt. No one wants Robby to do the cowardly and self-serving thing. No one wants the woman and her baby to die. The heroism of love, the self-forgetful passion of the heart, is what we all admire; but then the television screen goes blank, the lights come up at the theater, the radio fades, we close the novel, and how do most of us live?

The heart is utterly clear—love is all in all. This is the fundamental theme of all art. Objectification is the clouding of the heart, the dampening of the fire of love. Everyone admires and worships love, and holds it to be the source of all meaning and value in life; but hardly anyone serves love, hardly anyone is willing to pay the price love requires. Thus the vast majority of the human race lives in schizophrenia.

A few years ago a national news weekly conducted a poll of a thousand gradu-ating college seniors from throughout the country. The first question was, "What do you think the world will be like twenty years from now?" Over ninety percent responded that it would have all the problems it does now—war, crime, disease, famine, pollution, poverty, etc.—only they would be much worse. When asked what their own lives would be like in twenty years, however, again over ninety percent answered that they would enjoy a high-paying and successful career, have a beauti-ful spouse and family, live in a comfortable home in a suburban setting, etc. Schizo-phrenia.

One cannot have it both ways. If objectification is one's reality, then do not pre-tend to be a devotee of love. Self-deception is the great enemy of life, because it enables one to think one can have things any way one pleases. Reality has its own logic. At issue here is whether that logic is objectification or love. To pretend that love is the logic of life while living in objectification cuts one off from all reality, and no more destructive or self-defeating course is possible. If objectification—competition for power, enjoyment of pleasure, and establishment of security—is reality, then embrace it, as I who hold love to be reality must embrace love. Do not hold back. Give yourself entirely! Only then can the issue be decided between us.

There lies the rub. One can embrace love. One can give oneself entirely to love. Indeed, love permits nothing less. Objectification, however, is a coy mistress which allows itself to be seen but not touched. No one can embrace objectification, and one cannot give oneself to objectification. One may, and most people do, live by the logic of objectification; but what no one can do is regard oneself as living by the logic of objectification. Self-deception. Schizophrenia. And the means by which one deceives oneself is art.

Art in essence is the expression and exploration of the values of the heart. The whole point of art is to put self-interest aside so that the light of love may shine forth and illuminate the soul darkened by fear. In short, art helps the soul to find its way. For most people in our world, however, art has become entertainment, which helps the soul lose its way and feel good about doing so.

The difference between art and entertainment is not a substantive one. Art does not uphold any preset system of values. Art explores the hidden depths of the human heart. Art trusts in those depths, unlike the self-appointed moralists and busybody politicians who periodically crawl like insects across the pages of history, mistaking repression for virtue and censorship for moral fiber. The difference between art and entertainment is essentially in the action of the beholder.

Art reveals the reality of the heart. If one acts upon that revelation, if one seeks to live according to that reality, one is not far from the kingdom of heaven, not far from love. If art is the realm of fantasy, on the other hand, and if afterwards one for-gets about it so one may return to the "real" world, then one has experienced enter-tainment, not revelation. The heart remains isolated from life.

The vast majority of people are spiritual voyeurs. A voyeur is titillated by the sight of other people making love. A spiritual voyeur is titillated by the sight of other people living from the passion of the heart. Those who love are hated and feared while they live; but, after they die, when self-interest no longer intervenes, they are worshipped. Spiritual voyeurs even pay people to imitate people who live from the passion of the heart; and the more effective the imitation, the more it ministers to the psychological peculiarities of its audience, the more money it commands, thousands and even millions of dollars.

All who live in objectification are and must be spiritual junkies. They live in objectification, but they use art to give themselves the experiential illusion that they are living in love. They go to the theater or watch television or listen to the radio to get an emotional fix. They identify with the hero to convince themselves that they are heroes, then they go back to their less-than-heroic lives in the "real" world. Art becomes spiritual dope; and the more one takes, the more one needs to get high. The entertainment industry burgeons, and develops bigger, better, and more realistic trips. Even religion becomes entertainment, where one can identify with the ultimate hero, Jesus or Muhammad or Buddha or Krishna or Moses, or even God! Doubtless, one day soon the drama of film and the sense-reality of the theme park will be thoroughly integrated into affordable virtual reality, so that one will be able to actually feel that one is doing all the heroic, daring, wild and crazy things that heroes do, but with no personal investment or risk. The perfect drug.

What can be said of a society that bemoans the drug problem among its children, while at the same time the greater part of its adult citizens regularly indulge in the most potent drug of all? One cannot, however, solve the problem in an objectified way, such as Plato sought to do when he recommended the censorship of art. This would be like curing a patient with heart disease by cutting out his heart. Again, the problem is not with art, but what we do with it. Art becomes entertainment because we refuse to live the truth that it reveals. We do not refuse that truth because art has become entertainment. There is only one solution, and that is to live in love.

What the world needs now is love! Everyone sings this, everyone knows this, but what does every individual need? Empowerment. The world needs love, but the self needs power. This is the folly, the insanity and the self-contradiction of objectification. This is not tragic conflict, but pitiful madness, the madness we have brought upon ourselves. People ask how one can live total love in the "real" world, the world given over to objectification, and survive; but I say, how can the world of objectification survive? We are rats fighting for the most comfortable berths on a sinking ship. We must lose our lives to save life.

To love in a world of objectification is to live as one sane among madmen. Love learns the language of insanity, but only to lift people out of their insanity. Love appears, now as a god, now as a demon, to those too afraid to love. However, love never gives in to the logic of objectification, never sells itself for power, pleasure or survival. If it did, it would cease to be love.

One final but crucial point: Love alone saves, but one cannot love in order to be saved. The only saving love is to love for love's own sake. Only then can love be all in all.

When the reading ended, the students made some offhand remarks about the bitter ramblings of an aging intellectual hippy too smart for his own good. The boyfriend said that it all fit together too neatly, and Ariana's double pointed out, with sarcasm born of frustration, that he himself was a typical intellectual because, in her experience, when intellectuals preferred to ignore a challenge to their pet notions, they said it made no sense if it did not fit neatly together, and was too neat if it did. At this the boyfriend jumped up as if he had not heard, grabbed a football, and motioned to another boy to go out for a pass. Ariana's double and the young man whose spirit also had brightened at the reading were left alone, which seemed to suit them fine.

As darkness fell, Ariana lost contact with her double, and realized that the Teacher had disappeared as well. She suddenly had an overwhelming need to talk to him, to ask him what was going on, who this double was and what everything meant. She had understood the paper, but was bothered by the fact that she found it disturbing. Did that mean she was acquiring the fears and insecurities of the earthbound? Did it mean she herself could grow dim and dull? If that was possible, then anything could happen. As she wandered on the deserted stretch of sand, her only comforts were the regular lapping of the waves upon the shore and the moonlight, now shining directly through the gathering clouds, now causing its captors to glow like iridescent cotton with the warmth of its smothered presence.

She had no way of knowing where she was, or even when she was. Rather than traveling in a straight line, time seemed to dance upon the moonbeams. Gradually, however, the breaking waves grew louder until their sound was that of thunder, and the sparkling moonbeams became sharper and brighter until they were transformed into lightning. Ariana ran aimlessly through the endless night, not knowing where to go or if there was anywhere to go. She made for some hills in the distance, and saw the flickering light of a candle or campfire beckoning from the mouth of a cave. In desperation, she hurried to the hollow as if it were the only hope of shelter in all the realms of the cosmos. As she entered, a little man with big ears, bald head, and brown skin, dressed only in a simple white shawl and loincloth, smiled the warmest welcome she had ever received in any realm. She knew instantly who he was, and forgot all about her loneliness, the Teacher, and the abyss that the reading had uncovered in her soul.

2. Gandhi

"I hope you don't mind that I brought you to my ashram," his big eyes twinkled. "That other place was so inhospitable."

Again, she had missed the transition! Once he appeared, Ariana was so entranced and absorbed in studying him that she had failed to notice the point at which the darkness became gentle sunlight, the lightning wispy clouds, and the thunder exotic songs of colorfully plumaged birds. "Is this India?" were the first words she managed to say.

"No," he replied wistfully, "simply the setting I designed for our meeting. Do you like it?" His voice was a rich baritone that arose to squeaky soprano when he laughed or was otherwise excited, and occasionally deepened to a sonorous bass when he was saying something especially profound. In other words, the register of the voice matched the emotional range of the man. As Ariana came to understand this in the course of their interview, that voice came more and more to be a musical delight.

"If you knew where I was coming from, you'd have no need to ask!"

His eyes narrowed. "I know where you're coming from, and where you are going. I hope you find this place restful and refreshing."

"What do you mean, you know where I'm going?" she queried. "Where am I going?"

"My dear Ariana, I'd be happy to answer your question, but you will find that out soon enough, and we have time here to do justice to only one topic. Either we talk about you, or we talk about me."

As he pronounced the alternatives, she knew immediately why they had been brought together. "You've something to teach me," she declared, "something I'll need to know before I get to wherever I'm going."

He nodded. "Let's start with the question you've always had about me."

"I've always had lots of questions about you!" she laughed. "Let's face it, you may have lived in the public eye most of your life, but you were still an enigmatic man."

He bowed as if to a compliment. "The public eye sees only the surface. You wish to travel into the depths. Let's start at the surface then, shall we, and work our way deeper?" He rearranged himself, raising one knee and folding his hands upon it. "Shall we start with your question about the British?"

i. Political Program

Ariana suddenly felt like a cub reporter who, because everyone else is indisposed, is assigned to interview the president. She had to ask intelligent questions, and every word had to count. "Why did you come to think that British rule of India had to end?" she began. "You started out believing in the empire. You saw England as a civilizing influence spreading the democratic ideals of freedom and democracy throughout the world. After you returned to India from your twenty-year struggle in South Africa, you even supported the British war effort in the First World War!"

"The fight in South Africa wasn't so much with the British as the Boers," he replied. "But you don't want to know how I came to detest British rule. You want to know why. Do you know what colonialism is?"

"One country taking over another?"

"That's putting it succinctly," he smiled.

"But you already knew that when you supported the empire," she observed.

"Yes," he said, "but I didn't understand the basic principle of colonialism. Shall I illustrate?"

She had hoped she was beyond situations; but, while less frequent, they also seemed to be getting more realistic. This time she found herself, not in India, as she might have expected, but in a Latin American country, it seemed, though she could not be certain. The countryside was unsurpassably beautiful, and the people were unimaginably miserable. A few families, it seemed, controlled all the farm land. Instead of growing food to feed themselves, the farm workers labored at less-than-sustenance wages to bring in cash crops like bananas and coffee to be sold to the gringos up north, a business profitable to all parties concerned save the workers themselves. While the ruling class grew fat, the people lived in chronic malnutrition. Their life-expectancy was half that of an American, they were literally old by the time they reached forty, and their infant and childhood mortality rate was astronomical. Whenever they arose to throw off the yoke of oppression, however, the gringos sent money for the rulers to buy soldiers and guns; and, when all else failed, they sent their own troops as well. All the tyrants had to do was shout, "Communist insurgency!" and the Yankees came running.

After getting the general picture, Ariana found herself linked in awareness with a woman who, despite the loss of husband and uncles and brothers, as well as danger to her own children, fought back. She helped found an organization that worked to bring to light the kidnapings and tortures and murders through which the government of the rich maintained itself against the desperation of the poor. Sometimes it seemed to this woman that they were wasting their time, because the Americans did not withdraw their support from the government after the assassination of the morally indignant archbishop while he said mass in the country's cathedral, nor even after the slaying of four American nuns or six Jesuit priests. More important to her seemed the taking care of the children whom the violence left without homes and families. She came to spend more and more of her time in the organization's day-care.

Then the day-care was targeted for suppression. She and her helpers managed to get the children, infants, and toddlers all away, but many were wounded and killed in the mortar fire with which the government troops sent them on their way. Six months of hiding in the jungle killed off all but seven of the original thirty; and, with each death, her heart died again. For the first time, Ariana realized what a wonderful and terrible thing the heart was, how it could suffer agonizing death any number of times, and yet be reborn to suffer anew. Ariana lost touch with the woman just as she managed to find refuge for the surviving children in Mexico, and was considering traveling to the United States itself to plead directly with the American people to withdraw support from the tyrants exploiting her people.

"Do you know now where you were?" Gandhi asked when she returned to the peace of his ashram.

"El Salvador," she replied. "I knew as soon as I connected with that woman. She's quite a person! Maybe I'll meet her, I hope."

"Perhaps you already have," he said, and she remembered with wonder that she was already in embodiment even as they spoke. What was her alter ego doing now?

"Why show me El Salvador?" she asked. "Why not India?"

"India is past; El Salvador is present. We must fight the injustices of today, not the villains of yesterday."

"But maybe we also need to understand the injustices of yesterday so as not to perpetuate them," she said.

"Agreed, and we will talk about India," he promised; "but Americans are so proud of their principle of freedom, they consider themselves above the colonial fray. After all, weren't they once the victims of colonialism themselves? They refuse to face what they have done and what they continue to do to the Native Americans, the African Americans, and little peoples all over the word who get in the way of American business or political interests. Fortunately, God does watch closely over your native country. Every time America places self-interest before its own principles, the consequences are devastating, especially for itself. Take the most recent example—the Gulf War. The United States supported a ruthless dictator, thinking it could make him a tool of American policy. When he got out of control, it tried to contain him, and the innocent suffered through all of this."

"Are you saying the U.S. should never have gotten involved?" she asked.

"On the contrary, America created the monster. It was up to America to stop him. When the opportunity came, the American president stopped short for purely political reasons, and now the dictator is as dangerous as ever."

"I thought you were against war!"

"There are many ways to fight tyranny," he answered; "but if one uses violence, one should do so responsibly."

"And what does that mean?" she queried.

"Aim at eradicating the evil," he declared. "Then, if you fail, at least you will know the method itself was flawed, and not how you used it."

"If I get what you're saying," Ariana returned after a moment of reflection, "the United States has instant karma, as the Beetles sang. Whenever it violates its own integrity, punishment follows swiftly and mercilessly."

"Swiftly and mercifully," he corrected. "It is a blessing, a sign of spiritual advancement, that one either stays on spiritual track or destroys oneself."

"Spiritual advancement?" she exclaimed. "But America is the most materialistic country in the world!"

Gandhi smiled sadly. "Haven't you learned by now? Where there is the greatest opportunity for good, there is also the greatest opportunity for evil. The hardest tests come near the top of the spiritual mountain. And there is no harder spiritual test than power and the affluence that goes with it."

Ariana found herself biting her lip, and wondered if this was a habit of her earth-self, and if the impulse meant she and her double were coming closer together. "Give me another example of this instant karma," she demanded. "You said it happens all the time."

"The American involvement in Indochina, or, as it is known today, Vietnam," he replied. "During the Second World War, the Western democracies guaranteed the right of self-determination to all peoples, including the Vietnamese, who had been fighting for their independence for hundreds of years, first against the Chinese, then the French, and then the Japanese when they invaded Indochina in 1945, just months before the war's end. The French, however, had no intention of letting their former possession go its own way. American influence at that point might have been decisive in ensuring a peaceful transition to democratic independence. However, in exchange, it seems, for French cooperation with American foreign policy in Europe, the United States gave France a free hand in Indochina. That left Ho Chi-minh and his nationalists with only one source of support—the Soviet Union."

"And the rest is history," she concluded. "I get your point. Colonialism is a sin of which America is also guilty. But you still haven't told me its basic principle."

"That's simple," he said. "It's the same principle according to which a thief in a dark alley operates—take as much as you can any way that you can as quickly as you can."

"That ruthless?" she asked unbelievingly.

"Textbooks make colonialism sound like the rational development of national policy," he answered. "Textbooks make everything sound rational. Don't let yourself be fooled by the historians. Do you know why India is such a poor country today? I don't mean why it has poverty. Every nation has poverty. I mean why she herself is so poor."

"Because India failed to industrialize like the Western world?" she speculated.

"That's a common idea, even in India," he replied with muted bitterness, "but it belongs with the myth that Indians are starving because they refuse to slaughter and eat their cows."

"That's a myth?" Ariana asked before she could catch herself. Gandhi, however, turned suddenly mild.

"You really are naive, aren't you?" he chuckled in a kindly way. "Can you imagine what would happen in a sub-tropical country that lacked refrigeration if meat became a staple?"

"Disease?"

"Yes, disease, perhaps even worse than the Black Plague that wiped out half the population of 14th century Europe. And on top of that, what would the peasants do for milk, butter, cheese, and fuel if the cows were slaughtered?"

"Oh, yes," Ariana remembered her time with Ishwara, "I'd forgotten how dependent the Indian village economy is upon the living symbol of the Divine Mother."

"No," he declared, "the reason for India's poverty, as for that of most of the so-called third-world countries, is colonialism; and the behavior of the developed countries, the former colonizers to their former colonies, is equivalent to that of a thief who robs a man of all his wealth, then lends money back to his victim at interest, and is so enraged when the victim can't meet the payment schedule that he has him prosecuted to the last farthing."

"How did England destroy India's wealth?" she asked, still skeptical.

"Before the British came," he answered, "India had a stable agricultural economy with a thriving handicraft industry that enabled the peasants to supplement their farming income and thereby maintain a buffer zone against starvation when the crop failed, as crops periodically do all over the world. The British destroyed that system."

"Why?" Ariana persisted.

"Britain was the first industrial power in the world. An industrializing power, as Marx noted, needs three things: cheap labor, cheap raw materials, and expanding markets. England got her cheap labor at home through the Enclosure Acts, which robbed the peasantry of land that had been held in common for centuries and forced them into the cities. She got the rest from her colonies, especially India. Did you know that India originally was governed not by the British Crown, but by the East India Company, a private trading firm? Can you imagine what General Motors or IBM would do to a nation so rich in natural resources if placed totally at their disposal?"

"Economic rape," she murmured, beginning to see a dimension of horror in the world to which she had hitherto been oblivious.

"And that's what happened in India," he resumed. "For their first hundred years in India, the sole priority of the British was to maximize profits. The land was diverted from feeding the people to feeding England's industrial machine with raw materials that were literally a steal, and the British used a combination of underselling and forced monopolization to destroy domestic competition with English factory-made goods. Without markets, the Indian handicraft industry died, and so did millions of Indians who as a result lost their economic safety net. When Queen Victoria took direct command because the scandalous tyranny and corruption of the East India Company's administration could no longer be tolerated, the new system was already firmly in place, as in many ways it still is today. Don't misunderstand me. India is the victim of her own greed and venality. The problem is not England versus India, but the thoughtlessly brutal rich against the weak and despairing poor."

"And so you worked to get the powerful rich off the backs of the poor?" she asked.

"Yes, but that means nothing if the poor do not stand up and affirm their own humanity!" he declared. "Of course, the most spectacular aspect of my political program was the campaign for independence, but independence from England without the development of an independent spirit would simply have left India open to slavery in a different form. Slaves will be slaves no matter what the system under which they labor."

"What can be done to help another be strong?" she wondered.

"You ask about something very difficult," he replied thoughtfully, "perhaps the most difficult task in the world." Then he smiled warmly. "But also the most worthwhile! My poor effort to bring light into this darkness was the Constructive Program."

"I've heard of that," she said, "and I believe your followers have carried it on, but I don't really know what it is."

"Yes, they have carried it on," he confirmed, "and it is one ray of light in the dark foreboding of India's future. My idea was to help the Indian peasants find ways to help themselves, so the program never involved massive government funding. It has been staffed by volunteers, who have aimed at reestablishing the self-sufficiency and dignity of all India. On the one hand, therefore, I sought to resurrect the handicraft system so that India might reclaim her own resources and markets, and the field workers supplement their incomes."

"That's the reason," she exclaimed, "for the spinning wheel and the burning of British cloth! I never quite understood all that. But didn't Nehru, the socialist, and Patel, the capitalist, your left and right-hand men, laugh at you for wanting to return India to an earlier age?"

"Yes," he admitted, "Nehru and Patel—who by the way were their own men, not mine—believed industrialization along Western lines was the key to lifting India out of her poverty. They thought my economic ideas were pure nostalgia!" he chuckled. "In the four decades since my death, however, it has become quite clear to many independent economists, those not commissioned by the Indian government or the World Bank, that the root of India's economic distress is not under-production, but unemployment. Needed is a system that will give the average peasant the means of feeding his family, not employ a few middle-class technicians and make even fewer investors rich. India cannot hope to compete in industrial goods on the open market with the likes of the United States, Great Britain, Germany, France, Italy, Japan, and now China. She can hope, however to feed herself if she returns from cash-crop to subsistence farming, and if she patronizes her own handicraft industry. Such a policy, of course, would not generate a big enough cash-flow to support a modern army, navy, and nuclear-weapons program, but neither would it plunge India into steep national debt; and it would enable her to become a model for other victims of colonialism in the things that really matter, especially in providing the opportunity for a dignified, healthful and stable way of life for all her people."

"So one side of the Constructive Program is to retrain the peasants in handicrafts and reclaim the land for growing food," Ariana summarized. "What's the other side?"

"Wherever you find poverty, Ariana," he responded with that subtle blend of seriousness and gentle good humor for which he was famous, "you find despair. People give up and stop taking care of themselves. The problem in India is exacerbated by the caste system, and especially untouchability. Like African-Americans in the United States, fewer and fewer untouchables are willing to settle for the menial and dirty jobs to which they traditionally have been assigned. Yet, even today, there are caste Hindus who will wait a month for an available pariah rather than clean their own outhouses and toilets or dispose of their own garbage. Dirt builds up and breeds disease. Throughout my public life, I took every opportunity to shame my fellow Hindus into cleaning up after themselves." He made this last point with a twinkle in his eye. "And when I traveled through Noakhali in the last few months of my life, besides preaching the virtues of nonviolence to the first villagers of India to experience communal violence between Hindus and Muslims, I showed them how to build and maintain a proper latrine."

In that story she thought she had the essence of the man, but she was to discover that was not it by half. "I understand now, I think. Just as you can't learn to love another unless you first love yourself, so you can't learn to respect another unless you first respect yourself."

"What you say may be true, my daughter," he said, "but it's not quite my idea. In fact, my idea is just the opposite."

"What do you mean?" she asked, both bewildered and uncertain whether she liked his assumption of the role of paterfamilias.

"The third point in my social-political program was the foundation of the rest," he explained, "Just as there can be no freedom without self-respect, so there can be no self-respect without respect for the rights of others. At the heart of all my work has been the emphasis upon equality and friendship among Hindus of all castes, including untouchables, and among Hindus, Muslims, Sikhs, and all other communities and peoples in India."

"And women too?" she queried. "Do you count women among these 'peoples?' From what I understand, the lot of the Indian woman has not been enviable."

"Yes, women are included," he smiled, but his face then became stern. "India owes much to her women, and Indian men have much for which to ask their forgiveness. In any patriarchal society, men are encouraged to behave like spoiled little boys. India is no exception. Women, on the other hand, develop patience, endurance, long-suffering, gentleness, and respect for life—precisely those virtues my movement emphasized. Thus, in all aspects of satyagraha, women outshone men; and what the women of India have contributed to their native land's freedom has done much to unchain them from their traditional servitude. Much," he added sadly, "but not enough."

ii. Philosophy

For one of those 'eternal' moments to which Ariana was becoming accustomed since the contest brought her into contact with such profound and thoughtful spirits, Gandhi's head bowed low in sorrow. When he looked up again and smiled, she took the opportunity to continue the interview. She was beginning to feel that she had barely scratched the surface, and told herself that regard and respect for Gandhi would mean nothing, especially to him, if she did not have greater regard and respect for the truth. "Would you explain *satyagraha* to me?" she asked.

"Have you ever heard of it?" he asked in return, evidently feeling out where and how he should begin.

"Yes," she said,"and I've heard other people explain it. I've even read some of your explanations."

He laughed. "But now you want it from the horse's mouth?"

"I know it means something like 'truth-force,'" she offered as a beginning.

"Yes, it means exactly something like 'truth-force,'" he agreed. "*Satya* is the adjectival form of *sat*, which, in addition to 'truth,' may be translated as 'soul,' 'essence,' or 'essential being.' Graha means 'power' or 'force,' but it is like the force of water that flows gently and yet wears away the hardest rock. Satyagraha is the power of the inner being, the force of truth and the influence of love. In reality, it is the power of life. What usually goes by the name of power, the strength that is embodied in armies and bombs, in reality is utter impotence, because it can only destroy. God is truth, and God is love, and God is the only genuine power."

"Nonviolence, then, is what it's all about!" she almost sang as she glided about his hut, feeling at joyful peace. The walls were translucent and breathed in the sweet air, giving the sensation of both protection and exposure to the health-giving elements.

"Not precisely," he said, as he watched her enjoyment with obvious pleasure. "*Ahimsa*, nonviolence, is the fruit of satyagraha, but it is not the root."

She wondered what he meant, and immediately the atmosphere grew heavy and stark. She could not have said that any particular element changed, nor that anything remained the same. She knew only that this subtle but unmistakable change signaled the onset of another experience.

Sure enough, she was once again a he, a villager in a remote province of India. A shudra by caste and farm laborer by trade, he had a family of three sons and two daughters, and a wife who was as extraordinarily interested in life beyond the village as he was. As they worked in the fields all day, they talked of nothing but the new *mahatma*, the "great soul" who was going to throw the mighty British out of India without firing a shot. They might as well have been discussing events on another planet, as far as their fellow villagers were concerned, but it made them feel they were part of something not only large and important, but deeply spiritual. All their lives they had sought to draw nearer to God, but now they felt that God was drawing nearer to them.

This growing tranquility of spirit was sorely tested when rumor reached them of bandits in the area. There had been an attack upon a neighboring village, which reportedly had traded all the gold and silver of its wives and daughters to its former landlord for some obsolescent firearms with which he had armed his overseers. Now the landlord was going back to England, and the villagers, determined to fight their own battles, repulsed the marauders. He knew that their resistance had been effective only because it had been unexpected, and because the bandits believed they would find easier pickings elsewhere. He also wondered openly whether taking up guns or swords would not, as the Mahatma declared, corrupt their souls, even if it saved their bodies.

On the strength of his own and his wife's passion for peace, the villagers decided not to fight. Instead, the men would continue to work in the fields as usual, while the women stayed at home to calm the children's fears.

The attack came at sunset toward the end of the harvest, when the men were weary from the back-breaking labor of bringing in the crop, made doubly worse by the lack of women to help. The men heard shots and came running. A band of forty-odd bandits had already set about loading a truck with grain, while each in turn took a break to rape one of the village women. Another truck, this one accompanied by a jeep with a mounted rifle, pulled up, and the driver started shepherding the children into its flatbed while the gun swung around and covered the men. At that point the horror of it all broke over him, and he could no longer face what he had done. He ran, and the rest of the men ran after him. The bandits laughed derisively and let them go. The nearest army post was a day's journey on foot, and by then they would be long gone.

He never made it to the army post, and neither did he return to the village. Instead, he and a handful of his fellow villagers took to wandering, begging or pilfering food as opportunity and necessity dictated. He could feel the shame like an iron weight in his stomach, holding him in the vise of emotional paralysis. He could not bear the eyes upon him of anyone who knew what he had done. He tried to lose his fellows, and succeeded until only four of them were left; but these would not leave no matter how rudely he behaved toward them. They had been playmates as children, and he could see the concern for him in their hunger-dilated pupils.

He knew all along where he was going, even though at first he did not know that he knew. After several months of circling his prey's lair, he finally made his appearance at the Mahatma's ashram.

The Mahatma greeted him and his companions with ease and grace, as if they were old friends. The great man sat them down and offered them food, which they ate greedily. He had almost given up the idea of confrontation when the Mahatma asked the purpose of their visit.

"We tried your way," he answered with bitterness distilled and envenomed by months of lonely wandering. Then he described all that had happened. The Mahatma listened without once interrupting. "What have you got to say for yourself?" the peasant cried at the end of the story. "We tried your way, we obeyed your teaching, and look where it has gotten us!"

The Mahatma was suddenly stern. "If you did not have the courage to place your own bodies between those bandits and your homes and families," he said, "you should at least have had the courage to fight them. Better the courage of a soldier than no courage at all!"

Before he had time to react, he was once again she. Ariana had been returned to the ashram.

"So courage is the root," she whispered.

"Follow the courage in your heart," he declared, "even if it is only the courage to fight, and it will lead you to the highest form of courage—ahimsa."

"Nonviolence," she translated for her own benefit. "Courage is the root, and nonviolence is the fruit."

In reply, Gandhi joined his hands together and bowed.

"But why?" she asked. "I'm not sure I understand."

He bowed again, and the ashram again disappeared. Its place was taken by a cramped and busy office in a dusty and dirty town on a sweltering summer day. She was wearing a dress that was surprisingly cool, even though it covered her literally from neck to ankle, and taking dictation from someone who looked like he might be Gandhi's son. As he spoke, however, she realized that it was Gandhi himself, younger and with a full head of jet-black hair! He was going over the preliminaries of a letter addressed to General Smuts, the head of the South African government, detailing the abuse and humiliation the Indian population had endured. Gandhi believed the situation to be as dehumanizing for the victimizers as the victims. He had reasoned with the government, but found it adamant in its insistence that Indians be treated like criminals, required to register their fingerprints with the police and their homes subject to summary search. Moreover, South Africa refused to recognize the validity of non-Christian and non-Jewish marriages. Such an attitude on the part of the government toward an industrious and loyal segment of the population was intolerable. The Indians had talked and the government proven unresponsive. Now it was time for action. Gandhi was directing the Indian miners to strike and join their brothers and sisters in their march for dignity.

Charlie Andrews, an Anglican missionary and one of Gandhi's closest advisors and friends, appeared in the middle of the dictation. He carried a newspaper under his arm and evidently had something to report; but, since Gandhi did not notice, he sat on the edge of a desk and waited until the letter was finished. Then he opened the newspaper and placed it before his friend. "Have you seen this?" he said quietly. The headline declared that the railway workers of South Africa, who by the way were all white and who had nothing to do with Gandhi's movement, had gone on strike.

Noticing something was up, the rest of the office workers turned their attention toward Gandhi. When he read the article aloud, they were jubilant. Everyone knew that the combination of the two strikes would paralyze the economy and bring the government to its knees. Andrews alone looked concerned, and fixed his gaze upon his friend, as if waiting to see what he would do. Gandhi instructed Ariana to discard the letter she had just written and to take down another.

Everyone fell silent. They wanted to hear what terms Gandhi would grant the defeated. Then they went into shock when they realized he was not crowning their victory with magnanimity, which everyone expected, but calling off the strike unconditionally. "This is insanity!" one man cried, and the rest took up the theme.

"No one who wishes not to follow me need do so!" Gandhi snapped so he could be heard above the din. That brought silence, so, when he continued, it was in a gentle and persuading tone. He explained to them that satyagraha was not a way to take advantage of one's adversary. That was merely the nonviolence of the weak. Satyagraha was, in essence, communication. Suppose, for example, you work for an employer that seems not to take the proper safety precautions in his factory. You first discuss the matter with him, to be sure he understands what is wrong and that it is in his power to fix it. If the employer is culpable on both these counts and refuses to do right by his workers, then you resign. You do not resign to hurt the employer. Perhaps you are key to his operation, even irreplaceable; or, perhaps, he will have a substitute for you within the hour. In the latter case, it is so tempting to tell yourself that you need the job and might as well keep it, that to quit would be a futile gesture of protest. A true satyagrahi does not leverage or protest. A true satyagrahi does not cooperate with evil because it is evil.

At this point, several people protested, saying that, by Gandhi's own logic, non-cooperation should be undertaken whether it helps the enemy or hurts him, so why should they hold back simply because of the conjunction of the two strikes.

"Logically, you are right," replied Gandhi, "which only goes to show the limitations of logic. I thought we were seeking to demonstrate our good citizenship. Are you now prepared to make the government your out-and-out enemy? If satyagraha is communication, we must ask ourselves what message we would be sending by kicking the government, and indeed the nation itself, when it is down."

A number of people threw up their hands and walked out.

"And you, Ariana?" Gandhi addressed his secretary. "What do you think?"

"I think your principles are much clearer than their application," she said.

"You mean, 'Clearer than my practice?'"

She nodded, smiling at his ability to read her mind.

"I have always said that I would much rather be consistent with the truth as I perceive it today than as I understood it yesterday."

"That is why it's so exciting to work with you!" she cried, and he laughed.

"Yes, everyone says I'm full of surprises."

"Like the time those villagers told you they had to kill monkeys to save their crops," she continued.

"No fence would have been high enough to keep them out," he explained.

"You gave your blessing to the slaughter," she said, "just as you supported the British war effort in the First World War."

"And these things bother you," he did not ask, but stated. At this point, Ariana noticed, they were back in the ashram.

"Inconsistencies," she said, as much to herself as him. "I see so many inconsistencies."

"Do you really want an answer to the question you are raising," he queried, "or do you merely wish to feel morally superior?"

"How can you say that?" she demanded.

"In that case," he frowned, "I will take you at your word."

This time her self-awareness was totally submerged.

She was a young engineering student, a woman sitting in class, when the door opened and a young man entered, carrying an automatic rifle. At first, everyone thought it was a joke, that the gun was a toy; but, as the intruder marched up and down the aisles and everyone had a good look, the laughter died and the smiles faded. He ordered the men to one side of the room, nearer the door, and the women to the other. Then he told the men they could leave. Some hesitated, but a single brandishing of his weapon was enough to convince them to do as he said. As the last of the men walked out, she felt the paralysis of naked fear. If only one of them had stayed! She did not have long to dwell upon this abandonment, however, before the crazy man's bullets tore her and her friends' bodies apart.

Next came a complete blackout, and then Ariana was in the same classroom, only this time she was a he, one of the young men. He had no memory of having been she. Everything played out as before, only this time he was told he could leave. He hesitated, but then reasoned that defying the madman might provoke him to violence, and that, once free, he could go for help. Upon reaching the corridor he ran, but he had not made it even to the end of the building before the shots made his errand gratuitous.

Then Ariana, mercifully she thought, was returned to the ashram.

"Thank God it wasn't real!" she nearly sobbed.

"It was real," he countered, "but not for you. It happened at a Canadian university several years ago. However, what about your reaction?"

Ariana was trembling. "He had a gun!"

"So you thought the second time," he persisted, "but what about the first?"

Only then did she remember her experience as victim of a mass murderer. "I wanted someone to stay, someone to help. I wanted someone as big and powerful as that madman to make an effort to stop him."

"And yet," he observed mercilessly, "when the shoe was on the other foot, you yourself left."

"What would you have done?" she cried.

"I don't know what I would have done," he answered with infuriating calm, "because I never had the opportunity to confront a madman directly when other lives were at stake. I do know what I would not have done, however."

"You would not have left."

He nodded. "That is the dilemma. People wonder why they lack self-esteem or a positive self-image. They pay plenty of money to undergo therapy, attend workshops and seminars, etc. In reality, the solution is simple. If you wish to respect yourself, be a self worthy of respect. If you live in courage, you will respect yourself. If you do not live in courage, all the psychological tricks in the world will not help."

"But it's so hard!" she moaned.

"Yes, it is difficult," he agreed, "but courage is not optional, not if one wishes to be genuinely human. Most people have the attitude that one should be courteous, decent and helpful until one is in personal danger. Then one is excused. Such people excuse themselves from their own humanity. Courage is not optional. It is the very essence of selfhood. And nonviolence is the highest form of courage. One cannot be courageous for another, and one cannot excuse oneself from being courageous because of the cowardice of another. And one cannot force courage into another's heart."

"I think I see," she said softly, tears for some reason welling into her eyes. "What you demand of yourself you can only recommend to others."

"Satyagraha cannot be the law of the land," he smiled. "When all live by the truth of the heart, law will be obsolete."

"The truth of the heart," she mused."What is that truth? What is the essence of nonviolence?"

iii. Manipulation

Again, she was totally submerged. Her experiences with Gandhi, while brief, were also the deepest and most powerful yet. It was as if she were completely made over into another person and experienced, without a hint of make believe, that other person's reality as her own.

This time she was a young Belgian woman whose husband had been executed by the invading Nazis because he was a college professor who taught that people should think for themselves. She and her two children, a boy of seven and a girl of ten, were speeding jerkily through the night on a rail car that looked like it had been designed for the transport of cattle. The car was crowded with Jews, so she kept herself and her children apart in a corner, where she hoped they would not attract too much attention. They had been traveling for days with no food and little water, and not so much as a stop to empty the sloshing waste buckets or dispose of the mounting dead.

The train suddenly slowed, but Ariana did not think too much of it until she realized they were neither rounding a curve nor climbing a grade. The brakes were applied, and a few screeches brought the train to a dead halt. The occupants of the car became suddenly quiet, and instinctively moved away from the doors. No one complained when the shift in position crammed the passengers even closer together. Everyone hardly dared breathe.

With a jolt the doors slid open, and the German guards ordered the prisoners to line up alongside the rail line. As Ariana rushed her children into place, she felt the tip of what turned out to be a riding crop lightly on her shoulder. A German officer, perhaps the commandant, she thought, from the deference the other soldiers paid him, told her she was very beautiful, and asked her if she were Jewish. Upon learning that she was not, he declared she should not have to endure the insult of waiting in line with these swine. He would make things easier for her. The prisoners were being divided into two groups, one to be gassed and one to work. She had two children. She herself would choose which should live and which die.

Ariana protested, but the Nazi said that, if she did not choose, both children would die. She offered herself in their place, but he insisted that he had no intention of wasting beauty such as hers. He gave her to the count of ten. When he reached nine, she screamed out that he should take her daughter. The little girl looked up at her mother in horror. After that, Ariana fainted.

She regained consciousness in the ashram. She was lying down, and Gandhi was patting her forehead with a cool, damp cloth.

"I'm getting more physical all the time!" she whispered, smiling bitterly up at him.

"The marriage is approaching," he said cryptically. She did not, however, wish to pursue the subject. She felt something else was more important. "I'll never forget her face, or her scream. Even if it wasn't real, I'll carry it with me forever."

"It is the price one pays for falling in-between," he declared. "The logic of life should never submit to the logic of death."

"What would you have done?" she queried.

"Again, I can only tell you what I would not have done," he replied. "I would not have played the commandant's dehumanizing little game."

Ariana was shocked. "You would have let both children die?"

"That would have been his decision, not mine," the Mahatma said firmly.

She certainly could not accuse Gandhi of being an armchair moralist, but how could he say such a thing? "It must be nice to have everything laid out in black and white."

"Not everything!" he rejoined severely. "If we do not follow what is clear, however, how can we hope that the gray and foggy areas will ever diminish?"

She arose. "If we pretend to ourselves things are clear when they aren't, we will have only the illusion of seeing!"

Gandhi unexpectedly grinned. "You are right," he conceded. "Self-deception is the great enemy, so shall we examine what's at stake? As I see it, human beings have three options: to manipulate, to be the victims of manipulation, or to live the truth of the heart, to be true satyagrahis."

"What do you mean by manipulation?" she asked.

"You asked to know the essence of nonviolence," he replied. "It is to act in such a way that means and end are one. One cannot achieve a world of peace and justice through violent revolution and the dictatorship of the proletariat. Nor can one find happiness and prosperity through exploitation and mechanization. To recognize that the end is inherent in the means is the key to satyagraha. Because we do not have control over the results of our actions, good intentions justify nothing. In fact, as you suggest, good intentions can be a powerful form of self-deception. If I convince myself that my intentions are good, I can do anything. It is absolutely necessary to focus on the means."

"And manipulation is the opposite?" she offered.

"Yes," he confirmed. "Manipulation sets its sights on a particular goal, then casts around for whatever course of action seems most likely to achieve that goal. If, for satyagraha, means and end are intrinsically one, for manipulation the relation between the two is wholly extrinsic. Manipulation uses power to achieve its goal. Satyagraha derives its power from its goal."

"But isn't manipulation necessary to really do anything in this world?" she queried.

"The manipulation of objects, perhaps," he answered, "but not the manipulation of people. The manipulation of people is self-defeating and self-destructive."

She looked at him quizzically, but said nothing.

"What are the tools of manipulation?" he asked.

"Force," she replied, "and intimidation."

He smiled, as if at an apt student. "I hold a gun to your head, so you do what I say. Seems effective, doesn't it? I want to move this orange, so I pick it up and put it over here. I want to move that person, so I pick her up and move her over there."

"Crude, but effective," she agreed.

"Is it really?" he asked gently. "Effective, I mean? Naked force hardly ever accomplishes its objective. Push people and they have a tendency to push back. Force sets in motion an incalculable chain of events, when its very object is just the opposite. The attempt to control by force is the surest way to set things out of control. What other tools are in the manipulator's bag of tricks?"

"Deception," she said with alacrity.

"Yes," he affirmed, "and deception may work very well for a while. Sooner or later, though, the deceiver will be found out, and so lose everything gained by deception and then some. Anything else?"

"Bribery, blackmail . . ." she itemized.

"Bribery and blackmail!" he interjected. "They are even less reliable than force and deception! The tables are turned so easily. What guarantee is there that the bribe will not be taken without being acted upon, what assurance that the blackmailer won't be blackmailed in turn?"

"Absolutely none at all," Ariana replied with genuine conviction. She could see the inescapable truth in his argument.

"Is there nothing else?" he asked. "No more tools?"

"I can't think of any."

"My dear Ariana, you have left out manipaulation's most powerful and effective tool, as well as the most common in today's world."

"Seduction?" she guessed. The word had just popped into her head.

"Yes, seduction," Gandhi smiled mischievously, and another thought crossed her mind, that he himself could have been a great seducer had he so desired. "Seduction works through the most superficial aspect of a person, the self-image. Seduction is getting someone to desire what you want him to desire. It influences, controls, and even molds the self-image. The self-image is the most superficial aspect of a person; but, unfortunately, since most people live on the surface, seduction has plenty of victims upon whom to work its magic. And those victims are willing victims. In all other forms of manipulation, one is getting people to do what one wants. In seduction, people follow their own desires, and it is those desires upon which the seducer plays."

"Yes," she said, "I have seen many seducers among the earthbound."

"Have you?" he asked skeptically. "That's interesting, because seducers are usually invisible, at least as long as one is caught up in one's own self-image. It's curious, but seducers are hardly ever seen as manipulators. As long as people are given what they want, they usually don't look any deeper. Ironically, those who live the truth of the heart are almost always denounced as manipulators, because they challenge the soul to spiritual heroism, and that makes most people extremely uncomfortable."

He sank back in a rare mood of bitter despair. Then it passed, and he asked pointedly, "Now, can you see that one who lives by satyagraha is alone not subject to the power of manipulation? Intimidation has no power over him, because he does not fear death. Falsehood cannot mislead him, because one who sees with the heart cannot be deceived about anything essential, cannot be convinced that right is wrong *and wrong* right. Bribery and blackmail have no purchase over him, since there is nothing he values more than truth. Finally, seduction has no point of entry, for he does not identify with his self-image, but lives from his heart."

Ariana marveled at how simple it all was. "Yes, I can see that."

"Therefore, the way to put a stop to evil is not to go out and shoot or hang all the manipulators. This solution has been tried throughout history. It's called revolution, and those who do it invariably become worse manipulators than the villains they've replaced. The way to overcome evil is to root fear out of one's heart. Where fear has no place, manipulation has no power."

iv. Fasting Unto Death

Ariana sat in absorbed silence, feeling the ramifications of his wisdom deep within her soul. She knew he was not seeking converts. The last thing that concerned Gandhi was institutional or ideological affiliation, religious or philosophical. He was Hindu, but he always told would-be converts to his tradition that they should remain within their own. If you are a Jew, Buddhist, Christian, or Muslim, be a better one, don't become something else. If you do, religion will be for you nothing more than a social club. Religion for Gandhi was another word for life, and living it from the depths. If walked to the end, all roads lead to God.

After her brief but fruitful meditation, she was ready to ask him a question that had crossed her mind while he was speaking about manipulation. At first, she had instinctively filed the question away under the category of never-to-be-mentioned, but it refused to play dead. Like a frisky kitten, it kept nattering away at the fringe of her consciousness, occasionally hitting home with its claws. By the end of his discourse, however, she no longer feared to raise it. She felt she could ask him anything, and trusted that, no matter how he reacted, understanding would be his ultimate goal.

"On earth you fasted regularly, didn't you?" she began.

"Yes, my fasts were of two types," he answered. "One was private and personal, with the goal of spiritual and physical purification. Did you know that fasting can preserve and improve one's health?"

She had not, but given the tremendous stamina and vitality Gandhi had exhibited until the very end of his life at the age of seventy-eight, she had to believe it. "And the other?" she asked.

A shadow seemed to fall over his face. "My political fasts. My fasts unto death."

"What did those involve?" she asked, encouraging him to continue.

"Pain," he replied. "Suffering. Not so much of the body. Suffering of the spirit. These fasts were my alternative to despair. My personal fasts lasted as long as twenty-one days, and I was invariably fine. My political fasts never lasted more than a week, yet I came near to death each time."

"That wasn't just because you were in despair," she observed.

"No," he smiled sadly, "I also refused to take in much, if any, liquid. In my final fast, for example, I would not drink any water, and as a result my kidneys malfunctioned. I gained weight rather than losing it. The doctors said I was dying of toxemia."

Ariana fixed her gaze upon him. "Why?"

"Because that's what happens when one doesn't drink any water," he answered disingenuously.

"You know what I mean!"

From his response, Ariana figured that he must have inspired that tone of amused anger she heard now in her own voice in just about everyone he had ever known. He took a deep breath, sighed, and set himself completely at ease, as if finally they were ready to get down to business. If he had not been so utterly open about it, Ariana would have resented him for setting her up.

"To stop the violence," he said simply. "I fasted unto death four times. Once, to stop my campaign of noncooperation when it degenerated into rioting and murder. That was in the 'twenties. The second time was against untouchability, in the 'thirties. And finally, in 1947, I fasted twice to end the communal warfare between Hindus and Muslims in the streets of Delhi and Calcutta."

"And it worked every time, didn't it?" she said. Now that she felt the way open, she had no need to hurry.

"That depends upon what you mean by 'work,'" he replied sardonically. "The campaign ended, my fellow Hindus opened their temples to the pariah, and the fighting stopped. Today, however, India is developing nuclear weaponry, untouchables are still regarded by many as the dregs of humanity, and Hindu India and Muslim Pakistan take almost any excuse to go for each other's throats!"

"Surely you exaggerate!" she protested. "You can't really believe that your life counted for nothing!"

"That's not the issue," he said, calm again. "I was not seeking to accomplish anything."

"Pardon me, but I think you were seeking to accomplish a great deal," she exclaimed angrily; "and that, in your zeal for the cause of righteousness, you overstepped the bounds you yourself had set! You committed emotional blackmail! You were guilty of manipulation!"

She could not tell whether Gandhi's look was sad or stern.

"Don't get me wrong," Ariana continued. "I sympathize entirely. I even think that you did the right thing, even if for the wrong reasons."

"But you just want me to admit that they were the wrong reasons?" he smiled wanly.

"Something like that," she confessed, unable not to return his smile.

"If I am to confess to a crime," he said, "you must first explain to me the nature of that crime. How was my fasting blackmail?"

"You yourself know the answer to that," she insisted.

"No, I do not. But," he added with that twinkle in his eye, "I do know how it might be construed as blackmail."

"Spoken like a true lawyer!" she laughed.

"My dear, there is no such thing as a true lawyer," he quipped, and Ariana laughed even harder. He waited until her laughter subsided. "In this case, I will, nevertheless, help you out, not because you are a damsel in distress—self-reliance was always my motto, even for women!—but because it is an important issue. Some Christian missionaries said something similar to me, I believe during my fast against untouchability. They asked me if I were not violating my own principles, if I were not exercising coercion."

"And what did you say?"

"I will tell you that later," he replied coyly, and then added in full seriousness, "but it is important to remember that I was only a man, and therefore was perfectly capable of espousing standards by which I myself may have failed to live. I was more aware than anyone else of the need to keep watch over myself, especially when I exercised such influence over the masses. The slightest misstep would have turned me into another Hitler. Even now, if you could convince me that I had violated the spirit of nonviolence in so serious a matter, I would plead guilty to hypocrisy and any other charge you cared to bring against me. There would be something terribly wrong with me!"

"Or with your principles," she added.

"You are sharp!" he grinned. "In my life, I don't think I would have admitted that possibility; but now, when everything is at stake for all of us, I can see the obligation to do so. So, here goes. In my own terms, you are saying that I used the end, which was laudable, to justify the means; that I influenced people to do things, or not do things, not because of their moral estimate of the behavior in question, but out of their affection for me. Is that the gist of your argument?"

She nodded solemnly.

"And you wish me to mount a defense?" he asked.

"If a defense is possible," she replied.

"Very well," he assented, "this court is now convened. Let me begin by warning you, ladies and gentlemen of the jury"—he bowed to Ariana—"that my defense, while simple in and of itself, requires a somewhat complex presentation in order to be effective; so you will please take care to follow in its intricacies."

He arose, and began pacing about like a lawyer. She imagined this was a bit of heavenly theatrics because, as far as she knew, as a young lawyer on Earth, he had been shy and stiff in court.

"First of all," he resumed, "the prosecution's case fallaciously assumes that an action with conditions attached is ipso facto manipulative. In other words, because I fasted in order to accomplish something that presumably had nothing to do with fasting, I violated my own most fundamental principle that the end is inherent in the means. This assumption is plainly erroneous. If I approach my employer and inform him that I will do no more work until he pays the month's back wages he owes me, I am not blackmailing or manipulating him, even if I am presenting an ultimatum. I am merely holding him to the terms of my employment. To fail to do so would be to cooperate with his manipulation of me."

"Alright," Ariana agreed, "but that only proves you might be innocent. It doesn't prove you are."

"Reasonable doubt isn't enough to acquit here?" he smiled. "It doesn't matter. I'm only just beginning. Let us consider an analogy. It may appear sexist at first, but, I assure you, it's not, so please bear with me. Suppose a woman says to her husband that, unless he buys her that diamond bracelet she so desires, she won't make love with him anymore. Is that manipulation?"

"As a woman, I might be tempted to say no," she smiled; "but yes, it clearly and unequivocally is manipulation."

"Take a second case," he continued. "Suppose a man has had a stroke or heart attack, and the doctors have warned him against caffeine, yet he won't give up his coffee. If his wife says she won't sleep with him unless he does, is that manipulation?"

"On my terms or yours?" Ariana asked.

"Since this is an enquiry into an alleged incongruity between my behavior and my understanding, my terms alone are directly relevant."

"Well then, on your terms, I would say it again is clearly manipulation. She would be doing it for his good, but she would also be blackmailing him with the threat of withdrawing her affection."

"Finally," he said with only the merest nod of acknowledgment, evidently considering the second example as self-evident as the first, "let's look at a third case. Suppose a woman, after trying pleas, arguments and tears, says to her husband, 'I will not make love with you until you stop beating and abusing our child.' Is that manipulation?"

"Yes," she replied without hesitation. "It's for a good cause, but, on your terms, it's manipulation."

"I don't think so," he said unexpectedly.

"What do you mean?" she exclaimed. "How can it not be? In this means-end business, what makes it different from the rest?"

"It depends," he answered. "If one thinks of sex as candy, and of the woman as withholding a pleasurable reward, then one would see it as manipulation." He paused.

"Or?" she prodded.

"If one sees making love as an expression and consummation of love," he went on, "then isn't the woman saying to her husband, 'How can you love me, if you do not love the fruit of our union?' In other words, in the situation in question, love-making would be a lie and, in effect, cooperation with the husband's abuse of the child. In refusing sex, the woman would not be manipulating her spouse, but simply making visible and living according to the truth of the situation."

Ariana pondered. She saw what he meant, but she could not see how it applied to his fasting.

"In order to demonstrate that the analogy is precise in all ethically relevant points," he resumed, as if reading her mind, "I must show that my fasting falls neither into the first category of selfish manipulation, nor the second of manipulation for another's good, but into the third category, that of action out of moral necessity. In this regard, it is instructive to examine the cases in which I fasted, but even more instructive to look at the cases in which I did not."

"I don't understand," said Ariana, feeling as if he had said that to know blue you must look at what is not blue, a plainly endless task whose completion, were it effected, would still yield no recognition of blue.

"I fasted to stop my campaign when it turned violent, against untouchability, and to end the communal violence between Hindus and Muslims," he explained— "all causes close to my heart. Why, then, did I not fast against the partition of India? It broke my heart to see Hindus and Muslims go what they so foolishly thought could be their separate ways. I believed it entirely the wrong move, and one that would cause incalculable misery and hardship to all concerned. To me, it was the vivisection of my beloved mother India. Why didn't I fast then?"

Somewhere she had heard of a reason, but hesitated to offer it. However, since it looked as if he would not continue until she answered him, and since nothing else came to mind, she finally opened her mouth. "It wouldn't have worked."

Gandhi's eyes softened in pain. "So, you think I fasted only when I calculated the odds were in my favor?" he said softly, not defensively.

"There's that possibility," she asserted.

"And as a good prosecutor," he brightened, "you're using every trick in the book. Well, then, let's consider that possibility. Let's suppose that I only fasted when I knew I could win."

Ariana turned away, not at all enjoying this exploration of his motives, no matter what the spiritual necessity for doing so. "All eyewitnesses and students of the period agree," she said, "that nothing, not even a mahatma starving himself to death, could have stopped the partition of India. At a certain point in time, Hindu India and Muslim Pakistan became historical inevitabilities even you could not prevent."

"You mean the rest of India would not have followed me in maintaining unity no matter what I did?" he asked.

"Yes," she answered.

"I agree," he said.

She slowly returned her gaze to his beautifully ugly face. "You do?"

"My dear Ariana," he said with the twinkle returning to his eye, "when so many scholars and experts say nay, who am I to say yea?"

"Well then, you see my point!" she declared.

"Yes," he rejoined, "but I'm not sure you see mine."

"I didn't know you had a point," she said curtly, wondering why she could get him to agree on everything she said and still feel as if she had lost.

"Just one," he replied. "If my countrymen would not have followed me when I fasted against partition, then, when they did follow me, it could not have been solely out of affection."

"I don't quite see . . ."

"If they stopped the satyagraha campaign in the 'twenties, opened the temples to untouchables in the 'thirties, and ended the communal violence in Calcutta in the 'forties solely because I manipulated them through their devotion to me, then I could have gotten them to remain united against partition. I could have gotten them to do anything. Since all agree that clearly was not the case, they must have followed me in my fasts for other reasons. Something else must have been at work there."

"I understand what you're saying," she admitted, "but what could it have been?"

"Conscience, perhaps?" he suggested with a hint of irony. "The issues over which I fasted had one thing in common—they were morally clear-cut. Partition was not. I was the first to admit that individuals could have supported partition on moral grounds, feeling that it was the lesser of two evils. On the other hand, one cannot dehumanize or murder innocent people in good conscience. When one does that sort of thing, one leaves one's conscience at home. As for the campaign of noncooperation, I started it, and it was my responsibility to see that it stayed peaceful or end it. These were not cases of disagreement over the right course of action, but of people doing what they themselves, when they finally consulted their consciences, would realize was wrong."

"But, on your own terms," Ariana persisted, "did that give you the right to present an ultimatum?"

"Not a right!" he declared. "A duty! Like the woman in my third case, wasn't I saying to my countrymen, 'You call me bapu, father, but can you really mean it when you are senselessly slaughtering your own brothers and sisters?' I had tried every other avenue of communication, and they still thought they could continue to indulge their anger and bigotry while maintaining their relationship with me. Fasting unto death was the only way I could make clear to them the truth of the situation while giving them an opportunity to change."

"So, you called them to their own consciences?" she asked.

"Yes," he said, "and if conscience told them otherwise, they did not follow me, as was the case in partition."

Ariana allowed silence to fall between them. All the while they had been talking, the scene had been subtly changing. At some point, she could not have said when, the birds stopped singing. The sun had withdrawn behind a hazy cloud, and looked as if it were in danger of being snuffed out like a candle flame. And now, low but unmistakable, began the rumbling of what Ariana at first took to be the storm returning. The sound, however, was not right, both too regular and too staccato in another of what by now were to her those familiar conjunctions of opposites.

"One thing still bothers me," she finally said to a pensive Gandhi, who had withdrawn to a corner as if to await the judge's verdict. "What about the violence to your own body?"

"The body is a tool," he said, without looking at her. "It is an instrument for the communication of love. In India, fasting is a time-honored form of communication between a holy man and his disciples."

"Are you a holy man?" she teased.

She heard the smile in his reply. "If people cast me as one, I've got to speak to them in a language they will understand."

With a jolt, Ariana remembered what the Teacher had said about God meeting us on our own terms. She also remembered a scene from a movie about Gandhi in which the Mahatma, on his bed of fasting, had been confronted by a Hindu rioter who wanted him to eat because he was going to hell, but not with Gandhi's death on his soul. Gandhi replied that only God knows who is going to hell, and asked him what he had done. The man had killed a Muslim boy because the Muslims had killed his own son. Gandhi told him he knew a way out of that hell. He should find a boy whose parents had been killed in the violence and adopt him as his own. Up to this point, Ariana remembered thinking, Gandhi's advice was on a par with that of any psychologist or social worker: fill up the void, overcome your suffering by serving another. But then Gandhi slipped in the knife. He told the man to make sure the boy was a Muslim. Then Gandhi twisted the knife. He was to raise him as a Muslim. Here was no sentimentality, no trace of psychological pandering. Gandhi had told the literal truth, that was all. There was no other way out of that hell. Truly, the voice of God! Was it any wonder that many Hindus believed him to be, like Krishna, an incarnation of Vishnu?

"Oh, by the way," she said, as Gandhi sat himself down again and looked charmingly into her eyes, "What did you say to those missionaries?"

"I pleaded guilty!" he proclaimed. "I was exercising coercion, the same coercion Christ exercised from the cross!"

3. Hitler

As Ariana returned his gaze, she found herself wishing that life really could be that way, requiring nothing but faith, love, and courage. "It isn't that simple," she said at length. "There's good, but then there is also evil. There's you, but then there is also Hitler. It's interesting that you were contemporaries."

"Yes," he replied, "and we had a lot in common. We both recognized the political importance of the masses, and in that way brought our respective countries into the twentieth century. We both had a tremendous, even charismatic influence over the masses. We both held irregular power achieved through irregular channels. We both were of nondescript origin and stock. There was only one real difference, but that difference was everything—I chose the path of nonviolence, and Hitler the path of violence."

"That's what I mean!" Ariana broke in almost before he had finished. "If they were just paths, so that one could take one and leave the other behind, then what you teach would be fine. But they aren't. Evil and good exist in the world together. If good sits back and refuses to fight, then evil wins."

"I have never denied the necessity of fighting evil!" said Gandhi, his eyes flashing.

"I know, I know, but I can't help thinking you might as well have. You yourself said that satyagraha appeals to the conscience. What if someone doesn't have a conscience? You speak to a person's sense of right and wrong. What if someone doesn't care about right and wrong, like Hitler? Against a Hitler, fighting nonviolently strikes me as not fighting at all."

"Many people said the same in my own lifetime," he mused as if he were reminiscing.

"Yes, and you said they were wrong," she said. "Do you still think that?"

"I do!" he affirmed.

"What about your own example of the mass-murderer?" she challenged. "You said you would not have left that room; but if you wouldn't try to stop him, what good would staying do?"

"You assume the only way to stop a madman is through violence," he said, "and in the situation of the lone madman, you may be right. Perhaps it's like the monkeys ravaging the crops. On the other hand, Hitler was a madman at the helm of a populous and mighty nation. Stopping him with violence meant the loss of millions of innocent lives. I am not saying that in itself invalidates the use of violence, because stopping him with nonviolence would have cost millions of lives as well."

Ariana leaned passionately forward. "And I'm saying all the innocent people would have been lost, because nonviolence would not have stopped him at all!"

"Perhaps you are right," he said, not flinching one whit in the face of her onslaught. "There is no way of knowing with certainty. There is one thing, however, of which I am certain—nonviolence wasn't really tried. Certainly there was moral opposition to Hitler's regime in Germany in the 1930's, but for the most part it confined itself to normal political channels, no matter how inadequate those proved themselves to be. And, when those channels failed entirely, it became purely academic, a few professors declaring Hitler immoral but calling for no real resistance, and by that I mean not even demonstrating philosophically how the call of common human decency was higher than any political allegiance or loyalty oath. The most such resistance accomplished was to create a psychological split between abstract duty to humanity and concrete obligation to Hitler. It even bestowed a measure of tragic greatness upon those who embraced this split, giving to Hitler what they conceived to be his due—their wills, and to God what they conceived to be God's—their hearts. The only opposition to Hitler genuinely active in its stance was that of the Bolsheviks; but, as they were every bit as ruthless as the Nazis, there was nothing to choose between the two parties morally. Moreover, everyone knew they took orders from Moscow, whereas the Nazis had the virtue of being thoroughly German."

"You sound as if you've made a complete study of Nazi Germany," she remarked, feeling that she should have known better than to think she could have had more detailed knowledge of this issue than he.

"The Hitler era is one of the great test cases in human history," he said. "Anyone who wishes to fight evil in the world must take it into account. Don't take me at my word, however, for I represent a special interest group." He smiled. "See for yourself."

Before she had time to ask what he meant, a change came over everything unlike any she had experienced before. In a way, it resembled her condition at the end of her encounter with Ishwara. She had then felt on terms of spiritual intimacy with every aspect of being; but, compared to the present connection, that one had been vague and abstract. Now there was neither ecstasy nor banality, only reality. She felt a powerful integrity and a certain peace, but no bliss, joy, or light. It suddenly occurred to her that if God's mind had memory banks, a particularly depressing tape was being replayed for her now.

The panorama of Nazi Germany and the world in which it played out its brief and catastrophic part was laid out in her mind, and she had to choose the scenes upon which to focus. At first, she flitted back and forth, hither and yon, feeling her way through the anger, hysteria, fear, and confusion.

She was attracted to the infrequent points of shining light, an especially radiant one, she knew, being Gandhi in India. She realized, however, that she had spent much time in the light, and now had to go into the darkness. Nevertheless, she did not feel up to facing the inferno of the Holocaust itself without first acclimating her soul.

She ended up in what looked to be a combination headquarters and private study. He was there, as she knew he would be, with the clipped little moustache that both he and Charlie Chaplin had made so famous. He was pacing back and forth, as she also had imagined him, nervously awaiting the outcome of Germany's bid to reclaim the Ruhr, an industrial area in the westernmost part of Germany that France had occupied after the First World War. French troops had eventually withdrawn; but they had left behind a puppet government, and ordered Germany to forget any hope of rejoining this linchpin of the German economy to the rest of the defeated Reich any time soon. Now Hitler, in ignoring those orders, was risking the wrath of the victorious Allies. As he waited, he talked to his aides, and they pretended to be interested. Ariana, however, listened intently, and she wondered if God did so as well. If other people ignored us, did God make up for it by giving special heed? If so, what Hitler said would then have been a weird and demonic prayer.

In a jerky, desultory manner, Hitler talked about how the world was now being put to the test, and how he was the test. He was only one man, but now he had taken upon himself the persona of absolute and unconquerable evil. He was a magician who seized what he wanted through sleight of hand. He yearned for someone, any-one, his best friend or worst enemy, to see through his game, because only then would anyone appreciate his artistry. Everyone thought he succeeded simply by brute force. No one realized that this idea, "brute force," was itself a sophisticated psychological construct that derived its reality from the credence human beings invested in it.

He pointed to the invasion of the Ruhr as a prime example. Certainly, he had sent in several panzer brigades—an overwhelming display of force!

At this point, one of the staff officers, no doubt thinking Hitler might take it amiss if no one showed a more active interest in the utterly one-sided conversation, asked der Fuehrer if he did not mean to say a display of overwhelming force. As if he had been waiting for such a cue, Hitler exploded into a tirade against the folly, not only of the officer in question, but all so-called military experts who thought them-selves wise. He meant precisely what he said. It was the display that was over-whelming, not the force. That was the whole point. What force did Germany have at the moment after it had been bled white and pillaged by its enemies? His will and his will alone propped up the Third Reich! But he was just one man. If his enemies saw through the magic show before German industry was fully yoked to the war effort, the faintest breath of resolute resistance, whether from within or without, would knock down his administration like a house of cards. And they could be sure that, in the event of his fall, he would take the generals and their hangers-on with him.

No one dared mention that Germany was not at that moment at war.

Now Ariana had direction. She knew from what Gandhi had said, as well as her own historical studies, that no real opposition to Hitler had materialized. Neverthe-less, she would find those points of light that indicated some sort of spiritual striv-ing against the rising terror, so as to gauge the possible effect a genuine satyagraha campaign might have had.

She chose Denmark in the middle phase of the Second World War. A tiny penin-sular country jutting into the North Sea from the northern coast of Germany, it was easily overrun by the Third Reich's military machine. As had happened in Germany and Poland, and as was to happen in every country the Germans occupied, the

Gestapo, the Nazi secret police, eventually set about rounding up the Jews. The first step was to set them apart from the general population by commanding them to wear the yellow Star of David (the symbol, ironically, of the dynamic balance and harmony of the cosmos) in a visible place on their clothing. The day after this general order went out, the King of Denmark, who was a Christian monarch in a predominantly Christian country, appeared in public wearing the Star of David, along with his family, servants, guards, retainers—indeed, his entire household! All the Danes followed suit, and this sowed so much confusion among the Nazis that most of the Danish Jews were able to escape across the straits to neutral Sweden. They were the only Jewish community in Nazi-occupied Europe to escape destruction.

Next, Ariana was attracted to a light in Germany itself. She found herself at Dachau concentration camp near Munich, in the south. A band of prisoners were refusing to strike fellow prisoners, even though they were beaten instead. Ariana focused on this group for quite some time, and found that they pooled their rations, giving most to those who were weakest, sometimes even helping outsiders. They said prayers, Christian prayers, even if the SS guards beat them and denied them food for doing so. Then she realized with a shock that they were Jehovah's Witnesses! They were those same people who, she had heard from the earthbound, came ringing people's doorbells early on weekend mornings, peddling their own off-beat brand of Christianity. Now she understood why they were there, and why all of them were young men. The Witnesses refused military service to any nation, because they considered themselves citizens in God's kingdom. Evidently, they were managing to maintain that citizenship in face of the Nazis' brutal methods for reducing a human being to an isolated bundle of drives and fears.

As Ariana pondered these two sides of the sect, the fanatical and the heroic, the camp commandant read aloud a general order from der Fuehrer himself giving the Jehovah's Witnesses special privileges within the camps. Ariana could not believe her ears. She had to see for herself. This overwhelming curiosity carried her straight back into Hitler's presence.

He was less expansive now, huddling in an underground bunker with a less impressive audience of flunkies and hangers-on. Nevertheless, he talked as he had always talked, with the implicit assumption that everything he said was of utmost interest to everyone. Courage was the topic of the day, something about which he, with his Iron Cross, claimed to know a great deal. There was nothing he admired more than courage, and nothing he feared more, either. Take Churchill, for example. Churchill alone stood in the way of Germany's destiny—one man, but one man of courage. Take the passive resistance in Denmark, for example. Yes, the king of Denmark had been ideologically misguided, but he had also been brave, and so had his countrymen. They had no way of knowing that the Germans were in no position to risk a disturbance in Denmark, through which ran the supply-line to Norway, whose naval bases were essential to the U-boat campaign against Allied shipping in the North Atlantic. Indeed, if there had been more such brave men in Europe, Hitler's accomplishments would not have been possible. That was why he feared courage, because it alone could defeat him. That was why he admired those damned Jehovah's Witnesses. When it comes to honor, one must give even the devil his due!

Hitler pointed to his greatest work, the annihilation of the Jewish population, as a case in point. Besides being an irreversible victory for the Aryan race, it was a massive logistical feat. To move millions of people across Europe to the remote regions of Poland, exterminate them, and dispose of their bodies was no easy thing. Some of his aides had asked him why bother to move the victims, why not simply dispose of them, so to speak, in the comfort of their own homes. For two reasons, he explained, such an approach was impossible. One, it was essential that the Jews cooperate in their own annihilation. Two, it was desirable to upset the German people as little as possible. In other words, even though he had written about the final solution in his masterpiece, *Mein Kampf* (*My Struggle*) nearly two decades ago, all parties concerned had to have some way of maintaining the self-delusion that that was all blustering and propaganda. His enemies, Jewish and non-Jewish alike, were civilized men, and therefore possessed of the besetting weakness of civilization, reason. They thought that everyone acted as they themselves did, out of self-interest, and they could not see any self-interest in Hitler actually massacring the Jews. As his own generals periodically pointed out, it tied up valuable military resources, such as railroads and troops. What they were either too stupid or gutless to say was that the greatest of these wasted resources were the Jews themselves, a clever and highly educated people who could have provided technically skilled services if kept under lock and key. Keep the devil under lock and key! All these fools, however, didn't understand that one's idea of self-interest depended upon one's idea of self. Hitler's self was the will, and he would have his way over those who preached and worked for the corruption of the will, the civilized half-men of Europe, or go down fighting!

By this point, Hitler's audience was asleep. As before, however, Ariana's unseen but whole-hearted attention sparked the flame of self-disclosure. There was only one other man in the world who knew what the spirit was all about—not even Churchill understood—and he had just gotten a letter from that man. In that letter, the Mahatma of India had asked him to reconsider whither he was leading his country, and to reexamine his policy of violence. No doubt the British, ever jealous of their imperial wisdom and might, were saying to themselves that Gandhi had no appreciation of the full dimensions of Hitler's wickedness, but the letter itself proved that he alone did. This man alone saw that Hitler was doing what he was doing out of choice, and so it was logical to appeal to his will. Hitler could not be swayed by such an appeal, but he was moved by the man who made it—moved to loathing and contempt as much as admiration and respect, but moved. He moved everyone and everything else. Courage alone moved him. This man had shown the ultimate courage of looking into his own soul and there seeing the possibility of perfect love and absolute ruthlessness. As realities, Christ and Caesar were mutually exclusive; but, as possibilities, they went hand-in-hand.

Take the sheep, the Allies, for example. Certainly, a few fought back in the spirit of a Churchill, but even he was unable to touch that deep core of common humanity which the will eternally denies, and so eternally respects, and therefore which alone can defeat the will. They had courage of a sort, but Hitler himself was too big to be touched by this moral equivalent of children's daring. Only full recognition of the spiritual root of Hitler's power would enable them to defeat him, because only then would they be able to uproot him from their own souls. As it was, no matter what happened henceforth, he had won, because the ideal of the will, power, had taken possession of their souls. The Mahatma played nice music, but Hitler's was the tune to which everyone danced.

Ariana now was carried on, as if by the irresistible logic of her experience, to Dresden in the last months of the war. Located in eastern Germany, Dresden was one of the most beautiful cities of Europe. It had preserved much of its medieval architecture, including the original city walls, and was filled with art treasures, museums, and magnificent churches. The German High Command, whether in defiance of or accordance with a Hitler now cut off in Berlin Ariana could not tell, had declared Dresden an open city, which meant that it would offer no resistance to the Allies. Moreover, there was nothing in Dresden of military value. Allied POW's were the only direct reminder of the war, and they were kept beneath the earth in warehouses designed for the storage of meat in natural refrigeration. Nevertheless, the Allies—the "good" Allies, the British and Americans, not the "bad" Allies, the Russians—decided to fire-bomb Dresden. The British took the initiative, but the American chief of the Allied Expeditionary Force, Eisenhower, had to give the go-ahead.

As Ariana discovered, in fire-bombing a city one drops incendiary bombs, which are of little use against a fortified military position, but can wreak havoc upon civilian targets. One begins on the outskirts, for two reasons. One, in the suburbs one finds the most combustible materials, the wooden dwellings. Two, by creating a ring of fire around the city, one creates a vacuum in the city's center that sucks in the flames, generating heat of such intensity that it melts steel and concrete, thereby rendering conventional bomb-shelters useless. Had she not seen it with her own eyes, Ariana could never have imagined what such heat could do to the human body. More people died at Dresden than Hiroshima, at the very least, and perhaps even Hiroshima and Nagasaki put together. And, to Ariana's anguish, they were mostly old men, women, and children, because any male who could carry a gun was off fighting in the war. Among the few survivors were the Allied POW's, luckily held deep beneath the earth. Ariana kept asking herself the reason for this atrocity, kept telling herself that the Allies were on the side of goodness and light, and that Hitler could not be right. Was this all only vengeance for the fire-bombing of London and the rocket attacks upon Coventry, as Hitler's war was vengeance for Germany's defeat in World War I? Had the souls of his enemies really become possessed by Hitler?

As if in answer to her question, Ariana found herself in a large conference room which at the moment was occupied by only a few men. She knew immediately that they were the president of the United States and his closest military, political, and scientific advisors. Two days before an American plane had dropped an atomic bomb upon Hiroshima. Now the president had to decide whether or not to give the go-ahead to a similar mission against Nagasaki. It was August 8, 1945.

One of the naval advisors was explaining that Japanese kamikaze attacks had all but ceased, and that the enemy had been unnaturally quiet since the Hiroshima bombing. Another naval man—from the quantity of gold leaf on his uniform, probably an admiral—insisted that it all might be just a trick, and that it was not at all unusual to have a calm before a storm. A civilian advisor, probably a member of the cabinet, insisted that the Japanese were finished, and that the American government had reliable information that token of unconditional surrender was only days if not hours away.

Suddenly, an elegant-looking man motioned as if he were about to speak, and everyone fell silent. The problem was not with the Japanese, he insisted; it was with the Russians. As they all knew, that very day the Soviets had declared war on Japan and were in the process of overrunning Manchuria. Nobody cared if the Russians took that godforsaken wilderness, even if it was loaded with natural resources. After all, they had owned it way back before they became the first Western power to suffer defeat by Japan in 1905. Let them have it back. China, however, was another story. The civil war between Chiang Kai-Shek's Nationalists and Mao Zedong's

Communists, which had been put on the back burner during the struggle for survival against Japan, was heating up again; and Russia would like nothing more than to see China go red. It was necessary to send the Soviets a message.

Now the president spoke. He wondered if Hiroshima had not been enough of a message. The elegant gentleman replied that the Russians might think it a one-shot affair in order to save the hundreds of thousands of American and millions of Japanese lives that undoubtedly would be lost in a conventional military assault upon the Japanese mainland. They knew as well as the Americans that Japan was ready to surrender. The bomb, therefore, would say to them, in the least ambiguous terms, that the United States was willing to use such a terrible weapon to support its interests in Asia, Europe, and anywhere else the Communists chose to pursue a policy of aggression. Such a message would be the single most potent catalyst of peace in the post-war world.

In support of this position, one of the scientific advisors, who evidently had played an important role in the development of nuclear explosives, spoke next. He said that there were compelling scientific as well as political reasons for dropping another bomb on Nagasaki. First of all, from a purely methodological point of view, the bombing of Hiroshima was the first test of an atomic device upon an urban population. In science, one experiment did not count. One had to demonstrate repeatability. Moreover, the weapon to be used on Nagasaki would be of somewhat different design than the Hiroshima bomb and, at this nascent stage of atomic research, it was imperative to strike out in the right direction. Comparative data was absolutely essential, and who knew when the opportunity would arise again in the post-war world?

The president thanked his advisors and told them that, for security reasons, his final decision would not be known to them until after the fact. They laughed, as this was the chief's customary way of telling them he was going ahead with a projected course of action.

Ariana was frozen in disbelief, and then disbelief turned to fear. The fact that America, the champion of human rights and freedom, had actually dropped the bomb on Nagasaki was not half so frightening as her realization that many Americans, had they been privy to the secret session, would have found a great deal of reason in the arguments presented, as had the president himself. She remembered what Gandhi had said—textbooks can make anything sound rational. Now she knew why. Textbooks were written by experts, and experts turned reason into a style, a format. As long as something was tailored to the format, no matter how monstrous it might be in substance, it was "rational."

Ariana again wandered through a stormy night. She longed for Gandhi's ashram, but it was nowhere to be found. She wanted to tell the Mahatma that she understood his lessons, but wondered if she would ever see him again. She thought of the history of the world since 1945, and it did not offer much hope. She knew that some earthbound spirits pointed to the nearly half-century of an absence of global conflict as a vindication of the policy of nuclear deterrence. Suppose they were right, suppose things would have been even worse than Korea, Vietnam, and all the other "little" wars that had plagued the world in the interim, without nuclear umbrellas and the threat of massive retaliation. Now that atomic weapons were coming into the hands of one nation after another, now that the balance of nuclear terror favored destabilization, now that nuclear war could break out from any quarter of the globe, what would ensure the peace in its place?

Ariana was now certain of two things—only the heart sees clearly, and one tends to become the means one uses. If one does feel it necessary to use violence—and she was not, like Gandhi, prepared to rule out that possibility altogether—one should do so in fear and trembling, with full awareness that one is inflicting suffering and death upon real human beings. One should not go to war with bands playing and banners flying. Someone, she could not remember who, had once said that the most reluctant politicians make the best statesmen. She was also certain, after meeting Gandhi, that the most reluctant fighters made the best warriors. Once one dehumanized one's enemy in one's own mind, one had dehumanized oneself, and the real enemy had already won. Suddenly, she fell to her knees in the middle of the blackness and, tears in her eyes, thanked the Mahatma for helping her to see.

4. The Fire

As soon as she uttered that prayer, Ariana found herself back among the children whose game of tag she had left what seemed like an eternity ago. They all came up and laid healing hands upon her, the look of concern in their faces telling her, more than words ever could, how deeply her experience had brought change to them all.

She drank in their life-renewing energies with gratitude and joy; and they, for their part, gave in the same spirit, because to do so made her adventure their own. When she felt strong enough to stand, she looked up and saw the Teacher, as she knew she would. The children did not seem afraid, but still they backed away, as if his business necessarily took precedence over their own.

"I already am in embodiment, aren't I?" she said cheerily, for the first time able to face this fact without overwhelming fear. "I'm already earthbound!"

"You are in embodiment," he replied evenly, "but you are not earthbound. You are, however, split between heaven and earth. Soon the two will be joined again."

She smiled, and what she saw in his face in reaction to that smile made her realize that he truly loved her, and everything he had put her through was the working of that love. "That's the real marriage, isn't it?" she asked.

"Utter confusion reigns in the heavens," he declared, "and total chaos on earth. Ours has been a little exercise in allaying that confusion. Only if you bring the spirit of love you have discovered in your heart into the reality of the world is there any hope of stemming the chaos."

"Am I that important?" she asked skeptically.

"If you let yourself be," he replied cryptically, causing her to feel that she was starting all over again.

"I don't understand," she said wearily. "I guess I'll never understand anything!"

"Was Hitler important?" he exclaimed. "Was Gandhi?"

"Of course they were!" she declared, feeling as if he were treating her like a little child. "In different ways, of course. Gandhi was important for good, and Hitler for evil."

"Why were they important?" he demanded.

"Why?" she echoed. "Well . . . Because they were!"

"What was Hitler before taking over the National Socialist Party?" he queried.

"I don't know," she said. "From what I've heard, not much of anything."

"Before the First World War," informed the Teacher, "he was a failed artist and architect, living off a pension derived from his father's civil service. During that war, though he did win the Iron Cross, Germany's highest decoration for military valor, he did not rise above the rank of corporal. He didn't want the responsibility of command! And what was the National Socialist Party before Hitler joined it?"

She thought back to her studies, and then realized she was connecting with her earth-self! "Not much more than a tiny, albeit politically ambitious, social club," she answered.

"And what was Gandhi before he found his cause in South Africa?" the Teacher continued.

"A neurotic middle-class Indian lawyer," she replied, "too shy to speak in court!"

"That's one lesson Gandhi and Hitler teach us," he asserted: "the power one human being can have, for good or for evil! World war did not end in 1945, just as it did not begin in 1914. The world has been at war, spiritual war, since the dawn of history. Most people feel helpless in the face of this conflict. They think they must be someone important, like a political leader, artist, general, king, celebrity . . ."

"Or a Gandhi or Hitler?" Ariana broke in.

"Yes," agreed the Teacher, smiling for the first time since his arrival, "or a Gandhi or Hitler! People think they have to be important to have an effect in this struggle, but they never ask how one becomes important in the first place. People feel helpless only because they are fence-sitting. If they joined in the fray, they might very well go through tremendous suffering, but they would not feel helpless!"

"They're caught in the middle, aren't they?" she suggested.

His eyes asked her to explain herself.

"They don't want to face the Hitler in themselves, because they can't bear the truth that they themselves could be like him," she said. "So in their imaginations they turn him into a subhuman monster, totally unlike anyone else who's ever lived. And they do the same with Gandhi. They turn Gandhi into a superhuman saint, again totally unlike anyone else who has ever lived, because they don't want to face the Gandhi in themselves. If they did, they would have to face the possibility that they too could live in the courage, truth and love of a Gandhi, which means they could also suffer as he did!"

"And putting the two together?" he encouraged.

"They don't want to face the lesson Gandhi and Hitler together teach us, at all!" she proclaimed, learning from her own words. "The German people were perhaps the most civilized in the world, but they became accomplices in the worst mass murder the world has ever known! There is no middle ground. If we do not live in the spirit of a Gandhi, we become, at the very least, tools of the Hitlers of this world!"

"Yes," affirmed the Teacher, "it is our choice!"

Ariana pondered. "But," she said at length, "where is God, then, in all of this?"

"Nothing works mechanically or according to plan," he replied. "Love offers itself at every moment. The question is whether or not one opens to receive it."

"And the various religions?" she inquired, wondering if her "adventures" had all been for nothing.

"So many paths to the field of battle," he said. "Of course, every road *toward* is also a road *from*. Religion can be challenge or excuse, struggle or hiding place, life or oblivion. It is up to you."

"But I feel they mean more than that!" she objected.

His eyes narrowed. "I don't think you appreciate how much that is. Religion is the dimension of absolutes, for better or worse. It is where we decide what we count as real, and what we hold to be of ultimate worth. The East absolutizes the transpersonal depth of existence, whereas the West absolutizes personal immediacy. That is why Easterners often strike Westerners as inscrutable, distant, and inaccessible; whereas Westerners strike Easterners as petty, egotistical, wrapped up in their own little self-imaging world. Personality without depth becomes trivial. Depth without personality is monolithic and ultimately dead. The battle is right there, bringing the two together. Is that enough for you?"

"But that's so abstract!" she protested.

The Teacher looked down, evidently thinking, and then raised his eyes to hers once again. "You've had much experience with personal intimacy by now," he began.

"Of a virtual sort," she qualified, smiling in mild embarrassment.

"Weren't there basically two types?" he continued, ignoring her discomfort.

"I'm not sure what you mean," she answered.

"Wasn't there the relationship where you and your mate felt yourselves melt into each other in ecstatic unity, and even identity, of being?" he clarified.

"Oh, yes!" she confirmed, overcoming her initial reluctance to discuss this topic now that she could see where he was heading. "And there was the other type where my lover was more of a partner, and we remained distinct and separate selves in relationship."

"So," he reiterated, "personal intimacy is of two types?"

"Oh, no," she replied, "you need both. It's just that any given couple tends to emphasize one side over the other. You need the feeling of ecstatic unity, or there would be no intimacy. You need the sense of your own selfhood, or there would be no relationship."

"And you need both the transcendent spiritual depth and the immanent personal breadth," he declared, "or there is no life!"

Again she smiled. "Thank you."

"For what?" he asked.

"For not telling me everything, but pointing out where to begin."

"There's one other thing," he smiled in return. "We have focused on the heavenly realm, the sphere of absolute values. As heaven draws nearer to earth, as you draw nearer to your embodied self, the values of heaven will have to be integrated with the reality of the Earth. In this matter the aboriginal peoples of the world will be your guide. Always remember, the way of life is what unites us all, not in totalitarian order, but in egalitarian love."

"I will remember," she said uncertainly, but with faith that she would understand when the issue arose. "Is it time to go?"

"There will be no going or coming," he replied. "It will happen as naturally as the rain falls from the sky. But it won't be rain. It will be fire. For a season, you may laugh and play, as has been your custom. When you feel the intensity rise, you will know the day of the wedding feast is at hand."

She bowed deeply and, when she looked up, he was gone. The children gathered round, and she recounted all her adventures, leaving out not the smallest detail, lest one of her friends find it useful someday in his or her own quest.

Ariana continued to roam and frolic, though she found herself spending more time than ever working with the earthbound spirits. They seemed more congenial than before, because they were so close to the reality whose reflection had been so joyous and terrifying, so hopeful and foreboding, and, above all, so illuminating for her. For their part, they treated her with more respect than they did the angels, because her wisdom seemed to come from an at-once familiar and unfathomable depth.

Ariana summed up her wisdom in one simple teaching. It was not possible to prepare for the fire. If it were, it would not be the fire. However, it was possible to become the fire. Ariana challenged herself, and thereby everyone she encountered, to open bravely to the rapidly changing and unpredictable situation from the depths of the divine love in their own hearts. Uniting with that spirit of love was their only hope of ever becoming at one with the reality of themselves and the possibilities of life.

GLOSSARY.

Abu Bakr (ca. 573–674) In Islam, one of Muhammad's most trusted followers and first kalif (632–634).

African Americans (Also known as American Negroes or Blacks) American descendants of Africans, most of whom were brought to the United States as slaves.

ahimsa Sanskrit for "non-harmfulness" or "nonviolence".

Albigensians (Also known as Cathari or Bogomiles.) Dualistic Christian sect in southern France condemned by the Inquisition and destroyed by Christian Crusaders in the 13th century.

Alexander the Great (356–323 B.C.E.) Macedonian conqueror.

'Ali ibn Abu Talib (?–661) Muhammad's cousin and son-in-law, fourth kalif (656–661), and first Shi'ite Imam.

Allah Arabic for God.

anatman Buddhist doctrine of "no-soul", "no-self".

Andrews, Charlie Anglican minister and friend and companion of Mohandas Ganghi.

Anselm of Canterbury (1033–1109) Christian theologian.

anti-Semitism Literally, hatred of any Semitic people, but especially of Jews.

apocryphal gospels Gospels never accepted into the Christian canon.

Apostolic Letters Part of the Christian Bible including letters from early Church leaders to various Christian congregations.

Armenian Church See **Monophysites**.

Ashkenazim Jews whose ancestors came from central and eastern Europe.

Atman (Sanskrit) In Hinduism, denotes soul, self, or essence.

Atonement Christian doctrine that Christ is savior of the world.

Augustine of Hippo, Saint (354–430) North African prelate and, after Paul, greatest of all Christian theologians.

autism Psychological disorder involving severe difficulty in social interaction.

auto da fe' (Portuguese for "act of faith") Term used in the Spanish and Portuguese Inquisitions for the public reading of the sentences of condemned heretics. It came to be associated in the popular mind with the burning of heretics at the stake.

ayatollah (Persian for "sign of God") Highest grade of clergy in Shi'ite Islam.

Bar-Kochba (?–135) Leader of second great Jewish revolt against Rome.

Bathsheba (10th c. B.C.E.) Wife of King David of Israel and mother of Solomon.

Being and Nothingness (In French, *L'etre et le ne'ant*) Jean-Paul Sartre's massive ontological work defining human consciousness as "nothingness."

Bhagavad-Gita ("Song of God") Sacred Hindu scripture.

Bhakti, Bhakti-Yoga Spiritual path of devotion.

bhikkhu (Pali for "mendicant") Theravadin Buddhist monk.

Black Muslims See **Nation of Islam**.

Black Plague 14th-century outbreak of bubonic plague that killed half the population of Europe.

bodhisattwa "One destined to enlightenment."

Boers The descendants of the original Dutch, French, and German settlers of South Africa. They fought an unsuccessful war for independence from Great Britain (1899–1902), but the peace was a compromise with the Boers retaining control of domestic affairs.

Bolsheviks (Russian coinage, "majority-ites") Hard-line faction of the Russian Communist Party that won out over the Mesheviks and led the October, 1917 revolution. Thenceforth the term became synonymous with Soviet Communists and their adherants in other countries.

Brahma ("creator") Hindu god who orders the phenomenal universe.

brahmacharya In Hinduism, the first or educational stage of life.

Brahman In Hinduism, denotes ultimate reality, absolute being, "God beyond the gods."

Brahmin The priestly caste of Hinduism.

Brothers Karamazov, The (In Russian, *Bratya Karamazovy*) Novel by Dostoevsky written in 1879–1880.

buddha ("enlightened" or "awakened" one) The founder of Buddhism. (See **Gotama Buddha**.)

Caiaphas (1st century) Roman-appointed high priest of Israel and head of Sanhedrin, 18–36.

Caliph See **Kalif**.

Canaan Ancient name for Palestine.

chakra (Sanskrit for "wheel") Spiritual center connecting the physical with the spiritual levels of being.

Ch'an Chinese name for Meditation School of Buddhism.

chandala Untouchable or outcaste.

Chaplin, Charlie (1889–1977) World-famous actor, film-maker and comedian born in England and active for much of his life in Hollywood. He caricatured Adolf Hitler in the 1940 film, *The Great Dictator*.

Chiang Kai-shek (1887–1975) Leader of the Chinese Nationalist Party and of all China from 1925 to 1949. Thenceforth ruler of Taiwan until his death.

Christ ("annointed one") Also see **Jesus of Nazareth**.

Churchill, Winston (1874–1965) Prime minister of England during World War II.

Communism International workers' movement founded by Karl Marx (1818–1883) and Friedrich Engels (1820–1895) that took totalitarianism form wherever it came to power, most notably in the Soviet Union (1917–1991).

Confucianism Traditional philosophy/religion of China focusing on social relations.

Confucius (551–479 B.C.E.) In Chinese, K'ung Fu-tse. Chinese philosopher and founder of Confucianism.

Constantine the Great (274–337) Roman emperor (312–337) and founder of Constantinople who legalized and patronized Christianity.

Constructive Program Private organization founded by Mohandas Gandhi to foster economic self-sufficiency and healthful living among Indian peasants.

conversos (Spanish for "converts") In Spain, name given to Jews who converted to Christianity.

Coptic Church See **Monophysites**.

Counter-Reformation Roman Catholic attempt, beginning in 16th century, to counteract the Protestant Reformation through internal reform and missionary work.

Cromwell, Oliver (1599–1658) Puritan general and Lord Protector of England.

Crusades Medieval Western Christendom's attempts to regain the Holy Land from the Muslim Turks.

Cyrus of Persia (?–529 B.C.E.) Cyrus II, known as "the Great", king of Persia who allowed the Jews to return to Palestine.

Dachau Nazi concentration camp in southern Germany.

Daoism (or Taoism) Indigenous religion of China focusing on nature.

Dar al-Islam (Arabic for "house of surrender") Islamic name for community of those who live in obedience to God.

David, King Second king of Israel, ca. 1010–970 B.C.E.

David, Star of See **Star of David**.

dharma "duty"

dhyana "Meditation" in Sanskrit.

diaspora Greek for "dispersion".

Diocletian (245–316) Roman emperor (284–305) who divided the empire administratively between East and West, and who was the last emperor to seriously persecute Christianity.

Dome of the Rock Golden-domed Islamic shrine completed in 691 on site of old Jewish Temple in Jerusalem, said to be where Muhammad touched down on his mystical night journey to Jerusalem.

Dostoevsky, Fyodor (1821–1881) Russian novelist.

Duryodhana In Hindu legend, Arjuna's evil cousin.

East India Company, British A company founded in India that held trading monopoly from 1600 to 1813, and that in effect ruled India from the late-1700's to 1858, when India became a British crown colony. It dissolved in 1873.

Eight-Fold Path Buddhist path to enlightenment.

ekklesia Greek term used by early Christians to denote the community of the faithful.

enantiodromia Greek term denoting the passing of one thing into its opposite, or the idea that extremes meet.

Enclosure Acts (ca. 1760–ca. 1820) In England, legislation by Parliament that gave land that had been held in common by peasants into private ownership, usually by the gentry.

Enlightenment, Age of Term used to denote the 18th century in Western Europe, dominated by rationalism and the rise of natural science.

existentialism Modern Western philosophical school emphasizing personal experience and responsibility.

Exodus (Greek for "going out") Second book of the Judaeo-Christian Bible.

fasts unto death Mohandas Gandhi's public, political and conditional fasts against violence and untouchability. He called them "his alternative to despair."

Ferdinand and Isabella Catholic rulers of Spain in late 15th and early 16th centuries.

Filioque Controversy (Latin for "and the son") Disagreement between Eastern Orthodox and Roman Catholic Christianity over the nature of the Holy Trinity.

five pillars In Islam, the paramount religious duties incumbent upon the individual believer.

Flower Sermon Buddha's silent preaching to which Zen traces its origin.

forest-dweller Hindu third stage of life.

Four Noble Truths Gotama Buddha's original teachings.

Francis of Assisi, Saint (1181–1226) Roman Catholic saint in Italy.

Freud, Sigmund (1856–1959) Austrian founder of psychoanalysis.

Gandhi, Mohandas (1869–1948) Known as mahatma, "great soul". India's apostle of nonviolence and leader to independence from Britain.

Gentiles (from Latin for "peoples") Non-Jews.

Gestapo (Acronym for Geheime Staatspolozei) Nazi Germany's dreaded secret police.

Gospel, gospels (from Greek evangelion, meaning "good news") Part of the Christian Bible that tells of the life and esp. public ministry of Jesus.

Gotama Buddha (ca. 6th c. B.C.E.) Founder of Buddhism.

Gotama, Gautama Clan or family name of Gotama Buddha.

Grand Inquisitor, The Story by Fyodor Dostoevsky, part of *The Brothers Karamazov*.

Great Death In Zen, a stage in the attainment of awakening.

Greater Vehicle Mahayana Buddhism.

grihastha (Sanskrit for "householder") Hindu second stage of life.

gunas ("strands") In Hinduism, the three primary constituents of the phenomenal universe.

guru (Sanskrit for "teacher") Hindu spiritual master.

Hadith In Islam, the record of Muhammad's own sayings and deeds, as opposed to God's revelation through him in the Qur'an.

hajj In Islam, the fifth of the five pillars, the greater pilgrimage to Mecca.

Hallaj, Mansur al (858–922) In Islam, Persian mystic and martyr.

harijan (Sanskrit for "child of God") Hindu name for an untouchable or outcaste.

Herod Antipas (?–39) Son of Herod the Great and tetrarch of Galilee responsible, according to the Christian gospels, for the execution of John the Baptist.

Herod the Great (73–4 B.C.E.) Puppet king of Judea under Rome, 40-4 B.C.E.

high-caste In Hinduism, member of Brahmin or Kshatriya caste.

Hinayana (Pali for "small raft" or "lesser vehicle") Derogatory term for Theravadin Buddhism.

Hitler, Adolf (1889–1945) Dictator of Nazi Germany.

Ho Chi-minh (1892–1969) One of the founders of the Vietnamese Communist Party (1918) and president of North Vietnam (1954–1969).

Holocaust (Hebrew for "burnt offering") The Nazi attempted genocide against the Jews during World War II.

Holy Spirit In Christianity, the third person of the Holy Trinity.

Holy Trinity The Christian doctrine that there are three persons in one God: the Father, Son, and Holy Spirit.

Husain (626–680) In Islam, younger son of 'Ali and Fatima, Muhammad's grandson, and third Shi'ite Imam.

Hussein, Saddam (1935–) Dictator of Iraq from 1969. He is a Sunni Muslim.

Imam (Arabic for "leader") In Islam, the leaders of the Shi'a believed to hold religious as well as political authority.

imam In Sunni Islam, the prayer leader in a mosque. In the Shi'a, a middle-grade cleric.

Incarnation Christian doctrine of divinity of Christ.

Indochina Former name for Vietnam, along with Cambodia and Laos.

Inquisition (13th–19th centuries) Roman Catholic medieval and early modern tribunal for prosecution of heresy.

Intertestamentary Period Christian term for time between last of Old Testament prophets and coming of Christ, ca. 200 B.C.E.–1st c. C.E.

Irenaeus, Saint (ca. 130–ca. 200) Early Christian Church Father born in Greece who served as missionary bishop of Lyon in Gaul (present-day France).

Ishwara (Sanskrit for "Lord") Title of the high-gods of Hinduism, Vishnu and Shiva.

Islam Arabic for "submission" or "surrender".

Israel Hebrew for "he who wrestles with God".

Issa Arabic for "Jesus".

jati (Sanskrit for "birth") Hindu name for subcaste.

Jehovah's Witnesses International Christian religious sect founded in 1884 by Charles Taze Russel.

Jesus of Nazareth, Jesus Christ (ca. 4 B.C.E–29 C.E.) Founder of Christianity.

Jnana, Jnana-Yoga (Sanskrit for "knowledge") Hindu spiritual path of knowledge.

Job, Book of Part of the Wisdom Literature of the Bible especially concerned with the problem of evil.

John the Baptist (1st c.) According to the Christian gospels, last of the Hebrew prophets who proclaimed Jesus to be the messiah.

John, Saint (1st c.) One of Jesus' twelve apostles and author of one of the four gospels in the Christian New Testament.

Judas Iscariot (1st c.) According to the Christian Gospel, the disciple who betrayed Jesus to the Jewish authorities.

Jung, Carl Gustav (1875–1961) Swiss depth psychologist.

Kalif or Caliph (Arabic for "deputy") In Sunni Islam, successor to Muhammad's political and military but not religious authority. The Caliphate ended after World War I.

Kama (Sanskrit for "desire") The Hindu god of desire.

kamikaze (Japanese for "divine wind") Term for suicide attacks by Japanese pilots upon American warships in the final year of World War II.

Karbala, Battle of   (680) In Islam, Sunni massacre of the second Shi'ite Imam, Husain, and a small band of followers.

Karma   Sanskrit for "action".

karma, law of   In Hinduism, the idea that the choices one makes in one's present life influence the conditions into which one will be born in a future life.

Karma-Yoga   Hindu spiritual path of action.

kenosis   (Greek for "emptying") In the Christian New Testament (Philippians 2:7), Paul's characterization of the sacrifice whereby Christ became man.

Khomeini, Ayatollah Ruhollah   (1900–1989) Islamic Shi'ite cleric, revolutionary, and ruler of Iran (1979–1989).

Kierkegaard, Søeren   (1813–1855) Danish philosopher and theologian, noted as founding father of existentialism, and in particular Christian existentialism.

King, Martin Luther, Jr.   (1929–1968) African American civil rights leader and advocate of nonviolence.

koan   (from Chinese kung-an, "public document") In Zen Buddhism, a riddle or enigma designed to thwart the intellect and force one to see reality.

Koran   See **Qur'an**.

kosher   Hebrew for "pure" or "clean".

Krishna   (Sanskrit for "black") Ancient legendary incarnation of the Hindu high-god Vishnu.

Kristos   Greek for "anointed one", in Hebrew *messiah* and in English "Christ."

kshatriya   Nobles and warriors, the second highest caste of Hinduism.

kundalini   ("serpent-power") In Hinduism, the vital or life force.

Kurukshetra   Site of great battle in the Hindu epic Mahabharata.

lama   Abbot of a Tibetan Buddhist monastery.

low-caste   A member of the Hindu shudra or laborer caste.

Luke, Saint   (1st c.) Companion of Paul and author of one of the four gospels in the Christian New Testament.

Magna Carta   (1215) The "Great Charter" between King John and the English nobility.

mahatma   Sanskrit for "great soul".

Mahayana   ("big raft"—Greater Vehicle) The northern school of Buddhism dominant in China, Korea, Japan and Vietnam.

Malcolm X   (1925–1965) Born Malcolm Little. Martyred African-American Muslim who originally advocated black separatism but later embraced the Islamic concept of the equality of all human beings before God.

Mao Zedong (1893–1976) One of the founders of the Chinese Communist Party, leader of the Chinese Communist revolution, and ruler of mainland China from 1949 to his death.

Mark, Saint (1st c.) Companion of Paul and later Peter, and author of one of the four gospels in the Christian New Testament.

Marrano Jews In Spain, Jews who converted to Christianity under duress but continued to practice Judaism in secret.

Martin Luther (1483–1546) German leader of Protestant Reformation.

Mary, Maryam Mother of Jesus of Nazareth.

Matthew, Saint (1st c.) One of Jesus' twelve apostles and author of one of the four gospels in the Christian New Testament.

maya (Sanskrit for "veil") Hindu term for the phenomenal universe.

messiah (Hebrew for "anointed one") Term originally used to denote the kings and high priests of ancient Israel, who were anointed with a special oil when they took office. By 1st century, a savior figure awaited by the Jews who would deliver the people from their oppressors and usher in the Kingdom of God.

metaphysical (Greek for "beyond the physical") Not given directly in experience, hence having to do with basic assumptions or first principles.

Michelangelo Buonarroti (1475–1564) Italian sculptor, painter and poet.

modalism In Christian theology, the heresy that the "persons" of the Holy Trinity are really successive manifestations or modes of the one divine essence.

moksha Sanskrit for "salvation".

Monophysites In Christian theology, those who hold to the heresy that Christ had one divine nature, rather than being fully God and fully man. Represented today by the Coptic Church in Egypt, as well as by the Syrian and Armenian Churches.

monotheism, ethical monotheism The idea that there is only one, all-powerful and morally perfect God who is the creator of the universe.

Mormons Christian religious sect founded in the United States by Joseph Smith in 1830, formally known as the "Church of Jesus Christ of Latter-Day Saints".

Moses (ca. 13th c. B.C.E.) Legendary Jewish prophet and lawgiver.

Mozart, Wolfgang Amadeus (1756–1791) Austrian composer.

Muhammad (570/1–632) Arab founder of Islam.

Muhammad Ahmed (1844–1885) In Islam, Sudanese mystic, chieftain, and leader of revolt against Egypt. He and his followers believed him to be the Mahdi.

Muhammad, Elijah Leader of African-American separatist movement Nation of Islam, popularly known as the Black Muslims.

mukti Sanskrit for "liberation".

mullah (Arabic for "master") A lower grade of clergy in Shi'ite Islam.

Mussolini, Benito (1883–1945) Fascist dictator of Italy, 1922-1943.

Mutazilites Theological movement in early Islam that denied predestination and asserted the freedom of the human will.

My Dinner with Andre Louis Malle film.

nabi Arabic for "prophet".

Napoleon (1769–1821) In full, Napoleon Bonaparte, also known as Napoleon I. Emperor of the French (1804–1815) most famous for his conquest of much of continental Europe, his disastrous invasion of Russia, and his final defeat by the British Duke of Wellington at Waterloo. He died in exile on the island of St. Helena.

Nathan Prophet of Israel during reign of King David, 10th c. B.C.E.

Nation of Islam African-American religious movement that in the past advocated black separatism and superiority and was popularly known as the Black Muslims. In recent years it has drawn closer to the world community of Islam.

National Socialism German political movement advocating "Aryan" supremacy and the elimination of the Jews, led to power by Adolf Hitler (1933–1945).

Native Americans (Also known as American Indians) Tribal or aboriginal peoples indigenous to the Americas and their descendants.

netti, netti (Sanskrit for "not this, not that") In Hinduism, the affirmation that ultimate reality is not to be found in the phenomenal world.

New Testament Second part of Christian Bible.

Nicene Creed In Christianity, official statement of belief formulated by the Council of Constantinople in 381 and ratified by the Council of Nicea in 451.

Nicodemus (1st c.) According to the Christian Gospel of John, a prominent Pharisee who sought Jesus' teaching in secret.

Nietzsche, Friedrich (1844–1900) Highly individualistic German philosopher, influential upon the development of both existentialism and psychoanalysis.

Nile River A 3,000 mile long river that originates in east-central Africa and empties into the Mediterranean. Ancient Egypt depended for its very survival upon the Nile's irrigation.

nirvana (Sanskrit for "extinction") Buddhist term for the cessation of craving and end of rebirth.

nirvikalpa samadhi In Hinduism, awareness without duality, the highest state of consciousness.

Old Christians In Spain, name given to distinguish gentiles from Jewish conversos, or converts.

Old Testament The first part of the Christian Bible, identical in substance with the Jewish Bible.

Ontological Argument St. Anselm's argument for the existence of God.

Ontological Theory of Atonement The current author's theological formulation of a theme found in John's Gospel, the writings of Irenaeus, and Eastern Orthodox theology that Christ came to restore God's relationship with the human race and bring God back into the center of his creation, thereby saving it from dissolution and death.

ontology (Greek for "logic of being") Branch of philosophy dealing with what actually exists, as distinguished from what we can know (epistemology) and how we should live (ethics). In this definition, identical with metaphysics.

original sin Christian doctrine, first formulated by St. Augustine, that the human race has inherited guilt for the sin of Adam.

Orthodox Judaism The Ashkenazi subset of Rabbinical or Pharisaic Judaism.

outcastes The lowest of the low in the Hindu caste system. Also known as "untouchables".

paganism, pagan polytheism Worship of many gods.

Pandavas In Hindu legend, the five sons of King Pandu, including Arjuna.

paranirvana (Sanskrit for "nirvana in the body") In Buddhism, enlightenment.

pariah outcaste or untouchable.

partition of India After independence in 1947, the division of India into mostly Hindu India and almost exclusively Muslim Pakistan.

patriarchal society Male-dominated society.

Paul, Saint (?–ca. 62–64 C.E.) Jewish Pharisee who became the greatest of all Christian theologians and architect of institutional Christianity. Also known as Saul of Tarsus.

Peter, Saint (1st c.) According to Christian legend, Jesus' chief disciple. According to Roman Catholicism, first bishop of Rome and Pope.

pharaoh Title of ancient Egyptian kings.

Pharisaic Judaism See **Rabbinical Judaism**.

Pharisees Populist party in ancient Israel that gave rise to Rabbinical or Pharisaic Judaism.

Philip the Fair (1268–1314) Philip IV, king of France who prosecuted the Knights Templars for witchcraft and heresy.

philosophy, philosopher Greek for "the love" or "a lover of wisdom."

Pius XII (1876–1958) Orig. Giovanni Pacelli. Roman Catholic Pope, 1939–1958.

pogrom (Russian, literally "thunderous") Persecution of Jews.

Pompey (106–48 B.C.E.) Roman general.

Pontius Pilate Roman governor of Judea, 26–36.

pope, papacy Head of Roman Catholic Church.

Protestant Reformation See **Reformation, Protestant**.

pure-land In Mahayana Buddhism, intermediate realm between samsara and nirvana.

purgatory In Roman Catholic Christianity, intermediate realm between heaven and hell.

Qur'an The holy book of Islam.

rabbi (Hebrew for "master") In Jewish tradition, the preservers, teachers and interpreters of the Torah. In contemporary Judaism, leader of a synagogue or temple.

Rain Man Popular Hollywood film about an autistic adult.

rajas (Sanskrit for "heat") The guna of energy or emotion.

Raja-Yoga In Hinduism, the "royal road", the spiritual path of power.

Ramadan Ninth month of Islamic lunar year, in which Muhammad is said to have received the Qur'an and during which the faithful are to fast from sunrise to sunset.

Ramakrishna (1834–1886) Hindu mystic and saint.

rasul Arabic for "messenger" or "apostle".

recapitulation In Christian theology, one of Irenaeus' interpretations of the doctrine of the Atonement.

Reformation, Protestant 16th c. movement led by Martin Luther and John Calvin to bring Western Christendom back to what they believed to be the original teachings and spirit of Christianity. It led to the development of Protestant Christianity.

Revelation, Book of (In Greek, "Apocalypse") Last book of the Christian Bible.

Robespierre, Maximilien (1758–1794) A leader of the French Revolution.

ru'ach Hebrew for "breath", "wind", "spirit".

Sabellius (3rd century) Christian theologian and propounder of Sabellian Heresy, a form of modalism.

Sack of Constantinople (1204) Western Crusaders' attack upon the capital of the Byzantine Empire.

sacrament In Roman Catholicism, an outward sign instituted by Christ to transmit grace.

salat In Islam, the second pillar of faith, ritual prayer.

samadhi (Sanskrit for "putting together", in Japanese satori) State of intense concentration or trance in both Hindu and Buddhist meditation.

samsara (Sanskrit for "successive states") Buddhist term for the phenomenal universe.

samurai ("guardian") Japanese knight.

Sanhedrin Jewish Council of Elders.

sannyasa (Sanskrit for "laying aside") Hindu fourth stage of life, that of renunciation.

Sartre, Jean-Paul (1905–1980) French existentialist philosopher, novelist and playwright.

sat (Sanskrit for "being") In Hinduism, essence or truth.

Satan Hebrew *shaitan*, "the adversary."

sati, suttee (Sanskrit for "virtuous woman") In Hinduism, a high-caste widow's self-immolation in her husband's funeral pyre.

sattwa (Sanskrit for "light") Hindu guna of wisdom.

satyagraha (Sanskrit for "truth force") Mohandas Gandhi's own name for his philosophy of nonviolence.

Saul First king of Israel, 11th c. B.C.E.

saum In Islam, the fourth pillar of faith, the Ramadan fast.

Sephardim Jews whose ancestors came from the Mediterranean area, especially Iberia.

shahada (Arabic for "I believe") In Islam, the first of the five pillars, the confession of faith.

Shakespeare, William (1564–1616) English dramatist and poet.

Shakti (Sanskrit for "energy") Generic term for any Hindu goddess, and specific name of Shiva's consort, also known as Parvati.

Shakya Name of Gotama Buddha's tribe.

Shakyamuni (Sanskrit, "Sage of the Shakya tribe") Gotama Buddha.

Sheol (Hebrew, "grave") In ancient Israel, the underworld where the dead slept.

Shi'a, Shi'ites (Arabic for "party," "followers") Minority branch of Islam.

Shiva Hindu high-god.

shudra In Hinduism the caste of peasants and laborers.

Siddhartha Personal name of Gotama Buddha.

skandhas (Sanskrit for "heaps") The constituents of the phenomenal self.

Smuts, Jan Christian (1870–1950) Boer general and statesman, he served as Prime Minister of South Africa, 1919-1924 and 1939-1948.

Socrates (469–399 B.C.E.) Greek philosopher of Athens.

Solomon Third king of Israel, ca. 970–930 B.C.E.

SS (Abbreviation of Schutzstaffel, German for "protective squad") The elite guard units of Hitler's army responsible for administration of the concentration and death camps.

St. Helena   Volcanic island in the South Atlantic under British control where Napoleon spent the last years of his life (1815–1821) in exile after his defeat at Waterloo.

Stalin, Joseph   (1879–1953) Marxist revolutionary and brutal dictator of the Soviet Union (1928-1953).

Star of David   Six-pointed star symbolic of Judaism.

stupa   In India, a burial mound.

Substitution Theory of Atonement   In Christian theology, the idea that Christ died on the cross as a substitutionary sacrifice for sin. Classically formulated by St. Anselm of Canterbury.

suchness   In Zen Buddhism, what a thing is in itself.

Sufism   Islamic mysticism.

Sunna, Sunni   (Arabic for "path") Majority branch of Islam.

sunyata   (Sanskrit for "emptiness") Buddhist doctrine that there is no substantive being.

Synoptics   In Christian theology, technical term for the gospels of Matthew, Mark and Luke because of their similarity in comparison to the Gospel of John.

Syrian Church   See **Monophysites**.

Talmud   From Hebrew, "to study") Jewish rabbinical commentary upon the Torah.

tamas   (Sanskrit for "darkness") The guna of matter or inertia.

Tanakh   The Jewish Bible.

tantra   (Sanskrit, "system") In Hinduism and Buddhism, type of spiritual discipline involving direct or sublimated use of sexual energy to reach spiritual goal.

Taoism   See **Daoism**.

Templars, Knights   (ca.1120–1312) Roman Catholic order of warrior monks founded to fight in the Crusades and safeguard the pilgrim routes to the Holy Land

Temple, Jewish   First built by Solomon (10th c. B.C.E) and last destroyed by the Romans in 70 C.E., the Jerusalem Temple was the center of Jewish religious life.

ten *sefiroth*   The Ten Commandments, literally the ten "words" (Hebrew).

Theodosius the Great   (ca.346–395) Roman emperor of the East (379–395) who proclaimed Christianity the state religion of the empire.

Theravada   ("Way of the Elders") The Southern School of Buddhism dominant in Sri Lanka, Laos, Thailand, Myanmar, and Cambodia.

Thirty Years' War   In Christendom, devastating conflict essentially between Protestant and Catholic princes of Germany and then Europe, with Catholic France fighting on the Protestant side for political reasons.

Thomas, Saint   (1st c.) Jesus' disciple who, according to legend, brought Christianity to India.

Torah (Hebrew for "teaching", "law" or "guidance") Specifically, the first five books of the Jewish Bible: Genesis, Exodus, Leviticus, Numbers and Deuteronomy. Also known as the Pentateuch (Greek, "Five Books") and Books of Moses. Generically in Rabbinical Judaism, the entire Jewish Bible.

twice-born A male member of the three upper castes of Hinduism once he has gone through the ritual of the twice-born.

'ulama Teaching authority in Islam.

upper-caste A member of the brahmin, kshatriya or vaishya caste in Hinduism.

vaishya Merchants and traders, the third highest caste in Hinduism.

Vajrayana ("Diamond/Thunder/Lightning Vehicle") Tibetan Buddhism.

vanaprastha (Sanskrit for "forest-dwelling") The Hindu third stage of life involving withdrawal from the world.

varna (Sanskrit, literally "color") Hindu term for caste.

Vishnu Hindu high-god, the "Preserver".

Wailing Wall The western side of the ancient Jewish Temple's foundation wall in Jerusalem and the only part still standing. It is a holy place for Jews.

Westphalia, Peace of (1648) Treaty that ended Thirty Years' War.

Wiesel, Elie (1928–) Rumanian-born Jewish author, scholar, Nobel Prize winner, and survivor of the Holocaust. He now lives in the U.S.

witch-hunts Discovery and prosecution of alleged witches that took place mostly in the Protestant countries of northern Europe in the 16th–18th centuries. By some estimates, as many as 300,000 people were executed as witches, mostly women.

World Bank Formally the International Bank for Reconstruction and Development (IBRD). Founded in 1954 to facilitate investment in developing countries for the purposes of modernization and industrialization.

Yahweh (Hebrew, "I am that I am") Sacred name for the God of Israel.

Yoga In Hinduism, spiritual discipline.

zakat (Arabic for "purity" or "virtue") In Islam, the third pillar of faith, the "alms-tax".

Zen Japanese name for Meditation School of Buddhism.

INDEX.